CHICANE

Chicane is a media, content and creative consultancy that specialises in motorsports and their wider influence in society.

Founded in 2010 by Christopher Joseph, it is now in its ninth Formula One season.

Chicane has been the preferred media partner and consultancy at more than twenty-four international events involving Formula One teams, sponsors, circuits, suppliers, agencies, media and government organisations.

Chicane also produces carbon-neutral bespoke print and digital 'special edition' issues that focus on the four pillars of business, innovation, technology and sustainability, and seek to illustrate that Formula One is far more than a sport and much more than a business.

Chicane is based in Barcelona and London and its next project will be entitled The Fastest Lab on Earth. It highlights Formula One technology and how it is transferred and applied to our everyday lives.

 @chicaneTV

 chicane001

 www.chicane.one

The Fastest Show on Earth

The Mammoth Book of Formula One™

CHICANE

ROBINSON

ROBINSON

First published in Great Britain in 2015 by Robinson
This edition published in 2019 by Robinson

Copyright © *Chicane*, 2015, 2019

1 3 5 7 9 8 6 4 2

A CIP catalogue record for this book
is available from the British Library.

ISBN 978-1-47214-256-6 (paperback)
ISBN 978-1-47211-052-7 (ebook)

Typeset in Great Britain by Hewer Text UK Ltd, Edinburgh
Printed and bound in Great Britain by CPI Group (UK) Ltd, Croydon CRO 4YY
Papers used by Robinson are from well-managed forests and other responsible sources

www.littlebrown.co.uk

CONTENTS

ACKNOWLEDGEMENTS AND SOURCES

The editor has made every effort to locate all persons having any rights in the selections and materials appearing in this edition and to secure permission from the holders of such rights. The editor apologises in advance for any errors or omissions inadvertently made. Queries regarding the use of material should be addressed to the editor c/o the publishers.

F1, FORMULA 1, FORMULA ONE, FIA FORMULA ONE WORLD CHAMPIONSHIP, GRAND PRIX and related marks are trade marks of Formula One Licensing BV, a Formula 1 company. All rights reserved. Used with kind permission of Formula One World Championship Limited, a Formula 1 company.

Formula One in the United States
Key Contributor: Will Saunders for The History of Grands Prix in The United States and America's First Champion—Phil Hill.

Amy Hollowbush and Patty Reid at the Office of Mario Andretti for Mario Andretti and Andretti Race Record.

Teams and Drivers in Their Own Words
These chapters were written, abridged and compiled based upon information supplied and used with permission by the following copyright holders:

Williams
© Williams Grand Prix Engineering Limited

Antonio Giovinazzi
© Antonio Giovinazzi

Daniil Kvyat
© 2017. Official website of Daniil Kvyat, all rights reserved.

Glossary
A-Z Glossary

Allianz
© 2018 Allianz, all rights reserved.

Circuit Diagrams, Circuit Notes and Fast Facts
FIA © 2018 Federation International d'Automobile (FIA)

The following chapters utilized significant technical information supplied by and used by permission from the following copyright holders:

Aerodynamics
The text of this article is courtesy of Willem Toet, former Head of Aerodynamics Sauber F1 Team

Brakes
Brembo
© Brembo. All rights reserved.

Fuel & Lubricants
Total
© TOTAL S.A.

Powertrain
Mercedes High Performance Powertrains © 2018 Mercedes-Benz Grand Prix Limited. All rights reserved.

Tyres
Pirelli © 2018 Pirelli & C. S.p.A.—Pirelli Tyre S.p.A.

Additional writing and special thanks to Nathan Hughes, Trisha Telep, Philip Conneller, James McKeown and Will Saunders.

Special thanks to Matteo Bonciano, Pat Behar, Keith Sutton, Bradley Lord, Andy Stobbart, Anthony Peacock, Sophie Ogg, Stuart Morrison, Mike Arning, Steve Cooper, The Two Wills: Hings and Ponissi, Fabiana Valenti, Alberto Antonini, Maria Guidotti, Phillipe et Carl Gurdjian, Kate Beavan, Patsy Heavey, Mario Andretti, Graham Hackland, Mehul Kapadia, Amit Sharma, Bob and Pat Bondurant, Jochen Braunwarth, Pascal Freudenreich, Ecosse Elite, Linfluencers and 23 Rawle Street.

Overriding gratitude for exemplary patience to Duncan Proudfoot, Tom Asker and Steve Panton at Little, Brown and Robinson as well as to Elizabeth Lacey a.k.a 'boy' for proofreading.

PROLOGUE

"THIRTY MINUTES TO LIGHTS OUT"
An Introduction to Formula One

The thirty-minute period before the start of a Formula One Grand Prix Race is undoubtedly one of the quintessentially unique periods in world sport. The short half-hour lead-up to the race is both tense and frantic but most importantly it is indicative of the complicated nature of the sport and all that lies beneath the surface of a complex spectacle.

00:30 At thirty minutes before the start of the Formation Lap (warm-up lap), the pit lane opens and remains so for fifteen minutes. The cars are allowed to leave the pit lane and complete a reconnaissance lap while team personnel are allowed to get out onto the grid with the necessary equipment needed to start the race.

00:25 At the end of the reconnaissance lap the cars must stop at the rear of the grid, cut their engines and be pushed through the assembled race personnel, media and VIPs to their starting positions on the grid. Here they must remain with their engines turned off.

00:24 The cars are plugged into data monitoring and cooling systems. The race engineer gives the "one minute to fire up" instruction.

00:23 The ignition is turned on while the rear wheels are removed but kept in their heating blankets and the engine is started. Temperatures are measured and monitored before the engine is turned off again.

00:17 A warning signal is given that the end of the pit lane is to be closed in two minutes.

00:15 A second warning signal is given and the pit lane is closed. At this point no car will be permitted to enter the grid and must start from the end of pit lane. The front wing flap settings are cross-checked both on the grid and on the spares in the garage. The mechanics perform a wheel gun check to test the hydraulics.

00:11 Another ignition test and the drivers are summoned to their vehicles.

00:10 The ten-minute signal is given. Everybody except drivers, officials and team technical staff must leave the grid. The drivers suit up, fit their helmets and HANS (head-and-neck safety) devices, and are strapped into the cockpit by one of the mechanics.

00:05 Four red lights are illuminated on the gantry and an audible warning is given five minutes before the start of the formation lap.

00:03 Three lights are illuminated on the gantry and the three minute signal is given. All cars must have their race tyres fitted by this point.

00:01 Two lights are illuminated on the gantry when the one-minute signal is shown and by this time engines must be started and all team personnel must leave the grid, taking all equipment with them before the fifteen-second signal is given.

00:00:15 There is one light left illuminated on the gantry and the launch map is initiated by the driver.

00:00:00 The red lights go out and the green lights are illuminated to begin the formation lap led by the pole sitter.

The cars return to the grid after the formation lap and stop within their respective grid positions with their engines running. The Safety Car takes up its position at the rear of the grid.

A standing start will be signalled by the permanent starter (usually Mr Charlie Whiting of the FIA) by activating the gantry lights.

Once all the cars have come to a halt, the five-second light will appear followed by the four-, three-, two- and one-second lights until five red lights are illuminated on the gantry. At any time after the one-second light appears, the race will be started by extinguishing all five red lights.

The race to the chequered flag begins . . .

INTRODUCTION

THE INSIDERS' GUIDE TO THE FASTEST SHOW ON EARTH

In the quest for ultimate speed, Formula One combines the human, the technological and the financial in an exciting and compelling global circus watched by half-a-billion avid fans around the world. As the 'thirty minutes to lights out' countdown in the prologue shows, within the confines of the three-day race weekend there are many intricate details, subtleties and minutiae to be explored in Formula One, and even more within the wider industry and its sixty-nine years of heritage.

Welcome to the fully revised and updated edition of *The Fastest Show On Earth*. In response to the popular success of the first edition, I have revised and updated my take on Formula One to create a more streamlined, though still comprehensive, guide to Formula One for the 2019 season.

I have divided this edition into six very different yet complementary sections. The popular Drivers and Teams In Their Own Words sections have been retained as has the Formula One in the US section with an additional chapter on new American owners Liberty Media. In the Technical section I have drawn on expert analysis from within the industry to examine the effects that engines, tyres, brakes, aerodynamics and fuel have on the new era of racing. This extensive guide also includes the official FIA Circuit Guides complete with diagrams, data and fast facts, as well as the most comprehensive glossary of Formula One terms ever printed.

At every opportunity I have allowed those closest to the action to express their thoughts and ideas from their own unique perspectives, while I have added my point of view from inside the confines of the F1 ecosystem.

It has not been physically possible to include every aspect of Formula One in this edition nor has it been my desire to be encyclopedic in approach. The glossary included towards the end of the book explains all of the crucial terms in use within the sport from A to Z.

Please note that while every effort has been made to ensure that all information in the revised edition is up to date and accurate, the fact that it has been compiled during the 2018 season means that certain aspects may not have been resolved at the time of printing.

For an excellent source of further information readers are referred to the 'Understanding F1 Racing' section of www.formula1.com, the sport's official website. Here you will find in-depth information on topics such as logistics, suspension, testing, the steering wheel, the gearbox, race control, pit stops, flags, driver fitness, overtaking and the DRS, cornering and race strategy.

For those of you who wish to learn more about the rules and regulations—which change annually—referred to in the technical chapters, these can be found in their entirety at www.fia.com. In the 'Regulations' section you will be able to download the complete Sporting Regulations and Technical Regulations. Be warned, these documents run to fifty-seven and eighty-nine pages respectively.

You will also be able to view the first set of proposals from the F1 Commission, which advises on changes to both the Sporting and Technical Formula One Regulations for the 2019 season and beyond.

Much more than just a sport and far more than a business, Formula One is a world of fascinating sporting personalities and business-savvy individuals. I hope my approach will provide something for the casual observer being introduced to the sport, the race-going spectator, the avid fan wanting to know more, as well as the aficionados hungry to delve deeper into all that Formula One has to offer.

Christopher Joseph,
London, 2019

2019 F1 CALENDAR AND REGULATION CHANGES

FIA FORMULA ONE WORLD CHAMPIONSHIP

The 2019 FIA Formula One World Championship calendar is confirmed as follows:

17 March	AUS	Grand Prix of Australia
31 March	BHR	Grand Prix of Bahrain
14 April	CHN	Grand Prix of China
28 April	AZE	Grand Prix of Azerbaijan
12 May	ESP	Grand Prix of Spain
26 May	MCO	Grand Prix of Monaco
9 June	CAN	Grand Prix of Canada
23 June	FRA	Grand Prix of France
30 June	AUT	Grand Prix of Austria
14 July	GBR	Grand Prix of Great Britain
28 July	DEU	Grand Prix of Germany
4 August	HUN	Grand Prix of Hungary
1 September	BEL	Grand Prix of Belgium
8 September	ITA	Grand Prix of Italy
22 September	SGP	Grand Prix of Singapore
29 September	RUS	Grand Prix of Russia
13 October	JPN	Grand Prix of Japan
27 October	MEX	Grand Prix of Mexico
3 November	USA	Grand Prix of USA
17 November	BRA	Grand Prix of Brazil
1 December	ADE	Grand Prix of Abu Dhabi

FIA FORMULA ONE WORLD CHAMPIONSHIP—2019 TECHNICAL REGULATIONS REGARDING AERODYNAMIC CHANGES

Following a presentation made to the F1 teams at the Bahrain Grand Prix regarding proposals aimed at promoting closer racing and more overtaking in the Formula 1 World Championship, the

Strategy Group, the F1 Commission and the World Motor Sport Council approved a number of regulation changes for the 2019 season.

The changes, approved by e-vote, are as follows:
- Simplified front wing, with a larger span, and low outwash potential
- Simplified front brake duct with no winglets
- Wider and deeper rear wing

The vote follows an intense period of research into the FIA's initial proposals, which were made with the support of the F1 Commercial Rights Holder, conducted by a majority of the F1 teams. These studies indicated the strong likelihood of a positive impact on racing and overtaking within F1 and as such have now been ratified for implementation in 2019.

The approved changes are separate to the ongoing work being undertaken in regard to defining Formula 1's regulations for 2021 and beyond.

In addition to the aerodynamic changes ratified the FIA is continuing to evaluate a range of other measures aimed at encouraging closer racing and boosting overtaking in F1.

2019 TECHNICAL REGULATIONS AND 2021 POWER UNIT
The Formula 1 Strategy Group and the Formula 1 Commission has met at the FIA headquarters in Paris, in the presence of Jean Todt, FIA President, and Chase Carey, Chief Executive Officer of Formula 1.

Positive and constructive discussions were held regarding the future of Formula 1.

Firstly, regarding technical regulations for the 2019 season, the following changes were agreed, subject to World Motor Sport Council approval:

• Increase the fuel allowance for the race from 105 to 110 kg, in order to be able to use the engine at full power at all times
• Separate the weight of the car from that of the driver
• Require all drivers to wear biometric gloves to increase safety and facilitate medical rescue.

Discussions will continue on proposals relating to aerodynamics, with a view to taking a decision once research being conducted by the FIA, in consultation with the teams, has been concluded.

Secondly, the FIA presented its proposals for the 2021 power unit regulations:

• 1.6 litre engine
• V6 Turbo Hybrid
• Deletion of MGU-H exhaust energy recovery.

The FIA Technical Department will now meet with current and potential power unit manufacturers to discuss in more detail, with a view to concluding the 2021 regulations.

THE NEW ERA UNDER LIBERTY MEDIA

'We are excited to become part of Formula One. We think our long-term perspective and expertise with media and sports assets will allow us to be good stewards of Formula One and benefit fans, teams and our shareholders.'
—Greg Maffei, President and Chief Executive Officer of Liberty Media

'I am thrilled to take up the role of Chairman of Formula One. I greatly admire Formula One as a unique global sports entertainment franchise attracting hundreds of millions of fans each season from all around the world. I see great opportunity to help Formula One continue to develop and prosper for the benefit of the sport, fans, teams and investors alike.'
—Chase Carey, Chairman of Formula One

'I'm proud of the business that I built over the last 40 years and all that I have achieved with Formula One. I'm very pleased that the business has been acquired by Liberty and that it intends to invest in the future of F1.'
—Bernie Ecclestone

And so it was on 7 September 2016 that Liberty Media Corporation (commonly referred to as Liberty Media) agreed to buy a controlling interest in the Formula One Group responsible for the promotion of the FIA Formula One World Championship in a deal reported to be worth \$4.6bn (£3.3bn). One of the most important moments in the history of Formula One and one of the biggest deals in sports history was approved by regulators and finalised on 23 January 2017.

The controlling interest in the racing business was purchased from a consortium lead by the Luxembourg-based private equity firm CVC Capital Partners and included taking on \$3.4bn of F1's debt giving the takeover of F1's Jersey-based parent company, Delta Topco, an \$8bn enterprise value. The Formula One Group is listed in the NASDAQ as a tracking stock under the ticker FWONK and controls the various rights, management and licensing operations of the Formula One World Championship.

Liberty Media is a major media conglomerate with stakes in several sports and entertainment businesses such as the Atlanta Braves MLB team, Live Nation and Sirius XM, and is one of a number of media and telecom conglomerates that are owned and controlled by seventy-seven-year-old American businessman, landowner and philanthropist John Malone. With a net worth of over \$7.2bn, he shuns the limelight despite being one of the biggest media owners in the US.

This is in stark contrast to the man who turned Formula One from a relatively niche activity followed by a small group of aficiona-dos, which was commercially an almost amateur affair, into an inter-national sporting powerhouse. During his forty-year reign, Bernie Ecclestone ran F1 almost single-handedly or at least with the lowest head count I have ever encountered for an undertaking of such scale.

Idiosyncratic and mirthful in equal measure, he once insisted that I hand deliver a physical letter regarding a trademark permis-sion for a book project even though I had emailed the details across. Ringing ahead to verify the Princes Gate address, I was greeted by the somewhat film noir-esque 'Knightsbridge triple six eight.' Upon arrival at the residential looking HQ, I was buzzed in to be handed an electronic scan of his handwritten response. Months later at the US GP in Austin Texas, the Warhole-like figure sidled past whispering quietly, 'did you finish, then?', knowing full well the book was published and sitting on his desk. It was such atten-tion to detail that meant very little went on in Formula One without him knowing about it and even less without his approval.

There is no doubt that Bernie Eccelstone ruled over F1 with absolute authority as a master tactician but it was his dealmaking ability with presidents, princes and sheiks that turned F1 into one of the world's biggest sports. However, despite his commercial success which created annual global revenues somewhere in the vicinity of $1.8bn (£1.4bn), it is fair to say that in recent years he was seen as being more and more out of touch as an octogenarian leader in the digital age. Declining audiences and haphazard decision making about the nature of the racing on show meant that more and more people within the sport thought he was past his sell by date with no long-term plan in place. His legacy is undeniable and formidable, but equally it is true that the takeover of Formula One by Liberty as a giant US media and sport conglomerate represents a seismic change in the direction of the sport, which will explore its huge potential and multiple untapped opportunities.

NEW OWNERS, NEW LEADERS
The desire of the new owners to change the way the sport was run became evident with three key appointments. Chase Carey, the former executive vice-chairman of 21st Century Fox and a trusted Rupert Murdoch adviser, who had already been confirmed as the new chairman, was also installed as the chief executive. The original aim to have a two- to three-year transition period in partnership with Eccelstone was quickly forgotten and he was given the unusual honorary position of chairman emeritus, as a source of advice for the new owners, far removed from the decision making process.

Liberty also brought ex-Mercedes team boss Ross Brawn back to Formula One to lead the sporting and technical side of F1. The former Ferrari technical director was tasked with rationalising the regulations to enable close wheel-to-wheel Racing, and to improve the prospects for overtaking.

Brawn was joined in his role as Managing Director Motor Sports by former ESPN executive Sean Bratches as Managing Director of Commercial Operations. Bratches was a driving force in building ESPN into one of the world's leading sports franchises with expertise and experience in sales, marketing, digital media and distribution. The appointments gave Liberty an almost unprecedented opportunity to work together with the teams and promoters for a better F1 for them and, more importantly, for the fans.

TRANSITION AND EDUCATION

Liberty's first year in charge in 2017 was a new start for the sport, and there was genuine optimism in the paddock as new ideas were put forward by the new owners to release the shackles of the Ecclestone-era as they strove to create a bigger and brighter future. Almost immediately social media rules were relaxed for teams in the paddock and fan festivals began which provided more entertainment, inclusion and access.

Merchandising shops were reopened at circuits and a massive live demonstration event took place on the streets of Central London just prior to the British Grand Prix. A new logo was unveiled and a new theme song commissioned as Liberty moved to larger offices in London establishing new commercial, marketing, research and digital departments. However many fundamental issues were left unaddressed with the enormity of the transformation task evident to Sean Bratches:

'It is not something you just flick a switch and things happen. Things need to be invested in and nourished and brought to market. You will continue to see a cadence of announcements and changes. There is more to come.'

CONSOLIDATION, NEGOTIATION AND PROMOTION

2018 was a crucial year in charge of Formula One for Liberty in the post-Ecclestone era, and much was expected of them as they strove to take the sport into the twenty-first century. Having completely overhauled the organisation of the company, a proper business structure was created so that ideas could be researched and discussed before being implemented in an attempt to avoid the whimsy of the past.

The guarded enthusiasm that greeted the Liberty takeover soon turned to discontent when many of the ideas implemented seemed haphazard and not linked to the shared desire to increase revenues or popularity. When it was confirmed that revenues, and thus team payments, were down, relationships worsened and the spirit of cooperation was under threat.

The two major issues of 2018 were the 2021 engine specification and the inequitable payment of prize money to teams. While the five biggest teams and the engine manufacturers may understand where the commercial rights holder and the smaller teams are coming from, it will take skilled and detailed negotiations for Liberty to achieve consensus by the time the Concorde agreement that currently binds all parties expires in 2020. Prior to this, however, the issue of design became a major talking point in 2018 as Ross Brawn made it clear that every aspect of the cars are up for review in the quest to facilitate close racing. Getting the best twenty drivers on to the grid in an age of pay drivers was also an ambition that was expressed. On the commercial side Sean Bratches rolled out a series of new initiatives, including F1's first ever global marketing campaign based on a detailed brand study; F1 TV, a live OTT broadband product available in forty countries; the engagement of one creative and two media agencies; an expansion of the F1 Live events to four different cities; the addition of a new race from 2020 in Hanoi, Vietnam; the growth of audiences on social media and the establishment of an Esports league. All of these initiatives were designed to reposition the sport from a pure motorsport entity to a media and entertainment brand.

A CONTINUED REVAMP
While it is too early to judge the success or otherwise of many of the Liberty initiatives, there is a need for them to continue their overhaul of Formula One as the major rules revamp of 2021 approaches. New car rules and plans for a budget cap must be pushed through by Liberty in the best interests of the sport and they need to be done sooner rather than later.
Formula 1 is a sport with a rich history, according to F1 CEO Chase Carey:
'We want to preserve, protect and enhance that history by unleashing F1's potential, by putting our fans at the heart of a more competitive and more exciting sport. We are driven by one desire: to create the world's leading sporting brand. Fan-centred, commercially successful, profitable for our teams, and with technological innovation at its heart.'

FORMULA ONE IN THE US

THE HISTORY OF GRANDS PRIX IN THE UNITED STATES

The United States Grand Prix may have recently laid the foundations of a permanent home in Austin (2012), but the long history of Formula One races held in the US is a peripatetic patchwork tapestry; a legacy of tentative footholds tainted by circumstance (Watkins Glen, Indianapolis) and half-baked follies around concrete jungles (Detroit, Dallas, Phoenix).

Despite its status as an "emerging market" for Formula One, the United States has in fact hosted forty championship Grands Prix at eight different circuits during the sixty-nine-year history of the Formula One World Championship.

Indeed, the US has nominally played host to Formula One Grands Prix since the inception of the championship in 1950. From 1950 to 1960 the Indianapolis 500 counted towards the final championship standings, but the race was largely ignored by the F1 teams and drivers at that time and contested almost exclusively between American racers—making something of a folly of its championship inclusion.

It wasn't until 1959 that the first "proper" United States Grand Prix was held, when the Formula One circus pitched up in Sebring, Florida, for the concluding and deciding round of that year's world championship.

SEBRING AND RIVERSIDE—TENTATIVE FIRST STEPS

The Sebring International Raceway in Florida was a converted Air Force training base that had hosted motorsport since 1950. The first running of its most famous event, the 12 Hours of Sebring, took place two years later. By 1959, Formula One was searching for a genuine "American" race to supplement the Indy 500, and Sebring was chosen as the setting for the ninth and final round of the championship season.

The race, organized by Russian-born promoter Alec Ullman, saw an expanded roster of American entrants, with six of the nineteen-strong field racing under the stars and stripes. The American entry list included F1 regulars Phil Hill, Harry Schell, Dan Gurney and Masten Gregory—with reigning Indianapolis 500 winner Rodger Ward invited to add a genuine "American" flavour, only to be hopelessly outclassed at the wheel of a Kurtis Kraft-Offy Midget.

The real story of the weekend though was the three-man title shootout between Jack Brabham (Australia, Cooper), Stirling Moss (GBR, Cooper) and Tony Brooks (GBR, Ferrari). Cooper had revolutionized the sport since pioneering the rear-engined approach two years previously, and by 1959 rear-engined cars held a clear performance advantage in Formula One. Brabham held a substantial lead in the standings, with Moss requiring at least a second place and Brooks nothing less than a win to overhaul him.

In the event, the title battle was something of a damp squib. Moss led the early running from pole position, but retired with a gearbox failure on lap five. Brooks was hit by Ferrari teammate Wolfgang von Trips at the first corner and took a long pit stop to repair the damage. Brabham ultimately finished fourth after running out of fuel on the last lap and pushing his car over the line, securing his first World Driver's Championship—and the first for an Australian—as well as the Constructors' Championship for Cooper.

Despite the exciting climax to the season, the race was a disaster for Ullman. The attendance was barely half the size of that at the 12 Hours of Sebring, and after paying out the $15,000 purse (which included a plot of land for the race-winner, New Zealander Bruce McLaren), Ullman barely broke even. Sensing a need to enhance the commercial viability of the United States Grand Prix, Ullman switched coasts for the 1960 event.

The 1960 United States Grand Prix took place at the Riverside International Raceway in California. Again, the venue was an established setting for American sportscar racing, but was a completely new frontier for Formula One. Unlike the previous year, the United States GP would not play host to a championship showdown, with Jack Brabham having sewn up a second consecutive championship in Portugal two races previously.

British driver Stirling Moss romped to victory for Lotus, heading Lotus teammate Innes Ireland (GBR) and Bruce McLaren (NZ, Cooper) over the line. Of wider concern though was the fact that the race had once again failed to ignite public interest— and promoter Ullman was again left out of pocket once prize and appearance fees had been paid. Formula One wouldn't return to California for sixteen years, but in the meantime the first permanent home for the race established the United States Grand Prix as a regular fixture on the Formula One calendar.

WATKINS GLEN—TRIUMPH AND TRAGEDY

In 1956, Cameron Argetsinger, a sports car enthusiast and head of the recently formed Watkins Glen Grand Prix corporation, purchased 550 acres of land outside the tiny village of Watkins Glen in picturesque upstate New York—with the intention of building an international-standard permanent racing facility to replace the temporary street circuit which had hosted motorsport of every class since 1948.

Within a couple of years of its construction, Watkins Glen was hosting Formula Libra road races and these attracted such luminary names as Stirling Moss, Jo Bonnier, Phil Hill and Dan Gurney. Argetsinger though had designs on the ultimate American road-racing event, and after the commercial disappointment of the first two United States Grands Prix was able to take the race to Watkins Glen for 1961.

The inaugural race would mark the start of twenty years of unbroken Formula One racing at The Glen. The circuit proved one of the most popular in Formula One history, playing host to an annual autumn jamboree among the fall foliage and bearing witness to championship coronations, classic races and shocking tragedies during its tenure as host of the United States Grand Prix.

The first configuration of the Watkins Glen Grand Prix Race Course was a short, 2.35-mile blast around undulating terrain, with just eight corners encompassing one of the quickest and highest-speed laps on the Formula One calendar.

By the time of the maiden race in 1961, the US had already achieved an important milestone: Phil Hill had been crowned the first American World Champion at the wheel of the dominant "shark-nose" Ferrari 156. Unfortunately, Hill's Ferrari team declined to attend the United States Grand Prix after their driver Wolfgang von Trips and fifteen spectators were killed in an accident at the previous race in Italy, so the only chance the crowds would have to see their hero on track was during the pre-race parade as an Honorary Race Steward.

A total paying crowd of 60,000 fans across the weekend made the first race a guaranteed success from a commercial perspective, and the event brought about a popular conclusion on-track too, with the Briton Innes Ireland claiming his first and only Grand Prix success—which was also the maiden victory for the Lotus team.

The race quickly became tremendously popular with both the F1 fraternity and the paying public. The large starting and prize money on offer frequently exceeded the money available for all of the other races put together. The race was also well run and administered, winning the Grand Prix Drivers' Association award for the best-staged GP of the season in 1965, 1970 and 1972, and by the mid-60s the United States Grand Prix was an entrenched staple of the Formula One season.

American successes through the early years were few and far between though. A podium finish for Dan Gurney's Eagle in 1967 and Mario Andretti's sensational debut pole position in 1968 aside, the United States Grand Prix remained very much the preserve of European racers during the 1960s.

Despite victories for such racing greats as Jim Clark, Graham Hill, Jackie Stewart and Jochen Rindt, Watkins Glen wouldn't play host to a championship decider until 1970. The circumstances were laced with tragedy though, as Ferrari's Jacky Ickx attempted to chase down the points advantage of Lotus driver Jochen Rindt—who had been killed during the previous race in Italy. By finishing fourth, Ickx failed to take the victory required to keep the title fight alive, and Rindt was crowned Formula One's first, and only, posthumous World Champion.

The late 1960s and early 1970s was a treacherously perilous era for Formula One racing. Increasing speeds as cars became more powerful and aerodynamically sophisticated were not matched by improvements to the safety of the circuits—many of which were simply open roads bordered by trees, verges or other natural obstacles, with run-off areas and guardrails in their infancy. Between 1966 and 1970, eight drivers were killed at the wheel of Formula One cars. In an effort to improve both the safety and the spectacle of the Watkins Glen circuit, significant upgrades were made to the facilities ahead of the 1971 race.

The entire lower section of the track was torn up and redrawn, and a new "boot" section was added—lengthening the lap distance by over a mile to 3.4 miles. The improvements cost $2.5 million, and transformed the circuit into one of the most demanding challenges in racing: a gruelling up-and-down course where almost every corner was banked and long. Entries and prize-money hit record levels, with thirty drivers competing for a record race-winning pot of $267,000, and the first race on the new configuration was won by dashingly charismatic Frenchman François Cevert at the wheel of a Tyrrell as the popularity of the United States Grand Prix reached its zenith.

Unfortunately, tragedy would mar The Glen over the coming years. The 1973 event was dominated again by a narrative surrounding Cevert, but this time there was no happy ending. With his third World Championship sewn up and retirement due after the weekend of his 100th Grand Prix, Scotland's Jackie Stewart was ready to pass the baton of Tyrrell team leader to Cevert by letting the Frenchman take victory at the US GP in return for his "obedient" support during the season. Neither Tyrrell would take the start though; Cevert was killed during a violent high-speed crash at The Esses during Saturday qualifying, and Stewart withdrew from what would have been his career swansong. Cut down on the cusp of his prime, Cevert's death shocked the Formula One fraternity—and further catastrophe was to follow in 1974.

Against the backdrop of a three-way championship showdown between Jody Sheckter (South Africa, Tyrrell), Emerson Fittipaldi (Brazil, McLaren) and Clay Regazzoni (Switzerland, Ferrari), Austrian Helmuth Koenigg, in just his third Grand Prix, crashed at the fast, long Outer Loop—with the young Austrian killed instantly as his Surtees car split the Armco barrier in half. Fittipaldi took the title, but a second fatality in consecutive years cast a long shadow over The Glen.

Off-track, issues were beginning to mount too. The circuit and facilities were deteriorating from a lack of substantial investment, and increasingly rowdy spectators—who cared little for motor-sport —had taken to drunkenly setting fire to cars in the infamous "Bog" infield section. With Long Beach now hosting a rival "American Grand Prix" at a cosmopolitan street circuit in Los Angeles, The Glen's reputation waned rapidly through the late 1970s.

In 1978, an ultimatum from the FISA European motorsport governing body forced belated safety improvements, but the momentum was irreversible. In 1980, against a backdrop of mounting debts, Watkins Glen played host to its final Grand Prix. The race was a thriller, with Australian World Champion Alan Jones charging through the field to win after falling as low as seventeenth at the start, but with the promoters unable to either repay debts or secure loans to put on a race in 1981 it would prove to be Formula One's curtain call at The Glen.

LONG BEACH—THE WEST COAST MONACO

Set against The Glen's declining popularity was the rise of the United States Grand Prix West at Long Beach. A small city within Greater Los Angeles, Long Beach had a vastly different appeal to Watkins Glen—that of a cosmopolitan, urban, sun-kissed jaunt alongside the Pacific waterfront in Southern California.

After a trial Formula 5000 race in 1975 proved a successful demonstration run, Formula One made its debut at Long Beach in 1976. As with many street circuits, Long Beach was narrow, gruelling and predominantly slow, with its 2.04-mile lap encompassing thirteen corners—of which twelve were tighter than ninety degrees.

Set in early spring to provide a counterpoint to the autumnal race at Watkins Glen, the United States Grand Prix West proved a success from the off. The Swiss Clay Regazzoni won the first event for Ferrari in 1976, although the most popular victory was claimed by Mario Andretti in 1977—becoming the first and only American to win a Formula One championship Grand Prix on home soil (excluding winners of the Indianapolis 500 in the 1950s).

Changes to the circuit throughout its lifespan resulted in the curious quirk of the race being run to seventy-nine-and-a-half laps due to the pits and start-line unusually being at opposite ends of the track, but for the most part the layout remained constant until 1982. Sweeping changes ahead of the 1982 edition shortened the lap, and further amends ahead of the 1983 race saw the circuit truncated almost beyond recognition.

However, 1983 did see one of Formula One's most remarkable races, with Belfast-born John Watson recovering from qualifying twenty-second to charge through the field and take a scarcely believable victory—a drive that set a record for winning from a lowly starting position that stands to this day.

Watson's win was to prove Long Beach's swansong, however. Race organizer Chris Pook felt F1 was too expensive, and after an approach from CART (Championship Auto Racing Teams—known as Champ Car after 2004) decided to replace the Grand Prix with an Indycar race from 1984. The domestic series contained leading "home" drivers including Mario Andretti, and to this day the Long Beach Grand Prix remains one of the most popular motor races on the American calendar.

LAS VEGAS—A SHORT STAY ON THE STRIP

Perhaps Formula One's most bizarre foray in the US came in the early eighties, with a Grand Prix in Las Vegas run around a makeshift circuit in the car park of the Caesars Palace casino. The loss of Watkins Glen was an opportunity for Formula One to expand its offering in the States to new frontiers, and Vegas, which had been a non-starter in 1980, was confirmed as a second west coast race to close the 1981 season.

Constrained by the tight confines of the Caesars Palace perimiter, the circuit was a bizarre-looking sequence of three repeating "fingers", a short, flat, 2.2-mile anti-clockwise sequence of fourteen turns winding around a crooked "M" shape.

Although the track surface was relatively smooth, the circuit's anti-clockwise configuration caused significant problems for the drivers—leading to a common complaint of "Las Vegas neck". Combined with the dry desert heat, the Caesars Palace circuit became an ultimate endurance test for a generation of drivers whose notions of diet and fitness were far removed from the standards taken for granted today.

John Watson memorably described the circuit as "a racetrack made up of canyons of concrete", and the high average speed of over 100 mph failed to alleviate the boredom for drivers as the course repeatedly doubled back on itself to make the best use of the available space. The circuit was as uninspiring for spectators and television viewers as it was for the drivers, with the barren backdrop of dust, sand and highways failing to convey any of the associated glamour of Vegas.

Another unique feature of the race was its nomenclature. It was the first bespoke Formula One Grand Prix not to be named after the host country, with the race instead officially known as the Caesars Palace Grand Prix.

One benefit for race organizers of assuming Watkins Glen's slot on the calendar was that Caesars Palace played host to the season finale, and both editions of the race saw the title settled at the very last.

In 1981, Nelson Piquet (Brazil, Brabham) pipped Carlos Reutemann (Argentina, Williams) and Jacques Laffite (France, Ligier) to the title in a three-way showdown, overcoming exhaustion and severe neck strain—throwing up in his helmet during the race—to bring the car home in fifth place and beat Reutemann by one point.

For 1982, the equation was equally knife-edged, with Keke Rosberg (Finland, Williams) and John Watson (GBR, McLaren) battling for the Drivers' Title. A fifth place behind maiden winner

Michele Alboreto (Italy, Tyrrell) was enough for Rosberg, but a paltry crowd of 30,000 illustrated the extent to which the race had failed to capture the imagination.

Rosberg's coronation was to prove the final act at Caesars Palace. The 1982 season had seen three street races in the US, at Long Beach, Detroit and Vegas, and many within the sport felt that this was a saturation point—especially given the fact that none of these races had proven as well attended or as popular as Watkins Glen. After hosting two title deciders that were enthralling in spite of the setting rather than because of it, the race was pulled ahead of the 1983 season.

DETROIT, DALLAS AND PHOENIX—CONCRETE JUNGLES

Perhaps the least remembered of the "glasscrete" urban circuits that adorned the US in the 1980s, Detroit was a notoriously tricky car-breaker set in the heart of Motor City.

A 2.5-mile, seventeen-corner "point and squirt" style circuit, renowned for being exceptionally bumpy, slower than Monaco and containing the only level crossing in F1 history, Detroit was a fixture of the calendar from 1982 to 1988, displaying remarkable staying power compared to Dallas, Phoenix and Las Vegas.

Organizational problems dogged the event from the first running in 1982, with Thursday practice and Friday qualifying cancelled before John Watson provided a stunning show to win the race from a lowly seventeenth on the grid.

The race though did at least prove popular, with over 70,000 fans enjoying Michele Alboreto's victory in the 1983 event. A demolition derby in 1984 saw only eight finishers, but typically Detroit was unusually low on attrition for a street race during its lifespan. The race gained a reputation as a haven for street circuit specialists during the mid-eighties, with Nelson Piquet, Keke Rosberg and Ayrton Senna all tasting victory.

By 1988, the race was still attracting crowds of 60,000-plus, but the slippery track surface of the temporary circuit was proving troublesome—and the race organizers came in for fierce criticism from the drivers. Negotiations to upgrade the facilities and save the event failed, and the race was moved cross-country to Phoenix for 1989.

While Detroit may have had its problems as a destination for Formula One, the United States Grand Prix's most inglorious folly was a one-off stop in Dallas in 1984.

The layout of the temporary circuit in downtown Dallas' Fair Park was itself well-received, despite its tight and twisty nature, but the issues for which the Dallas Grand Prix are remembered were more deep-rooted.

A lack of run-off areas were and remain commonplace at street circuits, and the 100-plus-degree heat was an occupational hazard of scheduling a mid-summer race in Texas. The track surface, however, was a unique variable: a bubbling volcanic potion of metamorphic tarmac that flared and fractured throughout the weekend—much to the detriment of the low-ride height Formula One cars expected to traverse sixty-seven laps on raceday.

With rumours of cancellation abounding throughout the weekend, and a drivers' boycott proposed on Sunday morning, the entire weekend operated under a cloud—a mood heightened by Martin Brundle's leg-breaking accident during Friday practice.

Waved off by Larry Hagman and under the watchful eye of former President Jimmy Carter, when it eventually started the race itself was an attritional farce, with the unpredictable surface and abrasive conditions accounting for eighteen of the twenty-five-strong starting field.

Keke Rosberg won for Williams, attributing his success to a specially water-cooled helmet, allowing him to literally keep a cool head while those around were losing theirs—famously including pole-sitter Nigel Mansell, who unnecessarily tried to push his Lotus home after a late breakdown, ultimately collapsing onto the track with exhaustion and dehydration.

Citing the oppressive heat and farcical conditions, Formula One beat a hasty retreat from Texas after only one outing, replacing the Dallas Grand Prix with the infinitely more popular Australian race in Adelaide from 1985.

The last of Formula One's concrete jungle tour of uninspiring urban landscapes across America saw the circus set up camp in Phoenix for three seasons from 1989–91. Bizarrely, considering local ostrich races were rumoured to attract more fans than the Grand Prix, Phoenix was chosen to ring in the new season with a whimper in both 1990 and 1991.

Despite the unpromising portents, the 1990 United States Grand Prix was an absolute classic, thanks to the career-making performance of a hard-charging French-Sicilian by the name of Jean Alesi. Driving for Tyrrell, Alesi remarkably challenged the supreme McLaren-Honda of Ayrton Senna—impetuously passing the Brazilian for the lead before ultimately falling back into Senna's clutches and finishing second.

The 1991 race was a dismal procession, with Senna winning easily. Poor attendances and limited local interest (not a single American driver had started a race in 1990, no American team had entered a race since 1986, and no American had won a Grand Prix for more than a decade since Mario Andretti triumphed at the 1978 Dutch GP) saw Formula One beat a retreat from the United States—and the sport wouldn't return for almost ten years.

INDIANAPOLIS—TO THE BRICKYARD
The 1990s saw Formula One's global popularity and commercial power accelerate at an incredible rate. Although the decade was marred by the tragic death of Ayrton Senna, F1's biggest star, at the 1994 San Marino Grand Prix, the sport as a whole grew to reach new audiences on new frontiers—with a generation of new drivers, headed by Michael Schumacher, becoming global stars in their own right.

The United States though remained a closed door. Various attempts at engineered cross-pollination, including Nigel Mansell's intercontinental Indycar adventures in 1993–4, CART legend Michael Andretti's doomed stint racing for McLaren in 1993 and the efforts of Formula One supremo Bernie Ecclestone to parachute in leading "American" talent such as Canadian 1996 CART champion Jacques Villeneuve, failed to set pulses racing in the US.

In 1998 however, a deal was brokered between Ecclestone and Tony George, President of the Indianapolis Motor Speedway, to bring Formula One to the spiritual home of motorsport in North America. Two years of renovation and construction followed to adapt the venue for Formula One, during which time a 2.6-mile course was built on the infield of the famous oval—although F1 cars would still run on the iconic banking for half of the lap. A further concession to Formula One was the direction of the circuit, with the Grand Prix becoming the first-ever race at Indianapolis to run in a clockwise direction (as per the general practice in F1). The scheduling of the event also played into F1's hands, with the Grand Prix organized for early autumn to avoid any clashes with the major dates on the American racing calendar.

To the relief of all concerned, the event proved spectacularly popular. With American open-wheel racing disastrously split into the IRL and Champ Car factions, fans flocked to Indianapolis to see what had become unquestionably the premier open-wheel motor racing series in the world. An estimated 225,000 fans saw Michael Schumacher's Ferrari take victory at the first United States Grand Prix in nine years, setting a new record for a crowd at a Formula One race in the process.

Although incredibly successful from an attendance perspective, the history of the race was unfortunately tarnished by external circumstances and internal controversies. In 2001, the race was the first international sporting event to be held in the US since the September 11th attacks, and a sombre event, marked by many drivers bearing messages of support on their helmets and flanks, saw double-World Champion Mika Häkkinen take his twentieth and final Grand Prix victory. In 2002, the dominant Ferraris of Michael Schumacher and Rubens Barrichello attempted a staged "dead heat" finish—with Barrichello taking a last-gasp win but the team accused of disrespecting fans by manipulating the race result.

The most contentious event of all though, and indeed one of the most controversial races in Formula One history, came in 2005. After several tyre failures in practice, Michelin, who provided tyres to seven of the ten teams, declared that their race tyre could only safely last for ten laps unless measures were taken to slow the cars at the banked Turn Thirteen. The sport's governing body, the FIA, stated that any measures to slow the cars would present a competitive disadvantage to the three teams supplied by rival manufacturer Goodyear—who after all had arrived at the race with fully functional tyres.

The Michelin teams, unable to find a compromise with the FIA, were left with no choice but to withdraw from the race. The fourteen Michelin-shod cars peeled into the pitlane after the formation lap to howls of derision from the packed grandstands —who had not been kept informed of the developing situation. Soundtracked by a chorus of boos, the six Goodyear cars, led by the Ferraris of Schumacher and Barrichello, took the most bizarre start in Grand Prix history.

The race, won by Schumacher, was a sideshow to the PR disaster—with many questioning whether F1 could ever return to Indianaoplis after such a farce. Subsequent races in 2006 and 2007 passed off without incident, but the damage to Formula One's reputation was irrevocable. After the 2007 race, Tony George stated publicly that he was unable to match Ecclestone's financial demands, and the United States Grand Prix once again drifted off the F1 calendar—leaving behind it a familiar whiff of missed opportunity, greed and poor treatment of the most belittled group in sport: the fans.

AUSTIN—A FRESH START

The disgrace of 2005 may have lingered in the minds of fans, but to those with a commercial interest in Formula One the American market remained too important to leave dormant for long. In due course, 2009 and 2010 were soundtracked by a plethora of proposals, denials, plans and negotiations to restore the United States Grand Prix. Despite various statements from potential race venues including New Jersey and Weehawken and Monticello in New York, it was announced in May 2010 that Austin, Texas, had been awarded the Grand Prix on a ten-year contract, starting in 2012.

The purpose-built Circuit of the Americas (COTA), constructed on 800 acres of land to the east of Austin, opened its doors to Formula One in November. The late season Texan sunshine and Austin's cool, youthful vibe and buzzing nightlife rendered the race an instant success with teams and fans alike.

Of the three races at COTA to date, the spoils have been shared by Lewis Hamilton (two wins) and Sebastian Vettel (one win). The circuit has been universally praised, offering iconography such as the dauntingly steep Turn One, an "esses" sequence of bends that recalls the famous Maggots and Becketts complex at Silverstone and a triple-apex fast 180-degree corner that apes the infamous Turn Eight at Istanbul Park.

Respectful touches such as the "tailgating" areas alongside the circuit and the cowboy hats sported on the podium have shown an awareness of what a United States Grand Prix has to do to genuinely connect with American audiences. For the first time in the history of the United States Grand Prix, the race has a purpose-built home and a commitment from all parties to making the event a long-lasting and commercially viable success on and off the track. The relationship between Formula One and the United States has long been a difficult one, but Austin's fledgling success makes it seem as though the love might, finally, be reciprocally consummated.

AMERICA'S FIRST CHAMPION—PHIL HILL

Of the thirty-three drivers to have won the Formula One World Championship, only two have raced bearing the Stars and Stripes on their flanks.

While 1978 World Champion Mario Andretti is one of the most renowned figures in motorsport history, the charismatic head of a dynastic family who enjoyed popular success on both sides of the Atlantic, America's "other" champion remains one of Formula One's lesser-known legends.

Phil Hill may not be a name familiar to many Formula One fans, but he was a true titan of F1 and sportscar racing in the late 1950s and early 1960s—and a man fully deserving of his place on the roll call of Grand Prix racing history.

A LIFELONG PASSION

Phil Hill was a child of the Roaring Twenties, born into a prominent family in Miami in 1927 and subsequently raised in Santa Monica, California. The son of a postmaster general, from an early age Hill was distant from his parents and displayed tendencies towards social introversion and self-doubt—but his passion for automobiles saved him from an unhappy childhood.

At the age of twelve, Hill's favourite aunt bought him a Ford Model T—which her chauffeur taught him to drive and Hill dissected repeatedly in order to understand how it worked. After graduating from high school Hill enrolled at the University of Southern California to study business administration, but he quickly tired of studying and dropped out to become an assistant mechanic in a Los Angeles garage.

The proprietor of the garage was an amateur racer, and Hill's first exposure to auto racing came helping other drivers tune and set up their performance vehicles. In 1947, Hill bought an MG-TC two-seater, modifying it himself so he could start racing on the amateur circuit. He won his first professional race, a three-lap event at the Carrell Speedway in July 1949, and in the same year Hill's skills as a mechanic took him to England as a trainee with the Jaguar racing outfit—but buoyed by on-track success his aspirations were increasingly turning to a career behind the wheel.

After both Hill's parents died in 1951, he used his inheritance to buy a 2.6-litre Ferrari—beginning a lifelong love affair with the scarlet racers from Maranello. Although Hill was a regular winner, his emotional intelligence and preternatural introversion made him constantly worry about and question the dangers of racing—even leading him to quit driving for ten months after developing severe stomach ulcers.

Upon returning to full health, Hill forged a reputation as the best sportscar racer in America—winning a succession of races in Ferraris run and entered by their wealthy owners. Hill's successes brought him to the attention of Enzo Ferrari, and he was invited to join the Prancing Horse's roster for the 1955 24 Hours of Le Mans.

FIRST SPORTSCARS TO FORMULA ONE

Unfortunately for Hill, his promotion to the Ferrari race team could not have come at a worse time. The 1955 24 Hours of Le Mans saw the worst disaster in motorsport history, with eighty-three spectators killed when the car of Mercedes driver Pierre Levegh somersaulted into packed grandstands. For the sensitive Hill, the disaster caused fresh personal turmoil—but the American continued to race for Ferrari.

By now Hill had turned his aspirations to Formula One, but promotion to the Ferrari's Grand Prix outfit was a long time coming as Enzo Ferrari felt Hill lacked the appropriate temperament for single-seater racing. As it transpired, Hill's Grand Prix debut would come at the wheel of a Maserati, finishing a creditable seventh at Reims in the 1958 French Grand Prix.

Hill was subsequently elevated to the Ferrari Formula One team after the deaths of Luigi Musso and Peter Collins, and almost instantly proved his class with late-season podium finishes at the Italian and Moroccan Grands Prix.

By 1959 Hill was racing full-time for Ferrari, driving alongside a stable of thoroughbred teammates including Frenchman Jean Behra, Briton Tony Brooks and Hill's countryman, Dan Gurney. Hill finished the season fourth in the standings thanks to a strong return of three podiums from five races finished, helping to establish Hill as one of the leading drivers on the grid.

In 1960 the Ferraris endured a frustrating year, racing an obsolete front-engined Dino 246 against the rear-engined Coopers. Hill could only finish fifth in the championship, but he took his first Grand Prix win at the Italian Grand Prix in Monza. Starting from his maiden pole position, Hill also claimed fastest lap as he led home compatriot Richie Ginther and Belgian Willy Mairesse for a rare Ferrari one-two-three. Hill's victory was the first Grand Prix triumph for an American driver for over forty years, and the first win by an American in the "modern" era since the codification of the Formula One championship in 1950.

Hill would subsequently enter his home Grand Prix for Cooper after Ferrari declined to travel to the United States Grand Prix in Riverside, California. The American finished sixth on home turf, but much better was to follow in 1961.

1961: HILL REACHES THE SUMMIT
Hill's 1961 season would see him claim the Formula One World Championship, and it was a victory as much indebted to Hill's prodigious skill behind the wheel as his car: the iconic "sharknose" Ferrari 156.

The 156 was Ferrari's first rear-engined effort, and the Maranello outfit's response to the changing regulations for the 1961 season which reduced engine displacement from 2.5 to 1.5 litres. The "sharknose" epithet came from the dramatic air intake "nostrils" at the front of the car, and the 156 quickly became one of the most revered machines in Formula One history.

The three full-time Ferrari drivers for the 1961 season were Hill, fellow American Richie Ginther, and Wolfgang von Trips, a charming and flamboyant German of noble aristocratic heritage. While Hill travelled to races with a bulky tape recorder and would spend his time between sessions alone in his room listening to cassette recordings of old operas, von Trips would take debonair swings through the local nightclubs. Only Hill had tasted Grand Prix victory before, and started the season as de facto team leader.

The Ferraris were the class of the field from the outset. Only an inspired Stirling Moss denied the scarlet 156s victory at the opening race in Monaco, but a Ginther-Hill-von Trips two-three-four demonstrated the speed and reliability of the scarlet cars. The following race, the Dutch Grand Prix, saw Hill start a sequence of five consecutive pole positions, although von Trips took the chequered flag by less than a second for his first Formula One victory.

The tables were turned at round three in Belgium, with Hill heading home von Trips and Ginther for a Ferrari one-two-three—and the battle at the top of the standings already looked to be a straight fight between Hill and von Trips. Mechanical issues suspended the championship battle in France, but the race was still a Ferrari success with Giancarlo Baghetti taking victory in a privately entered 156.

The fifth race of the season at Silverstone saw Ferrari clinch their first ever Constructors' Championship, with von Trips heading home Hill and Ginther for another crushing one-two-three. The wet German Grand Prix at the fearsome Nürburgring saw Stirling Moss take his second win of the season in treacherous conditions—but second place for von Trips ahead of Hill in third put the German four points ahead in the standings with just two races left.

Heading to Monza, von Trips was on the cusp of destiny. A victory would have given the German the World Championship, but the race was to be marred by one of the most tragic accidents in Formula One history. On lap two, von Trips was duelling with Jim Clark's Lotus on the approach to the Parabolica corner when the two cars touched. Von Trips' Ferrari lurched to the left, launching up a verge and into a packed spectator area before becoming airborne as the car flew back across the track. Von Trips was flung from his car and killed instantly, along with fourteen spectators who had been struck by his careering Ferrari. Surprisingly the race continued, supposedly to help the emergency services' recovery effort, and Hill went on to take a comfortable victory.

With von Trips' death, the victorious Hill could not be overhauled in the standings, and the win sealed a maiden World Championship for the American. It was a tarnished title, won amid tragic circumstances, and Hill's celebrations were understandably muted on one of Formula One's darkest days. Hill went on to be a pallbearer at von Trips' funeral, remarking, "I never in my life experienced anything so profoundly mournful."

A VERSATILE TALENT

Throughout his Formula One career Hill retained a vested interest in other forms of racing, dovetailing his burgeoning skill in single-seaters with continuing success in top-class sportscar races.

As was common among leading drivers of the day, Hill's racing was not exclusively constrained by the schedule of the Formula One calendar. He entered Formula One as the reigning 24 Hours of Le Mans champion, having become the first American-born driver to win the race driving for Ferrari alongside Belgian team-mate Olivier Gendebien. Hill, who displayed a lifelong affinity for wet-weather racing, drove most of the night in torrential conditions to help secure a famous victory.

Hill had also taken a maiden victory at the 12 Hours of Sebring alongside Peter Collins in 1958, and for a time was the pre-eminent sportscar driver in the world alongside his fledgling Formula One career. Further prestige victories were secured in the 1000km Buenos Aires (1958, 1960), the 12 Hours of Sebring (1959, 1961) and the 24 Hours of Le Mans (1961, 1962). Hill also had the distinction of bookending his career with victory; having won his first professional race in 1949, he also won his final event, the Brands Hatch 1000km, in 1967 at the wheel of a Chaparral Chevrolet.

The skillset that enabled Hill to race with such distinction in sportscars was born of his love for and appreciation of a car's internal mechanics. As much as Hill was a chronically nervous and frenetic presence before a race, pacing endlessly and feverishly chain-smoking, he was a notably calm and careful driver— mechanically sympathetic and famously easy on his cars. In an era of high mechanical fallibility, Hill's style allowed him to frequently bring his cars home to the finish—and his natural speed meant this was invariably near the front of the field.

ELDER STATESMAN

Hill's triumphant success in Formula One saw him finally slay his inferiority complex, but his introspective turmoil about the nature of racing and his personal demons endured. Hill once claimed that, "racing brings out the worst in me. Without it, I don't know what kind of person I might have become. But I'm not sure I like the person I am now." He was also outspoken on the dangers of racing, openly stating after claiming the World Championship that, "I no longer have as much need to race, to win. I don't have as much hunger anymore. I am no longer willing to risk killing myself."

Hill came back with Ferrari in 1962 to defend his title, but after starting the season with three consecutive podiums, results tailed off drastically—and Hill left the outclassed Scuderia before the end of the season. The end of his relationship with Ferrari marked the conclusion of Hill's time as a frontline Formula One driver, and ever-diminishing results during 1963 with ATS and 1964 with Cooper yielded only a single points-scoring finish at the 1964 British Grand Prix.

Although he officially retired from single-seater racing in 1964, Hill's final Grand Prix entry came at the 1966 Italian Grand Prix with a one-off entry at the wheel of an Eagle. Hill though failed to qualify, and his Formula One career concluded with something of a whimper.

Hill continued intermittently to race sportscars through the 1960s, but by this time his lifelong interest in restoring classic cars had developed into a lucrative business, Hill and Vaughn, which Hill ran alongside business partner Ken Vaughn. Selling the business made Hill an independently wealthy man, allowing him and wife Alma to raise their three children in comfortable surroundings in Southern California.

Hill remained in the public eye through his media work, acting as a television commentator for ABC's *Wide World of Sports* and enjoying a decades-long and distinguished association with *Road & Track* magazine. In 1989, Hill was inducted as the sole sportscar racer in the inaugural class of the Motorsports Hall of Fame of America, and he was also inducted into the International Motorsports Hall of Fame two years later.

Always an eloquent speaker who was self-effacingly open about his inner demons, Hill seemed to reach a semblance of personal peace in his later years. "In retrospect it was worth it," he said. "I had a very exciting life and learned a lot about myself and others that I might never have learned. Racing sort of forced a confrontation with reality. Lots of people spend their lives in a state that is never really destined to go anywhere."

After being diagnosed with Parkinson's disease in later life Hill withdrew from public life, and he died from complications related to the disease after a short illness in August 2008, aged eighty-one.

MARIO ANDRETTI

Not many have driven a race car better than Mario Andretti. He could make a bad car competitive and a competitive car victorious. He won the Indianapolis 500, the Daytona 500, the Formula One World Championship and the Pikes Peak Hillclimb. He won the Indy Car National Championship four times and was a three-time winner at Sebring. He won races in sports cars, sprint cars and stock cars—on ovals, road courses, drag strips, on dirt and on pavement. He won at virtually every level of motorsports since he arrived in America from his native Italy at age fifteen. He is a racing icon, considered by many to be the greatest race car driver in the history of the sport.

Assessing his legacy is easy: he drove the careers of three men; he drove with a passion and joy that few have equalled—and he won. Mario Andretti took the checkered flag 111 times during his career—a career that stretched over five decades. And he was competitive all of those years: He was named Driver of the Year in three different decades (the sixties, seventies, eighties), Driver of the Quarter Century (in the nineties) and the Associated Press named him Driver of the Century in January, 2000.

The admiration for Andretti has been for his achievements on the racetrack. He is in the very elite, top-superstar category of his game. Yet, if you look at his whole life, he has seen a world that most people will never see. And the journey he has made is what made him a very rich man.

THE 1940S

Mario was born in Montona, Italy (now Croatia), about thirty-five miles from the northeastern city of Trieste. World War II broke out around the time he was born, at the beginning of 1940. When the war ended, the peninsula of Istria, which is where Montona was located, became part of Yugoslavia. So the Andrettis were inside a Communist country. The family stuck it out for three years, hoping that the only world they had ever known would right itself. In 1948, they decided to leave. Their first stop was a central dispersal camp in Udine. About a week later they were transferred to Lucca, in Tuscany.

For seven years, from 1948 to 1955, the Andrettis lived in a refugee camp in Lucca. They lived in one room with several other families—with blankets separating each one's quarters.

Unfortunately, it was not just "pick up and go". Formal requests for visas had to be submitted to the American Consulate. Only so many people got visas. And when they reached a quota, there were no more granted. And many people were trying to leave. Some were going to Argentina, some to Australia, some to Canada. Everyone followed their imagination. And some people stayed. It was a case of whatever you thought was your best bet.

THE 1950s

The Andrettis waited several years for US visas. When they were finally granted, the family of five left all their belongings behind and began their new life in America. On the morning of 16 June 1955, the Italian ocean liner *Conte Biancamano* arrived into New York Harbor. Settling in Nazareth, Pennsylvania, the family of five had $125 and didn't speak English. Mario and his twin brother, Aldo, were fifteen.

In 1954, a year before arriving in the United States, the twins had gone to Monza to watch the Italian Grand Prix. They were only fourteen years old, but motor racing was becoming more and more of a dream for both boys. In those days, it was more popular than any other sport in Italy. That was especially true in the 1950s, when Ferrari, Maserati and Alfa Romeo were the top players in Formula One. And the world champion at that time was Alberto Ascari—Mario's idol.

So imagine the thrill when, a few days after arriving in America, the Andretti boys discovered a racetrack—right near their home in Pennsylvania. It was a half-mile oval track, which was different to what they had seen in Europe. And the cars were modified stock cars, not sophisticated grand prix cars. But there was a lot of speed. And it looked very, very do-able to them. The twins were now on a mission.

To become a racer, you need your own car. And there are only three ways to obtain a car: Steal it (which was against their principles). Buy it (except they didn't have any money). Or build it yourself (their only real option). They set out listening to anybody who had even the slightest knowledge of a race car. They found out about engines, shocks, spring rates, suspension, chassis setup, and on and on.

With some local friends they built a car—a 1948 Hudson Hornet Sportsman Stock Car—and raced it for the first time in March of 1959. Four years after arriving in America, Mario and Aldo were racing. While Aldo didn't have the same good fortune, Mario's career flourished as he won twenty races in the sportsman stock car class in his first two seasons.

THE 1960s

Mario's "first victory of consequence" came on 3 March 1962, a 100-lap feature TQ Midget race at Teaneck, New Jersey. On Labor Day in 1963, he won three midget features on the same day—one at Flemington, New Jersey and two at Hatfield, Pennsylvania.

After joining the United States Auto Club in 1964, Mario finished third in the sprint car point standings, capped by a dramatic victory in a 100-lap race at Salem, Indiana. He also drove in his first Indy Car event at Trenton, New Jersey on 19 April 1964, starting sixteenth and finishing eleventh in the 100-mile race, and earned $526.90 on his professional debut.

Mario won his first Indy Car race in 1965, the Hoosier Grand Prix, and finished third in the Indianapolis 500, earning him Rookie-of-the-Year honors. He went on to win his first Indy Car Championship that year—with twelve top-four finishes—and became the youngest driver (at age twenty-five) to win that title. In 1966, he won eight Indy Car races, his first pole at the Indy 500 and a second straight national championship.

In 1967, Mario's passion for racing saw him compete and win in the Daytona 500 stock car race, take his second pole at the Indy 500, claim his first of three career victories in the 12 Hours of Sebring endurance race, finish as runner-up in the Indy Car national championship and be named Driver of the Year for the first time.

He even tried drag racing in 1968—driving a Ford

Mustang—and earned eight more Indy Car victories en route to second place in the Indy Car point standings. Realizing a lifelong dream, Mario qualified on the pole in his very first Formula One race at the 1968 US Grand Prix at Watkins Glen, but was forced out of the race with a clutch problem. But Grand Prix racing was in his blood and the decade of the Seventies would see his dream come true.

Mario's celebrated win in the Indianapolis 500 came in 1969. He led a total of 116 laps and established fifteen of twenty new records set during that event. Mario scored a total of nine wins and five pole positions that season and went on to win his third national Indy Car title. He ended the decade with a total of thirty victories and twenty-nine poles out of 111 Indy Car starts.

THE 1970s

The 1970s proved to be a decade of successful versatility for Andretti, beginning with his second victory in the 12 Hours of Sebring in 1970, followed by his first Formula One triumph in South Africa, driving for Ferrari in 1971. His mastery of endurance racing was at its zenith in 1972, when he co-drove a Ferrari 312P to victory with Jacky Ickx at the 6 Hours of Daytona, 12 Hours of Sebring, BOAC 1000 km at Brands Hatch and Watkins Glen 6 Hours.

He continued his attack on the open-wheel series, winning a total of seven Formula 5000 events in 1974 and 1975, while finishing second in points in both seasons. He also took the USAC National Dirt Track Championship title in 1974, with three wins.

Andretti returned full-time to the Grand Prix circuit in the mid-seventies. His quest for the world title began in earnest in 1976, racing for the legendary Colin Chapman at Team Lotus. Their first taste of success came in the year's final Grand Prix in Japan, a race Andretti won in a monumental downpour. Conditions, in fact, were so atrocious that Niki Lauda pulled into the pits and forfeited his chance to retain the championship.

In 1977, Mario was third in the world standings with seven poles and four wins, including Grand Prix victories in his native Italy (Monza) and again in the United States (Long Beach).

The culmination of his international career came in 1978, when he won the World Championship driving for Lotus, making him the first driver in motor racing history to win the Formula One and Indy Car titles. Mario dominated the scene with nine poles and six wins in the revolutionary "ground effect" Lotus, which he had worked so hard to develop, and joined Phil Hill (1961) as the only American ever to capture the world title. He was again honored by being selected Driver of the Year, in recognition of his accomplishments.

Andretti topped the sport's best again in 1979, taking the International Race of Champions (IROC) series. As the decade came to an end, his full-time return to Indy Cars was imminent.

THE 1980s

In 1980, Mario competed for one last season with Team Lotus but was plagued by mechanical problems. He switched to the Alfa Romeo team in 1981, in what was to be his last full-time stint as a Formula One driver.

When the call came from his old friends at Ferrari to replace the injured Didier Pironi in 1982, Andretti put the car on pole at Monza and finished third, much to the delight of his Italian fans. The final Grand Prix start of his career was in the last race of the season at Las Vegas; however, a mechanical failure caused his day to end early. All told, Mario earned twelve victories and won eighteen poles in a total of 128 Grand Prix starts.

As he returned to the States in the early 1980s to concentrate on Indy Car competition, Andretti teamed up with his son Michael and Philippe Alliot to compete at the 24 Hours of Le Mans in 1983, where they qualified and finished third, the highest finish for a non-factory team. It was also Mario's first season with the newly formed Newman/Haas Racing team.

The 1984 Indy Car season proved to be a memorable one for Andretti who, at forty-four, won his fourth national championship by winning six events, eight pole positions and setting ten track records. The season was capped with his third Driver of the Year selection, bestowed for the first time by unanimous vote, making Mario the only man to ever win the trophy in three different decades (1969, 1978, 1984).

As the eighties progressed, Andretti continued to make racing history with some personal milestones. With his son, Michael, they established the first-ever, father-son front row in qualifying for the 1986 Phoenix Indy Car event a feat they accomplished a total of ten times before the close of the decade.

In 1987, in the debut of the Chevrolet-powered engine, Mario sat on the pole eight times, including his third pole at the Indy 500. He went on to lead 170 of the first 177 laps before engine failure cut his day disappointingly short.

Mario won his fiftieth Indy Car race at Phoenix and his fifty-first at Cleveland in 1988. As the decade came to a close in 1989, Andretti took on what would be the ultimate teammate—his son, Michael. It marked the first father-son team in Indy Car history.

THE 1990s

With his two sons (Michael and Jeff) and his nephew (John Andretti), Mario attained another "first" as the four family members competed in the same Indy Car race at Milwaukee, 3 June 1990.

The following year, the four Andrettis raced against one another for the first time in the Indianapolis 500. Jeff was voted Rookie of the Year, joining Mario (1965) and Michael (1984) as the only three members of the same family to win the award.

In 1992, Mario achieved two new milestones. He became the oldest Indy Car pole winner when he earned his record-setting sixty-sixth pole at the Michigan 500 and, at Cleveland, he set an all-time record for most Indy Car race starts with 370 (Mario finished his career with 407 starts). He was also named Driver of the Quarter Century by a vote of all former Driver of the Year winners and a panel of twelve journalists.

As he began his thity-fifth year of professional racing in 1993, Mario continued to make headlines with his fifty-second Indy Car victory at the Phoenix 200, making him the first driver to win Indy Car races in four decades and the first driver to win races in five decades. This race also marked his 111th major career victory. Records continued to be made in 1993, when Mario set a world closed-course speed record (234.275 mph) in qualifying for the Michigan 500, as he earned his sixty-seventh pole. This record stood intact until 1996, a year after the track was repaved.

Mario decided that 1994 would be his final year of competition as an Indy Car driver. The season-long farewell campaign, entitled Arrivederci, Mario featured special tributes, salutes and honours at every race venue. As he sped around an Indy Car track for the last time on 9 October 1994 at Laguna Seca Raceway, the legend of Mario Andretti assumed its place in the record books and in the hearts of his many fans.

Although officially retired, for the next few years Mario continued to seek the one major trophy missing from his mantle, the 24 Hours of Le Mans. He competed an additional four times in the world's most prestigious endurance race, winning the WSC class and finishing second overall in 1995.

MARIO TODAY

Today Mario is a spokesman, associate and friend to top executives around the world. He works with Bridgestone Firestone, MagnaFlow, Mattel, Phillips Van Heusen, Honda and GoDaddy.

Healthy and fit, he looks as though he could slip right back into the cockpit of a race car and often does, in the two-seater which allows for a passenger to sit behind the driver and truly experience the speed and pressure that comes with open-wheel racing. Mario remains vibrant, pursuing other passions, still working at a number of personal business ventures including a winery and petroleum business. He plays tennis, enjoys waterskiing and flying his ultralight. He was in the first *Cars* movie. He's on Twitter and Facebook, carries a tablet computer and stays current in the digital era. He isn't just any seventy-eight-year-old, any more than he was just any racing car driver. He remains one of the most popular interviewers in racing and the most respected voice in motorsports. He is a much sought-after source by journalists from all over the world.

ANDRETTI—CAREER HIGHLIGHTS

- Four-time IndyCar National Champion (1965, 1966, 1969, 1984)
- Formula One World Champion (1978)
- Daytona 500 winner (1967)
- Indianapolis 500 winner (1969)
- Three-time Indianapolis 500 pole winner (1966, 1967, 1987)
- Pikes Peak Hill Climb winner (1969)
- Three-time 12 Hours of Sebring winner (1967, 1970, 1972)
- USAC National Dirt Track champion (1974)
- IROC (International Race of Champions) Champion (1979)
- Only driver to be named Driver of the Year in three different decades (1967, 1978, 1984) Named Driver of the Quarter Century (1992) by vote of past Drivers of the Year and a panel of twelve journalists
- Named Driver of the Century by The Associated Press (10 December 1999)
- Named Driver of the Century by *RACER* magazine (January, 2000)
- Named Greatest American Driver Ever by *RACER* magazine (May, 2002)
- All-time leader in IndyCar pole positions won (67)
- All-time IndyCar lap leader (7,595)
- All-time leader in IndyCar race starts (407)
- All-time leader in wire-to-wire IndyCar victories (14)
- Second all-time in IndyCar victories (52)
- Only driver ever to win IndyCar races in four decades
- Only driver ever to win races in five decades
- Oldest race winner in IndyCar history, with 1993 victory at Phoenix at age fifty-three
- Only driver to win the Indy 500, Daytona 500 and the Formula One World Championship
- From 1961 to 2000, competed in 879 races, had 111 wins and 109 poles (includes all forms of motorsports)

Mario's 111 career wins
52 IndyCar victories (USAC and CART)
12 Formula One victories (FIA)
 9 Sprint car victories (USAC)
 9 Midget victories (ARDC, NASCAR and USAC)
 7 Formula 5000 victories (SCCA/USAC)
 7 World Sports Car victories (FIA)
 5 Dirt track victories (USAC)
 4 Three-Quarter Midget victories (ATQMRA)
 3 IROC victories
 2 Stock car victories (NASCAR and USAC)
 1 Non-championship race

Formula one victories (12)
1971 South Africa (Kyalami); Questor Grand Prix (non-championship race at Ontario Motor Speedway)
1976 Japan (Mount Fuji)
1977 United States (Long Beach); Spain (Jarama); France (Dijon); Italy (Monza)
1978 Argentina (Buenos Aires); Belgium (Zolder); Spain (Jarama); France (Le Castellet); Germany (Hockenheim); Holland (Zandvoort)

Formula one pole positions (18)
1968 United States (Watkins Glen)
1976 Japan (Mount Fuji)
1977 Spain (Jarama); Belgium (Zolder); Sweden (Anderstorp); France (Dijon); Holland (Zandvoort); Canada (Mosport); Japan (Mount Fuji)
1978 Argentina (Buenos Aires); Belgium (Zolder); Spain (Jarama); Sweden (Anderstorp); Germany (Hockenheim); Holland (Zandvoort); Italy (Monza); United States (Watkins Glen)
1982 Italy (Monza)

Indycar victories (52)

1965 Hoosier Grand Prix

1966 Milwaukee 100; Langhorne 100; Atlanta 300; Hoosier Grand Prix; Milwaukee 200, Hoosier 150; Trenton 200; Phoenix 200

1967 Trenton 150; Indianapolis Raceway Park 150; Langhorne 150; St. Jovite 100; St Jovite 100; Milwaukee 200; Hoosier 100; Phoenix 200

1968 St Jovite 100; St. Jovite 100; DuQuoin 100; Trenton 200

1969 Indy 500; Hanford 200; Pike's Peak Hill Climb; Nazareth 100; Trenton 200; Springfield 100; Trenton 300; Kent 100; Riverside 300

1970 Castle Rock 150

1973 Trenton 150

1978 Trenton 150

1980 Michigan 150

1983 Elkhart Lake 200; Caesars Palace 200

1984 Long Beach Grand Prix; Meadowlands Grand Prix; Michigan 500; Elkhart Lake 200; Mid-Ohio 200; Michigan 200

1985 Long Beach Grand Prix; Milwaukee 200; Portland 200

1986 Portland 200; Pocono 500

1987 Long Beach Grand Prix; Elkhart Lake 200

1988 Phoenix 200; Cleveland Grand Prix

1993 Phoenix 200

Indycar pole positions (67)

1965 Langhorne; Indianapolis Raceway Park; Phoenix

1966 Phoenix; Trenton; Indy 500; Milwaukee; Langhorne; Atlanta; Langhorne; Milwaukee; Trenton; Phoenix

1967 Trenton; Indy 500; St Jovite; Trenton

1968 Trenton; Indianapolis Raceway Park; St Jovite; St Jovite; Indiana Fairgrounds; Sacramento; Michigan 250; Phoenix

1969 Hanford; Milwaukee; Langhorne; Trenton; Kent
1970 Phoenix; Milwaukee; Indianapolis Raceway Park; Sacramento
1972 Milwaukee
1973 Texas
1974 Trenton
1980 Michigan 150; Phoenix
1981 Watkins Glen
1982 Michigan 500
1983 Cleveland; Elkhart Lake
1984 Long Beach; Portland; Meadowlands; Cleveland; Michigan 500; Elkhart Lake; Mid-Ohio; Laguna Seca
1985 Long Beach; Milwaukee; Meadowlands
1986 Phoenix; Mid-Ohio; Laguna Seca
1987 Long Beach; Phoenix; Indy 500; Meadowlands; Pocono 500; Elkhart Lake; Laguna Seca; Miami
1992 Michigan 500
1993 Michigan 500

Endurance race record

Date	Race	Car	Co-Driver	Start/Finish	
2/6/66	Daytona 24 Hours	Ferrari	Pedro Rodriguez	3	
3/26/66	Sebring 12 Hours	Ferrari 365P2	Pedro Rodriguez	DNF	
6/19/66	24 Hours of Le Mans	Ford GT Mk II	Lucien Bianchi	DNF	
2/5/67	Daytona 24 Hours	Ford GT Mk II	Lucien Bianchi	DNF	
4/1/67	Sebring 12 Hours	Ford GT Mk IV	Bruce McLaren	1	1
6/11/67	24 Hours of Le Mans	Ford GT Mk IV	Lucien Bianchi	DNF	
2/3/66	Daytona 24 Hours	Alfa Romeo T33	Lucien Bianchi	5	
3/22/69	Sebring 12 Hours	Ferrari 312P	Chris Amon	2	
4/25/69	Monza 1000 km	Ferrari 312P	Chris Amon	DNF	
2/1/70	Daytona 24 Hours	Ferrari 512S	Arturo Merzario and Jacky Ickx	1	3
3/21/70	Sebring 12 Hours	Ferrari 512S	Nino Vaccarella and Ignazio Giunti	1	

7/11/70	Watkins Glen 6 Hours	Ferrari 512S	Ignazio Giunti		3
3/20/71	Sebring 12 Hours	Ferrari 312P	Jacky Ickx	2 DNF	
7/24/71	Watkins Glen 6 Hours	Ferrari 312P	Jacky Ickx	DNF	
11/9/71	9 Hours of Kyalami	Ferrari 312PB	Jacky Ickx	1	2
1/9/72	Buenos Aires 1000 km	Ferrari 312PB	Jacky Ickx		10
2/6/72	Daytona 6 Hours	Ferrari 312PB	Jacky Ickx	1	1
3/25/72	Sebring 12 Hours	Ferrari 312PB	Jacky Ickx	1	1
4/16/72	BOAC 1000 km at Brands Hatch	Ferrari 312PB	Jacky Ickx	1	1
7/22/72	Watkins Glen 6 Hrs	Ferrari 312PB	Jacky Ickx	1	1
4/25/74	Monza 1000 km	Alfa Romeo 33TT	Arturo Merzario	1	1
7/13/74	Watkins Glen 6 Hours	Alfa Romeo 33TT	Arturo Merzario	DNF	
6/18/83	24 Hours of Le Mans	Porsche	Michael Andretti and Philippe Alliot	3	3
2/04/84	Daytona 24 Hours	Porsche	Michael Andretti	1 DNF	
6/11/88	24 Hours of Le Mans	Porsche 962C	Michael Andretti and John Andretti	3	6
2/4/89	Daytona 24 Hours	Porsche 962	Michael Andretti	6 DNF	
2/12/91	Daytona 24 Hours	Porsche 962	Michael Andretti and Jeff Andretti	6	5 (DNF)
6/17/95	24 Hours of Le Mans	Courage Porsche C34	Bob Wollek and Eric Hélary	3	2
6/15/96	24 Hours of Le Mans	Courage Porsche C36	Derek Warwick and Jan Lammers	9	13
6/14/97	24 Hours of Le Mans	Courage Porsche C36	Michael Andretti and Olivier Grouillard	31	27 (DNF)
6/17/2000	24 Hours of Le Mans	Panoz LMP-1 Roadster S	David Brabham & Jan Magnussen	4	16

THE BEST OF THE REST—*OTHER*
NOTABLE US F1 DRIVERS

DAN GURNEY

Dan Gurney is highly regarded for his Formula One contributions, both on and off the track. He is the only driver to score the first F1 victory for three different constructors: Porsche (1962), Brabham (1964), and Eagle (1967). He himself had built the Eagle chassis. As a result, Gurney's name is still associated with race car aerodynamics. He was the first person to use what is now known as a "Gurney flap" on the wing of his car. He is also credited as being the first driver to spray champagne on the podium. Gurney made his F1 racing debut with Ferrari in 1959, finishing in the top three in two of the four races he entered. His second season racing for BRM was much less successful, with his car failing to finish most races. His only race finish with BRM saw him end up in tenth place. Between 1961 and 1965, Gurney drove for three different teams and was classified in the top six in the Drivers' Championship each year, but he would never finish better than fourth in the title race. Officially, he left the sport in 1968 but made a brief return with McLaren after the death of founder Bruce McLaren. Gurney won just four races of the eighty-six he started.

PETER REVSON

Revson started four races for Lotus in 1964, but returned to the United States to drive Indy Cars and closed-wheel sports cars. He made a guest appearance for Tyrrell at the 1971 Formula One United States Grand Prix. While he failed to finish the race, his driving was sufficiently impressive that he was signed by McLaren to drive for the 1972 season. He stood on the podium at four of the nine races he attended, and stayed with the team for an even more successful year in 1973. Revson won the 1973 British Grand Prix and the 1973 Canadian Grand Prix, both in wet conditions. However, he made the fateful decision to join the Shadow team when McLaren offered him a third car for the next season. While testing their car in preparation for the 1974 South

African Grand Prix, Revson suffered a fatal accident when the front suspension of his vehicle failed.

EDDIE CHEEVER
Cheever entered a few F1 races in 1978 before starting full time with Osella in 1980. However, the new team was unable to provide him with a competitive car and he only finished one of the races he entered that year. He joined Tyrrell in 1981, and had improved results, but still failed to secure any podium finishes. With Ligier in 1982 he finished in the top three at three races before changing teams once again. Cheever enjoyed his most successful season in 1983 with Renault, mounting the podium four times. However, he never tasted victory throughout his F1 racing career, which ended in 1989. He finished no higher than third in the 132 races in which he competed.

RICHIE GINTHER
Ginther started fifty-two races during the 1960s, finishing on the podium fourteen different times. He won the 1965 Mexican Grand Prix driving for Honda and finished third overall in the 1963 season, racing for the BRM team.

BILL VUKOVICH
Vukovich competed in five Indy 500 races when they were part of the Formula One World Championship. In 1951 he retired after just twenty-nine laps and finished a disappointing seventeenth the following year. However, he returned for the 1953 event, started from pole and went on to win the race. He won again in 1954 and was leading in 1955 when he crashed into a marker. The collision pitched the car into, then over, a concrete wall, fracturing Vukovich's skull. He died at the scene. Statistically Vukovich won 40 per cent of the Formula 1 races in which he competed, but drivers who competed only at the Indy 500 events are often omitted from the history of the sport.

THE REST
The following drivers started at least ten Formula 1 races during their driving careers: Michael Andretti, Tony Bettenhausen,

Ronnie Bucknum, Mark Donohue, George Follmer, Masten Gregory, Jim Hall, Brett Lunger, Jim Rathmann, Harry Schell, Scott Speed, Danny Sullivan and Rodger Ward. Two other drivers, Bob Bondurant and Skip Barber, competed in F1 racing during the 1960s and later formed two of the most respected and successful driving schools in the USA.

"THE AMERICAN"—BOB BONDURANT

Bob Bondurant recovered from a horrific near-death crash in 1967 to become a driving instructor for Hollywood actors such as Paul Newman and Tom Cruise. Today, his high-performance driving school has graduated over half a million people.

"I went as high as the treetops," recalls Bob Bondurant incredulously. "I remember looking down at the embankment from the air and thinking, 'Uh-oh, this is going to be a bad one!' And that's the last thing I remember."

It was 27 June 1967, the United States Road Racing Championship, and Bondurant's McLaren MK 1C had just careered around the 150-mph corner when disaster struck. As he neared 200 mph, the front steering arm broke and he slammed into the embankment. It was one of the most shocking crashes in the history of motor racing. Somehow, in a split-second, Bondurant was able to switch the engine off, take a deep breath, relax the muscles in his neck, shoulders, hands and wrists and pray for the best. He should have been killed that day. The car flipped eight times. All that was left of it was the rear suspension.

Bondurant woke up in hospital in casts. "How soon am I getting out?" he asked anxiously.

"Well, young man," said the doctor severely, "I saw your accident and it's the worst I've ever seen. Do you want the good news or the bad news?"

"The good news," suggested Bondurant.

"You have a mild concussion and three broken ribs and two broken legs below the knees, but they will heal. The bad news is I cannot allow you to sit up because the lower vertebrae in your back is damaged and if you sit up there's a risk you could become paralyzed. So don't sit up."

"Okay," he agreed.

"And you broke nearly every bone in your feet and ankles and you'll never walk again."

"Are you *sure*?" asked Bob Bondurant.

* * *

The Bob Bondurant School of High Performance Driving sprawls across 450 acres of scorched earth in Arizona's Sonoran Desert, eleven miles from Phoenix, on land leased from the Gila River Indian community. The fifteen-turn road course covers 1.6 miles and was designed by Bondurant himself, serving wannabe racers, the odd Hollywood film star, the occasional Black Ops team needing a crash course in covert, high-speed manoeuvres, as well as everyday drivers looking to upgrade their road safety skills. There's also a four-day Grand Prix course ($4,999 if you're interested).

Bondurant is a sprightly eighty-one-year old, although the hearing in one ear has been damaged from racing cars in the 1950s, in an era before health and safety, when the engine was mounted directly under the driver's ear. On most days, alongside his crack team of driving instructors—which includes Andy Lee, World Challenge Rookie of the Year in the 2012 GTS Championship—America's uncrowned world driving champion takes to the track at 180 mph, often with gleeful passengers who pay him for the pleasure. It's how he stays in shape, he says.

"When I put my helmet on," says Bondurant, "I'm like a different man."

Bondurant has fond memories of his time in Europe, racing Formula One, when his colleagues were the likes of Jochen Rindt and Jackie Stewart, and he remains a very proud member of the hallowed Club International des Anciens Pilotes de Grand Prix F1 (aka CIAPGPF1 Grand Prix Drivers Club). For a kid with the heart of a racer, the arrival of Formula One on the world motorsport scene when he was seventeen made a huge impression on the young Bondurant. At the time, he was cutting his teeth on an Indian Scout motorcycle near his family home in Los Angeles. At twenty-three, he was racing sports cars and winning races as well as accolades. But it was the Cobras that defined Bob Bondurant's career. In 1963, he joined Caroll Shelby's Cobra team and began chalking up an impressive number of wins, taking Europe by storm and securing a permanent place on the team. In 1964, he won the GT class at the 24 Hours of Le Mans. In 1965, while racing in Reims, France, where he helped to win the World Manufacturers' Championship for the US in his now trademark Cobra, the impressive American had his first brush with Formula One.

Enzo Ferrari summoned the man the Italians were calling "Bondurante Sir Cobra" to Italy for a meeting. John Surtees, reigning F1 World Champion, did the translating.

"Ferrari said, 'Would you like to live in Italy?'" recalls Bondurant. "And I said, 'Si, if I'm driving in Formula Uno.'"

But Ferrari was not to be rushed.

"When will you let me know?" asked Bondurant.

"When I decide," said Ferrari.

"One week? Two weeks?" Bondurant persisted.

"He looked at me very sternly and he repeated, 'When I decide.' So I shut my mouth."

Bondurant returned to digs in England, thinking he'd blown it, that he'd pressed the great man too hard. Three days later, however, the phone rang. It was Luigi Chinetti at Ferrari, requesting Signore Bondurante's presence in Italy. He was to report to the factory to be fitted for the Ferrari 158V8 that he'd be driving that October in the US Grand Prix in Watkins Glen, New York.

It was his Formula One debut. He began fourteenth on the grid, got a good start and soon made it up into sixth place. Then the track was beset by wind and rain. Bondurant says, "You race in Europe, you get used to racing in the rain, so you just do it." But halfway through the race, the elastic on his goggles came unstuck. The rain had stretched the elastic band and they kept blowing down over his eyes. His first time in a Formula One car, racing for Ferrari, he recalls ruefully, and this happens! What are the odds?

Bondurant soldiered on, pulling the goggles back up over his eyes and holding them there, driving one-handed for the rest of the race, sometimes at 170 miles per hour. To shift gears, he was forced to put his knee on the steering wheel to free up his right hand. He finished ninth, but it wasn't enough to make the grade with Ferrari. While throughout 1966 he continued to race for Ferrari in prototypes, at Sebring, Daytona and Le Mans, at the following Mexican Grand Prix, he drove a Lotus 33 for Reg Parnell, and after that he competed in five Grands Prix for Team Chamaco Collect, finishing fourth at Monaco.

As a rainstorm plagued the Belgian GP of 1966, Bondurant worked frantically beside Graham Hill to prise an immobilized Jackie Stewart out of his demolished—and dangerously leaking—car. Stewart was soaked in fuel and trapped in the car for over thirty minutes, his steering column pinned to his leg. The pair were eventually able to free the Scot using spanners from a spectator's toolkit. This was the incident that provoked Stewart's one-man crusade to improve driver safety in the sport.

About ten years ago, Bondurant received a phone call from a stranger who claimed he'd been at that ill-fated race in 1967. He was seventeen at the time, he explained, and had witnessed the crash and captured some of it on camera. Would Bondurant like to see the negatives, he asked.

"A lot of drivers never got to see the accidents they were in back then," says Bondurant. "Blowing up those negatives and looking at those pictures gave me so much closure. To see how badly the car was damaged—and that I survived it."

The photographs are now hanging in the museum at the Bondurant School of High Performance Driving, among Bondurant's lovingly archived collection of motor racing memorabilia.

The crash finished his racing career, but just eight months later, through sheer force of will, he was walking again, albeit painfully. He'd also just opened his first driving school at Orange County International Raceway.

"I just never gave up," he says. "I *never* give up."

Back in 1966, Bondurant had acted as technical director on the cult film *Grand Prix*, teaching its star, James Garner, how to race. He'd enjoyed teaching and realized a new vocation. "It's like the man upstairs said, 'Before you get maimed or killed I'm going to take you out of racing and help you teach other people.'" says Bondurant. It was the same bloody-minded determination that had enabled him to achieve so much as a racing driver that got him back on his feet and succeeding in business. While still in a cast and wheelchair, he was tirelessly canvassing sponsors for the school—despite, as he admits, not being the greatest of advertisements for a new driving school.

Bob opened his school with three Datsuns, a Lola T70 Can-Am

car and a Formula V. His first class consisted of just three students. The second week there were two students, Robert Wagner and Paul Newman, who were training for the film *Winning*. Bob was a technical advisor, camera-car driver, and actor-instructor in the film. Newman told Bob that he had turned down two better-paid films to do *Winning*, just because he wanted to see if he had the guts to be a racing driver. Bob was impressed by his daredevil attitude and a mutual respect and enduring friendship developed between the two men. Legend has it that there were only three people that Newman would ever call on the telephone, one of whom was Bondurant.

A move to Ontario Motor Speedway in California followed— and the addition of a few cars from Porsche—then to Sears Point in Sonoma. The school finally settled in Arizona in 1989 with a Ford partnership, switching to GM and Goodyear in 2005.

Along the way, Bondurant had started racing again, and was inducted into the Motorsports Hall of Fame of America. In April 2012, he expanded with a satellite school at Pikes Peak International Raceway (PPIR) in Colorado. Arizona's summers get too hot to run much of a corporate programme, so the partnership at PPIR takes up the slack. They've trained up to 500 people a day in Colorado.

"We've now graduated nearly 500,000 people," he says. A further expansion of the Bondurant School out to the Circuit of the Americas Formula One track in Austin is on the cards, too. Brand Bondurant represents an American connection to the tumultuous early days of Formula One—a living archive as, just two states to the east, Formula One finds a home in Austin.

MARIO UNCUT

MARIO ANDRETTI'S ON THE PHONE! INTERVIEW
—UNCUT

Mario Andretti is in his office in Pennsylvania when the call is put through.

"Hello this is Mario Andretti."

Christopher Joseph (CJ): "Hi Mario. I saw that you had some fun and games on the weekend down in Austin?"

Mario Andretti (MA): "Yeah. Finally we were able to just have a taste of what it will all be, obviously, the racing part of it, the surface was quite ready. A few touches here and there. No breaking points yet. But it was all great to be able to go down for the first time and sample what it's going to be."

CJ: "Everything is ready?"

MA: "Yes. It's amazing the amount of work that they've done since the last time I was there which was in June. If you would've seen it then and then now, it's almost a miracle happened. But there's work to do yet . . . You could tell the infrastructure's quite ready, just finishing touches here and there, as you can imagine. But then again I'm told that 1,100 bodies [are] on site everyday, forty different contractors show up, there's a lot of action going on. Quite honest, while we were out there playing on the track, you could look around and see work going on. They didn't even waste that day by being idle. But it's definitely ready to go . . ."

CJ: "How did you find it behind the wheel again and on an F1 track and a new track at that? What about up the hill, Turn One, your Turn One, is it going to be called the Andretti Turn by the way? How was that?"

MA: "Well, it's . . . [laughs] Who knows? I don't think they've named any corners yet but I call that a marquee corner when the track wasn't even paved. Something impressed me about it, it's going to draw comments from other drivers, I suspect. Again, you're always anxious to get on and get the first taste of it. That's what we're all about. Those are the days we always look forward to. That's our playground, if you will. I had different choices of cars to go out. The only disappointment of the day was not getting into the R30. It went out for five laps to shake it down and the engine blew. So, I didn't get to drive that."

CJ: "That's a shame but that's racing, I guess."

MA: "That's a shame but they promised me another day so that's good. And they had the 79 there, which was great, so I was able to tool about with that a little bit. And I took out some other cars, Ferraris and things."

CJ: "Did you take Bobby Epstein around?"

MA: "Yeah, Bobby, I took him out in the three-seater formula one car. I don't know if you ever seen those?"

CJ: "Yeah. Is that the Pirelli one you had?"

MA: "Yeah, that's the one. I did quite a bit of driving with that. They had a lot of passengers waiting in line. Then the engine overheated on that too."

CJ: "When you first decided to become the ambassador for the Circuit of the Americas, I was told you took quite a time to decide. You analyzed the role and what you could do? Is that the case?"

MA: "First of all, it's like any new project, you have many questions. And there were potential issues here and there, which you would expect from a project of this magnitude. When you go to the private sector on something like this, and you're trying to compete with venues that have been financed by governments, you wonder whether it's ever going to come off. That was my concern, of course. I was flattered that I was asked to be part of it, but I wanted to confirm many aspects of it. I started with Bernie. He gave me certain reassurances that the game is on. I said, well, that's good enough for me, and then, of course, I had to see for myself. I went down there in June. It was just before the Montreal GP. I was satisfied with what I saw as far as the plans, project and people involved. Then I just reported back to Bernie in Montreal and I said, I think things should be good there. That was it. And I feel strongly that the group behind it is very, very committed."

CJ: "So it's not just the case of Bobby and Red opening up a cheque-book so they can acquire you as an ambassador ... It actually was a question of you doing your due diligence and going down there to see if these guys were serious and could bring it in on time?"

MA: "Exactly. And the thing that impressed me the most was Bobby. He was there with his work boots on and dirty jeans and construction helmet. And, I mean, he was hands-on, and very passionate about what was going on. Then I got the same feeling again when I met him the second time, the third ... When you see someone that is investing but also wants to be part of it, keep their hand in it, I think that speaks volumes for me. You can see that they have a lot riding there, you can imagine."

CJ: "When I spoke to him he said it was probably the biggest thing he'll ever do in his life."

MA: "Yeah. I saw so much satisfaction in their faces when they were finally able to present it to the press and the world. That, to me, was very rewarding, in many senses. Of course, you just wish them well because of that. The overall plans, what they'd secured already, MotoGP and so forth, or some of the events they had planned for, and others, outside of motor racing, to keep the facility active year-round, I think, maybe those things make a lot of sense and because of that I hope their business model really works for all the reasons."

CJ: "You've pretty much raced on every US F1 track. Why do you think it will work this time in Austin at COTA as opposed to Indy, Phoenix, Detroit? I guess the last time we had a stable US race was back in Watkins Glen . . ."

MA: "Well if you look back at . . . okay, let's start at Watkins Glen. Why does Formula One leave Watkins Glen? Because there was no real commitment, reinvestment in bringing the facility up to the standards that Formula One required, standards that the rest of the world was adhering to. From there, it went somewhere else, then it went to, I think, Long Beach. So that seemed to be an interesting venue but one thing leads to another, it was still a temporary course, and there was some other issues. And from there it moved from Dallas to Phoenix to . . . You know, all temporary venues. Detroit. And the temporary aspect of it was exactly that. So, then, all of a sudden, I felt very good about Indianapolis, but here's my take on it. There's never been a successful dual venue for road racing. If it's an oval with a road course, the road racing side suffers. Why? Because there's no ambience. I mean, we've seen that even with some circuits like Germany and so forth, where they have a dual purpose ... They never survive. There's something about it. Take The Daytona oval where they have the road course. Why isn't that 24 hours Daytona successful from the standpoint of attendance?"

CJ: "That's a good question."

MA: "It lacks the ambience of road racing. Indianapolis suffered that tremendously. You know, you sit in a grandstand and what do you see? Cars go by on the straightaway and then you don't see the rest of it, you have to look at a television screen. So, again, that's why it didn't survive. Now, finally, I think, for the first time since, probably, the seventies, it's going to have a proper home, with a circuit built up to the standard that is required today to be competitive with the rest of the world. And the United States does not have another venue like this, not for road racing. Here they have many classics, and a really nice road course, but they're years behind the times as far as what I'm talking about. Again, that's why, for Formula One fans, for road racing fans it's time to rejoice. And quite honestly, I had the first question to cross my mind too is—is Austin going to work? Basically, the location. Well, to be honest with you, I think you have to look at accessibility from South America too. Just incredibly fertile ground for motor racing. You have the proximity of Mexico, you have Brazil and so on and so forth. And you could see from the response for tickets, it was amazing what they got from South America, for instance. It's got a lot of benefits, and it's easy to travel to, to Austin. It's not a big issue from that standpoint."

CJ: "What do you think then that Formula One in Austin and in the States has to do culturally to make this work? Because, I think, the first one is always easy and then you contract for another nine years. There's a cultural difference I think in motor sports between F1 and the rest of motor sports in the States. So what do the guys down in Austin have to do to make this work?"

MA: "I think the one thing that's going to work is the fact that it's a solid home, it's something you can definitely look forward to for the years to come. That in itself should be very strong for the continuity aspects, should be very strong to be able to bring the fans back, and I think the Formula One fan base—I keep saying this always—is underestimated here in the United States. I can't see why the event shouldn't be something that's so welcome by the fans and be attended for the years to come. I think it can only get stronger. That's the way I see it, because, again, you're going to have MotoGP coming back in and, obviously, you're going to have some GrandAm, some sports car racing, and all that. The place will continue to be showcased and I'm sure that the exposure it will receive is also going to be another tool that will be in the minds of the fans, the ones that will not be here this time but want to experience it. I feel strongly in that respect."

CJ: "What do you think F1 has to do itself to make it successful? Because it's a big return after five years, and as you know, it's a strange circus that comes to town when F1 visits."

MA: "Just be there. I don't think they need to do anything in particular, anything they don't do anywhere else. There's only one thing I would like to interject on that—I would love to see Formula One open up to the opportunity to have some guest drives. By that I mean, I know how I started, you can say times are different, this and that. But you know what? Times are different but a lot of things are the same. I got the opportunity by being the third driver on a top team when I broke into Formula One, and I won races as a third driver. Can you imagine we go to some of these new markets and so forth, to have a local hero be invited by McLaren or Ferrari or something to be the third man on the team. You know, after some proper testing or whatever."

CJ: "So, you mean not just driving practice Friday but actually driving in the race?"

MA: "Driving in the race, yes. I mean, it's happened before and I think this could be a big, big promotional item to bring the local fans. Formula One, in so many ways, being so international, it's very partisan too and there's a lot of national pride going into it, and a lot of fans who would love to see, maybe, one of their own, see how they measure up, but not with a weaker team, it would have to be with a top team. And if the talent could reveal itself, it could be here, another launch. The financial aspect needs to be considered but I think again Formula One should be thinking in those terms—as elite as it is, there are some drivers in different countries that I think would belong and make the most of the opportunity. It would do wonders, I think, for the event in that country."

CJ: "Do you think we need an American driver, and if not that, an American team, for F1 to really take hold in the States?"

MA: "I don't think so. I think it's still on the cards though, but I think it would be a lot better, it would be a lot more interesting, a lot more coverage, a lot more interest from the fans, the press standpoint, and so forth, because naturally you will be rooting for your own. When you have such an international event, to be able to fly your own flag has that particular pride to it. So all of these elements, I think, would be a big plus in promoting Formula One in the States. I think by having a venue such as this, those opportunities will open up."

CJ: "Being a businessman, what will we see business opportunity-wise for F1 in the US? This year, for instance, was the first time Unilever came on board, so we had some fast moving consumer goods. What else do you think we'll see?"

MA: "Well, here again I think when you look at the sponsorship in F1, obviously, you have a lot of global companies involved for the obvious reasons, and I'm sure those global companies do a fair amount of business in the United States. They would want to benefit from the exposure here. So then again, and this might also encourage some other companies here that would want to expand in international markets to be able to be in Formula One to have that opportunity to have the visibility. All of this plays in a positive direction. I think this could be the beginning of a lot of good things. There are many areas where you can see there could be more growth, more interest in what we have now because of the venue that's in place."

CJ: "What was your take on the whole Texas versus New Jersey race? Do we need two? Is it beneficial to have two American races?"

MA: "It's beneficial for America for sure. I think of any country in the world, America could easily host two Formula One races. New York, I think it would be a great market, it's a market that Bernie has been eyeballing for years. I hope that happens as well. It's been pushed back another year now. I've been in touch with the principals there, people involved, and they're working very hard . . . they're very professional, trying to make that happen as well. It can only help the fan base by having two events to look forward to. One can also feed off the other."

CJ: "I know that for Austin they've arranged for one-day flights from New York, Miami and Los Angeles direct into the race, which is a really cool idea."

MA: "I think Austin is going to be a very nice host city for this event. I think it will be a pleasant surprise for a lot of people that are not familiar with that particular area."

CJ: "When we wake up on November nineteenth, what do you think the opinion will be of what's happened on that day?"

MA: "I think it's going to be a great weekend. We might even crown the world champion right there."

CJ: "That would be nice."

M: "It would be nice for Austin, yes."

CJ: "How do you think the mind-set of the modern driver differs from your mind set during your period?"

MA: "I don't think the mind-set should differ, mainly because the mind-set is having this positive attitude of coming in with the idea of having a result that particular day. My mind-set was always to enter every event with the confidence of winning regardless of how realistically things looked at that moment. And that's the mind-set of every champion, every proper racing driver, to go out there and feel, you know what, things might not look too good but I still think I have a chance of winning today. The preparation for the champion drivers has always been the same—the ultimate in physical conditioning and the total focus of the driver on his job. And that's it. There's no difference. The only difference is in the metal, that is the car that you're sitting in. Today you have more tools to work with, and that's why you go faster."

CJ: "Do you think it's more car-focused today or just as car-focused as in your period?"

MA: "I feel especially in Formula One, the credit goes fifty-fifty. Obviously that could shift by 10 per cent either way at any given time, but the thing is the driver's still in command, and it's the driver's job to bring whatever equipment he's sitting in to the limit. In the past the cars were slower because they didn't have the cornering capability, but the driver worked just as hard as he does today. I've gone through the decades, and I know how this works because I've had the experience. I felt that I fit very well back in the sixties and I would fit very well right in 2012 if I was a little younger. I wouldn't have to change a damn thing as far as my approach to the sport as a driver."

CJ: "There's a great quote by Dale Earnhardt—'It's not the fastest guy, it's the one who refuses to lose.'"

MA: "I'll go along with that."

CJ: "If I may ask a question sent in by the fans?"

MA: "Sure, go ahead . . ."

CJ: "This one from Dr Vanda Collins. What was your late and great friend Ronnie Peterson like to have as a teammate?"

MA: "From the human side and the professional side, he was the perfect teammate. We had a great relationship on a human side as friends with our families, and we definitely had a respect for one another. We enjoyed the racing together and shared the team. We never had a cross word for each other at any time. When I lost him, it was like losing a brother or a son. No question about it."

CJ: "I think that's a great way to finish."

THE LONG AND WINDING ROAD TO
TURN ONE—*USGP 17:11:2012 1400.01.03*

"I didn't get into this as a Formula One or racing fan. My initial reaction was 'Why Austin? Why Texas?' I didn't get into it with the expectation that I'd be running the whole show one day. I think we're going to do well with Formula One racing. I think we will be here for a long time."
Bobby Epstein

"Red McCombs changed my life and so has this project and I am sure it has been the biggest thing that Bobby has done in his life. Perhaps it is the biggest thing we will ever do."
Rad Weaver

Bobby Epstein crackles over the phoneline in that silky southern Texas drawl that he has and immediately apologizes for being late as he was taking his son to *"soccer"*. Yes, even in Texas they play soccer.

Across the board from management, teams, drivers, sponsors and fans the inaugural United States Grand Prix was universally acclaimed yet not a lot is known about the people who made it happen on 17 November.

Turn One at the Circuit of the Americas (COTA) may yet become an iconic part of Formula One folklore but the first turn for the men who brought the race to Texas was a downturn in the economy, which brought an unexpected result.

"I bought the land. I bought it at the worst possible time and I used to joke that we'd put roller coasters and waterparks there one day because no one was going to build houses as the housing market had died," said Bobby Epstein.

"So when I was told that some marketing executives were looking at various properties in that part of town to bring a Formula One race here I listened. I listened very carefully."

I am listening very carefully now as I wonder what exactly this former bond trader thought was his biggest challenge and his biggest achievement.

"Besides ensuring the financial health of the project and navigating some of the very difficult waters I think I focused mainly on what happens outside the racing lines. I focused on the fan experience, the spectator point of view. I think that's where I knew I had something to contribute."

He continued: "From the start I asked for a great fan experience: Give us a large number of overtaking opportunities was my first instruction to the designers. We gave them more or less a blank canvas. We let them choose the land that they thought would fit from a driver's standpoint as well as give a unique fan perspective.

"Tilke were able to draw upon the best characteristics of the most respected features of different tracks from around the world and incorporate that into something that functions year round but can still be the premier track in the world. I think we ended up with something special."

THE SAN ANTONIO CONNECTION

Texas may be "wide open for business" as the slogan goes, so it is not surprising that it also took a great partnership to get the job done. Former baseball player Rad Weaver, who is a director on the board of McCombs Partners, the investment capital firm founded by the extraordinary Red McCombs, joins into the conversation to explain his role.

"Red and I were lead investors on the project. Bobby and I, in many ways have kind of held each other's hand through this project and worked together to help guide this thing through to race day."

McCombs Partners are canny investors who believe in people first but also in the strength of brands. So where will business both from and outside Texas make the most of the USGP?

"They will all learn how they can integrate their brands and activate their brands around F1 and how to make the most of the race weekend as a corporate event."

Looking ahead to the future, Rad said: "In my opinion a natural maturation process will take place through which the teams, COTA and Formula One as well as the brands will find the best way to maximize the exposure that Formula One provides. I think there's no question you will see the US get even more excited next year and more importantly US brands will get very excited."

While the USGP and COTA were definitely an all-American affair they did have some European assistance. Throughout the process they were guided by KHP Consulting in the most important aspects of cultural, social and economic engagement that are necessary to successfully stage a Grand Prix for the first time.

Katja Heim, their CEO, who has guided Bahrain, Shanghai and Abu Dhabi through the same challenging process, is also optimistic for the future. "Year one is normally when you struggle right up to the last minute to deliver the race on time and you think to yourself, 'My God, is everything ready? Is the paint dry? Is everything in the right place?'

"Year two is when people start to show a lot more interest and look to position their brands especially if you've done a good job as COTA have. You have to manage people's expectations and deliver even better than the first time.

"COTA's impact on Texas should exceed $500 million in 2013 while the Grand Prix itself is estimated to bring in more than $250 million to the local economy.

"Year three for the new Grand Prix is the most difficult year, like the difficult third album in music. You have to retain the fans from the first two years but still gather new fans while improving the quality of the product. Whatever you did right the first two times you have to do again, but as if this is the first race all over again. You might be older and more experienced but you have to be a lot wiser."

So Bobby, what was the most difficult part of bringing the race to Austin?

"Other than a disgruntled former partner, not having a contract for a race while simultaneously having a partially built track, lawsuits, impossible construction schedules, politics, the weather and needing a couple of hundred million bucks, the project was a piece of cake."

TEAMS: IN THEIR OWN WORDS

MERCEDES

When it comes to the history of Mercedes-Benz's involvement in Formula One motor racing it can be divided into two distinct eras: the Daimler-Benz years of 1954 and 1955 and the current team that returned to the Formula One World Championship in 2010.

Of course it is important to remember that prior to the establishment of the Formula One World Championship in 1950 Mercedes-Benz competed in Grand Prix motor racing in the 1930s when the legendary "Silver Arrows" with their exposed aluminium bodywork dominated pre-war Grands Prix. In fact, Mercedes have been active since 1901 when the first-ever Mercedes was raced to victory in the Nice-Salon-Nice race and in 1908 the first victory in a Grand Prix motor race for a Mercedes was secured in the French Grand Prix in Dieppe.

It is also important to point out that Mercedes, initially in association with Ilmor Engineering, has operated as an engine supplier since 1994, achieving eighty-six race wins. What is now known as Mercedes AMG High Performance Powertrains first supplied engines to Sauber in 1994 then to McLaren from 1995 to 2014, Force India since 2009, Brawn in 2009, the factory team since 2010, Williams since 2014 and Lotus from 2015.

1954
Mercedes-Benz at the behest of the Chairman of the Board of Management returned to Formula One in spectacular style with

a triumphant one-two victory by Juan Manuel Fangio and Karl Kling in the French Grand Prix in Reims. The Mercedes W196 R was upgraded after the British Grand Prix and Fangio, who had transferred from Maserati earlier in the season, went on to win the German, Swiss and Italian Grand Prix races. His forty-two Drivers' Championship points clinched the World Championship for Fangio from Jose Froilan Gonzalez and Mike Hawthorn.

1955
In 1955 Fangio, Kling and Hans Hermann were joined by Stirling Moss, Andre Simon and Piero Taruffi. The success of 1954 continued into the new season as the W196 R dominated the rest of the field. Fangio won his home race, the Grand Prix of Argentina, followed by victory in the Belgian Grand Prix and a one-two victory with Moss in the Dutch Grand Prix. Moss then went on to sensationally win the British Grand Prix at Aintree from Fangio. In what turned out to be the last appearance for the 1955 Silver Arrows, Fangio won the Italian Grand Prix unchallenged; it turned out to be his last victory for Mercedes-Benz. Fangio won the Drivers' Championship with a total of forty points to the twenty-three secured by Stirling Moss in second place. All of this was overshadowed, however, by the tragic disaster at the 24 Hours of Le Mans which killed Pierre Levegh and over eighty spectators. The French, German, Spanish and Swiss Grands Prix were cancelled as a result. At the end of the season the team withdrew from racing to concentrate on production car engineering, a decision that had been made prior to the tragedy in Le Mans.

2010
Amid much fanfare Mercedes-Benz returned to Formula One as a constructor for the 2010 season with Michael Schumacher and Nico Rosberg as drivers and Ross Brawn as Team Principal. Daimler AG acquired a 45 per cent stake in the Brawn GP team and, along with Aabar Investments (30 per cent), secured a long-term sponsorship deal with Petronas to enter the Championship as Mercedes GP Petronas Formula One Team. The modern era of the Silver Arrows began with a fifth and sixth place at the Bahrain Grand Prix, followed by fifth and tenth place at the

Australian Grand Prix. By season end the team had achieved three podiums and a total of 214 Championship points to finish fourth in the Constructors' Championship, with Rosberg finishing seventh and Schumacher ninth in the driver standings.

2011

With the purchase of the remaining 24.9 per cent stake owned by the team management, Daimler and Aabar completed the takeover of the team as Mercedes entered its second season in the modern era of the Silver Arrows. The MGP W02 was the product of intensive design and development work but results on the track did not live up to expectations. The team once again finished fourth in the Constructors' Championship with 165 points as Rosberg finished in seventh place with eighty-nine points and Schumacher one spot behind with seventy-six points in the Drivers' World Championship. There were no wins, no podiums and no poles, but the team built for the future with the appointments in the engineering department of Bob Bell as Technical Director, Geoffrey Willis as Technology Director and Aldo Costa as Engineering Director.

2012

For the 2012 season the team strengthened the ties between AMG and Mercedes-Benz, to become known as Mercedes AMG Petronas F1 Team, and at the Chinese Grand Prix Rosberg achieved the first victory since Fangio at the 1955 Italian Grand Prix. This was Rosberg's first victory in his 111th Grand prix and the first by a German driver in a Silver Arrow since Hermann Lang in the 1939 Swiss Grand Prix. However, in what was to be Schumacher's last season in Formula One, the team finished a disappointing fifth in the Constructors' standings on 142 points with Rosberg (ninety-three points) and Schumacher (forty-nine points) placed ninth and thirteenth respectively in the Drivers' Championship.

2013

Lewis Hamilton joined the team in 2013, replacing Michael Schumacher (308 GPs), in a three-year deal to race alongside

Nico Rosberg and immediately made an impact by finishing third in the second race of the season in Malaysia. After a series of four pole positions for the team Rosberg secured victory at the Monaco Grand Prix. More success followed with third in Canada for Hamilton and victory for Rosberg at Silverstone. After four consecutive pole positions Hamilton claimed his first victory for the team in the Hungarian Grand Prix. Three further podium finishes and points in every race in the second half of the season enabled the team to pip Ferrari for second place in the Constructor's Championship by six points in the season finale in Brazil. Ross Brawn retired as Team Principal at the end of the season to be replaced by the pairing of Toto Wolff (Executive Director Business) and Paddy Lowe (Executive Director Technical).

2014

A revolution in engine regulations in 2014 introduced a 1.6-litre turbocharged V6 engine with a built-in energy recovery system. Mercedes made the best use of these new rules to produce a dominant car due to the innovative design of the car's engine. The F1 W05 utilized the PU106A Hybrid which packaged the turbo and compressor at opposite ends of the internal combustion engine, giving the team an aerodynamic, battery and packaging advantage. The F1 W05 Hybrid became the most dominant car in Formula One history, with the team finishing the season 296 points ahead of their nearest rival Red Bull Racing to secure the Constructors' Championship with a massive 701 points. Lewis Hamilton and Nico Rosberg achieved a record breaking sixteen wins (split 11-5), eighteen poles (7-11), twelve fastest laps (7-5), eleven front row lockouts and eleven one-two finishes. Hamilton was crowned World Champion in Abu Dhabi finishing on 384 points, sixty-seven ahead of second-placed Rosberg on 317 points. The team won a reported $102 million prize for winning the Constructors' Title.

2015

The 2015 Formula One season was the second in the new era of Hybrid Power Units. As in the previous year, the contest for the title soon developed into a thrilling battle between the two Silver Arrows drivers. Lewis and Nico won 16 of the 19 races on the calendar, continuing the Silver Arrows' domination of the year before.

Reigning champion Lewis started off with a victory in the Australian Grand Prix with Nico finishing second to make it the first one-two result for the Silver Arrows of the new campaign. As the season progressed, eleven further one-twos were to follow.

The second of these came on the third race weekend in China. After Sebastian Vettel had lifted the winner's trophy in Malaysia, Lewis and Nico returned to winning ways in Shanghai, finishing first and second respectively. This was followed by a victory for Lewis in Bahrain and Nico's first two wins of the seasons in Barcelona and Monaco—the German's third successive victory in the Principality.

The next three races—Canada, Austria and Great Britain—were then a ding-dong battle between Lewis and Nico, with each of them taking it in turns to claim the top spot on the podium. After a disappointing result in Hungary, Lewis embarked on a six-race winning streak that sealed his third world championship title, starting with the Belgian Grand Prix and concluding in the USA. In fact, his championship lead was so great that he wrapped up the title in the fourth-to-last race in Austin.

Undeterred, Nico struck back with victories on the last three grand prix weekends of the season in Mexico, Brazil and Abu Dhabi. Meanwhile, the team secured the Constructors' Championship for the second time in a row with a formidable points total of 703.

Lewis added another chapter to his success story by winning his third F1 world championship title and joined an elite group of Formula One legends, equalling the record of his childhood hero Ayrton Senna—and of a certain Niki Lauda. He has regular face-to-face contact with Niki, of course, in the latter's capacity as Chairman of the Supervisory Board to the Silver Arrows team.

With his tenth win of the season in Austin, Lewis set yet another record, becoming the first driver in the history of Formula One to register more than ten Grand Prix victories in two consecutive seasons. Only three drivers have so far taken their win tally into double digits in a single season: Michael Schumacher (2002, 2004), Sebastian Vettel (2011, 2013) and Lewis (2014, 2015).

2016

Nico began the new season in Melbourne's Albert Park just as he had ended the previous one—with a win. In fact, the German finished the first four races in Australia, Bahrain, China and Russia as the victor—each time, starting from the front row.

Nico had now achieved seven wins in a row, following on from the last three races of 2015 in Mexico, Brazil and Abu Dhabi. What better way to take the momentum from the previous year with you into the new year? Lewis, meanwhile, finished three of the first four races on the podium, while technical problems meant he could manage no better than a modest seventh place in Shanghai.

Then came Barcelona—and an abrupt end to the Silver Arrows' winning streak, with both cars out of the race within just a few hundred metres. All that was wads quickly forgotten for Lewis, however, who final clinched his first victory of 2016 at the prestigious Grand Prix of Monaco—his adoptive home race. But it was hard work getting there. In a chaotic race, Lewis claimed the 44th victory of his career from third on the grid.

  With Nico finishing the Monaco Grand Prix back in seventh place, Lewis took the first sizable chunk out of his team-mate's championship lead. He continued in the same vein in the next race—the Canadian Grand Prix—once again ascending the top spot of the podium. But Nico never gave up for one moment. He hit back straightaway with a win at the European Grand Prix.

After a difficult weekend in Baku came the perfect month for Lewis: four victories in five weeks took him to the top of the World Championship standings for the first time that year. Where Nico had come away from Russia with a lead of forty-three points, he went into the summer break nineteen points adrift. With six victories from seven races, Lewis had made a truly impressive sprint in July.

After the summer break, Nico again made a clean start to the second half of the year as he had done to kick off the season. Taking wins in Belgium, Italy, Singapore and Japan, he not only scored vital points but also showed that he was not about to let setbacks stop him in his tracks. He showed that he had learned lessons from his experiences of the past years, achieving all four wins at circuits where he had never won before.

One of the major outcomes of the weekend in Japan was, of course, the winning of the Constructors' World Championship. With an unassailable lead of 208 points, the Silver Arrows had wrapped up their third successive title. In the run-up to the World Championship showdown in Abu Dhabi, the much-vaunted momentum once again favoured Lewis. The three-time champion won in the USA, Mexico and, for the first time in his career, Brazil, keeping the title fight wide open until the finale at the Yas Marina Circuit. However, is was Nico who wrapped things up with second place in the season finale to secure his first World Championship title in his eleventh Formula One season. A few days later, just before the FIA Prizegiving gala in Vienna, Nico shocked the world by announcing that: we would retire with immediate effect from Formula One.

2017

Lewis Hamilton started the year on the right foot in Australia by taking the first pole position of the 2017 Formula One season, but he was beaten to race victory by Ferrari's Sebastian Vettel.
The on-track battle with Ferrari in Melbourne set the tone for the first half of the year. Lewis bounced back by winning in China, but both he and new team-mate Valtteri Bottas—who scored his first pole position in Bahrain—lost out to Sebastian in Sakhir.
The next round in Russia proved to be a special one for Valtteri, as he stormed into the lead at the start and held off Sebastian in the closing stages to take his first win in F1.

Lewis and Sebastian's Championship battle hit the track in Spain, with the two World Champions fighting hard for victory. Lewis emerged ahead this time round and in Canada, but that was sandwiched by a disappointing seventh place in Monaco, as the team struggled to get the most out of the W08 around the Monte Carlo streets.

Azerbaijan was next on the calendar and proved to be one of the most action-packed races of the season. It featured three

Safety Car periods and a red flag, due to numerous incidents—
including Sebastian making contact with Lewis at the second
restart.

Lewis looked set for a good result until his headrest started to
work loose and he was forced to pit for repairs, eventually finishing fifth—one spot behind Sebastian.

Valtteri's second F1 victory arrived in Austria, before Lewis
led his team-mate home in a dominant Silverstone display. The
team struggled in Hungary, with Valtteri the lead car in third
place, before momentum started to build in Belgium and Lewis
began to claw back ground.

On his 200th F1 start, Lewis took a controlled victory at
Spa-Francorchamps, before backing that up with another victory
in Italy next time out—giving him the Championship lead for the
first time in 2017.

The start drama for Ferrari in Singapore allowed Lewis to take
a surprise win and he was second in Malaysia, before returning to
winning ways in Japan and the USA. Coupled with Valtteri's P5
at COTA, that was enough for Mercedes to secure its fourth
Constructors' crown.

Lewis headed to Mexico knowing he had a good chance of
taking the Drivers' title and he did so in dramatic style after
Sebastian made contact with him on lap one. He rallied back
from a puncture to finish P9 and take his fourth Championship.
Mercedes signed off 2017 with second place in Brazil and master-
ful race victory in Abu Dhabi for Valtteri, with Lewis fourth and
second in the final two races.

Key Personnel Profiles

Niki Lauda, Non-Executive Chairman

Nationality: Austrian
Date of Birth: 22 February 1949
Place of Birth: Vienna, Austria

2012	Non-Executive Chairman, Mercedes-AMG Petronas Motorsport
2002	Team Principal, Jaguar Racing Formula One Team
2001	Race Director, Jaguar Racing Formula One Team
1993	Strategic Advisor, Scuderia Ferrari
1985	Formula One: Marlboro McLaren International – 10th
1984	Formula One: Marlboro McLaren International – 1st
1983	Formula One: Marlboro McLaren International – 10th
1982	Formula One: Marlboro McLaren International – 5th
1979	Formula One: Parmalat Racing Team – 14th
1978	Formula One: Parmalat Racing Team – 4th
1977	Formula One: Scuderia Ferrari – 1st
1976	Formula One: Scuderia Ferrari – 2nd
1975	Formula One: Scuderia Ferrari – 1st
1974	Formula One: Scuderia Ferrari – 4th
1973	Formula One: Marlboro-BRM – 18th
1972	Formula One: STP March Racing Team – Not Classified
1971	Formula One: STP March Racing Team – Not Classified

Nikolaus Andreas 'Niki' Lauda is not only a racing legend but the no-nonsense Non-Executive Chairman of Mercedes-Benz Grand Prix Ltd.

A three-time Formula One World Champion behind the wheel in 1975, 1977 and 1984, Niki has added a four more titles to his tally since his appointment to the position of Non-Executive Chairman of Mercedes-Benz Grand Prix Ltd in September 2012.

Born on 22 February 1949 to a wealthy industrialist family in Vienna, Niki was expected to follow his father into the paper manufacturing industry—but the young Austrian had other ideas. With his early motor racing career financed by a series of bank loans, Niki rapidly progressed up the motorsport ladder—eventually joining Scuderia Ferrari in 1974 and scoring his first win that same year.

A first Formula One title followed a year later—but it was the 1976 season that was to define Lauda's career, after he suffered near-fatal injuries in an accident at the Nürburgring. Through sheer force of will, Niki would return to the cockpit just six weeks later at Monza.

Scarred but undeterred, Niki would ultimately concede the 1976 title to his great rival and later friend James Hunt, before adding a second World Championship to his list of honours the following season.

After adding a third crown in 1984, Niki retired from F1 at the end of the 1985 season, taking on a role with German commercial TV station RTL as the resident expert in addition to acting as an adviser to Ferrari in the mid-90s.

For the 2001 and 2002 seasons, Niki became first Race Director and later Team Principal at the British Jaguar Racing Formula 1 team. He would return to the boardroom in 2012 as Non-Executive Chairman of Mercedes-Benz Grand Prix Ltd.

Away from the racetrack, Niki has put his entrepreneurial talents to work for his second great passion—aviation. Lauda Air was born in 1979 and by the 1990s had obtained a worldwide scheduled flight concession, leading to close collaboration with Lufthansa and ultimately the takeover of Lauda Air by the German operator in 2002. Fly Niki was born 12 months later, itself eventually taken over by Air Berlin in 2011 and Niki's company Laudamotion at the start of 2018.

Toto Wolff, Team Principal & CEO

Nationality: Austrian
Date of Birth: 12 January 1972
Place of Birth: Vienna, Austria

2013   Appointed as a managing partner of Mercedes-AMG Petronas Motorsport and Head of Mercedes-Benz Motorsport
2013   Appointed Head of Mercedes-Benz Motorsport

2012   Appointed Executive Director of Williams Grand Prix Holdings PLC
2009   Invested in Williams F1
2006   Invested in HWA AG; winner of Dubai 24 Hours
2004   Founded Marchsixteen Investments
2002   FIA NGT World Championship, 6th overall with one win
1998   Founded Marchfifteen Investments
1994   Class winner, Nürburgring 24 Hours
1992   Began motorsport career in Austrian Formula Ford Championship

Torger Christian 'Toto' Wolff is Team Principal & CEO of Mercedes-AMG Petronas Motorsport alongside wider responsibilities as Head of Mercedes-Benz Motorsport.

Born into modest surroundings in Vienna, Austria, Toto's first taste of motorsport came when at 17, whilst watching a friend race at the Nürburgring. A short racing career of his own followed, competing in Austrian Formula Ford and scoring a class win at the 1994 Nürburgring 24 Hours.

Toto called time on his racing career just three years later, pursuing his business career and finding a new outlet for his talent—investment. After studying at the Vienna University of Economics and Business, Toto founded his own investment company, Marchfifteen, in 1998, followed by Marchsixteen in 2004.

Initially focusing on internet and technology companies in the 'tech boom' era of the 90s, the business developed strategic investments in medium-size industrial companies and listed companies.

One of these investments included the initial public offering of HWA AG—the company responsible for developing and racing Mercedes-Benz cars for the DTM (German Touring Car Championship), as well as Mercedes-Benz's successful Formula 3 engine programme. Toto divested his stake in HWA AG in 2015.

In 2002, Toto started a new venture, co-owning a racing driver management company alongside two-time Formula One World Champion Mika Häkkinen. The same year, Toto returned to racing, winning once en route to sixth in the FIA GT World Championship. Further success followed in 2006, when Toto claimed top overall honours at the 24 Hours of Bahrain.

In November 2009, Toto merged his passion for racing and investment by investing in the Williams F1 Team. By July 2012, Toto was the Executive Director of the team, playing a key leadership role as Williams scored its first win in eight years at the Spanish Grand Prix that season.

Less than a year later, Toto was announced as managing partner of Mercedes-AMG Petronas Motorsport in January 2013 after purchasing a 30 per cent stake of Mercedes-Benz Grand Prix Ltd.

Subsequently appointed Head of Mercedes-Benz Motorsport at the end of 2013, Toto went on to assume full responsibility for the entire Mercedes-Benz motorsport programme—from Formula One to DTM, sports cars and the Formula 3 engine programme.

An entrepreneur, an investor and a racer, motorsport runs in Toto Wolff's blood. Under his leadership, Mercedes-AMG Petronas Motorsport has clinched five consecutive Formula One World Championship, Driver and Constructor titles.

Andy Cowell, Managing Director of Mercedes-AMG High Performance Powertrains

Nationality: British
Date of Birth: 12 February 1969
Place of Birth: Blackpool, England

2013   Managing Director, Mercedes-AMG High Performance Powertrains
2008   Engineering and Programme Director, Mercedes-Benz HPE
2006   Chief Engineer, Engines, Mercedes-Benz HPE
2005   Chief Engineer, V8 Engine Project, Mercedes-Benz High Performance Engines
2004   Principal Engineer, V10 Engine, Mercedes-Ilmor

2000   Principal Engineer, F1 Design and Development, Cosworth Racing

1999   Head of Pre-Development, Formula One, BMW Motorsport

1997   Principal Engineer, F1 Design and Development, Cosworth Racing

1994   Senior Engineer, F1 Design and Development, Cosworth Racing

1992   Project Engineer, F1 Design and Development, Cosworth Racing

1991   Graduate Engineer, Cosworth Racing

Andy Cowell is Managing Director of Mercedes-AMG High Performance Powertrains. He is a Fellow of both the IMechE and the Royal Academy of Engineering.

When asked for his motivation to start working in F1, Andy explains that it is a childhood dream come true: 'I wanted to work in Formula One because of my childhood addiction to motorsport, helping my Dad compete in sprints and hillclimbs and avidly watching Formula One on the TV.'

Andy's career path was set after a year spent on the Reynard Scholarship Scheme during his Mechanical Engineering degree. He joined Cosworth Racing Ltd. on their graduate scheme straight from university and worked his way through the company's various technical departments before specialising in the design and development of Formula One engines.

By 1998, Andy was leading the engineering project group responsible for the top end of the innovative CK engine, as raced to victory by Stewart-Ford in 1999. He spent a year with BMW Motorsport in 2000, managing the engineering group responsible for the concept and detail of the 2001 BMW-Williams engine.

Andy returned to Cosworth as Principal Engineer for F1 design and development in 2001, managing new engine projects in 2001 and 2003, before joining the company then known as Mercedes-Ilmor in 2004 as Principal Engineer for the FQ V10 engine project.

14 years later, he remembers joining the Mercedes family as follows: 'On my first day with the team, I felt privileged to be

working with such a capable group and apprehensive about my ability to positively contribute.'

He worked as Chief Engineer on Ilmor's V8 engine project before taking on responsibility for the technical and programme leadership of all engine projects—including the KERS Hybrid system, which made its race debut in 2009 and for which the company was subsequently awarded the prestigious Dewar Trophy by the Royal Automobile Club.

Andy subsequently served as Engineering and Programme Director for Mercedes-Benz High Performance Engines from July 2008 to January 2013, responsible for technical and programme leadership of all engine and powertrain projects, plus the strategy and organisation of the engineering group.

Since January 2013, Andy has been Managing Director of Mercedes-AMG High Performance Powertrains, overseeing development of the PU106A V6 Hybrid Power Unit, which went on to successfully power the 2014 championship winning F1 W05 Hybrid and was also awarded the Dewar Trophy.

Under Andy's leadership, Mercedes-AMG High Performance Powertrains has powered the Silver Arrows to eight world titles in four years, winning both the Drivers' and Constructors' championships in 2014, 2015, 2016 and 2017.

The Mercedes-AMG F1 M08 EQ Power+, the hybrid power unit of the 2017 season, played a pivotal role in the team's historic success of defending the titles across a major regulation change. The same power unit achieved a conversion efficiency of more than 50% during dyno testing in Brixworth, making it the most efficient racing engine ever made.

Andy was awarded the IMechE James Clayton Award in 2013 for his outstanding contributions to engine design and development in Formula One—including the V10, V8 and incumbent V6 with Hybrid Energy Recovery System—while also being recognised for his leadership at Brixworth.

RED BULL RACING

Red Bull Racing came into existence late in 2004 with ambitions to challenge for grand prix victories and world championship titles—but this is not the work of a moment and at the time the team had neither the facilities nor the depth of experience to challenge the best in the business. Under the guidance of team principal Christian Horner—himself new to F1—that was to change.

Over the next four seasons solid foundations were laid on which later success was built. The team recruited in both quantity and quality, steadily expanding in numbers until it was capable of going toe-to-toe with the most illustrious names in racing. Many of those recruited came with proven championship-winning pedigree—but the growing team wasn't looking solely outward, it also promoted from within: Red Bull Racing was a young team in every sense.

Behind the scenes, progress was rapid but on track the upward curve was less pronounced. The team finished seventh in 2005 and 2006. The initial driver line-up was a mix of youth and experience: David Coulthard provided the latter, while Christian Klien, Vitantonio Liuzzi and Robert Doornbos were the former. Coulthard scored the team's first podium, finishing third on the streets of Monaco in 2006.

For 2007 Mark Webber came onboard to join Coulthard. The team finished fifth in 2007 but disappointingly dropped back to seventh again in 2008—but everything was going to change in 2009.

David Coulthard retired at the end of 2008 to be replaced by Sebastian Vettel. The young German driver was a product of the Red Bull Junior Team and already a race winner in a Milton Keynes-designed Toro Rosso. His arrival at the senior team coincided with a major reset in the sport's aerodynamic regulations. The new rules provided a level playing field and gave Red Bull Racing's technical team, led by Adrian Newey, the chance to shine. In the RB5 they produced a winner. Vettel took the team's first grand prix victory, leading home Webber in a 1-2 finish at the Chinese Grand Prix, the third race of the season. The car would win five times further in 2009, including Webber's debut F1 victory at the German Grand Prix. The team finished second in the Constructors' Championship but, perhaps more significantly, it won the final three races of the season and went into the winter with confidence high, very much the in-form outfit.

The following year saw us achieve the ambitions laid down five years earlier. Driving the RB6, Webber and Vettel were the class of the field in 2010 and title contenders from the start. Their consistent podium finishes secured the team a first title, the Constructors' Championship, at the penultimate round in Brazil. Both drivers went to the final race in Abu Dhabi with a shot at the Drivers' crown. Vettel emerged triumphant, winning the race to became the sports' youngest ever World Champion. It was his fifth win of the season and the team's ninth.

The Red Bull RB7 and Vettel dominated 2011. He took eleven of the team's dozen victories during the season, and fifteen of our eighteen pole positions. He took his second Drivers' Championship title in Japan with four races to spare. The Constructors' title was confirmed a week later in South Korea.

The raw statistics suggest the RB7 was a far superior car to the RB6—but many within the team would argue to the contrary. The RB7 was our first KERS-equipped car and our inexperience designing the hybrid system led to teething trouble that went on deep into the year. What really made the difference in 2011 was that Red Bull Racing had evolved as a team. There was maturity and confidence running through the organisation. Car development was rapid and successful, the manufacturing operation was highly efficient, in the garage the race team were an incredibly slick unit capable of rebuilding a car in record time and then performing a sequence of benchmark pitstops. The team had learnt how to win and it wasn't about to stop winning.

Formula One, however, is ultra-competitive and the competition fought back hard in 2012. The first half of the season was an incredibly tight-fought battle. The first seven races went to seven different winners representing five different manufacturers and at the midpoint of the year, both titles were up for grabs. Red Bull Racing managed to kick on in the second half of the season and four consecutive victories saw Vettel emerge as a strong title contender. Those wins also propelled the team to a significant lead in the Constructors' Championship. That title was clinched at the penultimate round in the USA, leaving Seb to take the title in Brazil at the season finale. He did so with what is probably the (second) most dramatic Brazilian Grand Prix on record, surviving a first lap crash complete with a spin and significant damage to the car. This left him dead last, facing the wrong way and with the prospect of a race back through the field in foul weather. Spectacular for fans; painful to watch for anyone in the garage.

History appeared to be repeating in 2013. The RB9 looked like the class of the field from the start—but somehow never seemed to produce the decisive advantage it promised. That changed after the mid-season break when Vettel went on the rampage, setting a new record for consecutive victories, ending the season with nine in a row. Both titles were secured in India, with three races to spare—which meant when F1 got to Texas it was a very relaxed crew that competed the sport's first sub-two seconds pitstop, changing all four wheels on Webber's car in 1.92 seconds.

Red Bull Racing are not the first team to win four double championships in a row, but the others had done so with decades of experience at the top of Formula One. Red Bull Racing's rapid rise to the pinnacle of the sport was a very different ascent—and arguably more remarkable than the trophies themselves.

Success in F1 is, however, ephemeral, and the 2014 season saw reality bite. The new hybrid power units heralded a change in the established order. Saddled with a sizeable horsepower deficit the RB10 lacked the competitive edge enjoyed by its predecessors. Nevertheless, the car was still good enough to provide Daniel Ricciardo with his first, second and third Formula One victories.

Ricciardo had replaced Webber, the latter having decided to retire from Formula One at the end of the preceding season. Ricciardo, another product of the Red Bull Junior Team had made a name for himself at Toro Rosso—though few predicted the immediate impact he would have at Red Bull Racing. Ricciardo outscored his quadruple World Champion team-mate to finish third in the standings—but also narrowly out-qualified Vettel. While the team came down to Earth in 2014, its new driver was flying high.

Vettel departed at the end of 2014 and was replaced by another product of the Red Bull Junior Team, Daniil Kvyat. Like Ricciardo and Vettel before him, Kvyat had developed his skills at Toro

Rosso before taking the step up. Not that the step was so great in 2015. Still plagued by a horsepower deficit, and struggling to get the car balanced, the team endured its worst campaign since 2008. Ultimately it would finish fourth in the Constructors' Championship—though the second half of the season saw a return to form of sorts as the team fixed its balance issues and rose the top of the midfield. It boded well for 2016.

Red Bull did indeed move up the table again in 2016. The team finished second in the Constructors' Championship and Daniel Ricciardo was third in the Drivers' table once again—though the name on everyone's lips was that of Max Verstappen. The young Dutchman was promoted from Toro Rosso to replace Kvyat after four races of the season. He got off to the best start possible, winning his first race for Red Bull Racing, the Spanish Grand Prix at the Circuit de Catalunya-Barcelona. Ricciardo added a second victory in Malaysia, having narrowly missed out in Monaco after taking his first pole position.

Being second best in 2016 was frustrating, albeit frustration tempered by the knowledge that a major regulation change was coming for 2017 and could, potentially, play to the team's strengths. It didn't particularly pan-out that way with the car struggling for early-season form. The team, however, excels at in-season development, and the RB13 was soon on the podium. Daniel managed a mid-season sequence of five top three finishes in a row, including victory at the inaugural Azerbaijan Grand Prix. It was, however, later in the year that the car started to look properly competitive, with Max taking victories entirely on merit in Malaysia and Mexico.

Despite these results, the team slipped to third place in the 2017 standings, a position which was replicated in the 2018 season.

It was announced on 3 August that Ricciardo had signed a two-year contract to drive for Renault Sport Formula One Team. He was replaced by Pierre Gasly from Toro Rosso.

2017
HIGHLIGHTS:
• Max wins the Mexican Grand Prix to take his second win of the season

- The Team get a double podium in Japan with Max 2nd and Daniel 3rd
- Max takes his first win of the season in Malaysia
- Double podium for the Team in Malaysia with Max taking 1st place and Daniel 3rd
- Team's 100th podium in China
- Daniel's 20th podium in Monaco
- Daniel's first win of the season in Azerbaijan
- The Austrian Grand Prix marked Daniel's fifth consecutive podium

PODIUMS:
- 3rd Chinese Grand Prix (Max Verstappen)
- 3rd Spanish Grand Prix (Daniel Ricciardo)
- 3rd Monaco Grand Prix (Daniel Ricciardo)
- 3rd Canadian Grand Prix (Daniel Ricciardo)
- 1st Azerbaijan Grand Prix (Daniel Ricciardo)
- 3rd Austrian Grand Prix (Daniel Ricciardo)
- 3rd Belgian Grand Prix (Daniel Ricciardo)
- 2nd Singapore Grand Prix (Daniel Ricciardo)
- 1st Malaysian Grand Prix (Max Verstappen)
- 3rd Malaysian Grand Prix (Daniel Ricciardo)
- 2nd Japanese Grand Prix (Max Verstappen)
- 3rd Japanese Grand Prix (Daniel Ricciardo)
- 1st Mexican Grand Prix (Max Verstappen)

2016
HIGHLIGHTS:
- 2nd Constructors' Championship
- 3rd Drivers' Championship (Daniel Ricciardo)
—One Win
—Seven additional podium finishes
- 1st and 2nd at the Malaysian Grand Prix
- 468 Championship points
- 16 podiums

WINS:
- Win Spanish Grand Prix (Max Verstappen)
- Win Malaysian Grand Prix (Daniel Ricciardo)

PODIUMS:
- 3rd Chinese Grand Prix (Daniil Kyvat)
- 2nd Monaco Grand Prix (Daniel Ricciardo)
- 2nd Austrian Grand Prix (Max Verstappen)
- 2nd British Grand Prix (Max Verstappen)
- 3rd Hungarian Grand Prix (Daniel Ricciardo)
- 2nd German Grand Prix (Daniel Ricciardo)
- 3rd German Grand Prix (Max Verstappen)
- 2nd Belgium Grand Prix (Daniel Ricciardo)
- 2nd Singapore Grand Prix (Daniel Ricciardo)
- 2nd Malaysian Grand Prix (Max Verstappen)
- 2nd Japanese Grand Prix (Max Verstappen)
- 3rd United States Grand Prix (Daniel Ricciardo)
- 3rd Mexican Grand Prix (Daniel Ricciardo)
- 3rd Brazilian Grand Prix (Max Verstappen)

2015
HIGHLIGHTS:
- 4th Constructors' Championship
- 187 Championship points
- Double podium (2nd and 3rd) at the Hungarian Grand Prix

PODIUMS:
- 2nd Singapore Grand Prix (Daniel Ricciardo)
- 2nd Hungarian Grand Prix (Daniil Kyvat)
- 3rd Hungarian Grand Prix (Daniel Ricciardo)

WILLIAMS: A RICH HERITAGE

1977

Williams Grand Prix Engineering Ltd is founded by Frank Williams and ambitious British engineer Patrick Head. The company is based in an empty carpet warehouse in Didcot, Oxfordshire, and enters a purchased March chassis in order to compete in F1 during the latter half of the season. It sets about designing a car to contest the 1978 FIA Formula One World Championship with a staff of just seventeen people. Frank Williams finds a consortium of Middle Eastern backers to support the team's efforts and the first car, the FW06, is shaken down at the end of the year with Australian ace Alan Jones behind the wheel.

1978

The team fields a one-car team during its first season of competition. Alan Jones immediately forms a close working relationship with Williams and Head, and the car is competitive. "AJ" finishes fourth in only the team's third race, in South Africa, and he bags a podium at the penultimate race of the year, the USA GP East. Staff numbers swell from seventeen to fifty and Frank buys an entry for a second car in 1979 from John Surtees, whose team is closing down.

DID YOU KNOW?

Alongside his driving duties for Williams in 1978, Alan Jones wins the Can-Am title in the United States.

1979

Williams finishes runner-up in the Constructors' Championship beaten by Ferrari, who also win the Drivers' Title with Jody Scheckter. Jones and Clay Regazzoni are forced to race FW06s until the Belgian Grand Prix when the ground effect FW07 makes its debut. Regazzoni wins the team's first race, at Silverstone, and Alan Jones is the man to beat during the second half of the year, winning four races. Off-track, Patrick Head understands the increasing importance of aerodynamics in F1, so the team buys a wind tunnel from Lola.

DID YOU KNOW?
Frank Williams has very fond memories of 1979. "The car was a beauty that year," he says. "Whenever it finished, it won. Suddenly Williams were the team to drive for."

1980
The FW07B is the car to beat. Jones dominates the season en route to winning the World Title and he is ably supported by his new teammate, Carlos Reutemann. The Constructors' crown falls to the team as well, leading Frank Williams to comment, "This is the best feeling in the world." The team takes six victories (five for Jones, one for Reutemann) and nineteen podiums during the year, much to the delight of new sponsor Leyland Vehicles.

DID YOU KNOW?
Alan Jones contracts pleurisy prior to the USA Grand Prix West, following poor weather at a Silverstone test session and a damp bed in South Africa. He still competes at Long Beach, but crashes out of the race.

1981
Carlos Reutemann and Alan Jones win four races and bag the team its second consecutive Constructors' Championship. Reutemann loses out on the Drivers' Title by one point at the final race in Las Vegas, leading him to announce his retirement. The team's meteoric rise is acknowledged by Her Majesty the Queen, when Frank Williams receives the Queen's Award for Export. The team's title sponsorship changes hands mid-season from Abilad Williams to TAG Williams.

DID YOU KNOW?
Alan Jones breaks his little finger in a fight in the middle of the season, following a traffic incident in London. He carries on driving despite four of his fingers having to be bandaged.

1982
Rosberg wins the world title by five points with only one victory. The team's other FW08 is shared by Reutemann, Derek Daly and Mario Andretti. Reutemann finishes second in the season opener in South Africa, but he retires from driving after the second race and Daly takes over the car. Andretti makes a guest appearance at Long Beach. The team develops a four-wheel drive, six-wheeled F1 car for 1983, but the technology is banned before the team has a chance to race it.

DID YOU KNOW?
There were eleven different winners from sixteen races in 1982—a record.

1983
With turbo engines fully entrenched in F1, the Williams FW08C struggles in 1983 with its normally-aspirated Cosworth V8. Rosberg does brilliantly to win at Monaco but there are few highlights for Jacque Lafitte in the team's least successful season since 1978. At the last race in South Africa the Honda-powered FW09 turbo makes its debut, with Rosberg coming home in an encouraging fifth place. Over the winter the team moves into new, bigger premises in Didcot.

DID YOU KNOW?
Williams gave Ayrton Senna his first Formula One test at Donington Park in 1983. As you might expect, the Brazilian was immediately on the pace.

1984
The season is blighted by unreliability as Williams and Honda get to grips with turbo power for the first time. When the engine holds together, the car is quick and Rosberg takes a brilliant victory in the USA Grand Prix in Dallas. Jacques Laffite endures a disappointing season. He scores just five points to Rosberg's twenty-point-five and the team announces in September that Nigel Mansell will replace him in 1985.

DID YOU KNOW?
The race morning warm-up was held so early in Dallas that
Jacques Laffite turned up in the pits wearing his pyjamas!

1985

The FW10 is Williams' first carbon fibre chassis and the
improved torsional stiffness of the car has an immediate impact
on performance. The FW10 is the car to beat from mid-season,
once reliability is established. Rosberg leaves tongues wagging
at Silverstone when he sets a pole position lap of 160.938 mph—
the fastest lap ever recorded by an F1 car at the time. At the
Austrian Grand Prix in August, Rosberg announces that he is to
leave the team after four seasons and switch to McLaren. Nelson
Piquet will partner Mansell from the start of 1986.

DID YOU KNOW?
One of Nigel Mansell's first jobs after joining the team was to take
Frank's children on the dodgems at a fairground near Zandvoort
in Holland!

1986

The year gets off to a devastating start, when Frank Williams
is seriously injured in a road accident in the south of France.
He crashes while driving to the airport after a pre-season test
at Paul Ricard and his injuries leave him confined to a wheelchair. The dominance of the FW11 allows Williams to clinch
its third Constructors' Title with Nelson Piquet and Nigel
Mansell. They enter the final race in Adelaide as overwhelming
favourites to claim the Drivers' Title too, but they suffer tyre
problems and are beaten to the crown by Alain Prost in a
McLaren.

DID YOU KNOW?
To cap his most successful season in F1, in which he scores five
wins, Mansell is named BBC Sports Personality of the Year in the
UK.

1987

Nine months after his car accident, Frank Williams is back at the helm of Williams. He is awarded a CBE in the Queen's New Year Honours list and, fittingly, 1987 is a dominant season for the team in which it wins the Drivers' and Constructors' Titles. The team becomes unstoppable from mid-season. Nelson Picquet wraps up the Drivers' Title at Suzuka when Nigel Mansell's season comes to a premature end, following a heavy crash. At the Italian Grand Prix Honda announces that it will end its partnership with Williams at the end of the season, one year ahead of schedule.

DID YOU KNOW?

The team debuts its fi rst active suspension car at the Italian Grand Prix and Nelson Piquet duly romps to an impressive victory.

1988

While it waits for the arrival of Renault power in 1989, John Judd steps into the engine breach with his normally-aspirated V8, but it proves a disappointing year for the team. The highlights are Nigel Mansell's two podiums, at Silverstone and Jerez. Mansell suffers a bout of chickenpox mid-season, forcing him to miss the Belgian and Italian Grands Prix. He is replaced by Martin Brundle and Jean-Loius Schlesser, the latter's race at Monza becoming infamous for a misunderstanding between him and race leader Ayrton Senna at the first chicane. Senna retires and Monza is the only race of the year that McLaren fails to win.

DID YOU KNOW?

Riccardo Patrese is fined a whopping $10,000 for impeding Julian Bailey during qualifying for the Spanish Grand Prix.

1989

Thierry Boutsen wins a couple of races (in Canada and Australia) and the team secure second place in the Constructors' Championship. Renault's V10 hits the ground running and, in the back of the FW13, which is introduced for the final four races of the year, it's a particularly potent force. The drivers score four podiums in four races, helping the team to leapfrog Ferrari in the Constructors' standings.

DID YOU KNOW?
At the season-opening Brazilian Grand Prix, Riccardo Patrese starts his 177th race—a record at the time for the most Grand Prix starts by a driver.

1990
The team starts the year with an updated FW13 and there are only two highlights: Riccardo's win at Imola and Thierry's tenacious drive to victory in Hungary, in which he leads the entire race and comes home just 0.2 seconds ahead of Senna. However, the team needs to up its game in 1991 so in September Mansell re-signs, joining new aerodynamicist Adrian Newey.

DID YOU KNOW?
Drug testing in Formula One was introduced at the 1990 British Grand Prix.

1991
This year marks the beginning of a very successful period for Williams-Renault. Riccardo Patrese in the FW14 takes the team's first win of the year in Mexico, and Nigel Mansell goes on to win five races to Patrese's two. Mansell's victory at Silverstone produces one of the most iconic images of the year when he gives Senna, whose McLaren has run out of fuel, a lift back to the pits after the chequered flag.

DID YOU KNOW?
Riccardo Patrese's victory in the Portuguese Grand Prix was the team's fiftieth win.

1992
The FW14B is still regarded as one of the most advanced racing cars ever built. It features a semi-automatic gearbox, active suspension, traction control and anti-lock brakes. Mansell wins

the opening five races of the year and wraps up the title at the Hungarian Grand Prix in August. With Patrese's impressive consistency Williams are Constructors' Champions for a fifth time. Nigel and Riccardo leave the team at the end of the season.

DID YOU KNOW?
Nigel claimed Williams' fiftieth pole position at the Portuguese Grand Prix.

1993
Alain Prost joins the team and Damon Hill is promoted from test driver to race driver in January. Prost wins the opening race of the season in South Africa, and Hill quickly gets up to speed winning three consecutive races (Hungary, Belgium and Italy), earning him a new contract for 1994. In the Constructors' Championship Williams scores exactly double the number of points of second-placed McLaren. In September the team announces Ayrton Senna as its lead driver for 1994, in place of Prost. The Frenchman retires from the sport as statistically its most successful driver.

DID YOU KNOW?
David Coulthard had his first test for the team in September.

1994
The year is marred by tragedy when Ayrton Senna is killed at the third race of the season. He crashes at the Tamburello corner at Imola and succumbs to his injuries while in hospital. Since his death, all Williams cars have been branded with the Senna "S" on or around the nose cone. Damon Hill runs Michael Schumacher close in the world title fight. He loses out at the last race following a controversial collision that takes both cars out of the race. The team's second FW16 is shared by David Coulthard and Mansell as the team retains the Constructors' Title.

DID YOU KNOW?
Hill and Coulthard's one-two finish in the Portuguese Grand Prix was the first British one-two in Formula One since Graham Hill

and Piers Courage did the same at the Monaco Grand Prix in 1969. 1995 Damon Hill wins four races but he is still thirty-three points adrift of Schumacher come the end of the year. David Coulthard takes his fi rst pole in Argentina and his first win in Portugal to finish third in his debut year. However, in August the team signs Jacques Villeneuve as Damon Hill's teammate for 1996 and moves to its current premises in Grove.

DID YOU KNOW?
Damon Hill was the highest paid British sportsman in 1995, ahead of boxer Chris Eubank.

1996
Williams is utterly dominant. The team wins all but four races and scores more than double the number of points of its closest rival, Ferrari. Damon takes driver's the crown at the final race in Japan from Villeneuve who has an impressive debut season. The French-Canadian stays on for 1997, but Hill moves to pastures new.

DID YOU KNOW?
When the team moved into its new factory in Grove, a section of the A34 had to be closed in order to move the wind tunnel from its old factory in Didcot.

1997
The FW19 is immediately quick, winning three of the opening four races and Villeneuve goes on to pip Michael Schumacher to the World Championship. To celebrate, Jacques' mechanics wear blond wigs in deference to his new look. Jacques also claims Williams' 100th pole and the team's 100th victory. Off-track, it is another change of engine for Williams as Renault quits F1 to be followed by the return of BMW in 2000.

DID YOU KNOW?
Heinz-Harald Frentzen scores his first F1 victory at the San Marino Grand Prix.

1998

Williams commits to a two-year supply of customer engines based on the Renault French V10 rebadged as Mecachrome. There is a major overhaul of the technical regulations aimed at improving the spectacle. The cars are narrower and they run on grooved tyres, much to the dismay of the drivers. "They feel so unstable compared to slicks," says Jacques Villeneuve. The team finishes third in the Constructors' Title and fails to win a race for the first time in ten years.

DID YOU KNOW?

The Williams FW20 did not suffer a single mechanical failure that was attributable to the team.

1999

Ralf Schumacher and Alex Zanardi debut for the team; Schumacher finishes on the podium in his first race but the FW21 lacks the pace of the Ferraris and McLarens to challenge consistently at the front. There is disappointment for the team at the European Grand Prix, which is held in atrocious conditions at the Nürburgring. Schumacher is leading the race and he looks set for his first win in F1 when a puncture forces him to make an extra pitstop, dropping him to fourth. The team also announces a tyre deal with Michelin for the following season.

DID YOU KNOW?

Frank Williams received a knighthood in the New Year honours list.

2000

Williams finishes a credible third in its first year with BMW. Schumacher takes three podiums and the FW22 demonstrates great consistency. Jenson Button is confirmed as Schumacher's teammate in January. Jenson retires from a points-scoring position in his first race and he finishes sixth in his second, the Brazilian Grand Prix. At the United States Grand Prix the team confirms that its test driver, Juan Pablo Montoya, will partner Schumacher in 2001. The season highlight was Ralf Schumacher's third place in Melbourne—just twenty seconds behind race winner Michael Schumacher.

DID YOU KNOW?
BMW Williams introduces a major new sponsorship portfolio for 2000. It includes global giants Compaq, Reuters and Allianz.

2001
The team scores more than double the number of World Championship Points of 2000 and it racks up four victories en route to third place in the Constructors' Championship. Schumacher takes his and BMW Williams' first victory at the San Marino Grand Prix and Montoya stands atop the podium for the first time at the Italian Grand Prix.

DID YOU KNOW?
When Ralf Schumacher wins the Canadian Grand Prix and Michael Schumacher finishes second, it's the first one-two for two siblings in the history of the sport.

2002
The team finishes second in the Constructors' Championship to Ferrari. The one-two finish in the Malaysian Grand Prix proves to be its only victory of the year. Juan Pablo Montoya is spectacular in qualifying, taking seven pole positions but Michael Schumacher wins eleven of the seventeen races and storms to his fifth world title. During qualifying for the Italian Grand Prix at Monza, Montoya records the fastest-ever lap by a Formula One car when he averages 161.449 mph en route to pole position.

DID YOU KNOW?
Despite being vehemently denied by team boss Frank Williams, there were rumours throughout the year that BMW was about to buy the team.

2003
For 2003, points are awarded down to eighth place and one-lap qualifying is implemented. Juan Pablo Montoya and Ralf

Schumacher both score points in twelve out of the sixteen races, but Ferrari pips the team to the Constructors' Championship. At the Nürburgring BMW announces the continuation of its partnership with Williams until 2009, while McLaren announces at the end of the year that Juan Pablo Montoya will join the team in 2005.

DID YOU KNOW?
Ralf Schumacher was fi ned $50,000 for causing a first-corner accident at the German Grand Prix.

2004
A late run of form is enough to ensure it beats long-standing rivals McLaren in the Constructors' Championship, finishing fourth. Montoya ends the year—and his Williams career—on a high in Brazil when he gives the team its only victory of the year. A mid-season technical reshuffle sees Sam Michael take the reins as technical director, while Patrick Head becomes the team's director of engineering. BMW, meanwhile, becomes the first manufacturer to exceed 19,000 rpm with its P83 engine.

DID YOU KNOW?
The threat of a typhoon over the Japanese Grand Prix weekend prompted organizers to cancel all of Saturday's on-track sessions, including qualifying.

2005
Mark Webber and Nick Heidfeld steer the team's fortunes to notch up a handful of podiums but no victories as the team drops to fifth place. The highlight of the season is a double podium at the Monaco Grand Prix, but, overall, it's a turbulent season for the team on and off the racetrack. There are several changes to the design team and BMW announces the termination of its partnership with Williams at the end of the season.

DID YOU KNOW?
The US Grand Prix at Indianapolis turns into a fiasco when Michelin withdraws from the race on safety grounds. As a result, neither Williams driver starts the race.

2006

The team joins forces with Cosworth for the new V8 era and it also has a new tyre supplier in Bridgestone. Nico Rosberg, son of 1982 world champion Keke, replaces Nick Heidfeld alongside Mark Webber. Rosberg hits the ground running at the season-opener in Bahrain, where he finishes seventh and sets the fastest lap of the race—the youngest driver in the history of the sport to do so. But it's an unrewarding year for the team, in which it finishes eighth in the championship. The team announces mid-season that Alex Wurz will replace Webber for 2007.

DID YOU KNOW?

Nico Rosberg was offered a place at Imperial College, London, to read aerodynamics before he entered Formula BMW in 2002.

2007

Williams joins forces with Toyota in 2007 and winds up fourth in the Constructors' standings. Alex Wurz takes the team's only podium of the year when he comes third in the Canadian Grand Prix. Nico Rosberg re-signs with the team in a deal that will keep him at Williams until the end of 2009.

DID YOU KNOW?

Nico Rosberg improved his average grid position from fourteenth in 2006 to ninth in 2007.

2008

A standard Engine Control Unit (ECU) is implemented by the FIA to ensure traction control and launch control are outlawed, and there's a new rule stipulating that each gearbox has to last for four races. Rosberg manages only two podiums as the team finish eighth in the Championship. Frank Williams becomes the sport's longest serving team principal (longer even than Enzo Ferrari). The team records its 50,000th racing lap in Turkey and it starts its 500th Grand Prix at Monza.

DID YOU KNOW?
In October Williams is listed as a 2008/09 cool brand joining others such as Tate Modern, Rolex and Aston Martin.

2009
The FW31—which has a double diffuser from the outset—lacks the punch of its rivals and the team comes home seventh in the Constructors' Championship. The return of slick tyres is celebrated by the drivers, as are the new extra wide front wings and narrow rear wings. Jenson Button of Brawn GP wins the world title. Austrian race driver and private equity investor Toto Wolff buys a minority shareholding in the team, and the Williams Technology Centre in Qatar is launched in October.

DID YOU KNOW?
At the end of the season the team heads to Losail in Qatar, where His Highness Sheikh Khalid bin Hamad Al-Thani becomes the first Qatari to drive an F1 car.

2010
Rubens Barrichello joins the team alongside Nico Hülkenberg. Williams returns to Cosworth for V8 power. Barrichello finishes fourth at Valencia and he's a regular points scorer for the remainder of the season. Hülkenberg gets up to speed quickly and at the penultimate race in Brazil gives Williams its first pole position since the Nürburgring in 2005 He comes home in eighth place as the team pips Force India by one point in the Constructors' Championship to bag sixth place overall.

DID YOU KNOW?
Frank Williams is honoured at the BBC's annual Sports Personality of the Year awards. He wins the Helen Rollason Award to add to his list of accolades.

2011
Pastor Maldonado lines up alongside Barrichello. The year proves to be difficult and the team finishes ninth in the Constructors' Championship. Technical Director Sam Michael and Chief

Aerodynamicist Jon Tomlinson make way for Mike Coughlan (Technical Director), Mark Gillan (Chief Operations Engineer) and Jason Somerville (Head of Aerodynamics). Williams Grand Prix Holdings Plc lists on the Frankfurt stock exchange in March.

DID YOU KNOW?
At the end of the season Patrick Head, co-founder of Williams and its director of engineering, steps down from his involvement with the race team in order to concentrate on Williams Hybrid Power.

2012
The FW34 is a much more competitive proposition as the car has a good balance and the driveability of Renault's V8 immediately goes down well with Maldonado and Bruno Senna. Maldonado wins the Spanish Grand Prix from pole position. The team finishes eighth in the Constructors' Championship but the raw pace of the car gives everyone confidence for 2013.

DID YOU KNOW?
Williams has won sixty-four races with Renault power—more than with any other engine manufacturer.

2013
The team retains Pastor Maldonado for 2013 but he is joined by 2011 GP3 Champion and longstanding Williams Test driver Valtteri Bottas. The FW35 remains Renault powered, meaning the team can build on the relationship formed in 2012.

Changes within top management saw Executive Director Toto Wolff leave while Claire Williams, Frank Williams' daughter, is appointed Deputy Team Principal and takes control of the day-today running of the team.

The car has a fully incorporated Coanda exhaust with similar rear bodywork to that of the 2012 Champions, Red Bull. This however doesn't work as desired in the early part of the season with handling being sporadic and difficult. Another mid-season overhaul of management sees Mike Coughlan depart and make way for Pat Symonds, formally of Benetton/Renault, in the role of Technical Chief.

A strong showing in a wet Canadian qualifying sees Bottas qualify third while Maldonado failed to repeat his victory in Spain from 2012. An abandoned blown exhaust towards the end of the season results in a change of form as Bottas scores his first-ever points, claiming an impressive eighth position at Austin, USA.

Maldonado announces he is to leave at the end of the season to be replaced by Ferrari's Felipe Massa, bringing with him bags of experience and a calm head under pressure. More changes ring out through the team with Dave Wheater coming in as Head of Aerodynamic Performance, Shaun Whitehead as Head of Aerodynamic Process, Jakob Andreasen as Head of Engineering Operations, Craig Wilson as Head of Vehicle Dynamics and Rod Nelson as Chief Test & Support Engineer.

DID YOU KNOW?
Mercedes is Williams' eighth different engine supplier since 1977.

2014
Widespread regulations changes for the 2014 Formula One season, with the introduction of new hybrid 1.6 litre turbo charged V6 power units, presented Williams with an ideal opportunity to improve its competitiveness on the racetrack compared to 2013. The decision to partner with Mercedes Benz as the team's new power unit supplier in a long-term deal proved pivotal, and the well powered FW36 showed strong early promise at the start of the season. A mixture of bad luck on the racetrack and difficulties in wet conditions hindered the team's ability to maximise its points haul in the first half of the 2014 season. But this was to change in the second half of the season as Williams out developed its rivals to emerge as the main challenger to eventual Championship winners Mercedes. The team picked up its first podium since 2012 at the 2014 Austrian Grand Prix, and this was to lead to another eight podium finishes to eventually claim third in the Constructors' Championship.

2015
Consistency was key in 2015 with only minor rule changes in effect; the same engine as 2014; and Felipe Massa and Valtteri

Bottas pairing up again for a second season at Williams. After a relatively steady start, and Valtteri missing the opening race in Australia with a back injury, the team picked up the pace and secured its first podium in Canada with Valtteri clinching third. Three more third place trophies followed: Felipe in Austria and Italy; and another for Valtteri in Mexico. Silverstone, a special track for the team as we secured our first victory there, didn't disappoint. Felipe and Valtteri jumped from third and fourth on the grid to find themselves in first and second on the opening lap. Unfortunately the weather wasn't on their side, but the team brought the cars home in fourth and fifth respectively. These regular top ten finishes, combined with four podiums, meant the team successfully defended third place in the Constructors' Championship.

2016

In 2016 Felipe Massa and Valtteri Bottas paired up for the third season in succession. While the driver line-up and regulations remained consistent, the team unfortunately slipped to 4th in the Constructors' Championship. Following a steady start to the championship, in which Valtteri secured his and the team's only podium of the year in Canada, Force India began to close the gap in the fight for 3rd place, with Sergio Perez securing two podiums in Monaco and Baku. Felipe announced his retirement from the sport prior to the Italian Grand Prix at Monza. An emotional farewell followed at the penultimate race of the year in Brazil, where he retired from the race and walked down the pitlane to a standing ovation from the Mercedes, Ferrari and Williams garages. The fight for 3rd with Force India went down to the wire, at the season finale in Abu Dhabi. Unfortunately, the fight came to a premature end when Valtteri retired from the race, meaning the team had to settle for 4th in the Constructors' Championship. Valtteri and Felipe finished the year 8th and 11th respectively in the Drivers' Championship.

2017

In 2017, Lance Stroll lined-up alongside Felipe Massa after the Brazilian completed a U-turn on his retirement and re-joined

Williams following Valterri Bottas' move to Mercedes. Lance endured a tough start to his rookie Formula One season, with three retirements before finishing 11th at the fourth round in Russia. Lance went on to score his first points at his home Grand Prix in Montreal with ninth position. Later that year, Lance became the youngest rookie Formula One driver to finish on the podium with third place at the Azerbaijan Grand Prix. More success followed, and Lance became the youngest Formula One driver to start on the front row after qualifying second for the Italian Grand Prix. In contrast, Felipe had a very consistent year, scoring points in no less than twelve races, but he also suffered his fair share of misfortune. Felipe had climbed his way up to third in the Azerbaijan Grand Prix and looked to be within contention of winning the race before a mechanical failure forced him to retire the car. The 2017 season concluded with the team finishing fifth in the Constructors' Championship for a second consecutive year. Felipe and Lance finished the year 11th and 12th respectively in the Drivers' Championship.

FERRARI—THE COMPLETE TIMELINE

1950
Ferrari takes part in the second race of the World Championship, the Monaco GP, held on 21 May on the city circuit. The drivers are Alberto Ascari, Luigi Villoresi and Raymond Sommer, with the 275 F1 and 340 F1 single-seaters.

1951
The year of the first win in Formula One for Ferrari with José Froilán Gonzáles at Silverstone. The 375 F1, with a naturally aspirated engine, consumes less, which enables the Scuderia to gain time during the pit stops.

1952
The first Formula One Championship is won with Ascari: seven wins in seven races for the Scuderia from Maranello and Alberto Ascari is the new World Champion.

1953
An important season with Ascari winning with the 500 F2: World Champion for the second time in a row. The Italian driver wins in Argentinia, in the Netherlands, in Belgium, England and in Switzerland.

1954
Formula One changes the rules: cylinder capacity is limited to 2.5 litres for naturally aspirated engines and to 750 cc for those with compressors. Ferrari chooses the first option and fights with Mercedes. The Germans calculate speed and gear changes for every single circuit, but in the end Ferrari wins the marques' title.

1955
The Drivers' Title is fought out with Mercedes, and Fangio wins. Ferrari works on materials, the chassis construction and an improved engine. The 500 series proceeds: after the 553 the Scuderia uses the 555 F1 aka "Supersqualo".

1956

A positive season for a new team of drivers, with World Champion Juan Manuel Fangio together with Luigi Musso, Eugenio Castellotti and Peter Collins, as well as in some races Olivier Gendebien, Alfonso de Portago and Maurice Trintignant. The single-seater, the D50 from Lancia and Ferrari, powers to the World Title with the Argentinian driver despite some problems with its reliability.

1957

The Scuderia Ferrari debuts with the new single-seater type 801, similar to the D50 for the V8 engine and De Dion rear axle. This was the last season with the Lancia V8 engines, but it wasn't as successful as previous years. Fangio did not race for Ferrari anymore, but a young Mike Hawthorn joined the team from Maranello.

1958

The new engine, the V6 from the Dino made its entry in this challenging season to fight against Stirling Moss with Cooper and later Vanwall. The Ferrari drivers Hawthorn, Musso and Collins raced with the 246 F1 and Fangio for Maserati. The Italian driver lost his life in Reims in July, while Collins died at the race on the Nürburgring. The second place gained by Hawthorn was worth the World Title, the third for the Scuderia Ferrari.

1959

While in 1958 the Scuderia could defend itself against Cooper, the team was less fortunate in 1959. The English team used a 2495 cc engine especially planned for Formula One. Brabham won the first race and the Title, while Ferrari replied with a bigger V6-engine with 2474.5 cc and 292 bhp. On the fast tracks the car was superior, but it wasn't enough this year due to problems with the braking system and parts of the chassis.

1960

A year of transition for the Scuderia Ferrari, competing with the last models with front engine and rear traction. Cooper dominated the races, but now Ferrari had Phil Hill, Wolfgang von Trips, Richie Ginther, Cliff Allison and Willy Mairesse, who won the first three places at the race in Monza, due to the new rear engine, starting point of the new 246 P and the 156 used in Formula Two.

1961
The year of the Championship won by the US driver Phil Hill: the mid-rear engine worked extremely well in the 156 F1. All Ferrari drivers gained excellent results in Belgium, England and in Monza, where Hill won the race, while Wolfgang von Trips died in a terrible accident. Both World Titles went to Maranello this year.

1962
The management and the technicians leaving, as well as the fierce competition, had an important impact on the performance of this season for the Scuderia Ferrari. Furthermore there were no compromises in terms of safety and the cars were heavier than the required minimum weight. Meanwhile the Scuderia had prepared a "mysterious" single-seater with eight cylinders and air cooling.

1963
New drivers for the Scuderia Ferrari: Lorenzo Bandini, Willy Mairesse and Ludovico Scarfiotti as well as the new-entry John Surtees, who was already the fastest on motorbikes. The single-seater (156 F1-63) was fitted with new suspension, bodywork and engine: a V6 with injection system and six gears. The competition was stronger on the track and Ferrari concluded the season with a fourth place.

1964
A completely new single-seater for the new motorsport season: the 158 F1 with a small and light eight-cylinder, a new concept. It was a difficult start with some retirements, but in Germany Surtees won the race, but in the classification the English driver was behind the competition of Lotus and BRM until the US Grand Prix. A second place in that event helped John Surtees to

seal the titles for the Scuderia Ferrari in the Drivers' and the Constructors' Championships.

1965
A difficult season with two single-seaters racing for the Team from Maranello: the 158 F1 and the 512 F1 with V8 and V12 engines respectively. Surtees and Bandini behind the wheel with Scarfiotti and Pedro Rodriguez, experienced some problems with the cars, unforeseen events and accidents. The season ended with an unsatisfying fourth place.

1966
Engine capacity was doubled to three litres for this campaign. The 312 F1 debuted in Syracuse with a victory by Surtees in a race that didn't count for the Championship. The season was not a success and Surtees was dismissed midway through the season, while Bandini gained results that did not count for the Championship.

1967
The car's official debut was at the Champions' Race at Brands-Hatch with Bandini and Scarfiotti behind the wheel. It was the last Grand Prix for Lorenzo Bandini, who lost his life in Monte Carlo on 7 May. After that terrible loss the season was not very satisfying and the competitors showed up with more advanced technology.

1968
Franco Gozzi was nominated Head of the Scuderia. The new 312 F1-68 was driven by Chris Amon, Andrea de Adamich and Jacky Ickx with mixed results, but there were constant technological innovations. The first victory was gained by Ickx in France in the rain, but it was not enough to shake up the classification, in which Ferrari was outstripped by Lotus and Brabham.

1969
This was a dark year for the Scuderia in terms of problems with the organization, the technology and financing. Pedro Rodriguez

and Chris Amon (just after mid-season) gained only one place on the podium, in Holland.

1970
After a difficult start to the season Ferrari was again ruling in Formula One thanks to the competitive 312 B with its 180-degree V12 engine. Next to Jacky Ickx, Ignazio Giunti and Clay Regazzoni were racing for the Prancing Horse. Regazzoni gained his first win in F1 in Monza. With four successes and a pair of one-two wins Ferrari gained second place in the Constructors' Championship. The Drivers' Title went posthumously to Jochen Rindt, who had died in an accident during the qualifying sessions for the Italian Grand Prix.

1971
The Scuderia, with Peter Schetty now at the helm, opened the season with a victory at the South African Grand Prix with the Italian-American Mario Andretti behind the wheel of the 312 B. The Firestone slicks were used for the first time in Spain. At the third race, held in Monte Carlo, the new 312 B2 went onto the track. Its engine had a shorter stroke for higher revs and improved performance as well as innovative rear suspension. It was an exciting project, which helped Ferrari especially in qualifying, but the car's racing reliability only led to a third place in the Constructors' Championship.

1972
Problems with the engine and with performance below expectations this was a difficult year for the Scuderia with fierce competition from England. On the challenging Nürburgring Jacky Ickx, behind the wheel of the 312 B2 starting from pole position, garnered the only win of the season, which ended with a fourth place in the Constructors' Championship.

1973
Despite the intention to start with only one car in the F1 Championship, in the end two 312 B2s were used, with Jacky Ickx and Arturo Merzario behind the wheel. At the fourth race,

held in Spain, the 312 B3-73 made its first appearance with a self-supporting chassis created by Englishman John Thompson. It was a difficult year for the Scuderia with no F1 wins. In July 1973 Luca di Montezemolo was hired as an assistant to the management.

1974
With Luca di Montezemolo as the head of the team and Clay Regazzoni and Niki Lauda behind the wheel of the 312 B3-74 designed by Mauro Forghieri, the Scuderia quickly forgot 1973, gaining ten pole positions and three victories. Lauda's win at the Spanish Grand Prix was the Scuderia's fiftieth F1 Grand Prix success. The Scuderia and Regazzoni were fighting for both titles right until the last race, staged at Watkins Glen (USA). In the end Emerson Fittipaldi—for the second time in his career—and his McLaren-Ford secured both the Drivers' and Constructors' Championship.

1975
After an eleven-year gap the Scuderia regained the Drivers' Title with Niki Lauda, thanks to his five wins, eight podium places, nine pole positions and securing points in twelve of the fourteen races. The Constructors' Title was also captured thanks to the contribution of Clay Regazzoni, who won the Italian Grand Prix. This was the end of the domination by the V8s with the first V12-cylinder winning the Championship with almost 500 bhp.

1976
On 1 August Lauda suffered an appalling accident on the Nürburgring: he was saved by two other drivers from the flames of his single-seater. The Austrian was severely hurt, and yet forty-two days later he was back on the track in Monza, gaining a fourth-place finish. The Championship was decided at the last race, held in Fuji, Japan. The Austrian retired after the second lap because of the torrential rain. James Hunt, who crossed the line third with McLaren, took the Drivers' Title finishing one point ahead of Lauda. The Constructors' Title went to the Prancing Horse.

1977

In 1977 Ferrari used the 312 T2, again driven by Niki Lauda and Carlos Reutemann. With three wins and six second places Lauda won the World Championship with two races to go, at which point the Austrian left the Prancing Horse. In the last two races of the Championship, which ended with four wins in total and the third Constructors' Title in a row, the Scuderia selected Canadian Gilles Villeneuve to race in the team with Reutemann.

1978

The Scuderia, under the new head of the team Marco Piccini, changed its tyre supplier from Goodyear to Michelin, introducing radial tyres for the first time in F1. With the 312 T3 Reutemann and Villeneuve—whose courage on the track thrilled the fans—were the main players in a year of ups and downs but a total of five wins. Mario Andretti won the Drivers' Title with Lotus 79, the first proper "wing car" in the history of Formula One.

1979

In Formula One everybody was talking about "ground effect" and single-seaters were planned to generate downforce for higher corner speed. The 312 T4 was a competitive and reliable car helping Jody Scheckter to win the title. Gilles Villeneuve—whose fierce duel with René Arnoux at the 1979 French Grand Prix entered history—gained second place in the Drivers' standings, while Ferrari, with 113 points and six victories, won their sixth Constructors' Title.

1980

The season was a negative one for Ferrari: the 312 T5 is mystifyingly uncompetitive despite being based on the previous year's World Champion car. The Scuderia only came home eighth in the Championship. Not even Gilles Villeneuve could tame this difficult single-seater and help Ferrari to gain places on the podium in a challenging season. At the end of the year Jody Scheckter retired from Formula One.

1981

For Ferrari 1981 was the start of the turbo era with the 1.5-litre turbo powertrain. Ultimately, however, the season turned out to be an extremely difficult one with loads of problems related to reliability, as was the case for the other teams. With Villeneuve and Didier Pironi the Scuderia concluded the Championship in fifth position in the Constructors' standings with two victories and a third place for the Canadian driver. Off the track, FISA and FOCA made peace thanks to Enzo Ferrari's intervention: this is how the first Concorde Agreement was born.

1982

A dramatic year for the Scuderia: Gilles Villeneuve died in qualifying at the Belgian Grand Prix while in Germany a terrible accident put an end to Didier Pironi's career. The Frenchman participated in ten out of the campaign's sixteen races, coming in just five points adrift of Keke Rosberg in the Drivers' standings. The 126 C2, used this season, had a lighter and more rigid chassis thanks to the composite material introduced in Maranello by British engineer Harvey Postlethwaite. The car was then raced by Patrick Tambay and, for the last two races of the season, by Mario Andretti. In the end the single-seater carried the Scuderia to the Constructors' Title with a total of eleven podium places and three victories.

1983

The Scuderia started the Championship with the 126 C2B, an evolution of the 126 C2 set up for the new rules and fitted with Goodyear tyres. The car was driven by the Frenchmen Patrick Tambay and René Arnoux. The car gained two victories before the debut of the 126 C3 at the British Grand Prix (ninth race out of fifteen). The victories with Arnoux at the German and the Dutch GPs confirmed the strength of the new single-seater and the Scuderia carried away the Constructors' Title again this year.

1984

To limit the engine capacity the Federation decided that the tank could only have a volume of 220 litres and the cars could not be refuelled. This led to incredible research in the area of petrol and lubricants and consequently to higher costs. In Maranello, eleven years after Arturo Merzario, there was an Italian back in the fold: Michele Alboreto, discovered by Ken Tyrrell. Alboreto came to race next to René Arnoux. It was a difficult season for the team, but also for the fans. The Scuderia concluded the 1984 Championship with a frustrating second place in the Constructors' standings behind McLaren.

1985
In the 1985 Championship Ferrari raced the 156-85. The 1.5l V6 car won six places on the podium and gained two victories in the first eleven races of the year. Alboreto—with his Swedish team-mate Stefan Johansson, who took over from Arnoux as of the second race of the season—arrived at the Italian Grand Prix fighting for the Drivers' Title with Alain Prost. However, technical problems with the car at the end of the season meant that Alboreto failed to gain a single point in the last five races, effectively "handing over" the World Title.

1986
The F1-86 was the protagonist of a season to forget. Due to reliability issues Alboreto and Johansson completed the season without a victory and a lowly fourth place in the Constructors' standings, more than 100 points behind the winning Williams team. At the end of the season Enzo Ferrari announced that John Barnard would come to Maranello. Barnard had been the first to introduce a carbon fibre chassis in F1 in 1981 (with the McLaren MP4/1). He had won five Drivers' and Constructors' Titles between 1984 and 1986 as the father of the MP4/2 project.

1987
The rules now permitted naturally aspirated engines with a displacement of 3,500 cc and no tank limit. The Scuderia started the season with the F1-87 with a 90-degree V6 turbo engine. After a disappointing first part of the Championship that brought two third places by Michele Alboreto, the Scuderia improved with a second place in Portugal. Gerhard Berger

secured pole and won in Japan and in Australia, with Ferrari gaining a one-two victory.

1988

On 14 August 1988 Enzo Ferrari died; he was ninety years of age. The season was dominated by McLaren with Senna-Prost, winning fifteen out of sixteen races. The Drivers' Title went to Senna. Ferrari interrupted the McLaren procession with an unexpected one-two win in Monza about a month after the death of its founder; this helped the Scuderia gain second place in the Constructors' Championship.

1989

Ferrari started a new era with the revolutionary F1-89. With innovative aerodynamics and pushrod suspension it was fitted with a semi-automatic seven-speed gearbox, activated on the steering wheel. The clutch pedal was only used at the start. It was powered by a naturally aspirated 65-degree V12 cylinder with 600 bhp at 12,000 rpm. The new driver, Nigel Mansell, won in Brazil and Hungary. Gerhard Berger had a terrible accident at the San Marino Grand Prix, where the car went up in flames at the Tamburello corner. The Austrian had light burns on his hands and couldn't race in the next event, but still won in Portugal and gained second places at the Italian and the Spanish races.

1990

The Scuderia started with the F1-90, sporting the number one thanks to World Champion Alain Prost. The single-seater was especially competitive and Prost won five races, while Mansell won in Portugal. Prost came to Suzuka, the penultimate race of the season, to challenge for the title with his old rival Ayrton Senna but a collision between the two put an end to their race and the Frenchman's Championship challenge.

1991

Jean Alesi joined Prost behind the wheel of the F1-91 for what turned out to be a disappointing season. After the Monaco Grand Prix Cesare Fiorio left in anger, while Alain Prost heavily criticized the single-seater. It was the beginning of the end of the relationship between the French driver and Ferrari. For the season's last race Gianni Morbidelli started for the Prancing Horse. The Championship, with Senna and McLaren winning the titles, ended without a win for the Scuderia. At the end of the year Luca di Montezemolo was back at Ferrari as Chairman and CEO.

1992

In 1992 the Scuderia drivers were Jean Alesi and new-entry Ivan Capelli. The single-seater F92 was a completely new approach but it wasn't fitted with active suspension and this allowed Williams to dominate the Championship. Nigel Mansell claimed the title with five races to go. For Ferrari it was a season to forget— no wins and a mere twenty-one points in the Constructors' Championship.

1993

In the summer of 1992 John Barnard returned to Ferrari. It was nevertheless another bitter season for the Scuderia. Alesi and Berger accumulated twenty-eight points, compared to the 168 from Williams-Renault, who secured the Constructors' and Drivers' World Titles (with Alain Prost). Prost ended his career at the end of the season having won four titles. In July of 1993 Jean Todt came to Maranello—after a successful motorsport career at Peugeot—to revitalize the team as Head of the Scuderia.

1994

A truly dramatic year for Formula One with both Roland Ratzenberger and Ayrton Senna losing their lives at the San Marino Grand Prix in Imola. Ferrari concluded the Championship with third spot in the Constructors' standings; the title was won by Williams. Meanwhile Michael Schumacher (Benetton-Ford) won his first Drivers' Title.

1995

The Scuderia's car for the 1995 season was the 412 T2, designed by Barnard in England. The engineer abandoned the fashion of the high nose and presented the clutch lever behind the steering wheel, plus an intelligent mechanical brake power distributor (which was a first in F1). Alesi and Berger were more competitive, securing eleven places on the podium. The World Titles went again to Michael Schumacher and Benetton-Renault, while the Scuderia came in third in the Constructors' Championship.

1996

In August 1995 Ferrari confirmed Michael Schumacher as an official driver alongside Eddie Irvine. They raced the F310 to four pole positions, three wins, three second and two third places. Michael Schumacher gained third place in the Drivers' Championship, behind Damon Hill (Williams-Renault) and his teammate Jacques Villeneuve. With 112 points Ferrari secured second place in the Constructors' Championship.

1997

In the fiftieth year of Ferrari Michael Schumacher won five races. At the last race of the season in Jerez he was one point ahead of Villeneuve. With twenty-one laps to go race leader Schumacher reacted decisively to an attack from the Williams driver and the two cars collided. Schumacher had to retire, while Villeneuve crossed the line third, winning the World Title. The FIA subsequently disqualified Schumacher from the standings at the end of the year, while confirming the points the German gained in the Constructors' Championship, thereby helping Ferrari to second place.

1998

Six wins for Schumacher, plus two second places and three third places, as well as three second places and five third places for Eddie Irvine, gave the Scuderia Ferrari 133 points and second spot in the Constructors' Championship. In 1998 slicks were replaced by grooved tyres and the F300 was a completely new design. The team from Maranello arrived at the last race in Suzuka with Schumacher fighting for the title with Mika Häkkinen and his McLaren-Mercedes. However, a tyre failure put paid to any Drivers' Title dreams. Häkkinen won the race, and with it the title by fourteen points.

1999

The Scuderia claimed the Constructors' title, thereby ending a barren spell stretching back to 1983. After Schumacher broke his leg at the British Grand Prix, Eddie Irvine challenged for the title. He arrived at the last race, in Suzuka, ahead of Häkkinen by four points in the Drivers' standings. But the Ferrarista only managed to cross the line third. Häkkinen won the race and the Drivers' Title for the second time in a row.

2000

Twenty-one years after Jody Scheckter's triumph the Drivers' World Title was back in Maranello thanks to the competitiveness of the F1-2000, which set the standard for the years to come. Michael Schumacher gained nine victories and won a season-long battle against Mika Häkkinen of McLaren at the penultimate race of the season in Suzuka. With a total of 170 points the team also reprised their 1999 Constructors' title success. For the Scuderia this was the start of one of the most successful cycles in the history of Formula One.

2001

Michelin joined Bridgestone in Formula One as an official tyre supplier and by the Hungarian Grand Prix, the thirteenth race of seventeen on the race calendar, Michael Schumacher had secured the Drivers' Title, the fourth of his career. At the end of the season the Scuderia had nine victories, fifteen places on the podium and a hat-trick of one-two wins for a total of 179 points to once again top the Constructors' standings. The main star of this incredible season was the F2011, nicknamed the "anteater" due to the shape of its nose. It sported a high chassis, with a concave lower section and relatively short and high sidepods.

2002

Ferrari dominated the 2002 Formula One campaign with fifteen victories in seventeen races. The eleven wins by Michael Schumacher and the four by Rubens Barrichello (including nine one-two successes) powered the Scuderia to the Constructors' Championship with 221 points—as many as the other ten teams combined. The 2002 single-seater was an entirely new project with smaller aerodynamic sides, a titanium-fusion gearbox, a different chassis design and construction and a new engine with a lower centre of gravity producing 835 bhp at 17,800 rpm.

2003

The 2003 Championship saw a re-invigorated competition thanks to the rivalry between Bridgestone and Michelin, resulting in eight different winners in the sixteen-race calendar. In the end it was Michael Schumacher again, clinching the World Title in the last race, held in Suzuka. The German driver beat the record of five World Titles held by Juan Manuel Fangio, becoming the most successful driver in the history of Formula One. Thanks to the F2003 GA, named in homage to Gianni Agnelli who had died in January 2003, the Scuderia gained its fifth successive Constructors' Title.

2004

Out of eighteen Grands Prix the Scuderia won fifteen (thirteen for Schumacher, two for Barrichello), including eight one-two victories. Their total of 262 points secured the Scuderia's fourteenth Constructors' Championship. Schumacher gained his fifth title in a row, the seventh of his career, in Belgium on the same track where he debuted in 1991. The F2004, fitted with the new ten-cylinder 053 engine producing 865 bhp at 18,300 rpm, exceeded all expectations in terms of performance and reliability.

2005

In the end the F2005, debuting with Schumacher at the Bahrain Grand Prix, failed to live up to expectations. The single-seater had plenty of potential but failed to compete with its rivals on the track. The season ended with just one win, gained in Indianapolis at a Grand Prix with just six cars on the track caused by a boycott of the teams running on Michelin tyres. The team achieved third place in the Constructors' Championship, won by Renault, while Fernando Alonso, with Renault, gained the Drivers' Title.

2006

Ferrari made up for a weak 2005 campaign as V8 2.4-litre engines were introduced, as were tyre changes during the race. The seven victories by Schumacher and the three by new-entry Felipe Massa weren't enough to stop Alonso and the Enstone team repeating their successes of the previous season. At the end of the campaign, with his retirement announced after the win in Monza, the Schumacher era in Maranello came to an end. In 180 GPs with Ferrari the German driver had won seventy-two races, gained fifty-eight pole positions, recorded fifty-three fastest race laps and won five Drivers' and six Constructors' Titles.

2007

The year 2007 will enter the annals of Formula One as one of the most embattled and intense seasons in the history of the series: two teams, Ferrari and McLaren, and their drivers, Massa, Räikkönen, Alonso and the rookie Hamilton fought for the World Title until the last race. In the season where Bridgestone again became the sole tyre supplier, the Scuderia achieved nine victories (six by Räikkönen, three from Massa) winning the Constructors' Championship with 204 points and also the Drivers' title—at the last race of the season in Brazil Kimi Räikkönen gained the upper hand on the McLaren duo.

2008

The Scuderia, with Stefano Domenicali as the new Team Principal and Aldo Costa as the Technical Director, defended the World Title with the F2008 on the track. At the end of an intense season Ferrari won its sixteenth Constructors' Title with eight victories (six for Massa, two by Räikkönen). As for the Drivers' Title, it was a sad day for the Prancing Horse at the last race, staged in Brazil. Felipe Massa won the race and was World Champion for less than forty seconds, that was when Lewis Hamilton (McLaren-Mercedes) crossed the line. At the last corner the English driver had grabbed fifth position in the race and the four necessary points to win the title by one point from the Brazilian Ferrarista.

2009

This campaign saw a host of regulation changes that radically changed the look of the cars. The front wing was much wider than in the past, the rear wing much narrower and higher, the diffusor further back, the bodies were without air-outlets and the aerodynamic devices reduced. The drivers had the possibility to move the flaps' angles from the cockpit and there was the introduction of the KERS (kinetic energy recovery system). Slicks were back, too. The F60—whose name celebrated the sixtieth participation of the Scuderia in the F1 Championship—could not offer a realistic challenge to teams such as Red Bull and Brawn GP. Ferrari gained just one success, with Kimi Räikkönen in Spa-Francorchamps, while a terrible accident during the qualifying at the Hungarian Grand Prix put an end to Felipe Massa's season; he was replaced by Luca Badoer and then Giancarlo Fisichella. The 2009 Championship, won by Jenson Button and Brawn GP, ended for the Scuderia with a disappointing fourth place in the Constructors' Championship.

2010

Race refuelling is banned and drivers reaching Q3 must start the race with the tyres they last used in qualifying. At Ferrari, Fernando Alonso comes in to replace Kimi Räikkönen alongside Felipe Massa. Fighting closely for the title are the Spanish Ferrari driver, Lewis Hamilton for McLaren and the two Red Bulls of Mark Webber and Sebastian Vettel. The F10 has a perfect start to the season, taking a one-two in Bahrain. Fernando wins in Germany, Italy, Singapore and Korea with the title fight coming down to the last event. The Abu Dhabi race is a heartbreaker for Ferrari, though, as Fernando finds himself behind Russia's Vitaly Petrov in his Renault, who has a good top speed and so is difficult to overtake; this gives the title to Vettel.

2011

The Championship is dominated by Red Bull as DRS is introduced and Pirelli become sole tyre supplier. Sebastian Vettel is again Champion, this time clinching the title in Japan, no fewer than four races before the end. The Prancing Horse F150 Italia car only wins one race, the British Grand Prix, with Alonso, who is very consistent, getting to the podium a further nine times. At the end of the season, the team is third in the Constructors' Championship with Fernando fourth in the Drivers' standings.

2012

The 2012 season is another exciting one for Scuderia Ferrari. The team, along with Fernando Alonso, are in the hunt for the title right down to the wire. The F2012 emerges from the Maranello factory and improves as the season goes on. Alonso scores some exceptional wins: in Malaysia the rain plays its part, as he wins from eighth on the grid, and he drives an incredible race in the European Grand Prix.

2013

The start of the season is encouraging, as there are two wins in the first five races—in China and Spain. However, from the mid-season onwards, Sebastian Vettel strings together a run of victories to take the title in India with three races in hand. Fernando Alonso is best of the rest, taking seven podiums. At the end of the season, with the team third in the Constructors' classification, Felipe Massa goes to Williams and Kimi Räikkönen returns to Maranello.

2014

The 2014 season was far from satisfactory for Scuderia Ferrari. For the first time since 1994, it failed to win a single race as the team dropped to fourth in the Constructors' classification. Alonso ended up sixth while Kimi Räikkönen could do no better than twelfth place, never seeing the podium. The Scuderia's car, named F14 T following an on-line poll among the fans, suffered in the face of the new engine regulations and because the aerodynamic package had limitations.

2015

Sergio Marchionne replaced the retiring Luca di Montezemolo as Ferrari President, Maurizio Arrivabene replaced Marco Mattiacci as Team Principle and Sebastian Vettel replaced

Fernando Alonso to create a revitalised Scuderia for the 2015 season. Vettel started well with a third in Australia followed by wins in Malaysia (his first in red and the team's first for 34 races), Hungary and Singapore. Vettel and Räikkönen finished third and fourth respectively in the Drivers Championship which was enough to give the team second place in the Constructors Championship with 428 points.

2016

There was much anticipation around the SF16-H in pre-season testing but the early promise was not realised so much so that by August technical director James Allison had left the team. In fact the team did not win a race in the entire 2016 season in a year they had hoped to challenge for the championship. Some poor strategy calls meant that Vettel could only finish fourth with Räikkönen in sixth so that the team achieved third place in the Constructors Championship with 392 points.

2017

The team got off to a flying start with Vettel securing victory at the season opener in Melbourne in a head to head battle with Lewis Hamilton. It was obvious from the get go that the SF70H was a genuine contender and by Monaco Vettel had a 25 point lead in the championship. However that was the extent of the teams progress and a disastrous Asian leg of the season where the team couldn't match their rivals on either pace or reliability meant that the Constructors Championship was decided by Austin and the Drivers by Mexico. Five wins and five poles were a stark improvement on the previous year enabling the team to carry their momentum into 2018.

In September of 2018 it was confirmed that rising star Charles Leclerc would partner Sebastian Vettel in 2019 replacing the Sauber bound Kimi Räikkönen.

MCLAREN: IN THE BEGINNING . . .

Bruce McLaren was born in 1937 in Auckland, New Zealand, and in 1963 founded Bruce McLaren Motor Racing in order to develop and race sports cars alongside his commitment as lead driver in the Cooper Grand Prix team.

He had arrived in the UK in 1958 with the "Driver to Europe" scheme that was designed to encourage antipodean drivers to compete with the cream of the world's drivers. His mentor was Jack Brabham who introduced Bruce to Cooper Cars, the small Surbiton (London)-based team who were poised to create a revolution with compact, lightweight Grand Prix cars powered by an engine behind the driver. Following an auspicious start to his F2 career in 1958 he joined the F1 team for 1959 and stayed with Cooper for seven years.

Bruce made an impact almost immediately by winning the 1959 US Grand Prix aged just twenty-two years and eighty days, at that time the youngest Grand Prix winner. He went on to win three more Grands Prix and countless sports car victories. Yet Bruce was no ordinary driver. His upbringing was steeped in cars and practical engineering at his parents' service station and workshop. By the age of fourteen he had entered a local hill climb in an Austin 7 Ulster and shown promise both as a driver and an engineer.

Back in the 1960s Bruce raced, as did most Grand Prix drivers of this time, in sports cars, Grand Touring cars and more humble saloon cars alongside his commitments to Cooper in Formula 1. He drove for Jaguar, Aston Martin and Ford with whom he won the 24 Hours of Le Mans in 1966.

He was a true competitor who excelled at innovating and developing racing cars. It was this passion that led Bruce to start his own company, first to develop and race a Cooper with a rear-mounted Oldsmobile engine that helped to kick start the "big banger" sports car era. In a show of loyalty to Cooper cars Bruce engineered two 2.5-litre Coopers for the 1964 Tasman series which he won.

MCLAREN BECOMES A CONSTRUCTOR

In 1964 Bruce and his small team built the first true McLaren sports car—the M1A—which became a top contender in sports car racing both in Europe and America. After proving its credentials the orders rolled in and twenty-four examples were built. Its successor, the M1B, was quicker still and carried Bruce's nascent team into the inaugural Can-Am (Canadian–American Challenge Cup) championship. These cars were faster than the Formula 1 cars of the age, providing a spectacle of colour accompanied by the deep rumble of highly-tuned, large American V8 engines. The inaugural year of this championship did not yield a victory for McLaren but Bruce came third in the series.

The following year, 1967, saw the start of one of the most dominant episodes in motor sport history.

Now in its trademark papaya orange livery, Bruce and fellow Kiwi Denny Hulme's Can-Am cars won five of the six races, with Bruce taking McLaren's first title. In the following five seasons what became known as the "Bruce and Denny show" rolled on with Hulme winning the title in 1968 and 1970, while Bruce claimed his second crown in 1969. Peter Revson won for McLaren in 1971. Between 1967 and 1971 the works McLarens won thirty-seven of the forty-three races, including nineteen one-twos. Such dominance won many admirers and many sales of racing sports cars and, just occasionally, a customer car won too. Over the duration of the Can-Am series McLaren was the dominant victor with forty-three victories, almost three times more than its closest competitor, Porsche.

McLAREN MOVES INTO FORMULA ONE

Back in 1965 Bruce had already decided to leave Cooper and build his own Formula One car for the first season of the new three-litre formula. Having built a "mule" chassis for testing in 1965, the first McLaren F1 car, the M2B, made its bow at the Monaco GP. Although saddled with underpowered and unreliable engines, Bruce scored a point for sixth place in only its third race, at Brands Hatch, with a further two points later in the season. It was a respectable start but the real mark left by McLaren's first F1 car was the innovation it featured.

Establishing a tradition that has long guided McLaren, the car's designer, Robin Herd, was recruited from the aerospace industry at Farnborough. Herd had worked with a material called Mallite—endgrain balsa wood sandwiched between two sheets of aluminium in a honeycomb, from which he constructed the entire inner and outer monocoque of the M2B. It was strong and light—a watchword for the aviation industry and a prescient and enduring quest for McLaren to this day.

It took only another season for the McLaren F1 team to make it to the top step of the podium, a feat achieved, appropriately, by Bruce himself at the 1968 Belgian Grand Prix. The Cosworth-powered M7A was among the fastest cars of the season and was liveried in McLaren orange for the first time. Denny Hulme won a further two races in 1968, the latter in Canada yielding the team's first one-two. Hulme went on to win four more Grands Prix in the following years.

Bruce's tragic death while testing at Goodwood in 1970 would have thrown lesser teams into disarray, but under the guidance of Teddy Mayer and with the support of Denny Hulme, who stayed loyal to his compatriot's team until he stepped down from Formula One and McLaren at the end of 1974, McLaren was on the cusp of achieving the ultimate success. The team's first Drivers' and Constructors' Championships came in 1974 when Brazilian Emerson Fittipaldi won three races and took the crown in the McLaren M23. The same model, now in its fourth season, also powered James Hunt to the 1976 Drivers' Championship after a season-long, and enthralling, battle with Niki Lauda and Ferrari.

McLAREN AT INDIANAPOLIS

In the 1970s McLaren had also been very active in the USA. Not only had McLaren created history with its Can-Am success but the team also coveted glory at the prestigious Indianapolis 500.

Following an unlucky accident that precluded Hulme from competing with the M15 in 1970, McLaren bounced back in 1971 with the F1-inspired M16. Powered by the ubiquitous turbo-charged Offenhauser engine and presenting the first wedge-shaped car at the Brickyard, Peter Revson and Mark Donohue were both super-quick but failed to take the win, Revson finishing second.

The following year Donohue won the Indy 500, and several other USAC races, in Roger Penske's M16B. It wasn't the orange car that won, but it was a McLaren. Two years later Texan Johnny Rutherford took the flag at the Brickyard in a McLaren M16 C/D and this time it was orange. The now venerable M16 line of cars progressed into D and E specifications with Rutherford finishing second in 1975 and winning again in 1976. Although this marked the end of McLaren's active involvement at Indy, customer examples of the M16 continued at the 500-mile race until 1981 when Vern Schuppan's example still managed third place.

THE IMPORTANCE OF CUSTOMERS
The 1980s were to see major upheaval at McLaren, setting the tone for McLaren's Formula 1 successes. Before moving on to this significant chapter in the history of McLaren there were some important learning points from the company's first seventeen years. First McLaren learned that success breeds success: with each new Can-Am car it experienced strong demand from customers who wanted the fastest cars available. The company also realized that it needed a production partner in order for it to be able to focus the efforts of the young company on developing its products. Accordingly McLaren established a partnership with Trojan to build customer cars. Between 1965 and 1976 Trojan built around 160 customer Group 7 Can-Am cars, fifty-two Formula 500/A cars and twenty-five Formula 2/B cars. In addition McLaren made no fewer than twenty-four cars for USAC racing in America.

The company's fame in the United States led it to form McLaren Engines based in Livonia, Michigan, in order to be close to its racing centres and provide on the spot support. Its experience of IndyCar racing delivered tremendous experience in aerodynamics due to the high speeds generated on the oval circuits—average speeds came close to 200 mph—and in the use of turbocharged engines at a time when almost all European racing was with normally-aspirated units. All this experience would prove valuable in the new era of the 1980s with Ron Dennis at the helm.

RON DENNIS STARTS A NEW ERA AT McLAREN AND REVIVES ITS SUCCESS

After McLaren's purple patch in the mid-1970s, the team's performance went downhill in 1978, '79 and '80. It was a time that saw the emergence of hugely powerful turbo cars from the big manufacturers competing against the small teams equipped with the normally-aspirated Cosworth engine that made its debut back in 1967. So in 1980 McLaren merged with Ron Dennis' Project 4 Racing team.

Ron's arrival was timely. He had worked in Formula 1 since 1966, joining Cooper Cars soon after Bruce McLaren departed, then started his own F2 team in 1971.

Not only did he bring a new drive and ambition to the famous team but he also brought back a skilled designer, John Barnard. Barnard was working in America where he designed the Chaparral 2K that won Indianapolis in 1980, but he had been at McLaren earlier in the 1970s where he worked on the M23 car that delivered two Formula 1 Drivers' Championships (Fittipaldi and Hunt) and McLaren's first Constructors' title (1974).

More significantly, Barnard was interested in a material new to racing car design, carbon fibre composite. This material was used in aerospace applications but had never been applied to a complete racing car monocoque. McLaren pioneered the use of carbon fibre in motor racing with its new car, the MP4/1, and revolutionized racing car construction. The carbon fibre chassis was built by Hercules Aerospace and brought new levels of rigidity and driver safety to Formula 1.

The MP4/1 series of cars raced for three years, delivering one victory in 1981, four in 1982 and another in 1983, by which time the turbo cars were outgunning the more nimble Cosworth-powered teams. Towards the end of 1983 McLaren's long-awaited turbo engine arrived in the form of a Porsche-designed V6 named TAG (Techniques d'Avant Garde). TAG principal Mansour Ojjeh became a shareholder in McLaren and shared in a period of rewarding success for the company. Ron attracted Niki Lauda out of retirement to join John Watson in 1982/3 on driving duties and both were to win races.

The 1984 season saw race wins turn into championships. Frenchman Alain Prost replaced Watson, but it was Lauda who took his third title, despite Prost winning seven Grands Prix to the Austrian's five. Guile and experience won over youth and pace, but McLaren had won its second Constructors' Championship and celebrated its most successful season so far with twelve victories from sixteen events. The MP4/2 B repeated its championship victories in 1985, Prost lifting the driver's trophy with five wins while Lauda managed just one before retiring. Prost went on to win the Drivers' Championship in 1986 and 1989 for McLaren.

THE SENNA AND PROST ERA
For 1988 McLaren entered what would be an enormously fruitful relationship with Honda, firstly with the Japanese company's 1.5-litre turbo engine then, when turbos were banned, with 3.5-litre V10 and V12 power plants. Also new for 1988 was Ayrton Senna. The explosive combination of Senna, the fastest driver in the world, and the master tactician and strategist Prost would yield two Championships (Constructors' and Drivers'). The first season of this partnership yielded almost the perfect score with Senna winning eight races and Prost seven, leaving just one for the other teams, and McLaren scored no fewer than ten one-twos. In 1989 the score was Senna six and Prost four, but the latter won the title.

Into the new decade, Senna had a new teammate in Gerhard Berger and he continued to dominate, winning Drivers' Championships in 1990 and 1991 with Berger's consistency helping the team to two more Constructors' Championships. The last year for McLaren and Honda was 1992 and although the team could not celebrate five Championships on the bounce, they won five races and finished second. Honda withdrew from Formula 1 leaving McLaren to use Ford and then Peugeot engines before linking up with Mercedes-Benz in 1995, a relationship that endured until 2014.

McLAREN'S FIRST TRIP TO LE MANS
In 1995 McLaren also entered Le Mans for the first time in its thirty-year history. The company's decision to build the F1, the

ultimate super sports car was never intended to spawn a racing car. However, the burgeoning interest amongst racing teams for a GT series using road-derived cars, and the eagerness of some McLaren owners to compete, stirred the competitive spirit at Woking. McLaren set about strengthening the iconic F1 road car for the parts that might not stand the punishment meted out in endurance racing.

The basis of the car was good—a carbon fibre tub for strength, high torsional rigidity and light weight and a 6.1-litre BMW V12 engine that issued 627 bhp. It was almost a modern Can-Am car for the road. The resultant racing version was named the McLaren F1 GTR and from an intended production of three, nine were produced in 1995 alone.

Weight was reduced by 90 kilos, bigger brakes and wheels, a roll cage, a faster steering rack, a reinforced gearbox, and a rear wing were added. Engine power was reduced over the standard car to 600 bhp in order to comply with Le Mans regulations. It must be the only car in the world that went to the track with less power than its road-going sibling.

The GTR's first outing was the first race in the BPR Global GT Championship at Monza, a series for professional racers and gentlemen drivers. Three GTRs entered and owner Ray Bellm had the honour of giving his car a debut victory with Maurizio Sandro Sala as co-driver. The GTR won its first six races and then headed for the big one—the 24 Hours of Le Mans. Six McLarens entered the race with drivers ranging from ex-GP aces JJ Lehto, Mark Blundell and Yannick Dalmas to long-distance specialists Derek Bell and Andy Wallace.

It was a wet race that placed a premium on delicacy of touch and, although the lighter prototypes were expected to be faster, the conditions played into the hands of the McLarens with Lehto in particular driving spectacularly well. At one stage in the night he was lapping ten seconds faster than any other car on the track. In the end, the black GTR of Lehto, Dalmas and Masanori Sekiya came home first by a single lap. The other McLaren GTRs finished third, fourth, fifth and thirteenth, with only one retiring due to a crash.

It was a remarkable achievement in that a real road car with only minimal modifications had taken on and beaten the best in the world's most gruelling race, at its first attempt and in the first year of production. The result also guaranteed that the McLaren F1 would claim an iconic status in the eyes of aficionados the world over.

It also secured for McLaren a first in that it is the only manufacturer to win the triple crown—The Formula 1 World Championship, the Indianapolis 500 and the 24 Hours of Le Mans. It remains a unique achievement.

The F1 story continues with a resounding victory in the BPR GT series in both 1995 and 1996 and the All-Japan GT Championship. The F1 revisited Le Mans in 1996, finishing fourth, fifth, sixth, eighth, ninth and eleventh and again in 1997 with a revised long-tailed GTR finishing second and third.

FORMULA ONE IN THE MODERN ERA
Back in the Formula One arena the relationship between McLaren and Mercedes Benz gelled and the driver team of Mika Häkkinen and David Coulthard complemented each other for six seasons of positive results. In this period the Finn won twenty Grands Prix and took the Drivers' title in 1998 and 1999, while the Scot won ten Grands Prix with another two to come after Häkkinen had retired. In 1998 McLaren won its eighth Constructors' Championship.

Another Finn, Kimi Räikkönen, replaced Häkkinen as Coulthard's partner and finished second in the championship in both 2003 and 2005, taking nine victories. He was joined by another exciting driver, Juan Pablo Montoya, for 2005 and 2006 who took three wins for McLaren before going back to America.

In 2007, reigning double World Champion Fernando Alonso arrived at McLaren to challenge for a third title while the gifted protégé of the McLaren and Mercedes-Benz team, Lewis Hamilton, would start his rookie year alongside an established master. Hamilton was quick "out of the box" and went on to win five Grands Prix and take a close second in the title race. Alonso also took four wins to finish third. Alonso was to leave after just a single season, but Hamilton went on to take five more victories in 2008 and secured the Drivers' Championship at his second attempt—the youngest driver ever to do so.

McLaren now has a heritage of fifty-four years, in fifty-two of which it has been represented at the pinnacle of the sport—Formula One.

RETURN TO HONDA POWER 2015–2017

After twenty year's powered by Mercedes engines McLaren reforged their championship winning partnership with Honda for the 2015 season. The new partnership of Fernando Alonso and Jenson Button struggled with what was rumoured to be an underpowered engine which suffered from reliability issues. Dogged by grid penalties for replacing power unit components the team could only manage ninth in the Constructors Championship which was their poorest finish since 1980.

2016 marked the Fiftieth Anniversary of McLaren's participation in Formula One and the champion team had a much more promising season. Despite having to play catch up with the other engine manufacturers the Honda powered Mclaren managed to achieve sixth place in the Constructors Championship on seventy-six points with Alonso and Button finishing tenth and fifteenth respectively.

However the season was overshadowed by the departure of legendary chairman Ron Dennis after 35 years at the helm which lead to the subsequent sale of his 25% stake in the company.

Team protégé Stoffel Vandoorne replaced the retiring Jenson Button for the 2017 season but it was decided in September after continued poor on track performance that McLaren would end their relationship with Honda at the end of the season. Despite an apparently excellent chassis the team managed only 30 points to finish ninth in the Constructors Championship.

RENAULT ENGINES 2018–A NEW ERA

For the first time in their history McLaren cars are powered by Renault engines from the 2018 season onwards. In April Zak Brown who was engaged as an executive director in 2016 was announced as the CEO of McLaren Racing as part of a restructuring of the McLaren Group. Following the resignation of Éric Boullier in July Gil de Ferran was appointed as Sporting Director.

In August Fernando Alonso announced that he would not

compete in Formula One in 2019 and Carlos Sainz junior was signed to a multi year deal to be joined by Lando Norris the teams' 2018 reserve driver, also on a multi-year contract.

HONOURS
Including twelve world drivers' championships and eight constructors' championships

Formula 1
182 Grand Prix Wins
155 Pole Positions
12 Drivers' Championships
8 Constructors' championships

Can-Am Series
43 race wins and five consecutive Constructors' Championships between 1967 and 1971

Indianapolis 500
Three race wins (1972 Mark Donohue M16B, 1974 Johnny Rutherford M16C/D and 1976 Johnny Rutherford M16E)

Le Mans
One win, on first attempt in 1995

Formula 1 Drivers' Championships
1974 Emerson Fittipaldi M23
1976 James Hunt M23
1984 Niki Lauda MP4/2
1985 Alain Prost MP4/2B
1986 Alain Prost MP4/2C
1988 Ayrton Senna MP4/4
1989 Alain Prost MP4/5
1990 Ayrton Senna MP4/5B
1991 Ayrton Senna MP4/6
1998 Mika Häkkinen MP4-13
1999 Mika Häkkinen MP4-14
2008 Lewis Hamilton MP4-23

Formula 1 Constructors' Championships
1974 Emerson Fittipaldi (All), Denny Hulme (All), Mike Hailwood
     (1-11), David Hobbs (12–13), Jochen Mass (14–15) M23
1984 Niki Lauda, Alain Prost MP4/2
1985 Alain Prost (All), John Watson (14), Niki Lauda (1–13,
     15–16) MP4/2B
1988 Ayrton Senna, Alain Prost MP4/4
1989 Alain Prost, Ayrton Senna MP4/5
1990 Ayrton Senna, Gerhard Berger MP4/5B
1991 Ayrton Senna, Gerhard Berger MP4/6
1998 Mika Häkkinen, David Coulthard MP4/13

RACING POINT FORCE INDIA

Racing Point Force India F1 Team is one of just ten competitors in the FIA Formula One World Championship. The team made its official debut at the 2018 Belgian Grand Prix, following the takeover by a consortium of investors led by Mr. Lawrence Stroll, but boasts the heritage of its predecessors in the guise of Force India and the other outfits operating out of the team's historical Silverstone base.

The current incarnation of the team can trace its origins to 2007, when Indian entrepreneur, Vijay Mallya, took over the Spyker team and renamed it Force India. The team experienced steady growth over the years, always living within its means and making sure it worked smart with the resources available.

The first season, in 2008, was about establishing a base from which to proceed, with veteran Giancarlo Fisichella joined by promising young talent Adrian Sutil to drive the Ferrari-powered VJM01. Indeed Adrian provided the highlight of the season, running a brilliant fourth in the closing stages of a wet Monaco Grand Prix until he was pushed off the road by Kimi Raikkonen's Ferrari. It was a difficult building year that saw the team finish tenth in the championship.

A switch for 2009 to Mercedes power and gearboxes from McLaren Applied Technologies provided the team with a solid starting point from which to develop the VJM02. The improvement in form was immediately obvious, as Fisichella and Sutil moved up the grid and began to challenge for points. Adrian was running a strong sixth in the rain in China when he unfortunately slid off the road.

The car had traditionally favoured faster circuits, and at Spa Fisichella took a shock pole position and then finished a brilliant second to Raikkonen in the race. By the next event at Monza the Italian was himself driving for Ferrari and third driver Tonio Liuzzi was promoted to a Force India race seat.

At that race Adrian underlined the speed of the car by qualifying second, setting fastest lap, and finishing fourth. At season's end Force India had moved up to ninth in the World Championship.

Sutil and Liuzzi continued the team's improving form into 2010. Adrian became a regular points-scorer, taking a best of fifth place in both Malaysia and Belgium, while Tonio had less luck but earned a good sixth in Korea. The progress was emphasised by seventh place in a championship which now included twelve teams, while Adrian earned eleventh in the drivers' version.

In 2011 the team continued to move forward as reserve driver Paul Di Resta was promoted to a race seat alongside Sutil, and Nico Hülkenberg joined as third driver. Adrian and Paul challenged for points at nearly every race and the team ultimately earned sixth place, narrowly missing out on fifth. Paul was the best placed rookie in thirteenth, while Adrian was an excellent ninth, beaten only by the drivers from Red Bull, McLaren, Ferrari and Mercedes.

2012 saw test driver Hülkenberg promoted to a race seat alongside Di Resta, while promising Frenchman Jules Bianchi joined as reserve driver for the VJM05. The team's path of growth did not stop and both drivers achieved excellent results in one of the most competitive seasons in recent years. Force India broke the 100-point barrier, scoring in sixteen out of twenty races and mixing with the sport's top teams.

Among some great results, the highlights of the season were fourth places by Paul Di Resta in the Singapore Grand Prix and an equal result for Nico Hülkenberg in the Belgian Grand Prix. In addition, the team very nearly tasted victory in the thrilling season finale in Brazil, where Nico led for thirty laps in changing conditions before eventually finishing fifth.

Adrian Sutil's return for the 2013 season saw his partnership with Paul Di Resta resumed. The pair produced some impressive performances at the wheel of the competitive VJM06, with Paul achieving a career-best fourth place in Bahrain and Adrian finishing fifth in Monaco with a gutsy performance. The team challenged for fifth place in the Constructors' Championship for most of the year, despite a mid-season change in regulations that affected the car's performance; a good string of results starting at the team's home race in India ensured the team reclaimed sixth place by the end of the championship.

The ever-increasing confidence in the team's performance was reflected by high-caliber appointments for the team's 2014 lineup, with Nico Hulkenberg returning to partner new recruit Sergio Perez in what was regarded to be one of the most interesting driver pairings in Formula One. Results didn't take long to come, with Perez scoring a sensational podium in the Bahrain GP, in only his third race with the team, and the team emerging as a contender behind the leading teams. A string of strong results, aided by the Mercedes engine's emergence as the best power unit on the grid, ensured the team pushed for fifth place until the final race of the season, eventually settling for sixth place and a record points haul of 155.

The seeds of change were sown, however, and 2015 saw an even stronger performance for the team. The confirmed line-up of Hulkenberg and Perez emerged as fifth fastest on the grid and by the end of the season, the team was celebrating its best-ever championship position. A podium for Perez in Russia, thanks to an inspired strategy call by the pit wall, was the icing on the cake as the team built on its previous success and set the foundations for even greater things to come in 2016.

The following two seasons saw Force India establish itself firmly at the top of the midfield battle. A slowish start of the 2016 season was turned on its head with two podiums in three races, Sergio Perez finishing third in both Monaco and Baku. A strong streak of races after the summer break saw the team leapfrog all its direct rivals in the championship and finish in fourth place for the first time ever with a whopping 173 points, a record that was set to last just one season . . .

A new line-up of Perez and French rising star Esteban Ocon helped the team retain its standing in the championship, more than doubling the points tally of its nearest competitors and setting the team's new highest total with 187. The VJM10, in its striking pink livery thanks to a new partnership with water technology company BWT, confirms its place as a growing force in the sport. With two consecutive fourth-place finishes in the championship, Force India carved out its spot as the 'world champions, pound for pound spent' in the words of F1 pundit Martin Brundle.

This lean, giant-killing outfit was ready to make its next leap up in the rankings, and halfway through 2018 a consortium of investors led by Canada's Lawrence Stroll purchased the assets of the team to provide it with the stability and investment needed to continue competing at the sharp end of the sport. Starting from zero points ahead of the Belgian Grand Prix, the team had its work cut out, but reacted in style to start scoring points with both cars in the two first races under its new guise.

The future looks bright for the ever-popular Force India team . . .

OTMAR SZAFNAUER, TEAM PRINCIPAL AND CEO

Racing Point Force India Team Principal and CEO, Otmar Szafnauer, heads up the team with responsibility for both the factory operations and trackside performance. Under his watch the team has emerged as a genuine podium contender, taking the fight to the leading teams. Otmar has a wealth of F1 and motorsport experience. He joined Ford in 1986 and became programmes manager of Ford Racing in 1993. In 1998 Otmar took up the position of Operations Director for the British American Racing team in F1. He then moved to Jaguar as COO and ultimately to Honda in 2002 where he held positions on the management board including that of Vice President of Honda Racing Development. In 2018, he was appointed as CEO and Team Principal of Racing Point Force India.

SCUDERIA TORO ROSSO

Scuderia Toro Rosso has been competing in the Formula 1 World Championship since 2006. With Red Bull Racing already in F1, the team was created with a view to finding two extra cockpits for the stars of the future coming through the ranks of the Red Bull Junior Driver Programme. Red Bull had dabbled in motor sport sponsorship for many years and in fact, Gerhard Berger was the first athlete the Austrian company supported. However, Red Bull's Dietrich Mateschitz wanted to aim higher and in 2004, he bought out the Jaguar Racing F1 team, based in Milton Keynes and rebranded it as Red Bull Racing. But what to do with the talented youngsters on the Red Bull books? The answer was to acquire the Minardi team in 2005, which started racing as Scuderia Toro Rosso a year later.

When the team was first established it operated partly as a satellite to Red Bull Racing, running a car designed mainly by Red Bull Technology. However, since 2010, Scuderia Toro Rosso has run completely independently, doing all the car design and manufacturing work in-house in Faenza. This necessitated a major expansion programme for the factory, with a brand new purpose-built facility coming on stream a couple of years ago. The Italian side of the operation is supported by the team's wind tunnel facility in Bicester, England. Team Principal Franz Tost has been at the helm since 2005, while the technical side is managed by Technical Director James Key.

The 2018 driver line-up of Brendon Hartley and Pierre Gasly both came through the Junior Driver Programme. In 2015, Carlos Sainz and Max Verstappen were the youngest ever driver pairing in Formula 1 with a combined age of just thirty-seven. Our reputation for bringing on young talent is brought out by other statistics relating to our drivers: Verstappen holds the record as the youngest driver to score points in F1, thanks to his seventh place in the 2015 Malaysian Grand Prix at the age of 17 years and 180 days. Sainz briefly held the record himself, having finished ninth in the previous round, the Australian Grand Prix, at the age of 20 years and 195 days old. Previous holders include Daniil Kvyat

(19 years 324 days), Jaime Alguersari (20 years 12 days) and Sébastien Buemi (20 years 149 days).

Currently the team has one win and one pole position to its name, both courtesy of Sebastian Vettel, who produced the fairytale result at the team's home race, the Italian Grand Prix in Monza, back in 2008.

FRANZ TOST, TEAM PRINCIPAL

As a young lad, Franz Tost's big hero was fellow countryman Jochen Rindt: his bedroom walls were covered with posters of the Austrian ace and when it was dissertation time at school, Franz's classmates would all groan, as they knew what was coming—another bloody eulogy to Rindt. Inevitably, Tost found himself behind the wheel, racing a Formula Ford. He was quick enough to win the 1983 Austrian FF Championship, but he felt he would not make it to the top as a driver so a degree in Sports Management from Innsbruck University was next on the agenda. This led to a job at the Walter Lechner Racing School at the Zeltweg circuit.

From there Tost moved to a team management role with EUFRA Racing and at the end of 1993, he took the post of team manager with Willi Weber's Formula 3 team. It was here that he crossed paths with Ralf Schumacher and Weber asked Tost to accompany the youngster to Japan. This led to looking after Ralf's interests at Jordan and then Williams, prior to taking on the role of Operations Manager with BMW's Formula 1 programme. From there, he took on the role of Team Principal with the newly formed Scuderia Toro Rosso in 2005.

Honda has had a long and illustrious history with Formula 1 dating back to the mid-1960s. The Japanese manufacturer entered three rounds in the 1964 Formula 1 World Championship with their RA271, surprising the paddock by rocking up with a full Japanese operations team, aside from American driver Ronnie Bucknum.

The RA271, powered by Honda's 1.5-litre V12 engine, would set the foundation for a successful first stint in the pinnacle of motorsport.

With their new RA272, it didn't take long for Honda to find their way to the top step of the podium, when Ritchie Ginther won the 1965 Mexican Grand Prix in only Honda's second year in the sport. Due to new engine regulations introduced in 1966, where engine sizes increased to 3.0-litres, teams fell behind the machining of their engines—including Honda—meaning the new RA273 made its debut with only three rounds left in the season at the Italian Grand Prix.

In 1967, World Champion John Surtees joined Honda to be its only driver, and Honda once again found success when Surtees beat Jack Brabham and Jim Clark to victory in the RA300's debut at the Italian Grand Prix.

Honda withdrew from Formula 1 after the 1968 season to focus on its automotive efforts in the United States, where overcoming the challenging legislative emissions requirement was an important step for the overall business for Honda. However, the Japanese manufacturer wouldn't be absent from Formula 1 for long.

1983 saw the return of Honda to Formula 1, although this time as an engine supplier. They teamed up with Spirit Racing for the season, and powered Williams for the final race in South Africa where Keke Rosberg finished in fifth position.

The following year got off to a good start with Williams, however, despite winning the Dallas Grand Prix at Fair Park, the season was plagued with retirements prompting Honda to develop a complete new engine for the next year. The RA165E was introduced for the 1985 season which powered Rosberg to victory at the Detroit Grand Prix. Williams-Honda finished the year strong, taking victories at the final three races with Nigel Mansell winning at Brands Hatch and Kyalami, while Rosberg won the season-finale in Adelaide.

It was clear at this stage that Honda was the engine to beat in F1, and in 1986 they powered Williams to the Constructors' Championship, with Mansell finishing runner-up to Alain Prost in the Drivers' Championship.

In 1987 Williams-Honda took their first double title, conquering the Constructors' Championship with 9 wins, while Nelson Piquet won the Drivers' Championship. Honda also had two more wins in the 1987 season, courtesy of the Lotus F1 team.

Honda entered its 'golden era' with McLaren in 1988, winning fifteen out of sixteen races to establish a dominant partnership lasting four years. Honda won four Constructors' Championships and four Drivers' titles before withdrawing from Formula 1 at the end of 1992, having achieved their objectives and to focus on stabilising the core of the business of consumer products. Their sabbatical from Formula 1 didn't last long, as they returned in 2000—again as an engine supplier—this time to BAR. Honda also powered Jordan Grand Prix for two seasons from 2001–2002.

The partnership with BAR resulted in fifteen podiums from 2000-2005 and a best finish of second in the Constructors' Championship in 2004. From 2006-2008, Honda competed once again as a constructor in the championship, finishing a best of fourth in the Constructors' Championship in 2006 with Jenson Button winning the Hungarian Grand Prix. Honda withdrew from Formula 1 at the end of the 2008 season due to the global financial crisis, vowing to return to the sport when the time was right. In 2015 they partnered once again with McLaren, however their results in the following three years prompted an early end to the partnership.

From 2018 Honda will power Toro Rosso, who has previously run Renault, Ferrari and Cosworth engines. This will be the first time that the team will have the backing of an independent engine supplier.

RENAULT F1—115 YEARS OF MOTORSPORT SUCCESS

Renault has long understood the value of motorsport to its brand.

Renault's first major motorsport victory came in the 1902 Paris-Vienna race at the hands of Marcel Renault. Three Type K lightweight cars were entered alongside four smaller voiturettes to do battle against the likes of Count Zborowski's powerful Mercedes and Henry Farman's Panhard. The event took place on steep, twisting roads, including a tough Alpine crossing. From that point on, Renault would be a very serious contender in motorsport at all levels.

In 1906 Renault entered the first-ever Grand Prix, held over two days on public roads outside Le Mans. Renault participated with its Type AK, a lightweight chassis fitted with a 12.9-litre four-cylinder engine. In spite of searing temperatures, a track that almost melted and more than twelve hours of racing, Hungarian Ferenç Szisz won the race for Renault. Victory contributed to an increase in sales for the French manufacturer in the years following the race.

THE JAZZ AGE AND LAND SPEED RECORDS

In the 1920s and 30s, Renault focused on rallying and the Land Speed record. In 1925 Renault won the Monte-Carlo Rally. Then in 1926 the 9.0 litre Renault 40CV Type NM des records was developed for speed trials, complete with a single seat, stream-lined coupe bodywork and exposed wheels. It went on to achieve a twenty-four-hour average of 107.9mph—significant speeds for a production-based car of the day.

In the thirties Renault developed the Nerva Series and continued with numerous speed record attempts on the roads of Europe and Africa. Powered by Renault's second eight-cylinder in-line unit and inspired by aviation engineering developments, the Nervasport finished second in the 1932 Monte-Carlo Rally, just two-tenths of a second behind the winner. Victory came in the 1935 Monte-Carlo Rally, the 1935 Liège-Rome-Liège race and second place, behind Bugatti, was achieved in the Morocco Rally too.

But the car turned in its most spectacular performance at the speed ring in Montlhéry. In April 1934, a specially prepared Nervasport won several endurance records in all categories. It covered more than 8,000km in forty-eight hours, at an average of over 100mph and a top speed of close to 125mph. The highly dynamic single-seater body designed by Marcel Riffard would influence the design of future Renault vehicles.

SHOOTING STARS IN THE 1950S
Renault recaptured the pioneering spirit of its early days in the 1950s with further attempts on the Land Speed record. After two years of wind-tunnel testing, in September 1956 Renault took the striking blue Étoile Filante (Shooting Star) to the Bonneville Salt Flats in Utah, USA. The outstanding vehicle featured a tubular, polyester-clad body and two large aircraft-like fins. It was propelled by an innovative turbine engine developing 270 hp at 28,000rpm and was equipped with the Transfluide transmission. In a nod to the aeronautics sector, it ran on kerosene and was practically vibration-free thanks to the rotation speed of the turbines. On its first run on solid ground, its developer Jean Hébert set a new land speed record, peaking at 308.85km/h.

Renault followed this remarkable speed achievement with further rallying success. It entered the petite and innovative rear-engined Dauphine in numerous events, including the Mille Miglia. It took the first four places in the 1956 event and won the Tour de Corse the same year. Two years later a Dauphine won the Monte-Carlo Rally.

THE START OF THE GORDINI PARTNERSHIP
In the early 1960s a sportier, high-performance version of the Dauphine was produced by Amédée Gordini, who had also created Grand Prix cars under his own name. The Renault-Gordini partnership proved to be highly successful, with the classic R8 Gordini, R12 and R17 appearing in subsequent years. The R8 Gordini excelled in rallies, hill-climb and racetrack meetings and proved so immensely popular that the Renault 8 Gordini Cup, a programme widely considered to be the forerunner of

brand-specific championships, was created in 1966. The Renault 12 Gordini engine also powered the first Formula Renault cars, with the first Formula Renault French championship held in 1971. Many eminent drivers and champions have since cut their teeth in the formula, including Jacques Laffite; Jean Ragnotti, Alain Prost, Sebastian Vettel, Kimi Räikkönen and Lewis Hamilton.

Gordini's facilities in Paris proved to be too small for the ambitious activities, so a new building outside the city was sought. The ideal location was found at Viry-Châtillon. The Gordini facility was inaugurated on 6 February 1969, and it was to be the launch pad for significant and lasting motor sporting success over the following decades.

VA VA VOOM AT VIRY-CHÂTILLON
The initial focus in Viry was a new 2-litre V6 engine, which was officially launched in January 1973. The engine soon proved to be competitive in the prestigious European 2-litre sportscar series. That was followed by a move into the FIA World Sportscar Championship with a turbocharged version of the engine.

Renault Sport was founded in 1976, and that year saw the birth of a parallel single-seater programme with the V6 engine in European F2.

LE MANS SUCCESS ACHIEVED; F1 DEBUT LOOMS
In sportscars the turbocharged Renaults proved to be incredibly fast, securing a string of poles and fastest laps. In parallel, in 1976 Renault Sport started track testing with a 1.5-litre version of the turbo engine for competition in Formula 1. A short programme of races was scheduled for 1977.

The V6 turbocharged RS01 made its debut in the 1977 British GP in the hands of Jean-Pierre Jabouille. Nicknamed the 'Yellow Teapot,' the car retired from its first race, but not before it had made a big impression. Four further outings at the end of the year provided more valuable experience.

Everything came together at Le Mans in 1978 when Didier Pironi and Jean-Pierre Jaussaud scored a historic victory in an Alpine-Renault A442B powered by Renault's turbocharged V6 engine. Another Renault came home fourth. With Le Mans success finally secured, Renault could now focus on Formula 1.

Its F1 education process continued until Jabouille earned the first points for Renault—and for any turbo engine—with fourth place in the US GP in 1978. A move to a twin-turbo set-up for the 1979 Monaco GP was one of the big breakthroughs. The team had finally begun to conquer the critical problem of turbo lag, and Jabouille duly scored the marque's historical first win on home ground in Dijon, having started from pole.

RALLYING TO VICTORY
In addition to circuit-based activities, Renault remained committed to rallying. It won the manufacturer's title in the 1973 World Rally Championship, before Guy Fréquelin claimed the 1977 French Rally Championship with the Alpine A310 Group 5. The Renault 5 Alpine garnered further fame with Jean Ragnotti, who finished second in the 1978 Monte-Carlo Rally. Ragnotti then piloted the Renault 5 Turbo to victory in the 1981 Monte-Carlo Rally and the 1985 Tour de Corse.

Renault also ventured into rallye raids with the Paris-Dakar Rally and a privately-entered Renault 20 driven by the Marreau brothers won the 1982 edition through the deserts of Africa.

After years of hard graft, Renault's F1 involvement began to pay dividends as it finished second in the 1983 World Championship with Alain Prost. The Frenchman had taken four wins to champion Piquet's three, but missed the title by just two points. The same year Renault became an engine supplier for the first time, joining forces with Lotus. Supply deals were also extended to the Ligier and Tyrrell teams in subsequent seasons. In Portugal 1985 Ayrton Senna scored his first-ever GP victory with Renault power, and the Brazilian proved to be one of the stars of the season.

F1 SUCCESS ENSUES
The works outfit was closed at the end of 1985 with focus instead directed at supplying engines to other teams. Indeed in 1986 the Senna/Lotus/Renault combination proved to the fastest on the grid, as the Brazilian took eight poles.

After a short period of absence, Renault returned to Formula 1 in 1989, but this time as an engine partner to the Williams team. In its first year of competition the new partnership won two Grands Prix, and two further wins followed in 1990. Nigel Mansell—who had used Renault power at Lotus—joined the team.

It was the start of an incredible era. By the end of 1991 the combination was the one to beat, and in 1992 Mansell proved so dominant that he secured Renault's first World Championship by August.

Former works Renault driver Alain Prost joined Williams in 1993, and he too won the title before retiring. Further championships followed for Damon Hill in 1996 and for Jacques Villeneuve in 1997. Williams-Renault also won the Constructors' title in 1992, 1993, 1994, 1996 and 1997.

In 1995 Renault expanded its involvement with a new collaboration with the Benetton team. Michael Schumacher won the championship in 1995, while Benetton won the Constructors' title—ensuring that with its two partners Renault scored six straight title successes between 1992 and 1997. Between 1995 and 1997 Renault engines won 74% of Grands Prix.

Renault officially departed Formula 1 at the end of 1997. Williams, Benetton and later the new BAR team used Renault-based engines under the Supertec, Mecachrome and Playlife names, and work continued in a small development project at Viry.

Renault simultaneously continued its rally involvement throughout the nineties and the Maxi Mégane was driven to victory in the Tour de Corse in 1997.

AN F1 RETURN

Again, Renault's official absence from F1 was to be a brief one. In early 2001 it was announced that the company had bought the Benetton team, and was to return in a full works capacity. The Renault name returned as Benetton's engine supplier that season, and then in 2002 the team was reborn as Renault F1 Team, with the chassis department still based at Enstone, UK, while working closely with the engine division in Viry.

In 2003 Fernando Alonso gave the new team its first pole in

Malaysia, and then the young Spaniard followed up with his and the team's first win in Hungary. The following year Jarno Trulli gave Renault victory in the most prestigious race of the year in Monaco.

In 2005 Alonso was the man to beat as he won the Drivers' title and Renault took the Constructors' version with eight wins between Alonso and team-mate Giancarlo Fisichella.

Despite the huge change from V10 to V8 technology for 2006, the Renault F1 Team was able to sustain its momentum. A further eight wins over the season saw Renault fighting with Ferrari for both titles, but Renault's innovation again proved victorious as it again captured both the Drivers' and Constructors' titles.

Supplying other teams had long been a Renault policy, and in 2007 a new partnership was formed with Red Bull Racing. The dark blue cars soon moved up the grid, and in 2010 Vettel emerged triumphant as the youngest champion in the history of the sport, while Red Bull-Renault earned the Constructors' championship.

As Renault refocused its activities around engine supply, Vettel proved unstoppable in the World Championship, breaking all the records as he secured consecutive titles in 2011, 2012 and 2013.

Alongside Red Bull Racing, Renault supplied Lotus F1 Team, Caterham F1 Team and Williams F1 Team. Throughout the era, the V8 engine developed by 250 engineers at Viry-Châtillon dominated, taking over forty per cent of the available wins and a record number of pole positions.

Away from F1, Renault Sport Technologies continued to develop its range of single-make championships with Formula Renault 2000 and the Clio Cup. The Clio Super 1600 enjoyed strong success on the rally circuit, winning several international titles between 2003 and 2005.

The 2005 season brought the creation of the World Series by Renault, following a merger between Eurocup Formula Renault V6 and the World Series by Nissan. Free to the public World Series by Renault meetings combined top-class competition with on-track F1 shows and family entertainment for 11 years. The series was also a springboard for most of the stars in the current F1 field.

THE START OF A NEW ADVENTURE

In 2014, Formula 1 welcomed a radical new wave of technology with the introduction of avant-garde powertrain technology. The new Renault F1 power unit revisited a previous engine generation's turbocharged architecture but combined it with powerful electric motors and an array of advanced energy-recovering devices that cut fuel consumption by forty per cent year on year while delivering comparable levels of performance and acceleration.

Renault continued to supply Red Bull Racing, sister team Scuderia Toro Rosso as well as Lotus F1 Team, but the era proved hard fought. A rethink of the corporate strategy was required, and at the end of 2015 Renault announced it would return to team ownership.

For 2016, the Renault name once again raced in F1 as a full manufacturer entry, taking charge of Enstone-based Lotus F1 Team once again. Renault Sport Formula One Team was reborn with a long-term commitment to the sport and aspirations to once more return to the top step of the podium and challenge for championships. The first challenger, the R.S.16 was the first Enstone-Viry collaboration in ten years and soon began running for points. The team continued its strong momentum the following year, with the R.S.17 ending the season with a string of points-scoring finishes.

Renault Sport Formula One Team ended the season in sixth position with a rapid car and two hungry drivers; one step closer to reaching its target.

SAUBER

TALES OF THE UNEXPECTED

Peter Sauber had never been particularly interested in cars, and motor racing did not do anything for him at all, not then at least. The fact that, in 2010, Sauber was able to celebrate the fortieth anniversary of Sauber Motorsport had a lot to do with chance in the early days, but afterwards it was down to sheer perseverance and, later on, a good deal of hard graft and skill.

Sauber's father owned an electrical company that employed around 200 staff and had premises in Zurich. Sauber's career path seemed to be mapped out. He trained as an electrical fitter with the aim of gaining further qualifications and following in his father's footsteps. But it would all turn out rather differently.

In 1967 Sauber used to drive to work every day in a VW Beetle—until a friend persuaded him to have some tuning work done. For a bit of fun he then entered it in a few club races in 1967. Far more significantly, it sparked his passion for tinkering with cars. He modified his Beetle to such an extent that eventually it was no longer fit for road use. This led to the next stage in Sauber's career: in 1970 he decided to set himself up as an independent builder of open two-seater racing sports cars. Out of the cellar of his parents' home in Zurich emerged the Sauber C1. He used the first name of his wife Christiane as the model designation.

That same year, he set up PP Sauber AG and moved into a specially built workshop on the premises of his father's company in Wildbachstrasse. With the C1 he won the 1970 Swiss sports car championship, but soon whittled things down to the occasional appearance as a racing driver. In 1974 he donned his helmet for the last time before turning his full attention to car construction. The "C" was retained as a trademark.

Sauber had set himself a difficult task: surviving on constructing racing sports cars in Switzerland seemed a doomed prospect. But he would not be deterred and was determined to battle on. The working day often stretched deep into the night, while money was in short supply.

SPORTS CAR SUCCESSES

Sauber achieved international prominence with the C5 in which Herbert Müller won the then acclaimed Interserie Championship in 1976. That was followed by his first forays at Le Mans. By this time Sauber Motorsport had four employees on the payroll. In 1981 Hans-Joachim Stuck and Nelson Piquet won the Nürburgring 1000 Kilometre race in a Sauber-built Group 5 BMW M1.

The following year was a decisive one for Sauber. He was commissioned by Swiss composite materials manufacturer Seger & Hoffmann to build a car for the Group C World Sports Car Championship: it was to become the Sauber C6. During this time he made contact with engineers at Mercedes who expressed an interest in motorsport—though all very much at a private level, as international motorsport had been an unmentionable subject for the Stuttgart carmaker since the tragic accident at Le Mans in 1955.

In 1985 Sauber began fitting Mercedes engines into his racing sports cars, moving that bit closer to the Stuttgart company. Just a year later, Henri Pescarolo and Mike Thackwell won the Nürburgring 1000 Kilometres in a Sauber C8. Further triumphs were to follow, ultimately prompting Mercedes' comeback to international motor racing. From 1988, Sauber and his crew acted as the Mercedes official works team.

Professor Werner Niefer, Chairman of Mercedes at the time, decided the cars should be painted silver, marking the revival of the famed "Silver Arrows". The highlight of this partnership was the year 1989, which brought not only the drivers' and manufacturers' titles in the World Sports Car Championship, but a one-two result in the legendary 24 Hours of Le Mans as well. The following year saw a repeat win of the World Championship title. Sauber Motorsport had grown to a workforce of fifty.

It was also during this time that the junior team was set up, based on an idea of Sauber's business partner of the time, Jochen Neerpasch. The drivers selected were Michael Schumacher, Heinz-Harald Frentzen and Karl Wendlinger. Peter Sauber paved the way for all three to enter Formula One.

FORMULA ONE

With the lustre of the World Sports Car Championship beginning to fade, Mercedes now looked to Formula One. In the summer of 1991 it was declared a joint project, and preparations went into full swing. Sauber set about building a new factory on the company site in Hinwil.

However, that November brought with it bad news: because of the straitened economic climate, the Mercedes board had decided against sending a works team into Formula One. Sauber had two options, one, to accept a financial settlement and withdraw, or alternatively to use the money as start-up capital for his own Formula One involvement. In January 1992 he took the plunge, and by autumn the first tests in the C12 were under way, with an Ilmor engine providing power. The company was then employing just under seventy staff.

On 14 March 1993, according to plan, two Sauber C12 cars driven by Karl Wendlinger and JJ Lehto lined up for the South African Grand Prix. With two World Championship points for fifth place claimed by the Finnish driver, this debut turned out an acclaimed success.

Contracts signed with Red Bull and Petronas in 1995 provided a solid foundation and enabled the Swiss team to establish itself as a fi rm fixture in Formula One. In 1995 and 1996 Sauber served as the works team for Ford, and from 1997 onwards the cars were powered by Ferrari engines bearing the name of the title sponsor Petronas.

The breakthrough was some time in coming, however. Finally, in 2001, three high points in the team's history arrived in rapid succession: the partnership with major Swiss bank Credit Suisse, fourth place in the Constructors' World Championship secured in mid-October and, just a few days later, the ground-breaking ceremony for the team's very own wind tunnel.

Sauber also decided to introduce some fresh blood into Formula One at this time, signing up Kimi Räikkönen and Felipe Massa to his team and later recommending Robert Kubica to the decision-makers at BMW.

BMW

Peter Sauber was on the lookout for a new engine partner in 2005. Now in his sixties, he was not disinclined to pass his life's work on into capable hands. An offer from BMW seemed like a good solution. The car manufacturer, which had been involved in Formula One with Williams since 2000, was keen to set up its own works team. On 22 June 2005, BMW announced its acquisition of a majority stake in the Swiss team.

The 2008 season—the third year of the BMW Sauber F1 Team—would mark the next milestone in the history of the team. The extension at Hinwil had in the meantime been completed and the workforce had grown to more than 400. The team's target for that year was to achieve its maiden victory—which turned out to be a one-two, with Robert Kubica winning in Canada ahead of Nick Heidfeld. In all, the BMW Sauber F1 Team notched up eleven podium places in 2008. Kubica claimed the team's first pole position in Bahrain and Heidfeld boosted the statistics with the first two fastest race laps. The team ended the World Championship in third place with 135 points.

Following a challenging start to the 2009 season, shock news broke on 29 July: at a press conference in Munich, BMW announced it was withdrawing from Formula One at the end of the season. The company bowed out with thirty-six points and sixth place in the World Championship.

STARTING OVER

The next press conference would be held on 27 November 2009, this time in Hinwil. Peter Sauber had reached an agreement with BMW and bought back his life's work. But the joy was tempered by disappointment as BMW had already decided to reduce the workforce. Employee numbers were whittled down from 388 to 260. It was with this pared-down workforce, with Ferrari as engine partner and drivers Kamui Kobayashi and Pedro de la Rosa, that the Hinwil team embarked on the 2010 race campaign.

The first half of the season was marred by numerous retirements for technical reasons, unprecedented in the team's history. After the first eight races, the team had a single World Championship point to its name. By the end of the season this had risen to forty-four, of which Kobayashi had picked up thirty-two, with De la Rosa and Heidfeld—who replaced the Spaniard for the last five Grands Prix—each contributing six points.

THE 2011 SEASON

The team hired another rookie, Sergio Pérez, for the 2011 season. The Mexican's arrival meant Kobayashi would have to take on leadership responsibilities in only his second full season on the F1 grid. The year began with the team getting to grips with the tyres developed by the new sole F1 supplier Pirelli, completing a promising programme of winter testing and jetting off for an opening race in which a strong team performance ultimately gave way to frustration.

Pérez and Kobayashi crossed the finish line seventh and eighth in Melbourne, only to be subsequently disqualified after a rear wing element was deemed to have contravened the rules. The team lost the ten points its performance had earned, but consolation arrived in the knowledge that the necessary speed was there. Strong showings duly followed in the next few races. In Monaco, for example, Pérez had just made it through to the top-ten qualifying shootout for the first time when he lost control of the C30 on the exit from the high-speed tunnel section and slammed into the barriers with devastating force. The Mexican youngster was initially motionless in the car. After what felt like an eternity the news came through that he had got away with severe concussion.

Kobayashi went on to show great mental strength to finish fifth in the race, the best result of the season for the Sauber F1 Team. Pérez also had to sit out the next race in Canada, with De la Rosa taking his place at short notice.

After a good first half to the season, which saw the team occupying what looked like a safe sixth place in the Constructors' World Championship, the team endured a drop in form. The cause of the downturn was rooted in a controversial technology: diffusers fed by the car's exhaust flow, even—thanks to sophisticated engine mapping—when the driver is off the throttle. The FIA announced a ban on the practice, only to subsequently reverse its decision.

In the meantime, the team had stopped development of an "outboard blown" diffuser for the C30, which put it at a disadvantage against rival teams still running the technology. Despite this handicap of well over a second per lap, the young drivers still managed to add to the team's World Championship Points haul. The Sauber F1 Team eventually finished seventh in the Constructors' Championship on forty-four points. Kobayashi was responsible for thirty of those, with Pérez recording fourteen points. Both Kobayashi and Pérez, together with Mexican reserve driver, Esteban Gutiérrez, were confirmed for the 2012 season as early as the summer.

THE 2012 SEASON

The Sauber F1 Team lined up for 2012 with the unchanged pairing of Pérez and Kobayashi in the race seats. And the season began strongly, Pérez coming home eighth and Kobayashi sixth at the opening race in Melbourne.

But that was only the start; even greater excitement was to follow in Malaysia, where Pérez delivered a sensational performance in fluctuating weather conditions. A clever tactical move in the early stages saw him make up a number of places, and the Mexican driver was subsequently the fastest man on a wet, then merely damp and finally drying track. Moving up into second place, he even put the race leader—Ferrari's Fernando Alonso—under pressure before briefly running wide and losing critical seconds. However, second was still an outstanding result and, most of all, it underlined what an excellent car the team had developed in the Sauber C31-Ferrari.

The next highlight of the season was not long in coming. Pérez qualified fifteenth for the Canadian GP, but a well thought-out strategy and the Mexican's ability to look after his tyres allowed him to work his way up to third—giving him and the team their second podium of the season at this still early stage.

The low point came at Spa. The weekend had begun perfectly; Kobayashi secured second place on the grid, with Pérez starting immediately behind him. However, the race had barely begun when both the Sauber cars were involved in the same collision caused by a rival driver. Their race was ruined and the disappointment was immense.

However, compensation for the Sauber F1 Team arrived just a week later in Monza, Pérez providing further evidence of his tyre-preserving prowess. The Mexican cut through the field like a hot knife through butter—most notably in the latter stages of the race after taking on more fresh rubber—to wrap up another second place.

The final highlight of the season came courtesy of Kobayashi in his home Grand Prix at Suzuka. The Japanese star had already qualified third to send his compatriots into raptures. Then he also made a fine start to the race, cementing his position at the business end of the field. Going into the final quarter of the race he came under increasing pressure from the ever-closing Jenson Button, but the local hero held firm to set the seal on his first podium finish in Formula One. For many in the team, the podium ceremony provided the season with its most emotional moment.

It was a very good year for the Sauber F1 Team, headlined by four podium finishes, 126 World Championship Points and sixth place in the Constructors' standings—a position higher once again than the previous year and an achievement that earned the praise of many outside observers.

HANDING OVER THE REINS

There was a major announcement on 11 October 2012—and with it a milestone in the team's history—it was the day that Sauber stepped down as Team Principal and passed on the baton to Monisha Kaltenborn.

THE 2013 SEASON

The Sauber F1 Team had a new pairing for the 2013 season. Nico Hülkenberg joined the Swiss squad for his third Formula One season. Esteban Gutiérrez was promoted from test and reserve driver to a race seat.

The season opener in Melbourne was chastening. Nico Hülkenberg was not even able to start the race due to a leak in the fuel tank of the C32; Gutiérrez finished his debut race in thirteenth spot.

However, the first points were not as far away as the team might have thought. Nico Hülkenberg collected the first four points of the season in Malaysia and followed up with a tenth place in China. After this, though, came a number of races that gleaned no points.

Scoring seven points and qualifying only twice for Q3 in the first half of the season was not the expected return of the Sauber F1 Team. In Hungary the team introduced an update package for the Sauber C32-Ferrari, and was confident it would improve performance during the second half of the campaign.

Finally, things turned round in Monza: Hülkenberg qualified third and finished fifth in the race, adding ten points to the team's tally. The remainder of the season saw at least one car qualifying in Q3.

In Singapore Gutiérrez made the top ten for the first time and delivered one of his best weekends of the season. In Korea both drivers qualified in the top ten with the Mexican rookie just missing out on his first point by finishing eleventh. Hülkenberg drove one of his best races in the season finishing fourth. The Sauber F1 Team advanced to seventh place in the Constructors' World Championship.

Only one weekend later, another highlight took place in Japan. Hülkenberg and Gutiérrez both finished in the top ten, pulling in another fourteen points for the team.

Disappointment struck in India, where Hülkenberg was forced to withdraw from the race early due to a broken brake disc. Gutiérrez missed the points because of a drive-through penalty. And it didn't look any better as the team left Abu Dhabi empty-handed as well. This time Hülkenberg got the drive-through penalty. In the last two races Nico Hülkenberg netted a further twelve points for the team.

With fifty-seven points, the Sauber F1 Team finished the 2013 season seventh in the Constructors' World Championship. Given that the team finished sixth twelve months earlier, this result was hardly satisfying. However, there were also positive aspects: the C32 was barely competitive in the beginning of the season, but the team improved significantly during the second half of the campaign by scoring fifty points. Nico Hülkenberg finished the Drivers' Championship in tenth spot, his best result in his Formula One career. Esteban Gutiérrez scored six points and was the best-placed rookie of the season.

THE 2014 SEASON

Failing to secure a single point and finishing in tenth position in the Constructors' World Championship, the team endured a frustrating campaign in 2014. This was the first time in their Formula One history that the team had failed to score even one point.

The team was dogged by reliability issues throughout the season, which resulted in a combined fifteen race retirements. Not surprisingly both drivers also struggled with power issues in qualifying to such an extent that the only time the team progressed into Q3 was when Adrian Sutil made it into the top ten shootout at the US Grand Prix.

In November it was announced that Marcus Ericsson and Felipe Nasr would replace Sutil and Gutierrez in the 2015 driver line-up. Only three teams on this year's grid—Ferrari, McLaren and Williams—have been in Formula One longer than Sauber. Between 1993 and 2014 a total of twenty-five drivers have lined up for the Swiss team in 384 Grands Prix.

THE 2015 SEASON

The Sauber F1 Team started with a new pair of drivers in its twenty-third Formula One season, relying on two young, talented and highly motivated drivers—Marcus Ericsson and rookie Felipe Nasr—for the 2015 season. Regarding the Sauber C34-Ferrari, quite a bit had happened as well—not only did the design change, but also the colours from grey to yellow-blue. Furthermore, the Swiss team made progress from a technical point of view. Moreover, in 2015 the Sauber F1 Team celebrated an outstanding anniversary: the United States Grand Prix at Austin marked the squad's 400th GP in twenty-three years of Formula One. By scoring thirty-six points and finishing eighth in the constructors' championship, the team increasingly improved compared with the previous year.

THE 2016 SEASON

Both Marcus Ericsson and Felipe Nasr were retained for the 2016 season. In July, after a long period of financial uncertainty, the Swiss based investment firm Longbow Finance acquired the shares of Peter Sauber and Monisha Kaltenborn to become the sole owners of the team. Pascal Picci of

Longbow took over Peter Sauber's role as chairman of the board whilst Monisha Kaltenborn was retained as Team Principal and CEO.

A ninth placed finish by Felipe Nasr at the Brazilian Grand Prix gave the team their only points of the season so that they finished tenth in the Constructors Championship on two points ahead of Manor on one point.

THE 2017 SEASON AND BEYOND—A TIME OF CHANGE

It was announced in January that German driver Pascal Wehrlein would replace Felipe Nasr to race alongside Marcus Ericsson for the 2017 season. However, following an injury to Wehrlein, it was

Ferrari reserve drive Antonio Giovinazzi who lined up on the grid at The Australian Grand Prix as well as The Chinese Grand Prix. Wehrlein returned to score four points for ninth place in Spain and one point for tenth place in Azerbaijan to give the team five points and a tenth place finish in the Constructors Championship. Just prior to Azerbaijan Monisha Kaltenborn was replaced by Frédéric Vasseur as Team Principal.

In July of 2017 it was announced that Sauber had signed a new multi-year agreement with Ferrari for up-to-date engines from 2018 onwards thus cancelling their planned switch to Honda.

In November Sauber announced that they had signed a multi-year technical and commercial partnership with Alfa Romeo so that from 2018 onwards the team would be known as Alfa Romeo Sauber F1 Team.

In 2018 Marcus Ericsson was joined by Charles Leclerc who in 2019 will swap with Kimi Räikkönen of Ferrari, who in turn will be joined by Antonio Giovinazzi.

RICH ENERGY HAAS F1

'We're still learning on the Formula One side. We don't want to be in the mid-pack forever. We want to get on top of the mid-pack. That's our goal.'
— Gene Haas, founder and President, Haas F1

The 2019 Formula One World Championship will be the fourth season for the Haas F1 Team and it is fair to say that they have exceeded expectations both on and off the track so far. In keeping with the spirit of our approach we have asked the newest team in Formula 1 to express themselves in their own words and to this end they have provided a detailed timeline from conception to the end of their first season along with a detailed insight into their multi-faceted founder.

FROM BREAKING GROUND TO BREAKING RECORDS
14 October 2013
Ground is broken on an 11,600 square-meter (125,000-square foot) facility adjacent to Gene Haas' NASCAR Cup Series team in Kannapolis, North Carolina.

6 January 2014
Gene Haas responds to the FIA's 'call for expression of interest' regarding a Formula One entry.

6 February 2014
Gene Haas proceeds with the requirements specified in the FIA's 'expression of interest.'

11 April 2014
FIA grants Gene Haas a Formula One license.

4 June 2014
Gene Haas announces Haas F1 Team will join the Formula One grid in 2016.

2 September 2014
Haas F1 Team launches its digital platforms, which includes www.HaasF1Team.com and a presence on Facebook, Twitter, Instagram and YouTube.

3 September 2014
Haas F1 Team announces technical partnerships with Scuderia Ferrari (power unit, gearbox and overall technical support) and Dallara (chassis design).

11 February 2015
With construction of Haas F1 Team's Kannapolis headquarters complete, personnel begin moving into their offices.

March 10, 2015
Haas F1 Team purchases the former Marussia F1 facility in Banbury, Oxfordshire, U.K. The 3.655 square-meter (39,350 square-foot) building serves as Haas F1 Team's European base, allowing for easier and quicker access to the team's overseas suppliers and streamlined logistics for when the team travels to Formula One venues in Europe.

22 September, 2015
Haas Automation is named the official machine tool supplier of Haas F1 Team.

29 September 2015
In a press conference at Haas F1 Team's Kannapolis headquarters, Romain Grosjean is announced as the team's first driver for its inaugural Formula One season in 2016.

30 October 2015
In a press conference at the Soumaya Museum in Mexico City, Esteban Gutiérrez is announced as the teammate to Grosjean for Haas F1 Team's debut season in 2016.

8 January 2016
Haas F1 Team's first racecar passes its FIA-mandated crash test.

12 January 2016
Haas F1 Team's first set of sea freight leaves for Australia.

4 February 2016
Grosjean spends first day in simulator in preparation for 2016 season.

5 February 2016
Gutiérrez spends first day in simulator in preparation for 2016 season.

9 February 2016
Grosjean has first seat fitting in Haas F1 Team's racecar.

10 February 2016
Gutiérrez has first seat fitting in Haas F1 Team's racecar.

15 February 2016
Haas F1 Team is the first team to arrive at the Circuit de Barcelona—Catalunya for preseason testing.

16 February 2016
Successful fire-up of the car's engine—the Ferrari 061.

20 February 2016
Haas F1 Team's racecar turns its wheels for the first time at Barcelona with Grosjean at the helm. The installation lap around the 4.655-kilometer (2.89-mile), 16-turn circuit comes during the team's production day.

21 February 2016
Haas F1 Team's first racecar, the VF-16, is officially debuted to the world with still and video imagery distributed via an online launch across Haas F1 Team's digital platforms.
The origin of naming the car "VF-16" goes back to the first CNC machine manufactured by Haas Automation, the VF-1, launched in 1988. The "V" stands for vertical, which is an industry standard designation for a vertical mill. Gene Haas adds "F1" to the

name to unofficially designate it as the company's "Very First One".

22 February 2016
After a physical unveil of the VF-16 at 7:50 a.m. CET at Barcelona, Haas F1 Team hits the track for its first official test at 10 a.m. sharp with Grosjean at the wheel. Thirty-one laps are completed, yielding 144.305 kilometers (89.7 miles) and a best time of 1:28.399.

23 February 2016
Gutiérrez drives the VF-16 for the first time during testing at Barcelona. He makes seventy-nine laps to log 367.745 kilometers (228.51 miles) with a best time of 1:25.524.

4 March 2016
Preseason testing at Barcelona ends. Haas F1 Team logs a total of 474 laps 2,206.47 kilometers, (1,369.86 miles) during the eight days of track time spread over 12 days (Feb. 22-25, March 1-4).

10 March 2016
Air freight packed up and sent to Australia. Haas F1 Team signs American racer Santino Ferrucci as a development driver.

14 March 2016
Cars and equipment arrive at Albert Park Circuit for the season-opening Australian Grand Prix in Melbourne.

18 March 2016
Grosjean and Gutiérrez participate in Haas F1 Team's first practice session at Albert Park Circuit in preparation for the Australian Grand Prix.

19 March 2016
Grosjean and Gutiérrez participate in Haas F1 Team's first qualifying session at Albert Park Circuit in preparation for the Australian Grand Prix. Grosjean qualifies 19th with a 1:28.322 and Gutiérrez qualifies 20th with a 1:29.606.

20 March 2016
Haas F1 team makes its official race debut in the Australian Grand Prix, becoming the first American Formula One team to compete in a grand prix since 1986. And after ending a 30-year drought for an American squad in Formula One, Haas F1 Team ends another drought for an organization's maiden F1 race. After starting 19th, Grosjean finishes an impressive sixth, earning the team eight points in the constructors standings. The last time a Formula One team scored points in its debut race was in the 2002 Australian Grand Prix when Mika Salo finished sixth for Toyota. Gutiérrez finishes 20th after a lap-17 crash with McLaren driver Fernando Alonso.

2 April 2016
Grosjean and Gutiérrez advance from Q1 to Q2 for the first time during qualifying for the Bahrain Grand Prix.

3 April 2016
Grosjean scores Haas F1 Team's best result when he finishes fifth in the Bahrain Grand Prix. With the sixth-place finish March 20 in the Australian Grand Prix, Haas F1 Team becomes the first team since 1973 to debut with consecutive point-scoring finishes. Ironically, it was another American team that held this record—Shadow Racing, which had Californian George Follmer scoring top-six results in the team's first two races.

1 May 2016
Grosjean finishes eighth in the Russian Grand Prix to earn Haas F1 Team's third points-scoring result in four races. These three point-paying finishes are the most of any new team in this millennium. When Jaguar debuted in 2000 and when Toyota came on the scene in 2002, each entity managed only two point-paying finishes in their entire first seasons for a combined total of six points.

12 July 2016

Haas F1 Team development driver Santino Ferrucci takes his first laps in a Formula One car during a test at England's Silverstone Circuit. The 18-year-old from Woodbury, Connecticut, pilots the Haas VF-16 for a total of 55 laps around the 5.891-kilometer (3.660-mile), 18-turn facility, marking the first time an American driver wheels an American Formula One car since Oct. 9, 1977 when Danny Ongais drove a Penske PC4 in the Canadian Grand Prix at Mosport International Raceway in Bowmanville, Ontario.

3 September 2016

Gutiérrez advances to Q3 during qualifying for the Italian Grand Prix, marking the first time Haas F1 Team is represented in Q3.

8 October 2016

Grosjean and Gutiérrez advance all the way to Q3 during qualifying for the Japanese Grand Prix. It marks the first time both Haas F1 Team drivers have moved on to Q3.

21 October 2016

Haas F1 Team practices for the United States Grand Prix at Circuit of the Americas in Austin, Texas. It marks the first time an American Formula One team has turned a wheel on American soil since the 1986 Detroit Grand Prix when Eddie Cheever and Alan Jones raced for Team Haas, which despite the name has no relation to Haas F1 Team. Industrialist Gene Haas owns Haas F1 Team while the late Carl Haas owned Team Haas.

23 October 2016

Grosjean makes 100th career Formula One start in the United States Grand Prix. He finishes tenth to give Haas F1 Team a point-paying finish in its first race on home soil.

11 November 2016

Haas F1 Team announces that Kevin Magnussen with drive alongside Grosjean in 2017. Gutiérrez will finish out 2016 season while exploring new opportunities for 2017.

27 November 2016

With the conclusion of the season-ending Abu Dhabi Grand Prix, Haas F1 Team ends its debut year with a very respectable eighth-place finish in the constructors standings with a total of 29 points, outpacing the factory Renault team (ninth), Sauber (10th) and Manor (11th).

On 25 October 2018 at the Mexican Grand Prix, it was announced that Rich Energy, the premium British energy drink brand, would become the title partner of Haas F1 team beginning with the 2019 FIA Formula One World Championship. The partnership will result in a significant livery change to incorporate the colours of Rich Energy, while the team name will become Rich Energy Haas F1 Team.

GENE HAAS, INDUSTRIALIST, TEAM OWNER, PHILANTHROPIST

Birthdate: 12 November 1952
Birthplace: Youngstown, Ohio
Hometown: Los Angeles, California
Residence: Camarillo, California
Marital Status: Single

INDUSTRIOUS BEGINNINGS
Find a challenge. Create a good, efficient and cost-effective solution. Repeat.

For Gene Haas, founder of Haas F1 Team in the FIA Formula One World Championship, that has proven to be his formula for success in business, racing and philanthropy.

Haas was born on Nov. 12, 1952 in the industrial town of Youngstown, Ohio. For someone born in what used to be known as the "Industrial Heartland of North America," it is appropriate that Haas has become a captain of industry, where his company, Haas Automation, is the largest CNC machine tool builder in North America.

Haas' family moved to Los Angeles when he was still a child, where his father worked as a designer of electrical cabinets for Hughes Aircraft and his mother was a schoolteacher. The second oldest of four children, Haas' family instilled at an early age the importance of hard work and responsibility. He delivered newspapers while in elementary school and at age 14 began working in a machine shop where he swept floors and kept the facility clean. After only six months, Haas was setting up lathes and conventional milling machines. He continued to work at machine shops through high school and college, mastering the machining techniques that would lead him to found Haas Automation in 1983.

Haas graduated from high school in Mission Hills, California, in 1970. After high school, he attended California State University-Northridge where he studied engineering and business. He graduated in 1975 with a Bachelor of Science degree in accounting and finance.

In 1978, after working for three years as an industrial programmer, Haas founded Proturn Engineering, a small contract machine shop in Sun Valley, California. Haas worked side-by-side with his two employees at Proturn Engineering, machining parts for the electronics and aerospace industries. It was during that time Haas developed a fully-programmable 5C collet indexer to boost productivity in his own shop. The Haas 5C was the industry's first device to automatically re-position parts accurately for machining by simply pressing a button, as opposed to having to reposition the material by hand—a cumbersome and time-consuming process.

The machine-tool industry received the economical and reliable Haas 5C Indexer with enthusiasm, and in 1983 Haas Automation, Inc., was born. The company started with three employees in a 465-square-meter (5,000-square-foot) facility. During the next four years, Haas expanded his product line to include a wide selection of fully-programmable rotary tables, indexers and machine-tool accessories. Haas Automation quickly became the leader in fourth- and fifth-axis parts positioning.

In 1987, Haas took what he learned from the 5C Indexer and designed and developed his first vertical machining center (VMC)—the VF-1. The prototype was introduced to the manufacturing world in 1988 at the International Machine Tool Show (IMTS) in Chicago. Haas listed the machine at the unheard price of $49,900. Industry experts were skeptical that an American company could manufacture and sell a machine tool for less than $50,000.

Haas Automation silenced the skeptics. The new product was a success. Today, virtually every manufacturer of vertical machining centers worldwide produces a similar machine in the $50,000 price range.

Over the next five years, Haas Automation began to grow. In 1992, Haas Automation moved to a larger facility in Chatsworth, California, to keep up with demand. In 1997, again seeking to keep up with the success of its growing product line and production demands, Haas Automation moved once more, to its current location in Oxnard, California, where all of its products are manufactured.

The 92,903-square-meter (1-million-square-foot) facility in Oxnard is one of the largest, most modern machine tool manufacturing operations in the United States. Haas Automation currently produces four major product lines: vertical machine centers (VMCs), horizontal machine centers (HMCs), computer numeric control (CNC) lathes and rotary tables.

Haas products are sold through a worldwide network of more than 170 Haas Factory Outlets in more than 80 countries providing the industry's best support and service.

Although he founded Haas Automation and serves as its president, Haas' primary role has always been heading up the engineering department. Ninety-five percent of all new design ideas originate through Haas himself. He sketches out his ideas and then turns them over to his engineers for refinement. After reviewing the engineers' work, Haas makes further modifications, as required. One of Haas Automation's strengths is its ability to take a new machine from initial concept, through design, and into production in just six to 12 months.

Haas' desire to push innovation and tackle new challenges goes beyond his interest in machine tools.

In 2007, Haas built Windshear, one of the most advanced automotive wind tunnels in the world. It opened to its first customer, a Formula One team, in September 2008.

The facility's centerpiece is a rolling road, which allows a full-size car to be restrained in place directly on top of a massive, treadmill- like stainless steel belt rotating at speeds up to 290 kph (180 mph). The rolling road accurately simulates the dynamics of a car on the racetrack, unlike traditional fixed-floor tunnels. The high-tech rolling road is able to accelerate from zero to 290 kph in less than one minute, with temperatures controlled within 1 degree Fahrenheit.

Windshear was the first wind tunnel of its kind in North America and only the third rolling-road wind tunnel of its scale in existence. Windshear is available for hire to all motorsports teams and auto manufacturers. NASCAR, INDYCAR, sports car and NHRA teams utilize Windshear, as does the United States Council for Automotive Research (USCAR), which has conducted tests on production cars at Windshear.

TEAM OWNER—A RACING LIFE BEFORE F1

In addition to his professional accomplishments, Haas is passion- ate about auto racing. He has competed successfully in off-road racing and sponsored numerous race teams through the years in CART, INDYCAR, Formula One and NASCAR.

In 2002, Haas formed his own NASCAR Cup Series team, Haas CNC Racing. Originally headquartered in Concord, North Carolina, Haas CNC Racing began as a single-car team with chassis and technical support from Hendrick Motorsports. The team made its debut on Sept. 29, 2002 at Kansas Speedway in Kansas City with driver Jack Sprague.

The team raced only two more times in 2002, but by 2003, Haas CNC Racing was running the full NASCAR Cup Series schedule.

In 2006, Haas CNC Racing relocated to a new, state-of-the- art, 13,000-square-meter (140,000-square-foot) facility in Kannapolis, North Carolina, where it began fielding two, full- time NASCAR Cup Series teams.

On July 10, 2008, Haas announced that he had partnered with Stewart, then a two-time NASCAR Cup Series champion. The new operation, known as Stewart-Haas Racing, became official in January 2009. The team fielded two NASCAR Cup Series entries—one for Stewart and another for Ryan Newman.

Haas immediately began to see results of his new partnership.

Stewart finished eighth in the season-opening Daytona 500 at Daytona (Fla.) International Speedway to score the first top-10 for SHR in just its first point-paying race. In late March, Stewart and Newman placed both cars among the top-10 in a race for the first time when Stewart finished third and Newman finished sixth at Martinsville (Va.) Speedway. In early May, SHR placed both cars among the top-five in a race for the first time when Stewart finished second and Newman finished fourth at Richmond (Va.) International Raceway.

Then on May 16, Stewart scored the first NASCAR Cup Series victory for SHR in the non-points All-Star Race at Charlotte (N.C.) Motor Speedway. The following week, on May 21, Newman scored the first NASCAR Cup Series pole for SHR in the Coca-Cola 600 at Charlotte.

SHR recorded its first point-paying NASCAR Cup Series victory when Stewart won the Pocono 500 at Pocono (Pa.) Raceway by 2.004 seconds over runner-up Carl Edwards. It marked the first time a driver/owner won a point-paying NASCAR Cup Series race since Ricky Rudd on Sept. 27, 1998 at Martinsville.

Stewart would go on to score SHR's second NASCAR Cup Series win at Daytona in July and its third at Watkins Glen (N.Y.) International in August.By Sept. 12, following the conclusion of the NASCAR Cup Series race at Richmond—the cutoff race for the NASCAR Playoffs—SHR was the only organization to place all of its teams in the playoffs.

With its inaugural season complete, SHR had placed both of its cars among the top-10 in the season-ending point standings. Stewart finished sixth in points while Newman finished ninth.

In 2010, SHR recorded three NASCAR Cup Series wins. Newman reached victory lane first when he won at Phoenix International Raceway in April. Stewart won twice—first at Atlanta Motor Speedway in September and again in October at Auto Club Speedway in Fontana, California. Stewart would go on to qualify for the playoffs and finish the season seventh in points. Newman finished fifteenth.

In August 2011, SHR announced it was adding a third team for INDYCAR star Danica Patrick, who would join the team for a limited NASCAR Cup Series schedule in 2012.

In September 2011, Stewart and Newman qualified for the playoffs. Stewart won five of the final 10 races, including the season finale at Homestead-Miami Speedway. With the victory, Stewart ended the season in a numerical tie with Carl Edwards, as each driver had 2,403 points. But Stewart won the championship by virtue of a tiebreaker, as his five wins on the season trumped Edwards' lone victory. It was the closest NASCAR Cup Series championship in history. While it was Stewart's third NASCAR Cup Series title, it was the first for SHR.

SHR picked up in 2012 just as it left off in 2011, as Stewart scored wins at Las Vegas Motor Speedway and Fontana. Newman also picked up a win early in the season at Martinsville. Stewart went on to win at Daytona in July and at Atlanta in August. In total, Stewart, Newman and NASCAR newcomer Patrick combined to collect five NASCAR Cup Series wins, 18 top-fives and 30 top-tens, along with a pole. Stewart qualified for the play-offs and finished ninth in points.

Patrick made the jump to a full-time NASCAR Cup Series schedule in 2013, joining SHR teammates Stewart and Newman, and she did it in a big way by winning the pole for the Daytona 500. Patrick's pole win was the first NASCAR Cup Series pole ever won by a woman. Stewart would score the first win of the season for SHR at Dover (Del.) International Speedway in June and Newman would follow by winning the Brickyard 400 at Indianapolis Motor Speedway in July. Newman left the team at season's end for another opportunity.

In 2014, SHR grew again with addition of a fourth car for Kurt Busch, sponsored by Haas Automation. Also joining SHR was Kevin Harvick. The duo combined to win six races in 2014, with both drivers qualifying for the playoffs. Busch won at Martinsville in April while Harvick took victories at Phoenix in March, Darlington (S.C.) Raceway in April and Charlotte in October before scoring back- to-back wins in November at Phoenix and Homestead to secure the 2014 NASCAR Cup Series championship. It was the second NASCAR Cup Series title for SHR and it came only two years after Stewart won the team's first championship.

SHR recorded five wins in 2015. Harvick took three

victories—Las Vegas in March, Phoenix in March and Dover in October. Busch won at Richmond in April and at Michigan International Speedway in Brooklyn in June. Both drivers qualified for the playoffs, with Harvick finishing second in the championship by a single point.

Three of SHR's four drivers made the playoffs in 2016, as Harvick, Busch and Stewart all scored victories. Harvick won four races—Phoenix in March, Bristol (Tenn.) Motor Speedway in August, New Hampshire Motor Speedway in Loudon in September and Kansas Speedway in Kansas City in October— while Busch won at Pocono in early June and Stewart won at Sonoma (Calif.) Raceway in late June. It was another successful NASCAR season, but SHR opted not to rest on its laurels. It announced that it would switch manufacturers to Ford beginning with the 2017 season.

Its inaugural year with Ford started off with a bang, as Busch won the season-opening Daytona 500. Harvick also joined Busch in the winner's circle, taking victories at Sonoma in June and Texas Motor Speedway in Fort Worth in November. Both drivers represented SHR in the playoffs, with Harvick advancing all the way to the Championship 4 for the third time in the last four years.

NASCAR isn't the only growth area for Haas' motorsports ambitions. On April 11, 2014, Haas was granted a license by the Federation Internationale de l'Automobile (FIA) to join the starting grid of the FIA Formula One World Championship in 2016. In its inaugural season, Haas F1 Team finished eighth in the constructor standings with a total of 29 points, the most of any new team in this millennium. The outfit followed up that run with an even stronger sophomore campaign, earning 47 points and maintaining its eighth- place standing.

The first American Formula One team since 1986 operates out of an 11,600-square-meter (125,000-square-foot) facility adjacent to Haas' NASCAR Cup Series team in Kannapolis, North Carolina. Haas F1 Team also has a European base in Banbury, Oxfordshire, U.K., allowing for easier and quicker access to the team's overseas suppliers and streamlined logistics for travel to European Formula One venues.

PHILANTHROPIST

Haas established the non-profit Gene Haas Foundation in 1999 to help fund community humanitarian causes as an official commitment to corporate and social responsibility. The Foundation supports local, state and international communities through grants to charities, non-profit organizations and other philanthropic foundations. Since its inception, the Gene Haas Foundation has awarded nearly $25 million to almost 1,000 organizations such as the YMCA, United Way, Salvation Army, Boys and Girls Clubs of America, Food Share, National Breast Cancer Foundation, American Red Cross and many others.

Haas is also a firm believer in education. The Gene Haas Foundation supports a variety of programs, particularly in the technical and engineering fields at schools, colleges and universities worldwide, including Ranken Technical College, Rensselaer Polytechnic Institute, and his alma mater, California State University-Northridge. Additionally, the Gene Haas Foundation has provided grants and scholarships for the American Association of University Women, the NAACP, the Society of Manufacturing Engineers Education Foundation and numerous others.

To augment the Foundation's work, Haas and Haas Automation established a worldwide network of Haas Technical Education Centers (HTECs), which play a vital role in many local training centers, community colleges and universities. HTECS provide an environment that allows students to take theory out of the classroom and apply it within modern manufacturing. Students learn machining and metalworking skills through a hands-on approach, using the types of Haas CNC machine tools they will encounter upon entering the workforce.

DRIVERS

LEWIS HAMILTON

Date of birth: 7 January 1985
Born: Tewin, UK
Lives in: Monaco
Height: 1.74 m
Weight: 66 kg

Lewis Hamilton was born on 7 January 1985 in Tewin, England. At the tender age of eight, Lewis sat in a kart for the first time and was immediately bitten by the racing bug. Mercedes-Benz soon recognised the British youngster's enormous talent, becoming one of his sponsors right at the start of his career.

Lewis not only showed incredible pace on the track but also climbed the career ladder at an impressive rate. After he had blown the competition out of the water in every category of karting and won the McLaren Mercedes Champions of the Future series, McLaren Mercedes enrolled him on their young driver programme in 1997. In 2001, he moved up into British Formula Renault, winning the title two years later.

Lewis' winning streak continued unabated in the Formula 3 Euro Series. He was crowned junior champion whilst still in his second year and subsequently progressed to the GP2 Series with ART Grand Prix. Despite his rookie status, Lewis dominated the Championship—taking five victories on his way to the title. This success immediately led to his promotion to the very pinnacle of motor racing—Formula One.

Lewis made his Grand Prix debut with McLaren Mercedes on 18 March 2007 as team-mate to reigning World Champion Fernando Alonso whilst still only 22 years old. Despite his youth, he remained in contention for the title right up until the season finale in Brazil—challenging top drivers with considerably more experience. The numerous records set by Lewis in his rookie season highlighted his class—including the most race wins, pole positions and points scored in a debut season.

What had already been an extraordinary career reached new heights in 2008, with a first Formula One World Championship crown. At the time of his title victory, Lewis was 23 years, 9 months and 26 days old—taking the accolade of youngest ever Formula One World Champion from Fernando Alonso. Four years later, after six successful seasons with McLaren Mercedes, Lewis sought a new challenge—joining the works Mercedes team for the 2013 season.

Lewis secured his first podium in a Mercedes Formula One car in only his second race at the Malaysian Grand Prix, with a maiden victory following eight races later in Hungary. A total of one victory, five podiums, five pole positions and one fastest lap saw Lewis finish his first campaign with Mercedes-AMG Petronas Motorsport in fourth place overall on 189 World Championship points.

2014 heralded the dawn of a new era for Formula One—and a second World Drivers' Championship crown for Lewis. 11 victories, 16 podium finishes, seven pole positions and seven fastest race laps from 19 races saw him take the title after a season-long battle with Mercedes team-mate Nico Rosberg—culminating in a dramatic finale at the season-ending Abu Dhabi Grand Prix. Highlights of a memorable year included fighting from the back of the grid to the podium in Germany and Hungary, plus a home victory at Silverstone.

One year later, Lewis would repeat that feat in equally impressive fashion. A dominant title defence brought 10 victories, 17 podium finishes, 11 pole positions and eight fastest laps from 19 races en route to a third World Driver's Championship—equalling the great Ayrton Senna and compatriot Sir Jackie Stewart.

Lewis achieved a similar level of success in the 2016 season, scoring the most race wins (ten) and most pole positions (twelve) of any driver. The Brit kept his World Championship hopes alive until the final weekend of the season in Abu Dhabi—but ultimately had to settle for the runner-up spot behind team-mate Nico Rosberg.

For 2017, Lewis came under intense pressure from Sebastian Vettel, trailing the Ferrari driver for the first part of the season before a stunning run of form catapulted him into the Championship lead at the Italian Grand Prix. Lewis secured his fourth World Title in Mexico with two rounds to spare. He ended the year with the most race wins (10) and pole positions (11) of any driver.

Lewis continues to reach new heights in the Formula One hall of fame. By the end of 2017, he had moved into first place on the all-time pole positions leader board (72), as well as becoming the driver with the most front row starts (118). With his fifth Drivers World Championship in 2018, Lewis is now joint-second with Juan Manuel Fangio on the all-time list of World Titles, behind only Michael Schumacher.

Debut: Australia, 18 March 2007
Best Championship: World Champion – 2008, 2014, 2015, 2017, 2018
First Win: Canada, 10 June 2007
2018 Formula One: Mercedes-AMG Petronas Motorsport- Champion
2017 Formula One: Mercedes-AMG Petronas Motorsport- Champion
2016 Formula One: Mercedes–AMG Petronas – 2nd
2015 Formula One: Mercedes–AMG Petronas – Champion
2014 Formula One: Mercedes–AMG Petronas – Champion
2013 Formula One: Mercedes–AMG Petronas – 4th
2012 Formula One: McLaren Mercedes – 4th
2011 Formula One: McLaren Mercedes – 5th
2010 Formula One: McLaren Mercedes – 4th
2009 Formula One: McLaren Mercedes – 5th
2008 Formula One: McLaren Mercedes – Champion
2007 Formula One: McLaren Mercedes – 2nd
2006 GP2 Series: ART Grand Prix – Champion

2005 Formula Three Euro Series: ASM – Champion
2004 Formula Three Euro Series: Manor Motorsport – 5th
2003 Formula Renault UK: Manor Motorsport – Champion
2002 Formula Renault UK: Manor Motorsport – 3rd

VALTTERI BOTTAS

Nationality: Finnish
Date of birth: 28 August 1989
Place of birth: Nastola, Finland
Lives: Monaco
Height: 1.73 m

Valtteri Bottas was born on 28 August 1989 in Nastola, Finland, entering his very first kart race at the age of six. Over the ensuing decade, the karting circuits of Finland and Europe would become his home from home, where he won numerous Championships and was a member of the Finnish national karting squad for seven years.

In 2007, at the age of seventeen, Valtteri made the step up to single-seater racing. He immediately won two races in the Formula Renault 2.0 NEC series and finished his rookie season in third position. Twelve months later, he lifted not one but two Championship trophies, sweeping all before him in his second Formula Renault 2.0 NEC campaign. With twelve victories from sixteen races, Valtteri won the title at a canter. That same year, he also won five races, and the championship, in the Formula Renault Eurocup.

In 2009, as a member of the ART Grand Prix squad, Valtteri graduated to the Formula 3 Euro Series, driving a Mercedes-powered car for the first time in his career. The Finn adapted to the new format very successfully, finishing the 2009 and 2010 seasons in third place. In both years, he won the prestigious Formula 3 Masters in Zandvoort—the only driver to win this event twice in succession. Other well-known Mercedes-powered winners of the F3 Masters are Lewis Hamilton (2005), Paul Di Resta (2006), Nico Hülkenberg (2007) and Jules Bianchi (2008), all of whom went on to compete in Formula One.

In the following year (2011), Valtteri switched to the GP3 Series, which was then in its second season as a support event to Formula One. This put Valtteri in the shop window for F1 teams and also gave him the chance to accumulate preliminary experience of Grand Prix circuits. He acquitted himself well, securing four victories on the last four weekends of the season to beat his team-mate James Calado to the title.

Valtteri was given his first Formula One test outing by Williams in 2010 and continued in this role in 2011 alongside his GP3 commitments. For the 2012 season, he decided to concentrate solely on his duties as a Formula One test driver and not to compete in any more races. In this capacity, he took a Williams car out in the first free practice session on fifteen of the twenty Grand Prix weekends that year, thereby acquiring valuable experience of the top tier of motor racing. In November 2012, he at last received the long-awaited call from his management team: 'Your time has come.'

Valtteri made his Formula One debut at Albert Park, Melbourne, in the 2013 Australian Grand Prix, thereby becoming the ninth driver from his country Finland to compete at this level. His debut season turned out to be a difficult one— but he at least outscored his team-mate Pastor Maldonado by four points to one. Valtteri's moment of glory came in qualifying for the Canadian Grand Prix when, on a drying track, he gave a virtuoso performance to claim P3 on the grid. In the race itself, though, he stood no chance against the opposition on a dry track. He therefore had to wait until the penultimate race of the season before scoring his maiden World Championship points for an eighth-place finish in the United States Grand Prix.

After a change of engine supplier at Williams for the 2014 season, Valtteri was back in a Mercedes-powered vehicle for the first time since his spell in Formula 3. He registered his best season so far in the highest echelon of motorsport, claiming six podium appearances and scoring 186 championship points to finish the campaign in fourth position, behind the Mercedes-AMG Petronas Motorsport duo of Lewis Hamilton and Nico Rosberg and three-time race winner Daniel Ricciardo. That year,

Valtteri his team-mate Felipe Massa secured third place for Williams in the Constructors' Championship. His best results were two runner-up spots in the British and German Grands Prix.

In the 2015 season, Valtteri once again outscored his team-mate Felipe Massa, despite missing out on the start of the season due to a back injury. He made two podium appearances and finished the year with 136 points. In the 2016 season, his fourth in Formula One, Valtteri secured his team's sole podium finish, which came in the Canadian Grand Prix. He again came out on top in the internal contest against team-mate Felipe Massa by a score of eighty-five to fifty-three points.

For the 2017 season, Valtteri becomes became the 11th driver to compete in Formula One with the Silver Arrows in a Mercedes, following in the footsteps of drivers such as Juan Manuel Fangio, Sir Stirling Moss, Michael Schumacher, Lewis Hamilton and Nico Rosberg. It was a breakthrough year for Valtteri that saw him score his first pole positions (four) and race wins (three). The Finn scored more points in his first season with Mercedes-AMG Petronas Motorsport than in his entire Formula One career before and ended the 2017 season in P3.

Debut: Australia, 17 March 2013
Best World Championship: P3 – 2017
First Win: Russia, 30 April 2017
2018: Formula One: Mercedes-AMG Petronas Motorsport – Car No. 77
2017: Formula One: Mercedes-AMG Petronas Motorsport – P3
2016: Formula One: Williams Martini Racing – P8
2015: Formula One: Williams Martini Racing – P5
2014: Formula One: Williams Martini Racing – P4
2013: Formula One: Williams F1 Team – P17
2012: Formula One: Williams F1 Team – Test & Reserve Driver
2011: GP3 Series – Champion
2010: Formula Three Euro Series: ART Grand Prix – P3
Formula Three Macau – P3
Formula Three Masters – Champion

2009: Formula Three Euro Series: ART Grand Prix – P3
Formula Three Macau – P5
Formula Three Masters – Champion
2008: Formula Renault 2.0 Eurocup – Champion
Formula Renault 2.0 NEC – Champion
2007: Formula Renault 2.0 NEC – P3

SEBASTIAN VETTEL

Birthdate: 3 July 1987
Birthplace: Heppenheim, Germany
Height: 175 cm
Weight: 62 kg
Civil Status: Single, two children
Hobbies: Football, sports in general

From the moment that Sebastian Vettel secured his first pole position and first victory at the rain-affected 2008 Italian Grand Prix it heralded the arrival of a unique talent. In a Toro Rosso car that was much more midfield than front-runner he became the youngest driver in history to win a Formula One Grand Prix aged only 21 years and 74 days. In a season in which he was named Rookie of the Year Vettel proved that he was fast, intelligent and technically adept. More importantly he showed that could drive an F1 car quickly and that he had the ability to do this consistently.

In 2009 Vettel graduated to Red Bull Racing where he went on to win the Chinese Grand Prix to become, at the age of 21 years and 287 days, the youngest Grand prix driver in history to win for two different teams. He claimed second place in the title race behind Jenson Button by winning the Abu Dhabi Grand Prix

giving him four victories along with four more podiums for the season.

2010 became a landmark season as Red Bull Racing won their first Constructors' Championship and Sebastian Vettel became the youngest ever World Drivers' Champion with a dramatic victory at the Abu Dhabi Grand Prix to beat Fernando Alonso to the title by a mere four points.

Following a contract extension Vettel was utterly dominant in 2011 finishing the season with 15 poles, 11 victories, 17 podiums from 19 races and a record total of 392 points. His closest rival Jenson Button could only achieve 270 points.

2012 began with seven different drivers winning the first seven races of the season and in a tense season finale in Abu Dhabi Vettel finished sixth to secure his third consecutive World Drivers' Championship by only three points over Fernando Alonso.

Once again in 2013 Vettel was supreme with a run of nine consecutive victories at the end of the season as he secured the World Drivers' Championship for a record fourth time with three races in hand at the Indian Grand Prix. He became only the third driver in the sixty-four years of Formula One, along with Fangio and Schumacher, to win four consecutive championships.

The change in engine regulations in 2014 saw Vettel struggle to come to terms with the new car and with his new teammate Daniel Ricciardo who won three races whilst the German became the first reigning champion since Jacques Villeneuve to fail to win a race.

Vettel's lifelong dream of driving for Ferrari came true when it was announced that he would take up a three-year contract to drive for the Scuderia from 2015 partnering close friend Kimi Raikkonen.

He approached his first season at Ferrari with a level of dedication and determination so that he was able to win three Grands Prix to Räikkönen's none. He was the only driver able to beat the dominant Mercedes all season.

2016 was a totally different story however as Vettel was unable to match the race pace of Mercedes or even Red Bull for that matter. Without a victory all season long he ended up in fourth position outside of the top three for the first time since 2008.

The perseverance of the previous seasons paid dividends in 2017 when Vettel and Ferrari became genuine title contenders winning the first race of the season in Australia and going on to be championship favourites by Monaco. However reliability problems and race errors through a disastrous Asian leg of the season meant he ended the year as runner-up to arch rival Hamilton with a total of five race victories.

CAREER:
1995–2002: Karting winning various titles
2003: 2nd in F.BMW ADAC with Eifelland Racing
2004: F.BMW ADAC Champion with ADAC Berlin-Brandenburg e.V.
2005: 5th in F3 Europe with ASL-Mucke Motorsport
2006: 2nd in F3 Europe with ASM Formule 3 and tester for BMW Sauber F1 Team
2007: 14th in the F1 World Championship with BMW Sauber and Scuderia Toro Rosso (6 points)
2008: 8th in the F1 World Championship with Scuderia Toro Rosso (35 points)
2009: 2nd in the F1 World Championship with Red Bull Racing (84 points)
2010: F1 World Champion with Red Bull Racing (256 points)
2011: F1 World Champion with Red Bull Racing (392 points)
2012: F1 World Champion with Red Bull Racing (281 points)
2013: F1 World Champion with Red Bull Racing (397 points)
2014: 5th in the F1 World Championship with Red Bull Racing (167 points)
2015: 3rd in the F1 World Championship with Scuderia Ferrari (278 points)
2016: 4th in the F1 World Championship with Scuderia Ferrari (212 points)
2017: 2nd in the F1 World Championship with Scuderia Ferrari (317 points)
2018: 2nd in the F1 World Championship with Scuderia Ferrari

CHARLES LECLERC

Born in Monaco, Charles was surrounded by the world of Formula 1 from a young age. When asked about the source of his passion for racing, Charles recounts a fond memory of his first encounter with the sport, 'I must have been four years old. My family and I spent an afternoon with friends during Monaco Grand Prix. We sat on their terrace, which was located just above the exit of turn one, Sainte Dévote. My friend and I played with toy cars and listened to the sound of the Formula 1 engines howling. You have certain memories of your childhood—like milestones—which are deeply engraved in your memory. This is one of my first and most vivid ones.'

Like any other four year old, Charles woke up one morning having decided that he did not want to attend pre-school that day. He told his father that he was feeling ill, and accompanied him to a social meeting with his father's best friend, Philippe Bianchi. As chance would have it, the meeting took place at Bianchi's karting track, not far from Charles' family home.

Little time passed that morning before Charles jumped into one of the karts and completed his first lap, attached to Philippe Bianchi's kart with a rope. After just one lap, the rope was removed, and Charles spent the rest of the day speeding away. 'It must have been during one of the first ten times that I sat in a kart,' Charles explains, that the funniest incident occurred. 'I was about four years old and had already learned how to start the kart up by myself. My father and I arrived at the track, and I just climbed into my kart and drove off. My father stood at the side of the track waving his arms frantically and shouting my name, but I did not understand why and kept on driving. After completing several laps I finally stopped. It turns out that I wasn't wearing a helmet. That's how oblivious I was to the rest of the world, even as a child, as soon as I had the chance to drive. Nothing else mattered.'

Soon after his first exploratory karting excursions, it became clear that racing was more than just an after-school activity for Charles. 'From the day that I actually started competing against others, I was there to win. I wasn't going about it like I was going to play tennis on a Sunday.'

Charles' ambition and passion are what enabled him to win various karting categories and advance to single-seater racing in 2014. He finished his first two seasons (2014 and 2015) as Rookie champion, with his overall results being second place in the 2014 Formula Renault 2.0 Championship, and fourth place in the 2015 FIA Formula 3 European Championship. In 2016, Leclerc became the GP3 Series Champion.

Most recently, the young Monégasque driver became Formula

2 Champion (2017)—so far ahead of his competitors in terms of points that his victory was clear even before the last race of the season had taken place.

An important role-model and companion on his journey to the top, whom Charles speaks very fondly of, was Jules Bianchi. A family friend and fellow racer, Jules is often credited by Charles as being a major influence and someone who he looked up to very much, 'I spent most of my life racing Jules. We spent almost every free weekend at his father's track. I haven't raced a single person as often as I have raced him, and I think that it will not be possible to ever break that record.'

In 2014, Jules Bianchi was involved in a fatal accident while racing in the Formula 1 Japanese Grand Prix. At the age of 19, Charles was confronted with a second tragic loss, namely that of his father Hervé Leclerc in 2017.

'It is quite strange that in my professional career, I have had the best year of my life in 2017, while it has been a tough year for me personally,' he explains, 'I have had to grow up very quickly due to both the nature of my profession as well as personal circumstances. I think that the biggest achievement in terms of my performance so far has been my pole position in the Baku GP qualifying [2017], just days after my father passed away. I went into the weekend without any expectations, but at the same time, knew that I had to make my father proud. Racing for him, in his memory, gave me strength. I owe everything to my father and Jules, and I dedicate each race and each victory to them.'

As a Ferrari junior driver, Charles especially looks forward to experiencing the power of the 2018-spec Ferrari engines in the upcoming season as part of the Alfa Romeo Sauber F1 Team. 'Having the 2018 engines in place will be a big boost for the team. The newly formed partnership with Alfa Romeo is also exciting news.'

He continues, 'I am thankful for all of the support I have received from Ferrari. The support I have been receiving from fans all over the world, especially over the past year, has also been overwhelming. I look forward to my first season in Formula 1 and will do my best to make everyone proud.'

Charles made his Formula 1 debut as a full-time race driver for the Alfa Romeo Sauber F1 Team in the 2018 FIA Formula 1 World Championship. His car was marked with the number 16.

On 11 September 2018, Ferrari confirmed that Charles would partner Sebastian Vettel in 2019, replacing the Sauber-bound Kimi Räikkönen.

CAREER HIGHLIGHTS

2017: FIA Formula 2, Champion

2016: GP3 Series, Champion

2015: FIA Formula 3 European Championship, 4th (1st Rookie)

2014: Formula Renault 2.0, Vice-Champion (1st Rookie)

2013: Karting KZ1, Winter Cup Winner; CIK-FIA World Cup Vice-Champion

2012: Karting KF2, WSK Euro Series; Champion: CIK-FIA European Championship; Vice-Champion: CIK-FIA U18 Championship Vice-Champion

2011: Karting KF3, CIK-FIA Trophee Academy Champion; CIK-FIA World Cup Champion

2010: Karting KF3, Monaco Kart Cup Winner (youngest in history); France Vice-Champion (youngest in history)

2009: Karting Cadet, France Champion (youngest in history)

2005–2008: Karting France, PACA Champion (2005, 2006, 2008)

MAX VERSTAPPEN

Date of birth: 30 September 1997

Car number: 33

Born: Hasselt, Belgium

Height: 1.80 m

Weight: 67 kg

Since his arrival into Formula in 2015 as the sport's youngest ever race starter at the tender age of 17 years and 166 days, Max Verstappen has been confounding expectation, rewriting the record books and raising the game of rivals across the grid.

The son of former F1 driver Jos Verstappen and Belgian kart champion Sophie Kumpen, Max was perhaps destined for a career in motorsport and turned his first laps at the wheel of a go-kart at the tender age of four-and-a-half. By his early teens Max had become a regular title winner on the international karting circuit and in 2013, he won the European KF and KZ championships. He completed his haul of major karting trophies by winning the 2013 World KZ championship, then the sport's highest category.

Max's transition from karts to single-seaters was just as impressive as his progress through the junior ranks. Opting to jump in at the deep end, Max signed for Van Amersfoort Racing to contest the 2014 FIA European Formula 3 Championship. Against top class and considerably more experienced opposition, he won a staggering ten times on his way to third in the championship standings.

Having proved himself in the ultra-competitive F3 arena, Max's next step was obvious—at least to him. Sidestepping the traditional route towards the next rung of the racing ladder, sixteen-year-old Max vaulted straight to the top. Joining the Red Bull family, it was announced, in August 2014, that he would race for Toro Rosso in Formula 1 in 2015.

Max's first experience of an F1 car came just four days after his seventeenth birthday, at the 2014 Japanese Grand Prix. The free practice outing for Toro Rosso made the Dutchman the youngest driver ever to take part in a grand prix weekend.

Just under six months later he became F1's youngest-ever racer when he made his debut at the 2015 Australian Grand Prix. A short two weeks after that he grabbed another record, becoming F1's youngest points-scorer with seventh place at the Malaysian Grand Prix.

In his rookie season Max finished in the points on ten occasions (including two fourth-place finishes, in Hungary and the USA) and amassed a haul of forty-nine championship points. He also demonstrated the thrilling aggressive but incredibly precise racing style that has since become his trademark.

A second season with Red Bull's junior F1 squad began in styles with three points finishes from his first three races, but the desire to challenge for bigger prizes, in all quarters, was clear and ahead of the Spanish Grand Prix, Max was drafted into the Red Bull Racing line-up alongside Daniel Ricciardo.

Max's impact was nothing short of spectacular, as after qualifying fourth on Saturday, he drove an immaculate race on Sunday to claim his first F1 victory and become the sport's youngest winner.

It was a major highpoint, but across the season's remaining seventeen races Max continued to provide electrifying racing entertainment, taking seven podium finishes in all and banking 204 points on his way to fifth place in the Drivers' Championship standings.

With new technical regulations coming into force last year, there was plenty of hope that Max's 2017 campaign would rise above his debut season for the Team but across the first dozen races the Dutchman was let down by a spate of reliability issues.

After the summer break Max's bad luck looked set to continue as an engine issue ruled him out of the Belgian GP after just seven laps and his Singapore GP was almost over before it started as a start line collision ended his race.

However, two weeks later in Malaysia the tables turned, and after a textbook drive Max claimed his second career victory. He almost doubled his season tally a week later but was ultimately forced to settle for second place behind Lewis Hamilton.

However, perhaps his finest moment of 2017 came in Mexico. After qualifying on the front row for the third time in his career, Max muscled past pole position man Sebastian Vettel in Turn Two to take the lead. From there Max drove flawlessly to eventually claim his third career win some twenty seconds ahead of second-placed Valtteri Bottas.

PIERRE GASLY

Date of birth: 7 February 1996
Car number: 10
Born: Rouen, France
Height: 1.77 m
Weight: 70 kg
Marital status: Single

Pierre Gasly has been knocking on the door of Formula 1 ever since winning the 2016 GP2 series in dramatic fashion, taking the title at the final round in Abu Dhabi. Actually, you could say he started knocking at the age of two, when he first used to go to kart tracks to watch his elder brothers. The talented twenty-one-year-old has petrol in his veins, given that his grandfather used to kart and his father tried his hand at a variety of motor sport disciplines. The Frenchman hails from the city of Rouen, famous for a race track that used to host the French Grand Prix a long time ago.

Like all his peers, Gasly's racing began in karts, in which he competed from 2006 to 2010. Pierre's first taste of single-seater racing came in the competitive French F4 Championship in 2011, when he finished third in the championship before moving up to the two-litre Formula Renaults the following year. He came third that season before taking the title in 2013. By this time, his speed and determination had caught the eye of the Red Bull talent scouts and he joined the Junior Programme, moving up to the 3.5 Renault series in 2014. He was runner-up behind another well-known Red Bull Junior, none other than Carlos Sainz. That year, he also got his first taste of GP2 before tackling the whole 2015 season in this Formula 1 feeder championship, with mixed results. However, last year, it all came good when he joined the Prema Power team, bringing home the Champion's trophy at the end of a thrilling season.

Since 2015, Gasly has combined racing with being on duty as the reserve driver for Red Bull Racing. However, with no seats available in Formula 1 at the end of 2016, he was given the chance to broaden his experience, by racing in the very competitive Japanese Super Formula Championship. Before joining us for his F1 debut, in the 2017 Malaysian GP, Pierre had already impressed in Japan, taking two wins and three podiums in his maiden season in the land of the Rising Sun. Pierre missed the United States GP to contest the final round of the Super Formula season, as he was only 0.5 points behind the championship leader. Unfortunately for Pierre, Typhoon Lan's presence around the Suzuka circuit meant that both races were cancelled, meaning he had to settle for runner-up in the championship to Hiroaki Ishiura.

Pierre returned to the Toro Rosso Formula 1 team for the Mexican GP and raced in the following three races of 2017, before being announced as one of Toro Rosso's 2018 drivers, partnering Brendon Hartley. Pierre already knew the team well enough as he tested for them at Barcelona in 2015 and 2016.

On 20 August 2018 it was announced that Pierre would switch to Red Bull in 2019 to partner Max Verstappen. He will become the tenth driver to race in Red Bull's senior team

NICO HÜLKENBERG

Nico Hülkenberg joined Renault Sport Formula One Team with an impressive racing career ahead of his eye-opening Formula 1 debut in 2010. Championship titles were secured in Formula BMW, A1GP and the GP2 Series. Nico also achieved a pole position in his rookie F1 season and won at Le Mans on his debut with Porsche in 2015.

Key Details
Date of Birth: 19 August 1987
Place of Birth: Emmerich am Rhein, Germany
Nationality: German
Website: www.nicohulkenberg.net
Car Number: 27

Milestones
1st Race: 2010, Bahrain Grand Prix (Grid 13th, Race 14th)
25th Race: 2012, Monaco Grand Prix (Grid 10th, Race 8th)
50th Race: 2013, Italian Grand Prix (Grid 3rd, Race 5th)
75th Race: 2014, Brazilian Grand Prix (Grid 12th, Race 8th)
100th Race: 2016, Monaco Grand Prix (Grid 5th, Race 6th)
125th Race: 2017, Great Britain Grand Prix (Grid 5th, Race 6th)

Q&A
How are you looking forward to the season ahead?
It seems like a very long time since I sat in a car and raced and that is very much what I want to be doing. Certainly, when I have visited Enstone and seen everything going on with the

development of the Renault R.S.18 I'm very enthused about the season ahead. Add that to the news from Viry about the development of the power unit and everything looks and sounds good; it's all positive and there are exciting times ahead.

How well primed is The Hulk?
I'm ready to rumble. I'm feeling positive and optimistic in myself. We're in a good position.

What could be possible in the season ahead?
We know what we want to achieve, but it's a competitive sport and we know there are other teams out there with the same aspirations. We won't know how good a job we've done with our car as everyone else has also been working hard on their car over the winter. This is what makes testing so interesting, and it's when we're on track that we'll see how much progress has been made in the off-season.

How will your second season with the team be different from your first?
You want every season you contest to be better than the one before. 2017 was my first with the team, and there's an element of learning different processes and personnel, but ultimately the goals are the same. For this year we want to build on the good position we built last season. 2017 was about bedding in, now I want to get ready to go. I get a good feeling, we have put a lot of work in over the winter and hard work usually pays off. I'm eager to get out there. Put me in the car.

How different is the team relative to where it was a year ago?
It's bigger and there are more buildings in Enstone. The team is growing and it's a rewarding experience to be part of this growth. The factory facilities are being improved and modernised. Everything is heading in a healthy direction and at healthy speed.

On track what differences do you expect to see?
Hopefully we'll be battling for positions a bit further up the order. The cars will look quite similar apart from smaller shark fins and

the addition of the halo. I like the look of the R.S.18 and I know everyone at Enstone and Viry has been dedicated to improving all areas of the package.

When we race, we'll have new tyres and I'm looking forward to some softer allocations for Grands Prix. This should mean more opportunities for multi-stop races, which should make things more interesting.

How do you rate the Renault Sport Formula One Team driver line-up?
It's strong. Daniel Ricciardo is an excellent addition to the team. Hopefully I can show him a few tricks!

Key Dates
2017
Nico was announced as a Renault Sport Formula One Team driver for 2017 in October 2016 and made his race debut for the team at the season-opening Australian Grand Prix in Melbourne.

2014–2016
Nico returned to Force India for a three-year spell, and after the first three races of the 2014 season he sat in third position in the Drivers' Championship, behind the Mercedes juggernaut of Hamilton and Rosberg. He finished fifth four times that year, ending the season ninth in the standings. 2015 saw Nico finish tenth in the Drivers' Championship. Outside of F1, Nico made his World Endurance Championship debut, driving for Porsche. Pairing Nick Tandy and Earl Bamber, Nico finished sixth in the Spa 6 Hours then the trio took victory at Le Mans in what was Nico's debut at the iconic race. In Nico's final season at Force India, he finished ninth in the F1 Drivers' Championship, assisting Force India to take fourth in the Constructors' Championship.

2013
For 2013 Nico joined Sauber, impressing with third on the grid at the Italian Grand Prix for the Ferrari-powered C32, taking fifth in the same race. His best finish of the season was fourth in the Korean Grand Prix and he ranked tenth in the standings that year.

2011–2012

With Williams opting for Pastor Maldonado at the squad, Nico moved to Force India in a reserve position for 2011, driving in Friday practice sessions. He was promoted to a race seat the following year, qualifying for the season-opening Australian Grand Prix six places ahead of team-mate Paul di Resta. In that year's Belgian Grand Prix he finished a career-best fourth. Nico looked set for glory in the season-ending Brazilian Grand Prix, however a safety car period robbed him of a 45-second lead in the race so he was eventually to finish in fifth. He closed the 2012 season in eleventh.

2010

2010 saw Nico's Formula 1 debut with Williams, racing alongside the highly experienced Rubens Barrichello. In his third race, the Malaysian Grand Prix, he out-qualified Rubens and he scored his first Formula 1 point in the same race. After finishing a season-best of sixth in the Hungarian Grand Prix, Nico secured pole position on a difficult damp Interlagos track, with two of his qualifying laps on slick tyres fast enough for his P1 position. His fastest qualifying lap was over a second ahead of next quickest, Sebastian Vettel. Nico ended the year fourteenth in the standings.

PRE-FORMULA 1

After a successful karting career, Nico's car racing started in German Formula BMW where he dominated the 2005 season, following in the footsteps of countryman Sebastian Vettel as champion. 2006 saw a graduation to German Formula Three and a race win, but it was the second season of the A1GP series, which started late in 2006—contested in identical Lola chassis with more than 500 horsepower from their Zytek V8 engines—when people really took notice of the rising star. Driving for A1 Team Germany, Nico claimed nine wins from the season's 22 races, including six in a row. His emphatic performance secured Germany the crown and cemented Nico's position as the most successful driver in A1GP history.

Two seasons in the F3 Euro Series from 2007 onwards followed, with third in the standings and four wins in his first outing, and the championship title and seven wins in the second.

In 2009, Nico became one of only three drivers to win the GP2 Series in their first season, following in the footsteps of Lewis Hamilton and Nico Rosberg. He secured his crown with five wins and five other podium finishes.

DANIEL RICCIARDO

Nationality: Australian
Hometown: Perth, Western Australia
Date of birth: 1 July 1989

2019 is Daniel Ricciardo's ninth season in Formula One and his first driving for Renault Sport Formula One Team.

With over 140 grands prix to his name, Daniel Ricciardo has developed a reputation for hard driving, thrilling overtaking and demon qualifying. Autosport magazine has twice voted him their driver of the year (across all branches of motorsport) and the Laureus World Sports Awards made him their Breakthrough Star in 2015 for his performances in the 2014 Formula One World Championship, his first season with Red Bull Racing during which he took three victories and finished the season third in the Drivers' Championship. He's added four more victories since and has racked-up an impressive number of podium finishes.

Daniel came through Red Bull's ranks, launched on the path to a successful motorsports career via the well-established Junior Team. Hailing from Perth, Western Australia, after learning his trade in the Australian Formula Ford and Asia-Pacific Formula BMW competitions, he took the plunge and followed in the footsteps of the southern hemisphere greats by moving to Europe to pit his skills against the best of his generation.

Daniel initially took residence in Italy, contesting the 2007 season in Formula Renault 2.0. He joined our programme in 2008 and won the Formula Renault 2.0 WEC championship. The next year he took the prestigious British Formula 3 title—traditionally a gateway to great things in Formula One. He finished 2009 with a three-day group test at Jerez in the RB5, finished top of the timesheets, completed nearly 300 faultless laps and making our engineers sit up and take notice with his speed, confidence and precise feedback. They also noticed he seemed to be enjoying it quite a bit too.

Off the back of his Formula 3 record and his speedy acclimatisation to the F1 cockpit, Daniel stepped up for 2010, becoming test and reserve driver for Scuderia Toro Rosso while also competing in the World Series by Renault. Daniel narrowly missed out on the FR3.5 title after impressive victories at Hockenheim, the Hungaroring, the Circuit de Catalunya and the showpiece round in Monaco.

He stayed with Toro Rosso for the 2011 season, advancing his education by regularly driving in free practice. He also raced a truncated campaign in FR3.5 and again won the prestigious Monaco Grand Prix support race, complete with pole position and fastest lap. These striking performances in the first half of the year led to Daniel being loaned to Spanish F1 team HRT for the final 11 rounds of the 2011 F1 season. He made his F1 race debut at Silverstone, and strong performances for the backmarker led to confirmation of a race seat with Toro Rosso in 2012.

In two years with Toro Rosso, Daniel established himself as a future star of Formula One. Lightning qualifying performances were backed up with grands prix that blended aggression and intelligence: Daniel pushed the limit—but he also brought the car home. During his two years at Red Bull Racing's sister team, Daniel punched above his weight to score points in 13 of his 39 grands prix and established a reputation as a gritty, confident racer, sure in his decisions and capable of getting the best out of his machinery. He was awarded the Lorenzo Bandini Trophy for 2013 in in recognition of his efforts. When Mark Webber announced his retirement from F1, Daniel was the natural and ready-made replacement for Red Bull Racing.

The immediate question in the minds of many was how Daniel would shape up with four-times World Champion Sebastian Vettel as a team-mate. "A lot of people have been asking the question," said Daniel at the time. "Obviously, it's my biggest challenge yet . . . but hopefully it's his biggest challenge too."

To the outside world, Daniel exceeded expectations in 2014 but the view from inside was that he did the job as anticipated. He didn't come into the team cold: Daniel had tested our cars on many occasions, frequently been our driver for Live Demo appearances and, perhaps most pertinently, served his time as our simulator driver, logging long days in Milton Keynes, providing factory support as the race team travelled the globe. To our engineers he was a known quantity: fast, smart and capable of providing the type of feedback that proved crucial in a season dominated by technical development.

Daniel hit the ground running at Red Bull Racing with his wins in Canada, Hungary and Belgium and outscored his illustrious team-mate. Since then he's been a model of consistency, delivering impeccable performance after impeccable performance. With a car that hasn't always been as competitive as we would wish, he's become a master of maximising the opportunities on offer: stealing podiums that were not really his to take, and adding to his victory tally with the 2016 Malaysian Grand Prix and last year's race in Azerbaijan.

Victory in Baku was one of Daniel's nine visits to the podium during 2017. It was a good example of Daniel doing what Daniel does best: on a day when all about were losing their heads, he kept his, avoiding the walls, staying away from trouble and delivering a string of aggressive, millimetre perfect overtaking moves to progress from the back of the field to P1. As has been the case in the past, once he had the lead, he never looked like relinquishing it.

While clinical once the visor is down, out of the car Daniel is a very laid back Aussie, keen on spending as much time as possible outdoors, always searching for the next adventure and eager to get into pretty much any sport you care to mention—but predominantly anything involving wheels.

This is slightly at odds with his alter ego, The Honey Badger, which features prominently in his helmet design. In his own words: "It's pretty cute, you wouldn't think much of it—but, in reality, it's a raging ball of anger that tears things apart. It's a bit like me: don't be fooled by the sunshine exterior, press the right buttons and I can be a very dark individual." Based upon all the available evidence, nobody believes this to be true—but Daniel Ricciardo is indeed a very focused racing driver.

ROMAIN GROSJEAN

In seven full seasons of Formula One competition, Romain Grosjean has continued to showcase the speed and consistency that was a hallmark of his highly decorated junior career. Collecting championships and numerous race wins as he ascended Europe's ultra-competitive open-wheel racing ladder, Grosjean's talents have continued to impress as the Frenchman joined Haas F1 Team in 2016.

Competing in Formula One full-time since 2012 with Lotus F1 Team, Grosjean has scored ten podiums, twice finishing a career-best second—the 2012 Canadian Grand Prix and the 2013 United States Grand Prix. With back-to-back top-ten finishes inside the championship standings in 2012 and 2013, Grosjean proved he was capable of mixing it up with the established talents in Formula One, building on the promise of his earlier career and quickly earning a strong reputation in the sport.

The 2003 season marked Grosjean's first foray into open-wheel racing after having started his career in karting in 2000. Racing in the Formula Renault 1.6 Swiss Championship, Grosjean steered his way to a clean sweep of ten wins from ten races to earn his first motorsport title. From there he graduated to the French-based Formula Renault 2.0 Championship, earning one win in 2004 before going on to launch another championship assault in 2005.

Recording ten wins to lift the title that season, Grosjean's next step was to move up to the prestigious Formula 3 Euro Series—a proving ground for numerous Formula One racers including many of his current contemporaries such as Lewis Hamilton and Sebastian Vettel.

Learning both the car and the circuits in 2006, Grosjean finished the season with one podium to his credit and a thirteenth-place classification in the points. Switching teams in 2007 and armed with a full year of experience, Grosjean's second season in the Formula 3 Euro Series paid dividends. Recording six wins, Grosjean captured the championship with a round to spare and, in doing so, caught the attention of two major teams that would help advance his career.

First he was announced in 2008 as a test driver for the Renault F1 Team—the factory squad that had recently claimed back-to-back world titles with Spain's Fernando Alonso. At the same time he confirmed he would compete in Formula One's official feeder category, the GP2 Series, now known as F2.

Racing for two-time GP2 Series champions ART Grand Prix, Grosjean's 2008 season started on a high as he contested and won the inaugural GP2 Asia Series, held before the regular GP2 Series got underway. Four victories from five double-header rounds secured Grosjean yet another championship. He would go on to score two regular-season GP2 wins en-route to a fourth overall finish in the category in 2008.

Opportunity knocked in 2009 as his role of test driver with the Renault F1 Team suddenly translated into that of full-time Formula One driver. Given the chance to contest the final seven rounds of that season's Formula One World Championship while partnering with Alonso, Grosjean's debut came at the European Grand Prix in Valencia, Spain in August 2009. His best finish was thirteenth at the Brazilian Grand Prix.

While Grosjean maintained his relations in Formula One as a test driver for tire manufacturer Pirelli in 2010, he turned his talents to a variety of racing commitments. He contested the Auto GP Series with DAMS, ably steering his way to four victories and the series title. At the same time, he joined the FIA GT1 World Championship with Matech Competition. Showing his versatility driving a GT car as opposed to an open-wheel machine, Grosjean won in his first time out for the team and collected a second victory before the season was done.

DAMS also gave Grosjean the opportunity to return to the GP2 Series, which ultimately led to a full-time race seat with the team for 2011—a platform that would propel Grosjean back into Formula One full-time.

His return to GP2 in 2011 bore immediate success. He once again claimed the GP2 Asia Series title before setting himself up for a shot at the GP2 Series crown—the one championship that had so far eluded his grasp. Grosjean didn't disappoint, leading DAMS to the top step of the podium five times to finally be crowned GP2 Series champion.

Grosjean's successes in 2011, combined with his test role with Lotus Renault GP, finally elevated him back into Formula One full-time for the 2012 season. Partnered alongside Formula One World Champion Kimi Raikkonen, Romain earned a race seat with Lotus F1 Team.

Qualifying third on the grid for the season-opening Australian Grand Prix behind former World Champions Lewis Hamilton and Jenson Button, Grosjean's pace was showcased perfectly—a trait that would be evidenced throughout the season. His first career Formula One podium finish came just three rounds later as he claimed third at the Bahrain Grand Prix. A second-place finish in Round Seven at the Canadian Grand Prix remains his career-high, while a third podium finish in Hungary followed. Grosjean placed eighth in the driver standings at the end of the year, having scored ninety-six points in his first full-time season.

Grosjean matured behind the wheel as he competed in 2013, and his consistency impressed the sport's observers as he built on the foundation he laid the previous season. Demonstrating an ability to extract the most from his machine and its tires, he raced his way to a total of six podium finishes that year, including a run of three straight in Korea, Japan and India. He equaled his grand prix career-best finish of second at that season's United States Grand Prix. Seventh overall in the final driver standings, Grosjean's points-scoring consistency led to a tally of 132 points for his best finish to-date in Formula One.

The 2014 season saw the introduction of a new engine formula, with turbochargers returning to the sport for the first time since 1988. The development curve was steep for many teams. Grosjean recorded two eighth-place finishes in Spain and Monaco, but regularly outpaced his teammate throughout the year.

There was renewed energy for Lotus F1 Team and Grosjean as they kicked off the 2015 season buoyed by a new power unit. Able to challenge at the front of the grid once again, points-paying finishes became a regular feature for Grosjean and he returned to the Formula One podium in August with a stellar drive to take third at the Belgian Grand Prix.

In a press conference at Haas F1 Team's headquarters in Kannapolis, North Carolina, it was announced that Grosjean would bring his experience and ambition to Haas F1 Team—the first American Formula One team in three decades.

Grosjean made his presence known immediately when Haas F1 Team's debut season began. He finished a solid sixth in the season-opening Australian Grand Prix and then followed it up with an even more impressive fifth-place result in the second race of 2016 at the Bahrain Grand Prix. When the season was over, Grosjean had scored all twenty-nine of Haas F1 Team's points to place it eighth in the constructor standings. It was the highest point tally for a new team in this millennium, for when Jaguar debuted in 2000 and when Toyota came on the scene in 2002, each entity managed only two point-paying finishes in their entire first seasons for a combined total of six points.

Grosjean backed up those drives in Haas F1 Team's sophomore year, collecting eight top-ten finishes with a best of sixth in the Austrian Grand Prix. He scored a total of twenty-eight points to maintain the team's eighth-place standing in the constructor ranks.

Grosjean's veteran poise and leadership will again be counted on during Haas F1 Team's fourth Formula One season in 2019.

CAREER HIGHLIGHTS
2017: FIA Formula One World Championship with Haas F1 Team; finished 13th in championship standings with 28 points; best race finish: sixth in Round 9 at Austrian Grand Prix on July 9
2016: FIA Formula One World Championship with Haas F1 Team; finished 13th in championship standings with 29 points; best race finish: fifth in Round 2 at Bahrain Grand Prix on April 3
2015: FIA Formula One World Championship with Lotus F1 Team; finished 11th in championship standings with 51 points and one podium; best race finish: third in Round 11 at Belgian Grand Prix on Aug. 23
2014: FIA Formula One World Championship with Lotus F1 Team; finished 14th in championship standings with eight points;

best race finish: eighth (twice) in Round 5 at Spanish Grand Prix on May 11 and in Round 6 at Monaco Grand Prix on May 25

2013: FIA Formula One World Championship with Lotus F1 Team; finished seventh in championship standings with 132 points and six podiums; best race finish: second in Round 18 at United States Grand Prix on Nov. 17; podiums: third in Round 4 at Bahrain Grand Prix on April 21; third in Round 9 at German Grand Prix on July 7; third in Round 14 at Korean Grand Prix on Oct. 6; third in Round 15 at Japanese Grand Prix on Oct. 13; third in Round 16 at Indian Grand Prix on Oct. 27; second in Round 18 at United States Grand Prix on Nov. 17

2012: FIA Formula One World Championship with Lotus F1 Team; finished eighth in championship standings with 96 points and three podiums; best race finish: second in Round 7 at Canadian Grand Prix on June 10; podiums: third in Round 4 at Bahrain Grand Prix on April 22; second in Round 7 at Canadian Grand Prix on June 10; third in Round 11 at Hungarian Grand Prix on July 29

2011: GP2 Series with DAMS; won championship with five victories; GP2 Asia Series with DAMS; won championship with one victory

2010: Auto GP with DAMS; won championship with four victories; FIA GT1 World Championship with Matech Competition; earned two victories in the four races in which he competed; test driver for tire manufacturer Pirelli

2009: FIA Formula One World Championship with Renault F1 Team; started final seven races of season; best finish: 13th in Round 16 at Brazilian Grand Prix on Oct. 18; GP2 Series with Barwa Addax Team; finished fourth in championship standings with two victories (completed six of 10 rounds before departing for Formula One)

2008: GP2 Series with ART Grand Prix; finished fourth in championship standings with two victories; GP2 Asia Series with ART Grand Prix; won championship with four victories; test driver for Renault F1 Team

2007: Formula 3 Euro Series with ART Grand Prix; won championship with six victories

2006: Formula 3 Euro Series with Signature Team; finished 13th

in championship standings with one podium
2005: Formula Renault 2.0 French Championship with SG Formula; won championship with 10 victories
2004: Formula Renault 2.0 French Championship with SG Formula; finished seventh in championship with one victory
2003: Formula Renault 1.6 Swiss Championship with Advance Racing; won championship with 10 victories
2000-2003: Competed in International Karting Championship series

KEVIN MAGNUSSEN

Date of birth: 5 October 1992
Car number: 20
Born: Roskilde, Denmark
Lives in: Dubai
Height: 1.74 m
Weight: 68 kg
Marital Status: Single

Born into a racing family in 1992, Kevin Magnussen was welcomed into another racing family in 2017 as the native of Roskilde, Denmark, and the son of former Formula One driver and current sportscar racer Jan Magnussen became a member of Haas F1 Team.

Magnussen joined the American outfit for his third full season competing in the FIA Formula One World Championship. He promptly delivered, scoring five top-ten finishes with a best of seventh in the Azerbaijan Grand Prix. Having previously driven for established marques McLaren and Renault Sport, Magnussen is now a Haas F1 Team regular alongside teammate Romain Grosjean.

Magnussen made his Formula One debut with McLaren in 2014, earning an impressive second-place finish in the season-opening Australian Grand Prix. He became the first Formula One rookie to deliver a podium finish in his debut race since Lewis Hamilton achieved the feat, also with McLaren, at

the 2007 Australian Grand Prix. Eleven more point-paying
finishes followed, allowing Magnussen to finish a respectable
eleventh in the championship standings.

Despite the strong first-year showing and being a member of
the McLaren Young Driver Program since 2010, Magnussen had
to settle for a reserve driver role at McLaren in 2015 when the
team signed two-time Formula One champion Fernando Alonso
to pair with 2009 champion Jenson Button. Nonetheless,
Magnussen made the most of the opportunity, helping to develop
the team's MP4-30 racecar and keeping his name front-and-cen-
tre for a full-time drive in 2016.

That drive materialized with Renault Sport, but the 2016
season proved to be a challenging one with the team finishing
ninth in the constructor standings, twenty-one points behind
Haas F1 Team. Magnussen, however, scored seven of the team's
eight total points, highlighted by a seventh-place finish at the
Russian Grand Prix.

The scrappy performance showcased Magnussen's tenacity
behind the wheel, something the Dane has displayed throughout
his career.

Like many Formula One drivers, Magnussen's motorsports
journey began in karting before transitioning to larger and more
powerful open-wheel machines. Plaudits were quickly earned,
with Magnussen moving outside of Denmark to race across
Europe in the traditional proving grounds of Formula One.

Magnussen's first season in open-wheel was stout. He scored
eleven wins for Fukamuni Racing en route to the 2008 Danish
Formula Ford championship. That success led to a dual campaign
in 2009 where Magnussen competed in the Formula Renault 2.0
NEC Series and the Formula Renault 2.0 Eurocup Series, both
with Motopark Academy. Magnussen's accomplishments
included earning rookie-of-the-year status in the NEC Series
while scoring a win and twelve podiums before finishing second
in the championship.

Remaining with Motopark Academy, Magnussen graduated to
the German Formula 3 Series in 2010 where he again captured
rookie-of-the-year honorus while scoring three victories, eight
podiums and a third-place finish in the championship. His

progress and success led to an invitation to join the respected McLaren Young Driver Program.

A second season in Formula 3 followed, this time in the prestigious British series with stalwart outfit, Carlin. Magnussen delivered once again as he amassed seven wins from eight podiums and finished second in the 2011 championship. Carlin subsequently retained Magnussen for its 2012 Formula Renault 3.5 Series campaign. In his first European-based championship season, Magnussen delivered a win and three podiums to earn his first Formula One test drive with McLaren.

The 2013 Formula Renault 3.5 Series saw Magnussen switch to the leading DAMS team. His previous season's experience was translated into a dominant title-winning campaign. Magnussen won the championship with five wins and thirteen podium finishes. His banner year included a second opportunity to test with McLaren, which ultimately led to the team offering him his first Formula One seat in 2014.

CARLOS SAINZ JR

Date of birth: 1 September 1994
Born: Madrid, Spain
Height: 1.78 m
Weight: 66 kg
Marital status: Single

At seven years old Carlos junior began to drive in Karts at his father's Indoor Karting in Las Rozas, Madrid, but he started to compete seriously in the summer of 2005 when he was ten.

In 2006 racing for the teams Alemany, MGM and Benikart, he won the Cadete Category of the Madrid Championship, finishing third in the Industry Trophy (Parma-Italy) and second in the Champions Race at the end of the year.

During the three following years, he contested the Junior Category. In his first year with the Genikart Team, he won the City of Alcañiz Automobile International Trophy and finished third at Macau in the Asian-Pacific Championship.

In 2008 in the same category, he won the Asian-Pacific

Championship at Macau and finished second in the Spanish Championship, being the best Spaniard classified in the Europe Championship, the German Championship, the Trophy Andrea Margutti (Italy) and the Monaco Kart Cup.

In 2009 he was part of the Tony Kart Junior Team and contested some races at Genikart Team, winning the famous Monaco Kart Cup as well as the Classification for the West European area (England, France, Switzerland, Portugal, Andorra and Spain). He also finished second in the European Championship's Final and second in the Spanish Championship, adding a final third at WSK International Series.

In 2010, and after several tests, Red Bull chose him to be a member of their Junior Team and after four days of testing he won the BMW Scholarship following the qualifying competition. At just fifteen years old he contested the Formula BMW European Championship and took part in three races of the Formula BMW Asian-Pacific Championship with the Antonio Ferrari's Eurointernational team clinching the Formula BMW European Championship. During the same season, he achieved victory in the Formula BMW Asian-Pacific Championship held in Macau. John Smith continued to support him in his career as they had done in the previous season.

In the 2011 season his evolution as a driver continued as the young Spaniard contested two of the most prestigious championships at European level: the Northern European Cup (NEC) and the Eurocup Formula Renault 2.0

In 2012, the Red Bull Junior Team driver competed with Carlin Motorsport in the British Formula 3 Championship and the European FIA F3 earning in his debut year a brilliant victory at the legendary Spa-Francorchamps circuit under a heavy downpour. The wins did not stop there, as Carlos achieved four victories in the British Formula 3 Series to finish in sixth place, while in the continental competition he finished fifth. Carlos ended his season at the prestigious Macau Grand Prix Formula 3, where despite qualifying in fourth a bad start left him with few options to fight for the win as he ended the race in seventh. At the end of 2012 the oil company Cepsa came on board as a sponsor for all competitions.

In 2013, Carlos combined GP3 Series racing with several meetings of the World Series. In an amazing debut at the Monaco Grand Prix the Spanish driver fought for the top positions in his first outing at the wheel of the powerful Formula Renault 3.5. However his GP3 season was marked by misfortune and bad luck, but the young Spaniard repeatedly demonstrated his talents achieving two podiums. The key moment arrived in midsummer when Carlos Sainz sat behind the wheel of a Formula 1 car for the first time during the young driver test held at the Silverstone Circuit. The Spanish driver enjoyed a day with the Scuderia Toro Rosso car and also at the wheel of the Red Bull RB9, the premier car in the Championship.

In 2014, Carlos made history becoming the first Spanish driver and member of the Red Bull Junior Team to win the World Series by Renault. The Spaniard won the title for French team, DAMS Racing, to become the youngest driver to win the title, and in record-breaking fashion, winning seven races.

After driving in the Abu Dhabi test for Infiniti Red Bull Racing it was announced in November of 2014 that Carlos would join the Scuderia Toro Rosso completing the driver line-up with Max Verstappen.

Carlos made his Formula 1 debut in the 2015 Australian Grand Prix where he took two points courtesy of a ninth-place finish. He would go on to pick up 18 points during his rookie season with a season highlight of seventh in the USA Grand Prix.

2016 was a bright year for the up-and-coming Spaniard, showing consistent results throughout the calendar. Five points-scoring finishes from the opening seven races put him in a good position to show-off his talent. He finished the season on 46 points with impressive drives to sixth in Spain, USA and Brazil.

Carlos was announced as a Renault Sport Formula One Team driver for 2018 in September 2017 prior to the Singapore Grand Prix, where he took a career-best result of fourth. Before that, Carlos enjoyed eight points-scoring finishes with a notable drive to sixth in Monaco. On his Renault debut, Carlos impressed and claimed what proved to be a highly valuable seventh place in Austin, ultimately putting the team in a positive position to secure sixth place in the Constructors' standings.

On 16 August 2018 it was announced that Carlos had signed a multi-year deal to replace Fernando Alonso at McLaren for the 2019 season.

2017 Laps Raced: 881 (216 with Renault Sport Formula One Team)
2017 KM Raced: 4,425 (1,036 with Renault Sport Formula One Team)
Best Finish: 4th, Singapore
Best Qualifying: 6th, Monaco

Milestones
1st Race: 2015, Australian Grand Prix (Grid 7th, Race 9th)
25th Race: 2016, Monaco Grand Prix (Grid 6th, Race 8th)
50th Race: 2017 Great Britain Grand Prix (Grid 13th, Race DNF)

LANDO NORRIS

Date of birth: 13 November 1999
Born: Bristol, United Kingdom
Height: 1.70 m
Weight: 64 kg
Marital status: Single

A stellar rise through the karting ranks followed by an outstanding first couple of seasons racing in junior single-seater championships have placed Lando Norris firmly on the motorsport map.

A gifted karter, he remains the youngest driver to ever set a pole position at a national meeting, won the Super One Series 'O' Plate in 2010, then in 2012 he became Formula Kart Stars champion and runner-up in the MSA Super One British Championship.

A year later, he won titles in the CIK-FIA KFJ European, CIK-FIA KFJ Super Cup, WSK Euro Series KFJ, CIK-FIA International Super Cup and World Karting Championship. In addition, he became WSK Masters Series vice-champion and made history by becoming the youngest karting world championship winner, taking the CIK-FIA KF World Championship title at the age of 14, an accolade previously held by triple world champion Lewis Hamilton.

His graduation to single-seaters has only underlined that initial promise. In 2016, he won a slew of single-seater championships— Formula Renault 2.0 Northern European Cup, Formula Renault 2.0 Eurocup and the the Toyota Racing Series Championship in New Zealand.

He then crowned his season with perhaps the most prestigious award presented to any promising young racing driver—the coveted McLaren Autosport BRDC Young Driver Award, which was presented to him at the Autosport Awards, in December 2016.

For 2017, Lando contested the European Formula 3 championship, eventually winning the title in October—all while dovetailing his racing activities with a fully fledged role as a test and simulator driver for the McLaren Honda Formula 1 team.

Following his success in F3, Lando became the official test and reserve driver for McLaren in 2018, as well as making his debut in F2 with Carlin Racing.

In September 2018, it was announced that Lando will partner Carlos Sainz as part of McLaren's driver line-up for the 2019 Formula 1 season.

Lando Norris said:

'To be announced as a race driver for McLaren is a dream come true. Although I've been part of the team for a while now, this is a special moment, one I could only hope would become reality.

'I'd like to thank the whole team for this amazing opportunity and for believing in me. I'm also extremely grateful for the commitment McLaren has already shown in my development, allowing me to build my experience in a Formula 1 car in both testing and on Fridays during the past two race weekends.'

CAREER HIGHLIGHTS

2018: McLaren Test and Reserve Driver; F2 Championship
2017: European Formula 3 Champion; McLaren Test and Simulator Driver. Winning the F3 championship means Lando

has won every single-seater championship he has contested in full, at his first attempt

2016: Formula Renault 2.0 Northern European Cup Championship; Formula Renault 2.0 Eurocup Championship; Toyota Racing Series Championship; McLaren Autosport BRDC Young Driver Award winner

2015: MSA Formula Championship

2014: CIK-FIA KF World Championship—made history by becoming the youngest karting world championship winner (aged 14)—a record previously held by Lewis Hamilton.

2013: CIK-FIA KFJ European Championship; CIK-FIA KFJ Super Cup Championship; WSK Euro Series KFJ Championship; WSK Masters Series vice-champion

2012: Formula Kart Stars Champion; Runner-up in MSA Super One British Championship

2010: won Super One Series 'O' Plate

SERGIO PEREZ

Date of birth: 26 January 1990
Nationality: Mexican
Lives in: Switzerland
Height: 1.75 m
Weight: 68 kg
Marital status: Married

Now entering his sixth year with Racing Point Force India, Sergio Perez is widely regarded as one of the fastest and most consistent drivers on the grid. The twenty-eight-year-old, fresh from finishing seventh in the world championship for the second season in a row, will be looking to 2018 to build on his recent success and help the team in its fight for the top three in the championship.

Born in 1990 in Mexico, Sergio comes from a motorsport family: having raced cars himself, his father Antonio was active in driver management. In this environment, it was natural for young Sergio to start his career in karting at the age of six, winning junior categories and quickly progressing to shifter karts.

A move to single-seaters at the age of fourteen and the start of a long-standing partnership with Escuderia Telmex saw him take part in the Skip Barber National Championship in the United States; the following year, in 2005, Sergio moved to Europe to compete in Formula BMW.

After two years in this category, including a two-race stint in A1GP for Team Mexico, Sergio graduated to British Formula Three, dominating the National Class in 2007 and claiming four wins on his way to fourth in the International Class in 2008. A first appearance in the GP2 Asia Series saw him complete a lights-to-flag win in Bahrain and earn a call-up to GP2.

In his second year in the Formula One feeder series, Sergio won races in prestigious venues such as Monaco, Silverstone, Hockenheim, Spa-Francorchamps and Abu Dhabi to mount a title challenge and finish runner-up to Pastor Maldonado. His performance earned him promotion to Formula One with Sauber.

In his first season in the pinnacle of motorsport, in 2011, five finishes in the points helped cement his position in Formula One. Confirmed at Sauber for 2012, he claimed three podiums, including two second places, on his way to tenth in the Drivers' Championship (sixty-six points). Sergio demonstrated an incredible ability to extract the best out of the car in changing weather conditions, pushing eventual winner Fernando Alonso closely in Malaysia and performing incredible comebacks in Canada and Italy.

A move to McLaren for 2013, replacing Lewis Hamilton alongside former World Champion Jenson Button, gave Sergio vital experience of the workings of a top team: eleven points finishes, including four consecutive ones in the final four races of the season, set him up as a consistent driver, earning him a place in the Sahara Force India Formula One team line-up for 2014.

Checo's life at Sahara Force India started in the best possible way, with a podium in only his third race with the team [Bahrain]. Some memorable performances in Canada, Austria and Singapore among others, saw the Mexican claim twelve points finishes on his way to tenth in the championship.

In 2015, an impressive string of points finishes in the second part of the season, crowned with a podium performance at the Russian Grand Prix, saw Checo clinch a career-best ninth place in the standings (seventy-eight points) while propelling the team to fifth in the constructors' championship. It was a memorable year for Checo, who also experienced the emotion of taking part in his first home Grand Prix in Mexico.

2016 turned out to be an even more spectacular season for Sergio. An incredible podium under the rain in Monaco heralded the start of a strong run of form destined to last the whole season; a further visit to the rostrum in Azerbaijan and a string of ten consecutive points finishes saw the Mexican break through the 100-points barrier for the first time in his career (and in the history of the team) and clinch seventh place in the drivers' standings, a lifetime best.

Paired with a new team-mate to form one of the most exciting line-ups in Formula One, Checo was at the top of his game in 2017, breaking the 100-point barrier once more and equalling his best championship position of seventh. Classy drives like those in Barcelona and Singapore helped cement his reputation and propelled the team to a record-breaking season while his relationship with Esteban Ocon kept the team in the media spotlight. Sergio's stellar season saw him confirmed for 2018, the Mexican driver and the team confirming the reciprocal faith and determination to climb to the next level.

LANCE STROLL

Date of birth: 29th October 1998
Car number: 18
Born: Montreal, Canada
Height: 1.82m
Weight: 76kg
Marital status: Single

Lance began his karting career in fine style in 2008 at the age of ten. He was nominated as rookie of the year by the Federation de Sport Automobile du Quebec in 2008 and driver of the year the following year. In 2010 Lance won four titles in the Florida Winter Tour before moving to the CIK-FIA World Championship in 2012 where he finished fifth overall. He competed in the series again in 2013 where he was again awarded as the best rookie.

Lance made the move away from karting in 2014, winning the Italian Formula 4 Championship with seven wins, thirteen podiums and five pole positions. In 2015 he competed in the Toyota Racing Series in New Zealand, where he picked up four wins and ten podiums from sixteen starts, sealing the title in the process. Following this, he made his debut in the Formula 3 European series, taking one win and six podiums to finish fifth overall with Italian outfit, Prema Powerteam. Lance was also part of the Ferrari Driver Academy before joining the Williams Young Driver Development Programme in November 2015.

Alongside the programme in 2016, Lance had been competing in the Formula 3 European Series with Prema Powerteam. He secured the title in dominant fashion with fourteen wins and fourteen pole positions to his name.

In his debut Formula One season, Lance broke two records by becoming the youngest rookie podium finisher with a third-place finish at the Azerbaijan Grand Prix, as well as becoming the youngest front-row starter, after starting second in the Italian Grand Prix. Lance recorded seven points-scoring finishes during his rookie season, which saw him finish 12th in the Drivers' Championship.

It was confirmed on 30 November 2018 that Stroll, whose father Lawrence led the Force India takeover, will join Racing Point Force India for the 2019 season replacing Esteban Ocon.

CAREER HIGHLIGHTS

2019: Race Driver for Racing-Point Force India
2018: Race Driver for Williams
2017: Race Driver for Williams
2016: Formula 3 European Series with Prema Powerteam, series Champion
2015: Young Driver Development Programme, Williams
2015: Ferrari Driver Academy

2015: Formula 3 European Series with Prema Powerteam, 5th overall
2015: Toyota Racing Series New Zealand, series champion
2014: Formula 4 Italy, series champion.

ALEXANDER ALBON

In the very last piece of the driver jigsaw puzzle, Scuderia Toro Rosso announced on the day after the 2018 Abu Dhabi Grand Prix that Alexander Albon will drive for the team in the 2019 Formula 1 season alongside Daniil Kvyat.

The twenty-two-year-old British/Thai driver has had a very impressive season in Formula 2 this year and, up until last weekend in Abu Dhabi, he was one of only two drivers who could have won the title. A start line collision in the feature race ended his hopes, but he still finished third overall in the F1 feeder series with a total of four wins.

Like all his contemporaries, Albon started racing in karts, winning various championships. He joined the Red Bull programme in 2012 and in 2016 he finished second in GP3 to his team-mate Charles Leclerc. 2018 was his second season in F2. Although born in London, Albon races under the Thailand flag. It means that 2019 will be the first time there has been a Thai driver on the Formula 1 grid since Prince Birabongse, who raced in the early fifties.

Franz Tost, Red Bull Toro Rosso Honda Team Principal:
'Alexander had an impressive Formula 2 season in 2018. He won four races and finished the Championship third. The way he is able to overtake many of his rivals in the races shows that he is ready and matured to race in Formula 1. Scuderia Toro Rosso is very much looking forward to 2019, as with Daniil and Alex we have two young, very strong and competitive drivers.'

Alex Albon:
'It's such an amazing feeling to know that I'm in Formula 1. Throughout my single-seater career, I went through a few ups and downs. I was dropped by Red Bull in 2012, so from then I

knew my road to Formula 1 was going to be a lot harder. I worked really hard and tried to impress every time I got in the car, and I have to say a big thank you to Red Bull and Dr Marko for believing in me and giving me a second chance. I've always been motorsport mad, and since I first got in a car it has been my dream to be in Formula 1. To be given this opportunity is just incredible.'

DANIIL KVYAT

Birth Date: 26 April 1994
Place of Birth: Ufa, Russia
Residence: Monaco
Height: 183 cm
Weight: 68 kg

At the age of eight, Daniil moved to Moscow with his parents, where he made his first appearance behind the wheel go karting.

Kvyat started go kart racing on a regular basis, and immediately began to put in strong performances. In the autumn, he had his first professional testing session for racing karts with the Stolitsa Kart team. In January 2005, Kvyat made his professional debut in motorsports winning his very first race in Sochi.

'The first thing that stood out was his fantastic feel for the car. He didn't have experience, but he had the will to win, the passion, the desire for victory and a fantastic work rate.'—Oleg Guskov, first coach.

Head of the Red Bull Junior programme and motorsport consultant Helmuth Marko started following Kvyat and eventually during the summer of 2009 Daniil participated in his first testing session in an open-wheel car arranged by Red Bull.

Daniil continued to race successfully in karting but his debut season in open-wheel racing was not easy. However after a number of competitive seasons in the feeder series he graduated to the next level.

In the 2013 season Kvyat found himself as a driver in the MW Arden team in the GP3 series, which was founded by the Red Bull Racing Formula 1 Team Principal Christian Horner. Carlos

Sainz Jr joined Kvyat as a teammate after a mediocre season in Formula 3.

The season start was a real challenge. Struggling to find appropriate settings for the cars, both Kvyat and Sainz failed in the season opener. They managed to catch up with the leaders after a few rounds once the Arden engineers mastered management of the Pirelli tyres. Daniil scored his first podium in the series at Hungaroring in July, then won the race in Spa in August to decrease the points deficit between him and the leaders in the drivers' standings.

Kvyat was very close to scoring maximum possible points at Monza: he took pole position, won the first race and was just one step away from another victory in the second race. Starting from P8 he overtook six opponents to become a runner-up in the race with a minimal gap to the winner.

Alongside his GP3 campaign, Daniil was also racing in the European Formula 3 Championship. He won his first race in Zandvoort after which he was offered a contract as a Formula 1 driver by Helmuth Marko head of the Red Bull Junior Team.

Kvyat was to substitute Daniel Ricciardo in the Toro Rosso cockpit, following his transfer to Red Bull Racing Formula 1 Team.

As a part of the preparation for his Formula 1 debut Daniil participated in several race weekends with the team in the USA and Brazil.

Daniil Kvyat finished his GP3 season with a win in Abu Dhabi, which secured him the title in the series. In his first season in Formula 1, Kvyat raced with Jean-Eric Vergne, a Frenchman, who had raced for Toro Rosso for two seasons already.

Having proved himself as a strong driver in one team with Vergne, Kvyat won promotion to the Red Bull Racing team. He was chosen to replace the four-time world champion Sebastian Vettel in Red Bull's flagship team.

The start of the 2015 campaign with Red Bull Racing was difficult due to issues with the Renault engine. After resolving reliability issues Daniil and his team began to harvest the points regularly.

Finishing second in the Hungarian Grand Prix, Kvyat scored

his maiden podium in Formula 1 thus setting the best result of Russian drivers in the history of the championship.

Red Bull Racing finished that season in fourth place in Constructors' Championship, while Daniil surpassed his far more experienced teammate Daniel Ricciardo in the Drivers' Championship, making the most overtakes during the season.

The 2016 season start was a challenge again but Daniil finished in P3 in the third round bringing home the first podium for Red Bull Racing in the new season.

However, after an incident during the start of his home Grand Prix when Kvyat contacted his teammate and Sebastian Vettel's car, team management decided to demote Daniil back to Toro Rosso.

Daniil spent some time adapting to the team and the new car, and returned to good shape, posting several strong performances in qualifying and races by the end of the season and securing his place in Toro Rosso for 2017.

On 26 September 2017, Toro Rosso announced the decision to replace Kvyat for the forthcoming Malaysian Grand Prix with Frenchman Pierre Gasly following a sustained run of underwhelming form from the Russian. Whilst confirming the decision to stand Kvyat down, in a statement, Toro Rosso added that the driver switch should not be considered a permanent parting of the ways, saying 'This is not a case of goodbye for our Daniil as he still remains part of the Red Bull Family.'

And so it was after spending the 2018 season as Scuderia Ferrari's development driver Kvyat was confirmed as one of Toro Rosso's drivers for the 2019 season replacing the Red Bull-bound Pierre Gasly.

ANTONIO GIOVINAZZI

Antonio Giovinazzi was born on 14th December 1993 in Martina Franca, in the Italian province of Taranto. He began karting in 2006 and won that year's Italian National Trophy as well as the European championship in the 60cc category.

He made the move to single-seaters aged 19, racing in the

Formula Pilota in China in 2012. The following year, he competed in the European Formula 3 championship driving for the Double R Racing team and also took part in the Formula 3 Masters. In 2014 he raced for the British Carlin team and the next year he competed in the Russian round of the DTM at the wheel of an Audi RS5 entered by Phoenix Racing.

He made his GP2 debut in 2016 with the Prema Powerteam, taking his first victory in the category at the Grand Prix of Europe and finished second overall in the championship with a total of five wins to his name. For 2017, he takes on the role of Scuderia Ferrari's third driver.

Antonio Giovinazzi was born on 14th December 1993 in Martina Franca, in the Italian province of Taranto. He began karting in 2006 and won that year's Italian National Trophy as well as the European championship in the 60cc category.

He made the move to single-seaters aged 19, racing in the Formula Pilota in China in 2012. The following year, he competed in the European Formula 3 championship driving for the Double R Racing team and also took part in the Formula 3 Masters. In 2014 he raced for the British Carlin team and the next year he competed in the Russian round of the DTM at the wheel of an Audi RS5 entered by Phoenix Racing.

He made his GP2 debut in 2016 with the Prema Powerteam, taking his first victory in the category at the Grand Prix of Europe and finished second overall in the championship with a total of five wins to his name. For 2017 he took on the role of Scuderia Ferrari's third driver and replaced the injured Pascal Wehrlein for the Australian and Chinese Grands Prix in the Sauber F1 car.

In 2019 he will race full time for the Alfa Romeo Sauber F1 Team alongside Kimi Räikkönen.

RACING HIGHLIGHTS
2016: GP2 Series, 2nd; Asian Le Mans Series LMP2
2015: Zandvoort Masters of Formula 3, 1st; FIA Formula 3 European Championship, 2nd; 3 Hours of Thailand, 1st
2013: Cooper Tires British Formula 3 International Series, 2nd
2012: Formula Pilota China, 1st

KARTING HIGHLIGHTS
2011: CIK-FIA World Cup for KF2, 3rd; Bridgestone Cup
Europe – KF2, 2nd;WSK Master Series – KF2, 1st
2010:WSK Master Series – KF2, 1st
2009: 20° Trofeo Andrea Margutti – KF2, 3rd; European
Championship Qualification Central Region – KF2, 3rd
2008: 38° Torneo Industrie – KF3, 2nd; Copa Campeones
Trophy KF3, 2nd
2006: Italian National Trophy 60 cc., 1st; Euro Trophy by 60
Mini, 1st; 36°Torneo Industrie – Minikart, 1st

KIMI RÄIKKÖNEN

Age: 37
Weight: 62 kg
Height: 175 cm

Kimi Räikkönen was born to race.

From his very first seat time in a pedal kart at the tender age of
three, he showed a passion and talent for speed. Whether it's a
Formula One car, roadcar, motorbike, kart, pushbike, snowmo-
bile or pair of skis—Kimi has only one speed: flat out.

RISE TO CHAMPION
Kimi's sky-rocket rise to Formula One World Champion was
truly sensational. His graduation to Formula One direct from
Formula Renault redefined fast track career progression; to this
day no driver in history has made such a dramatic entry. From his
very first Grand Prix with Sauber, Kimi made an impression on
both drivers and fans, and not long into his rookie season
McLaren made a successful bid to sign Kimi on a five-year
contract. For Kimi, this was not enough and with fame in his
sights he joined Ferrari, the most illustrious name in Formula
One.

The 2007 season was one of the most exciting battles in
history, and Kimi's fight to win the drivers' title was an international hit. 2008 was marred by bad luck which hampered his title
defence, despite finishing third in the championship and winning

the DHL fastest Lap Award. 2009 was marked by a historic victory at Spa in a year when the established teams struggled due to new regulations.

NEW CHALLENGES

2010 marked a new challenge for the Flying Finn; a move to the World Rally Championship where he competed for a second season in 2011 doing what he does best; breaking the speedometer and making sure his co-driver had a change of underwear.

Kimi returned to Formula One for the 2012 season, signing a two-year contract with the popular Lotus team. His return proved without doubt that he hadn't forgotten how to drive an F1 car. He was the only driver to finish every race and scored points in all but one; his season including seven podiums, a historic win in Abu Dhabi and third in the drivers' championship. It marked a highly successful and much longed-for return to the F1 cockpit, reigniting the passion of the Iceman's fans across the globe.

RETURN TO THE PRANCING HORSE

2014 saw Kimi returning to Ferrari. The Flying Finn had a tough season as consistent handling problems dogged him throughout; but things improved for 2015—not least because his son Robin Ace Räikkönen was born. Other highlights included podium finishes at Bahrain, Singapore and Abu Dhabi. 2016 saw Kimi marry his wife Minttu and in turn he was much more at home in the Ferrari with more podium finishes.

2017 saw Kimi battle to fourth place in the championship and there are high hopes for the striking new Ferrari SF71H to put the Scuderia back in title contention for 2018 and beyond.

In 2019 he will return to Alfa Romeo Sauber F1 Team on a two-year contract.

ROBERT KUBICA

Nationality: Polish
Born: 7 December 1984
Height: 1.83 m
Weight: 69 kg

CAREER HIGHLIGHTS

2019: Race Driver for Williams F1 Team
2018: Reserve & Development Driver for Williams
2017: Test with Renault F1 Team and Williams
2014-2016: World Rally Championship
2013: World Rally 2 Championship Champion – four wins
2012: Returned to rallying
2011: Injured in rallying accident
2010: Race Driver for Renault F1 Team, eighth overall – three podiums
2006–2009: Race Driver for BMW Sauber F1 Team
2005: World Series by Renault Champion – four wins, three pole-positions, eleven podiums
2004: Formula 3 Euro Series, seventh overall, three podiums. Second in Macau Grand Prix
2003: Formula 3 Euro Series, twelfth overall – one win, two podiums
2002: Formula Renault Italy 2000, second overall – four wins, three pole-positions, six podiums
2001: Debut in single-seaters
1995–2000: Karting, multiple title winner

Robert developed a love for motorsport at an early age and started karting as soon as he got his race license aged ten. In just three years, Robert had amassed six karting titles. He moved onwards and upwards to more competitive series, which resulted in even more success. Robert became the first foreigner to win the International Italian Junior Karting Championship, came second in the European Junior Karting Championship and also won the Junior Monaco Kart Cup, amongst other successes.

In 2000, Robert's progression continued with a test driver role in Formula Renault 2000, as well as a maiden pole position in single-seaters. Renault immediately placed Robert in their driver development programme and entered him in several Renault series, which would lead to more podium finishes.

2003 saw Robert graduate to the Formula 3 Euro Series with Renault, before moving to the Mercedes team, with whom he broke the lap record in Macau.

A year later, Robert moved up to the World Series by Renault, winning the championship in his rookie year. With four wins and eleven podiums, his talent was recognised with a prized Formula One test with the Renault F1 Team later that year.

In 2006 Robert began his Formula One career with BMW Sauber, becoming the first Polish driver to start an F1 race. Robert recorded a podium finish within just three race starts, making him the second driver to ever do so. In the following years he continued to achieve race wins, podium finishes and a pole position, before moving to Renault in 2010.

Considered one of the sport's most promising young talents and tipped to be a future world champion, Robert topped the pre-season test times in February 2010 before his career was put on hold. Robert suffered severe injuries in a rally accident which ruled him out of racing for several years, before a rehabilitation program put him back on the path to Formula One.

In 2017, Robert undertook several Formula One tests with Renault and Williams, and was announced as the team's Reserve & Development Driver for the 2018 season.

At the Abu Dhabi Grand Prix of 2018 Kubica's return to Formula One was made complete when it was announced that he would drive for Williams alongside George Russell for the 2019 season.

GEORGE RUSSELL

George Russell is a Mercedes-AMG Petronas Motorsport supported British Racing Driver and the reigning 2017 GP3 Series Champion with ART Grand Prix.

George is a twenty-year-old British rising star from Kings

Lynn, who is aiming to make the final steps up the motorsport ladder and reach the goal of Formula One.

His career began with humble beginnings in karting from 2006. His talent was clear to see from an early age, as he swooped to the MSA British Cadet Champion and British Open Champion in 2009, announcing himself to the world of British Motorsport.

In 2010 he moved to the Rotax Mini Max category where he became Super One British champion, Formula Kart Stars British Champion and also won the Kartmasters British Grand Prix in a dominant season.

Russell graduated to the Premier Junior Karting class (KF3) the following season, where he won the SKUSA Supernationals title and became the CIK-FIA European Junior Champion in 2012 and 2013, to complete his lucrative karting CV.

George embarked on his first season of single-seater racing in 2014, claiming the BRDC Formula 4 Championship title at the first attempt.

George also picked up numerous podiums in the Formula Renault 2.0 ALPS Championship that he completed a part season in, as well as victory at the Jerez in the Formula Renault Eurocup finale in a one-off appearance.

In the same year, he won the prestigious McLaren BRDC Autosport Award for his achievements. After just one year in Formula 4, he switched to the FIA Formula 3 European Championship for the next two seasons.

As a member of the HitechGP squad, driving a car powered by the Mercedes-AMG Formula 3 engine, George finished the 2016 season in third position, having scored two victories and made ten podium appearances along the way.

George made an immediate impact on his debut at the prestigious Macau Grand Prix, taking pole position on his first visit to the iconic Guia Circuit. Hs performances attracted the attention of the reigning Formula One World Champions.

In January 2017, he was announced as the latest additional to the Mercedes-AMG Petronas Motorsport line-up, following in the footsteps of Pascal Wehrlein and Esteban Ocon.

George competed in the GP3 Series—a support series to

Formula One. racing for frontrunners ART Grand Prix in 2017. The Mercedes-Benz Junior met his expectations in GP3—as he went on to take four victories, seven podiums and four pole positions on his way to winning the Driver's championship with two races left to spare.

These performances saw him be rewarded with a pair of Formula 1 Free Practice outings with the Sahara Force India Team, which he duly impressed on both occasions.

In 2018, George made the step up to the FIA Formula 2 Championship with ART Grand Prix, while also juggling his duties as Mercedes-AMG Petronas Motorsport Reserve Driver.

In F2, Russell has amassed more victories than any other driver, as well as the most pole positions, laps led and total amount of podiums—despite multiple unreliability issues.

It was announced on 12 October 2018, that George would compete in the 2019 FIA Formula One World Championship with Williams Racing, on a multi-year deal.

CIRCUITS

AUSTRALIA

THE AUSTRALIAN GRAND PRIX
15–17 March 2019

The 2019 FIA Formula 1 World Championship kicks off at the season's traditional curtain-raiser, the Australian Grand Prix at the Melbourne Grand Prix Circuit in Albert Park.

The temporary track around the Albert Park lake provides a tough test for drivers, engineers and their new machinery. A street circuit, the Albert Park surface lacks grip early in the weekend and for drivers the early practice sessions on a narrow layout featuring close barriers are about building performance slowly as the tracks 'rubbers in'—no easy task as they prepare to run their new cars for the first time. For teams, the high track evolution at this unrepresentative venue makes set-up something of a moving target, again a tricky prospect as they attempt to optimise performance of cars with just two weeks of pre-season testing data to draw upon.

CIRCUIT DATA—ALBERT PARK CIRCUIT
Length of lap: 5.303 km
Lap record: 1:24.125 (Michael Schumacher, Ferrari, 2004)
Start line/finish line offset: 0.000 km
Total number of race laps: 58
Total race distance: 307.574 km
Pitlane speed limits: 60 km/h in practice, qualifying, and the race

Australian GP
ROUND 01

RACE DATE ....17 March 2019
CIRCUIT NAME ....Albert Park Circuit
NO. OF LAPS 58
START TIME ....16.10 local/05.10 GMT
CIRCUIT LENGTH 5.303km
RACE DISTANCE 307.574k
LAP RECORD 1.24.125
Michael Schumacher
(2004)

Braking

Speed kmh

Lateral G-force

150
3
-1.0

Gear

Timing sector
Sector time
Lap time

T3
35.3
1:26.7

Circuit
Start
Finish
Light panels
Run-off areas
Gravel traps

Sector 1
Sector 2
Sector 3

Safety car — S
Medical car — +
Marshals — M

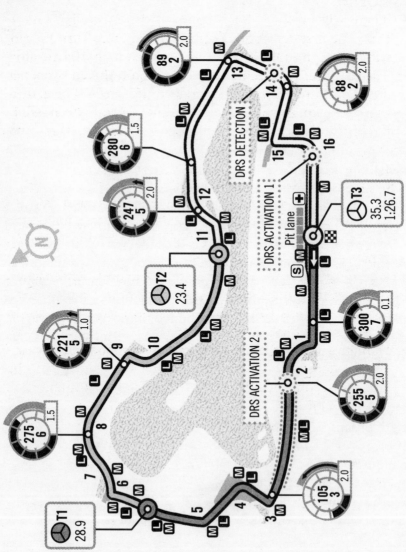

N

89
2
2.0

88
2
2.0

DRS DETECTION

13
14

280
6
1.5

247
5
2.0

12
11

15
16

T2
23.4

DRS ACTIVATION 1

Pit lane

T3
35.3
1:26.7

221
5
1.0

275
6
1.5

9
10

8
7
6

300
7
0.1

1
2

DRS ACTIVATION 2

255
5
2.0

5
4
3

T1
28.9

105
3
2.0

CIRCUIT NOTES
- The kerb on the exit of Turn Five has been lengthened by five metres
- The kerb on the exit of Turn Twelve has again been ground down to remove a bump that proved troublesome in 2017
- The kerbs on the exits of Turns Thirteen and Fourteen have been renewed, using 50 mm negative kerbs.

DRS ZONE
- There will be three DRS zones at the Australian Grand Prix. The first detection point is 170 m before Turn Eleven, with the Zone One activation point coming 104 m after Turn Twelve. The second detection point, shared by Zones Two and Three, is 13 m before Turn Fourteen. The activation point for Zone Two is 30 m after Turn Sixteen, while the activation point for Zone Three is 32 m after Turn Two.

AUSTRALIAN GRAND PRIX FAST FACTS
- This will be the 35th F1 Australian Grand Prix and the 24th to be held at Melbourne's Albert Park. The race joined the calendar in 1985, with the first race being held in Adelaide. It moved to Melbourne in 1996.
- The most successful driver here is Michael Schumacher, who won four times from nineteen attempts. He recorded a hat-trick of wins from 2000-2002 and then won again in 2004—all for Ferrari.
- Hamilton holds the outright record for podium appearances in Australia, with eight. Allied to his pair of wins, he finished second in 2011, 2016, 2017 and 2018, and took third in 2007 and 2012.

BAHRAIN

2019 BAHRAIN GRAND PRIX
29–31 March 2019

The Formula One continues its early season long-haul programme this weekend with a visit to the Bahrain International Circuit, home of Bahrain Grand Prix. Round one of the 2019 FIA Formula One World Championship Australia was a relatively gentle introduction to the season for 2019's cars but Bahrain provides a stiffer challenge. Heat and dust are both notorious engine breakers, while the stop-start nature of the track provides a harsh test for both brakes and tyres.

While the conversion of the Bahrain Grand Prix to a night race has improved the spectacle for fans, it brings with it challenges for both teams and drivers. The rapidly cooling track affects the balance of the car in ways that are inconsistent with a standard, mid-afternoon event.

The other consequence of racing at night is that it makes FP2, conducted in the early evening, the only practice session from which meaningful set-up data is gathered. FP1 and FP3, both of which take place in the mid-afternoon, are not expected to be fruitful in the search for a good race balance, with the circuit tending to move from oversteer on the hot track, towards understeer as the asphalt cools.

CIRCUIT DATA—BAHRAIN INTERNATIONAL CIRCUIT
Length of lap: 5.412 km
Lap record: 1:31.447 (Pedro de la Rosa, McLaren, 2005)
Start line/finish line offset: 0.246 km
Total number of race laps: 57
Total race distance: 308.238 km
Pitlane speed limits: 80 km/h in practice, qualifying, and the race

Bahrain GP
ROUND 04

RACE DATE ....31 March 2019
CIRCUIT NAME ......Bahrain International Circuit
NO. OF LAPS 57
START TIME ....16.10 local/15.10 GMT
CIRCUIT LENGTH.....5.412km
RACE DISTANCE 308.238km
LAP RECORD ....1.31.447 Pedro De la Rosa (2005)

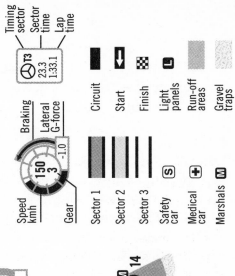

Timing sector
Sector time
Lap time

T3
23.3
1:33.1

Speed kmh
Braking
Lateral G-force
Gear

150
3
-1.0

Circuit

Start

Finish

Light panels

Run-off areas

Gravel traps

Sector 1

Sector 2

Sector 3

S Safety car

+ Medical car

M Marshals

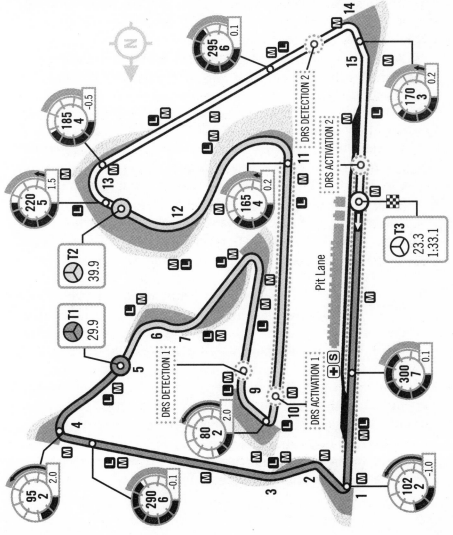

CIRCUIT NOTES
- Other than routine maintenance no changes of significance have been made.

DRS ZONE
- The DRS sectors at the Bahrain International Circuit are broadly similar to last year, with 100 m added to the second zone. The detection point of the first zone is 10 m before Turn Nine and the activation point is 50 m after Turn Ten. The second zone's detection point is 108 m before Turn Fourteen, with activation occurring 170 m after Turn Fifteen.

FAST FACTS
- This is the sixteenth Bahrain Grand Prix. The first event took place in 2004 and it has been held every year since except 2011.
- Sebastian Vettel is the most successful driver in Bahrain with four wins. Vettel won the 2012 and 2013 races for Red Bull, adding a third in 2017 and a fourth in 2018 for Ferrari. Ferrari are the most successful constructor with six victories, with Michael Schumacher winning the inaugural race in 2004 and Felipe Massa adding back-to-back victories in 2007 and 2008. Lewis Hamilton also has back-to-back victories in Sakhir, winning for Mercedes in 2014 and 2015. The other winners are Jenson Button (2009) and Nico Rosberg (2016).
- Despite never having won the Bahrain Grand Prix, Kimi Räikkönen has more podium appearances at this race than any other driver. His eight podiums comprise three third places (2005-2007) and five seconds (2008, 2012, 2013, 2015, 2016).
- Starting from pole hasn't been very useful in Bahrain: only five times has the pole position driver converted the advantage into victory, with Vettel being the most recent to do so in 2018. The eventual winner, however, has never started from further back than the second row, with both Alonso (2006) and Button (2009) winning from P4.

CHINA

2019 CHINESE GRAND PRIX
12– 14 April 2019

Following a first thrilling visit of the season to the Middle East at last weekend's Bahrain Grand Prix, Formula 1 rapidly returns to action with its first Far-Eastern race of the year, the Chinese Grand Prix, round three of the 2019 FIA Formula 1 World Championship.

The imposing Shanghai International Circuit possesses a number of characteristics that make for a challenging weekend, for both drivers and engineers.

The SIC is a circuit of contrasts. On the one hand it's recognised as a 'front-limited' circuit that puts high levels of stress on the front tyres, especially through the opening tight and twisting complex of corners known as the 'Snail', where the emphasis is on good balances and downforce. On the other hand, set-up is pulled in the opposite direction by the track's two long straights, where teams seek to reduce drag in the search for straight line speed. It's a delicate balancing act that often eludes even the best prepared team.

Matters are further complicated by the fact that the prevailing cool temperatures at this time of year mean that getting front tyres switched on is tricky on the relatively smooth surface. Failure to do so can result in high levels of graining and wear.

CIRCUIT DATA—SHANGHAI INTERNATIONAL CIRCUIT
Length of lap: 5.451 km
Lap record: 1:32.238 (Michael Schumacher, Ferrari, 2004)
Start line/finish line offset: 0.190 km
Total number of race laps: 56
Total race distance: 305.066 km
Pitlane speed limits: 80 km/h in practice, qualifying, and the race

Chinese GP
ROUND 03

RACE DATE ....14 April 2019
CIRCUIT NAME ....Shanghai International Circuit
NO. OF LAPS 56
START TIME ....14.10 local/06.10 GMT
CIRCUIT LENGTH.....5.451km
RACE DISTANCE 305.066km
LAP RECORD..........1:32.238
Michael Schumacher (2004)

Timing sector
Sector time
Lap time

T3
42.1
1:36.3

Braking
Lateral G-force

Speed kmh

150
3
-1.0

Gear

Circuit
Start
Finish
Light panels
Run-off areas
Gravel traps

Sector 1
Sector 2
Sector 3

S Safety car
✛ Medical car
M Marshals

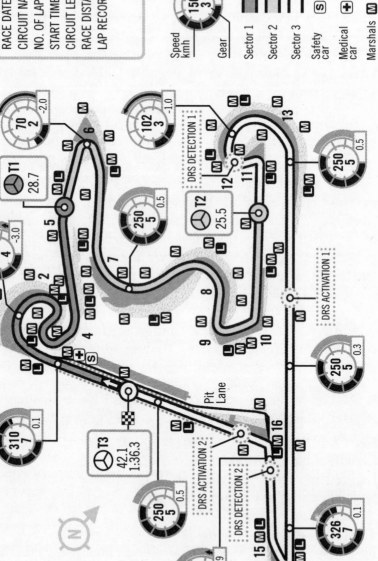

CIRCUIT NOTES
The concrete (inner) section of pit lane has been resurfaced.

DRS ZONES
The DRS zones at the Shanghai International Circuit will be as last year. The detection point of the first zone is at Turn Twelve and the activation point is 752 m before Turn Fourteen. The second zone's detection point is 35 m before Turn Sixteen, with activation occurring 98 m after Turn Sixteen.

FAST FACTS
- This is the sixteenth edition of the Chinese Grand Prix. The first event took place in 2004 and it has been held every year since at the Shanghai International Circuit.
- Lewis Hamilton is by far the most successful driver at the Chinese Grand Prix. The Briton has won the event five times—in 2008 and 2011 for McLaren and in 2014, 2015 and 2017 with Mercedes. Next on the list are Fernando Alonso (2005 and 2013) and Nico Rosberg (2012 and 2016). The trio are the only multiple Chinese GP winners from the eight drivers to have won in at the SIC.
- Three other current drivers have won in China: Kimi Räikkönen in 2007, Daniel Ricciardo in 2018, and Sebastian Vettel in 2009. The other winners are Rubens Barrichello (2004), Michael Schumacher (2006), and Jenson Button (2010).
- The victories scored by Hamilton and Rosberg make Mercedes the most successful constructor at this race, with five victories. Ferrari are next with four and McLaren have three wins here.
- Hamilton again leads the way on podium appearances with eight. In addition to his five wins he has one second place (2010) and two third places (2012, 2013). Only six other current drivers have appeared on the podium in China: Räikkönen has six appearances; Alonso and Vettel have five apiece, while Max Verstappen, Ricciardo and Valtteri Bottas have one each.

- Hamilton also holds the record for most pole positions in China: 2007, 2008, 2013-15 and 2017. That's two more than nearest rival Vettel who started from the front of the grid in 2009, 2010, 2011 and 2018.
- In the fifteen events here the race has been won from pole position nine times and four of the last five races have been won from the front of the grid.
- The Shanghai International Circuit was the scene of Red Bull Racing's first win in Formula 1, with Vettel winning from pole position..
- In 2018 Hamilton broke Räikkönen's record of twenty seven consecutive finishes in the points. The Finn's record encompassed a stretch between the 2012 Bahrain GP and the 2013 Hungarian GP. Hamilton last failed to finish at the 2016 Malaysian GP, when an engine problem ended his race after forty laps. Meanwhile, the double DNF suffered by Red Bull Racing in Bahrain brought to an end a run of thirty-nine consecutive races in the points for the Milton Keynes team.

AZERBAIJAN

2019 AZERBAIJAN GRAND PRIX
26–28 April 2019

The early-season sequence of flyaway races draws to a close this weekend with F1 heading to the Baku City Circuit, home of the Azerbaijan Grand Prix for Round Four of the 2019 FIA Formula One World Championship.

The only grand prix held below sea-level doesn't follow the conventions of street circuit design. Baku features the low grip, tight turns and unforgiving barriers expected of the type, but also encourages overtaking as well as ultra-high speeds on the 2.1 km pit straight, on which drivers spend over twenty seconds at full throttle.

Keeping brakes and tyres warm for the excellent passing opportunity into the Turn One left-hander has been problematic in the past—and this is likely to be exacerbated by the move from a late-June race to the cooler temperatures of late April. Another major issue for teams to consider during practice is finding an acceptable compromise between performance on the fast start-finish section of track and on the low-speed middle sector of the lap. The race's short history suggests there isn't a one-size fits all solution.

CIRCUIT DATA—BAKU CITY CIRCUIT
Length of lap: 6.003 km
Lap record: 1:43.441 (Sebastian Vettel, Ferrari, 2017)
Start line/finish line offset: 0.104 km
Total number of race laps: 51
Total race distance: 306.049 km
Pitlane speed limits: 80 km/h in practice, qualifying and the race
CIRCUIT NOTES
- The kerb at the apex of Turn Eight has been replaced.

Azerbaijan GP
ROUND 08

RACE DATE ....28 April 2019
CIRCUIT NAME ....Baku City Circuit
NO. OF LAPS..........51
START TIME ....16.10 local/12.10 GMT
CIRCUIT LENGTH 6.003km
RACE DISTANCE 306.049km
LAP RECORD 1:43.441
Sebastian Vettel
(2017)

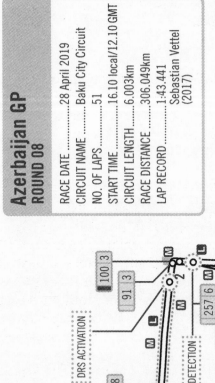

Timing sector
Sector time
Lap time

T3
35.3
1:26.7

Circuit
Start
Finish
Light panels
Run-off areas
Gravel traps

Speed kmh

288 7
Braking — Gear

Sector 1
Sector 2
Sector 3
Safety car S
Medical car +
Marshals M

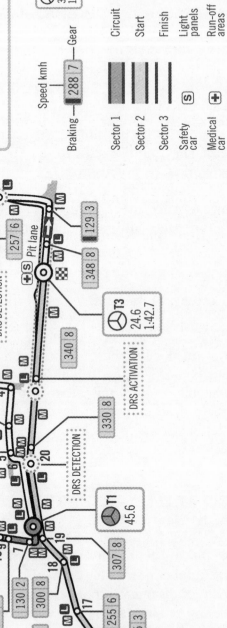

DRS ZONES

- There are two DRS zones in Baku. The detection point of the first is at the SC2 line, while activation is 54 m after Turn Two. The detection point of the second zone is at the apex of Turn Twenty, with activation 347 m after Turn Twenty.

FAST FACTS

- This is the third Azerbaijan Grand Prix and the fourth Formula One grand prix to be held on the Baku City Circuit. The circuit made its debut with the 2016 European Grand Prix.
- Nico Rosberg won the inaugural event in Baku for Mercedes, recording a Grand Chelem of pole (his 25th), victory, fastest lap and every lap led. The 2017 winner was Daniel Ricciardo for Red Bull Racing. The Australian won from tenth on the grid having crashed in qualifying. In 2018 Lewis Hamilton won from second on the grid.
- The Baku City Circuit is one of six tracks to have hosted grands prix of different titles. The others are Brands Hatch (British and European), Jerez (Spanish and European) The Nürburgring (German, Luxembourg, European), Imola (Italian and San Marino) and Dijon (French and Swiss). There is also a case to be made for the Indianapolis Motor Speedway, which has hosted both the United States Grand Prix and the Indianapolis 500, the latter being a round of the F1 World Championship between 1950 and 1960.

SPAIN

2019 SPANISH GRAND PRIX
10–12 May 2019

After a quartet of early flyaway races the 2019 FIA Formula 1 World Championship begins its European season at the Circuit de Barcelona-Catalunya, home of the Spanish Grand Prix.

The Barcelona track, the favoured off-season test venue for F1's teams, has always been something of a bellwether circuit, with a well-worn maxim stating that if a car is quick around the Montmeló circuit, it is likely to perform well at any of the calendar's twenty other race venues.

The judgement is based on the circuit's layout, which features a good mix of fast-, medium- and slow-speed corners, as well as swift changes of direction and a long start-finish straight. It's a combination that tests a broad range of car characteristics and after the particular demands of the opening races, taking in temporary tracks and races in cool and high temperatures, Spain's grand prix circuit is perhaps the first time this season we will get a definitive guide to each team's relative strengths.

CIRCUIT DATA—CIRCUIT DE BARCELONA-CATALUNYA
Length of lap: 4.655 km
Lap record: 1:18.441 (Daniel Ricciardo, Red Bull, 2018)
Start line/finish line offset: 0.126 km
Total number of race laps: 66
Total race distance: 307.104 km
Pitlane speed limits: 80 km/h in practice, qualifying and the race

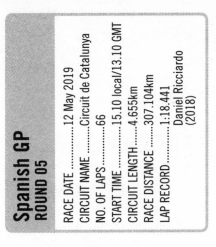

Spanish GP
ROUND 05

RACE DATE ....12 May 2019
CIRCUIT NAME ....Circuit de Catalunya
NO. OF LAPS 66
START TIME............15.10 local/13.10 GMT
CIRCUIT LENGTH....4.655km
RACE DISTANCE 307.104km
LAP RECORD 1.18.441
Daniel Ricciardo
(2018)

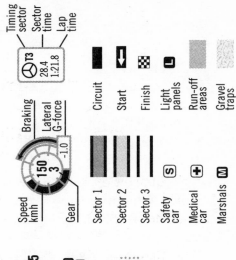

			Timing sector
			Sector time
			Lap time

T3
28.4
1:21.8

Braking

Lateral G-force

Speed kmh

150
3

Gear   -1.0

▮	Circuit
▼	Start
▦	Finish
L	Light panels
▨	Run-off areas
░	Gravel traps

Sector 1
Sector 2
Sector 3

S Safety car
✚ Medical car
M Marshals

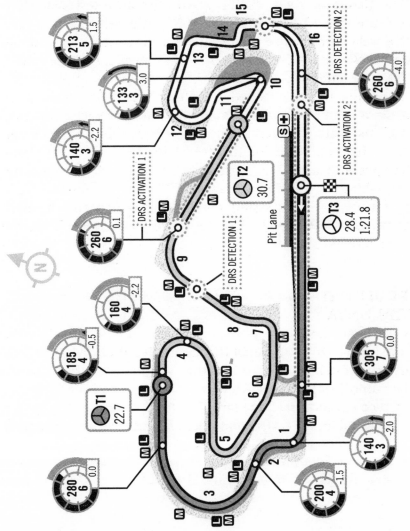

N

213 5   1.5
133 3   3.0
140 3   -2.2
260 6   0.1
185 4   -0.5
160 4   -2.2
280 6   0.0
200 4   -1.5
140 3   -2.0
305 7   0.0
260 6   -4.0

T1 22.7
T2 30.7
T3 28.4 1:21.8

DRS ACTIVATION 1
DRS DETECTION 1
DRS ACTIVATION 2
DRS DETECTION 2

Pit Lane

CIRCUIT NOTES

- The entire track has been resurfaced.
- A 10 m wide section of asphalt has been replaced by gravel around the outside of Turn One.
- The artificial grass on the exit of Turns Two and Seven has been removed.
- The guardrail has been re-aligned to the left of the run-off at Turn Four.
- New double kerbs have been installed on the exit of Turns Five and Sixteen and the artificial grass removed.
- The run-off areas on the exit of Turn Twelve and around the outside of Turn Thirteen have been increased.

DRS ZONE

Two DRS zones will be in use. The first has a detection point 86 m before Turn Nine and an activation point 40 m after. The second detection point is at the Safety Car line, with activation 157 m after Turn Sixteen.

FAST FACTS

- This will be the forty-ninth Formula 1 World Championship Spanish Grand Prix and the twenty-ninth edition at the Circuit de Barcelona-Catalunya. The circuit first held the race in 1991 and has been the home of the Spanish Grand Prix ever since.
- Four other venues have hosted Spanish GPs. The first event place at Barcelona's Pedralbes street circuit in 1951, with a second race taking place in 1954. After slipping off the schedule, the grand prix returned in the late 1960s, alternating between Madrid's Circuito del Jarama (1968, 1970, 1972, 1974) and Barcelona's Montjuïc (1969, 1971, 1973, 1975). Following the cessation of F1 racing at Montjuïc, Jarama hosted races from 1976-1979 and in 1981, while the Circuito de Jerez featured from 1986 to 1990.
- Michael Schumacher is the most successful driver at the Spanish GP, with six wins (1995-96, 2001-04). All the German's victories were scored in Barcelona.

- Ferrari are the most successful team at the Spanish Grand Prix with a dozen wins, eight of which were scored at the Circuit de Catalunya. The Scuderia's first win in Spain was at the 1954 Pedrables race courtesy of Mike Hawthorn and its most recent was in 2013 with Fernando Alonso. McLaren is next on the list with eight Spanish GP wins, although only four were scored in Barcelona.
- Four Spanish Grand Prix winners will line up on the grid this weekend: Kimi Räikkönen (2005, 2008), Sebastian Vettel (2011), Lewis Hamilton (2014, 2017) and Max Verstappen (2016).
- Schumacher again leads the way on pole positions at the Spanish GP, with seven—in 1994 and 1995 and then with a straight run from 2000-2004. Hamilton has the most Spanish GP pole positions of a current driver, with four. All four were achieved with Mercedes, in 2014 and 2016-18.
- Grid position counts for much here. In only three of the twenty-eight grands prix run to date at the Circuit de Barcelona-Catalunya has a win been scored from beyond the front row of the grid. Michael Schumacher took victory from third place on the grid in 1996, Max Verstappen, scored his maiden grand prix win after starting the 2016 edition from fourth place, while Alonso has the current record having scored his 2013 win from fifth place on the starting grid.

MONACO

2019 MONACO GRAND PRIX
23–26 May 2019

Formula One heads to Monte Carlo this week for Round Six of the 2019 FIA Formula One World Championship, the illustrious Monaco Grand Prix.

On a circuit little changed from its essential pre-war layout, the Monaco Grand Prix is something of an anomaly within the modern calendar. While the closeness of the barriers and the proximity of the grandstands makes the cars appear incredibly fast, this is the lowest speed circuit of the year and unique in having a reduced race distance, 40 km shorter than standard to ensure the laps fit into the required timeframe. Its status as the shortest circuit means, however, that spectators are afforded more laps in Monaco than at any other grand prix.

The intricate nature of the Circuit de Monaco sees teams employing as much downforce as possible and fitting bespoke steering racks to cope with the famously-tight hairpin. While the layout doesn't demand it, the nature of the race ensures teams pay close attention to their cooling requirements: with overtaking difficult, cars often form trains, disrupting airflow for those behind.

CIRCUIT DATA—CIRCUIT DE MONACO
Length of lap: 3.337 km
Lap record: 1:14.260 (Max Verstappen, Red Bull, 2018)
Start line/finish line offset: 0.000 km
Total number of race laps: 78
Total race distance: 260.286 km
Pitlane speed limits: 60 km/h in practice, qualifying and the race

Monaco GP
ROUND 06

RACE DATE ....26 May 2019
CIRCUIT NAME ....Circuit de Monaco
NO. OF LAPS 78
START TIME ....15.10 local/13.10 GMT
CIRCUIT LENGTH 3.337km
RACE DISTANCE 260.288km
LAP RECORD 1:14.260
Max Verstappen (2018)

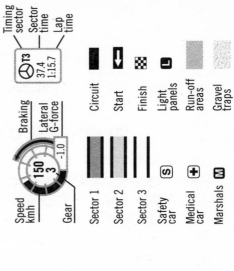

Timing sector — T3
Sector time — 37.4
Lap time — 1:15.7

Speed kmh — 150
Gear — 3
Braking
Lateral G-force — -1.0

Circuit
Start
Finish
Light panels — L
Run-off areas
Gravel traps

Sector 1
Sector 2
Sector 3
Safety car — S
Medical car — +
Marshals — M

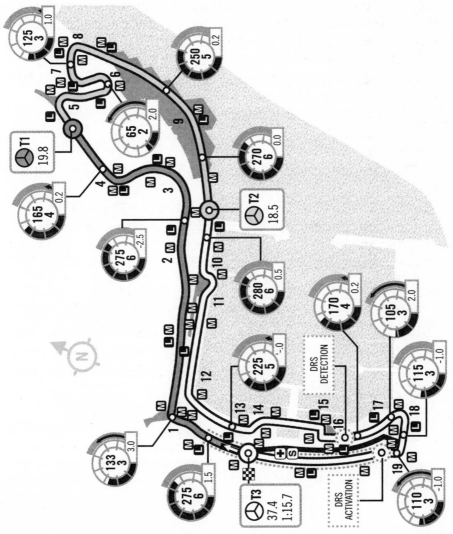

N

T1 — 19.8

T2 — 18.5

T3 — 37.4 / 1:15.7

DRS DETECTION
DRS ACTIVATION

125 / 3 / 1.0
250 / 5 / 0.2
65 / 2 / 2.0
270 / 6 / 0.0
165 / 4 / 0.2
275 / 6 / -2.5
280 / 6 / 0.5
170 / 4 / 0.2
105 / 3 / 2.0
225 / 5 / -1.0
115 / 3 / -1.0
133 / 3 / 3.0
275 / 6 / 1.5
110 / 3 / -1.0

CIRCUIT NOTES
The circuit has been resurfaced between Turns Seven to
Fifteen and Nineteen to One. The fast lane in the pits has also
been resurfaced.

DRS ZONE
There is a single DRS zone in Monaco, with the detection point
located 80 m after Turn Sixteen and the activation point located
18 m after Turn Nineteen.

FAST FACTS
• The Monaco Grand Prix appeared on the original Formula
One World Championship calendar in 1950. It reappeared in
1955 and has been ever-present since. This is the sixty-sixth
Monaco Grand Prix.
• With six wins, Ayrton Senna is Monaco's most successful
driver.
• McLaren are the most successful team in Monaco with
fifteen victories, split between Prost (1984-1986, 1988), Senna
(1989-93), Mika Häkkinen (1998), David Coulthard (2000,
2002), Räikkönen (2005), Alonso (2007) and Hamilton (2008).
• Mercedes took their fiftieth victory with Hamilton's win
here in 2016.
• Of the sixty-five Monaco Grands Prix to date, twenty-nine
have been won from pole position, including ten in eleven
years between 2004 and 2014.
• Olivier Panis is the only winner to start outside the top ten.
His 1996 triumph for Ligier came from P14. That race holds
the record for the highest number of retirements as a percentage of starters, with 85.7% of the field (eighteen from twenty-one) failing to see the chequered flag.
• While many drivers call Monaco home, Leclerc is one of
very few Monegasques to take part in the race. Louis Chiron
raced in 1950 and 1955 (with a DNS in 1956 and a DNQ in
1958) finishing third in 1950. He competed many times in the
pre-World Championship Monaco Grand Prix, winning in
1931. Olivier Beretta finished eighth for Larousse in 1994.

CANADA

2019 CANADIAN GRAND PRIX
07–09 June 2019

The 2019 FIA Formula One World Championship approaches its one-third point as teams make their way to Montréal for Round Seven of the campaign, the Canadian Grand Prix.

While this weekend's race takes place at a second consecutive temporary circuit after Monaco, the Circuit Gilles Villeneuve, located on the Île Notre-Dame in the St Lawrence River, presents teams and drivers with a very different set of challenges than the tight confines and low speeds of the Principality's twisting streets.

Here, a series of fast straights lead into heavy-braking corners. The high end-of-straight speeds and the stop/go nature of the circuit lead to it being classed as the season's toughest on brakes. The frequent braking events lead to high temperatures within the discs and pads and the effect is compounded by the fact that the straights, particularly on the first half of the lap, do not allow sufficient time for cooling.

The temporary nature of the circuit also means that track conditions evolve significantly across the weekend and this, allied with the relatively smooth surface, means that grip is often at a premium.

CIRCUIT DATA—CIRCUIT GILLES VILLENEUVE
Length of lap: 4.361 km
Lap record: 1:13.622 (Rubens Barrichello, Ferrari, 2004)
Start line/finish line offset: 0.000 km
Total number of race laps: 70
Total race distance: 305.270 km
Pitlane speed limits: 80 km/h in practice, qualifying and the race

Canadian GP
ROUND 07

RACE DATE ....9 June 2019
CIRCUIT NAME ....Circuit Gilles Villeneuve
NO. OF LAPS 70
START TIME ....14.10 local/18.10 GMT
CIRCUIT LENGTH......4.361km
RACE DISTANCE 305.270km
LAP RECORD ....1:13.622   Rubens Barrichello
(2004)

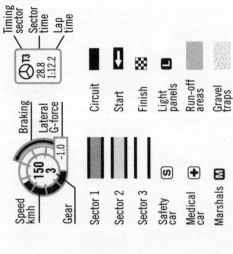

Timing sector
Sector time
Lap time

T3
28.8
1:12.2

Braking
Lateral G-force

Speed kmh
150
3
−1.0
Gear

Circuit
Start
Finish
Light panels
Run-off areas
Gravel traps

Sector 1
Sector 2
Sector 3

Safety car — S
Medical car — +
Marshals — M

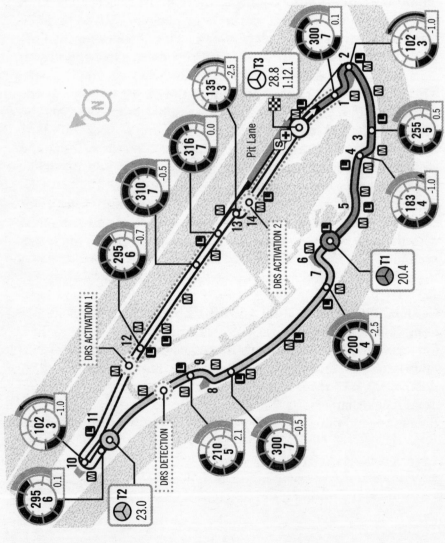

N

300 7 0.1
102 3 −1.0
135 3 −2.5

T3
28.8
1:12.1

Pit Lane

255 5 0.5
316 7 0.0
183 4 −1.0

310 7 −0.5

295 6 −0.7

13
14

DRS ACTIVATION 2

T1
20.4

12

DRS ACTIVATION 1

200 4 −2.5

11

10

DRS DETECTION

102 3 −1.0

295 6 0.1

T2
23.0

210 5 2.1

300 7 −0.5

CIRCUIT NOTES

- The wall on the drivers' left after the exit of Turn Two has been replaced and a new debris fence fitted. The walls on the both sides of the track between Turns Three and Six and at the back of the run-off at Turn Six have also been replaced, with new debris fences fitted.
- The walls in the escape road at Turn Three have been re-aligned to provide a larger run-off and easier access for removing cars. The wall in the run-off at Turn Ten has been re-aligned to provide better protection for rescue vehicles. The walls straight on at Turn Fourteen have been also been re-aligned.
- The tyre barriers at Turns Two (inside), Four, Six, Ten, Thirteen and Fourteen have been replaced by TecPro barriers.

DRS ZONE

There will be three DRS zones. A new zone has been added, with a detection point 15 m after Turn Five and an activation point 95 m after Turn Seven. The previous zones remains unchanged. They share a detection point 110 m before Turn Nine, with activation points 155 m before Turn Twelve and 70 m after Turn Fourteen.

CANADIAN GRAND PRIX FAST FACTS

- This will be the fiftieth Canadian Grand Prix and the fortieth to be held in Montreal. The race has been held at two other venues: Mosport in 1967, '69, from '71-'74 and '76-'77, and Mont-Tremblant in 1968 and 1970.
- Michael Schumacher holds the record for most Canadian Grand Prix wins, with seven. His first came with Benetton in 1994 and after joining Ferrari in 1996 he claimed another six in Montreal, in 1997, 1998, 2000 and from 2002-'04, all with the Scuderia.
- The most successful constructor at the Circuit Gilles Villeneuve is Ferrari with eleven wins, two ahead of McLaren. The British squad is more successful in Canada overall, however, with thirteen victories, one ahead of Ferrari.

- Sebastian Vettel is set to start his eleventh Canadian Grand Prix this weekend. The German has never failed to finish in Montreal and is the only current driver with more than one Canadian Grand Prix to his name to have scored points every single time he has raced here. Räikkönen can boast the most points finishes of a current driver (fourteen) but an otherwise perfect scoring record is blemished by a 2008 DNF, when he was crashed into by Hamilton in the pit lane.
- Since the current circuit configuration came into use in 2002 the race has been won from pole position nine times from sixteen events, with four occurring in the last four years. Räikkonen, in 2005, and Jenson Button, in 2011, hold the record for wins from furthest back on the grid on this configuration. Both won from P7 on the grid.

FRANCE

2019 FRENCH GRAND PRIX
21–23 June 2019

Following a decade-long hiatus, the French Grand Prix returned in 2018. This year, teams and drivers are heading to Le Castellet and the Circuit Paul Ricard for Round Eight of the 2019 FIA Formula One World Championship.

The race returns to Ricard for only the second time since 1990, and is the second time it will run on a full course layout since 1985—albeit a modified version of the circuit formerly used, including a chicane midway along the famous Mistral Straight.

Built on a plateau, the Mistral wind is just one of the variables drivers and teams will have to deal with this weekend. Ricard in this configuration represents a mixed offering across the three sectors—as might be expected from a flexible racing complex designed to include a multitude of circuit configurations.

The track features two high-speed straights and several heavy braking zones but also intricate, technical, low-speed sections, while the famous Signes corner at the end of the Mistral straight will be one of the fastest corners in F1 this year. Put together, it teases teams with the possibility of going in very different directions on set-up—and Friday's practice sessions are likely to be very busy and see them experiment with a wide range of downforce levels.

CIRCUIT DATA—CIRCUIT PAUL RICARD
Length of lap: 5.842 km
Lap record: 1:34.225 (Valtteri Bottas, Mercedes, 2018)
Start line/finish line offset: 0.000 km
Total number of race laps: 53
Total race distance: 309.690 km
Pitlane speed limits: 80 km/h in practice, qualifying and the race

Pirelli GP De France
ROUND 08

RACE DATE ....23 June 2019
CIRCUIT NAME ....Circuit Paul Ricard
NO. OF LAPS 53
START TIME ....16.10 local/14.10 GMT
CIRCUIT LENGTH......5.842km
RACE DISTANCE 309.690km
LAP RECORD 1.34.225
Valtteri Bottas
(2018)

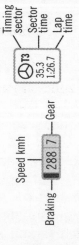

Timing sector
Sector time
Lap time

T3
35.3
1.26.7

Braking — | — Speed kmh

288 | 7

— Gear

⬛ Circuit

⬇ Start

🏁 Finish

L Light panels

Run-off areas

Gravel traps

Sector 1

Sector 2

Sector 3

Ⓢ Safety car

✚ Medical car

Ⓜ Marshals

N

T2
27.7

T3
40.0
1:30.0

T1
22.3

DRS DETECTION

DRS ACTIVATION

DRS ACTIVATION

DRS DETECTION

Pit lane

320 8
170 4
290 7
135 3
85 2
260 6
145 3
145 3
105 3
340 8
330 8
165 4
200 5
305 8
270 6
165 4
155 4
140 3
95 2

DRS ZONE

There will be two DRS zones at Paul Ricard. The first zone has a detection point 75 m before Turn Seven and an activation point 170 m after Turn Seven. The second zone has a detection point at Turn Fourteen and activation 115 m after Turn Fifteen.

FAST FACTS

• This is the sixtieth running of the Formula One World Championship French Grand Prix. The race is one of the original rounds of the World Championship and has been held from 1950 to 1954 and 1956 to 2008. The 1955 race was cancelled following the Le Mans disaster.

• This is the sixteenth French Grand Prix to be held at the Circuit Paul Ricard. The race first came here in 1971, returning in 1973, 1975-6, 1978, 1980, 1982-3, 1985-1990. The events between 1971 and 1985 were held on the original 5.810 km course and the races 1986-1990 on a shortened 3.813 km circuit.

• The French Grand Prix has also been held at Reims (1950-51, 1953-54, 1956, 1958-61, 1963, 1966), Rouen (1952, 1957, 1962, 1964, 1968), Clermont-Ferrand (1965, 1969-70, 1972), Le Mans (1967), Dijon (1974, 1977, 1979, 1981, 1984) and Magny-Cours (1991-2008)

• Michael Schumacher is the most successful French Grand Prix driver with eight wins. Ferrari are far ahead of the field as a constructor with seventeen victories, including the last three races of the previous era. It only has two victories at Ricard, however, and trails McLaren and Williams who both have three victories at this circuit.

• Both of Ferrari's wins at the Circuit Paul Ricard were scored by drivers that are now senior management figures at rival teams: Niki Lauda in 1975 and Alain Prost in 1990.

• Alain Prost is the most successful driver at Ricard. He took four of his six French Grand Prix victories at this circuit. His wins were split between three different manufacturers, victorious for Renault in 1983, McLaren in 1988 and 1989, and finally with Ferrari.

- Pole has conferred a small advantage at Ricard in the past, with nine of the fifteen previous races won from P1 on the grid. The third row is the furthest back a winner has started: Ronnie Peterson (1973) and Nelson Piquet (1985) were both victorious from P5.

AUSTRIA

2019 AUSTRIAN GRAND PRIX
28–30 June 2019

Following last weekend's French Grand Prix Formula 1 heads to the home of Red Bull with Round Nine of the 2019 FIA Formula 1 World Championship taking place at the Red Bull Ring, home of the Austrian Grand Prix.

The rural circuit features one of the season's most picturesque backdrops with the short 4.318 km track draped across the foothills of the spectacular Styrian mountains. And since its return in 2014 it has provided fans with some spectacular action thanks in most part to the high-speed nature of the layout and to the shortness of the lap, which helps to promote close racing.

Made up of just 10 corners, with the kink between Turn One and the old Turn Two now recognised as a corner, the Red Bull Ring is essentially made up four straights ending in tight corners and that means that good traction and straight-line speed are key attributes in the quest for success here.

CIRCUIT DATA—RED BULL RING
Length of lap: 4.318 km
Lap record: 1:06.957 (Kimi Raikkonen, Ferrari, 2018)
Start line/finish line offset: 0.126 km
Total number of race laps: 71
Total race distance: 306.452 km
Pitlane speed limits: 80 km/h in practice, qualifying, and the race

CIRCUIT NOTES
- The verge on the left approaching Turn 3 has been widened at the request of MotoGP.
- The opening in the corner of the run-off area at Turn 4 has been closed and a new one created further around the run-off.

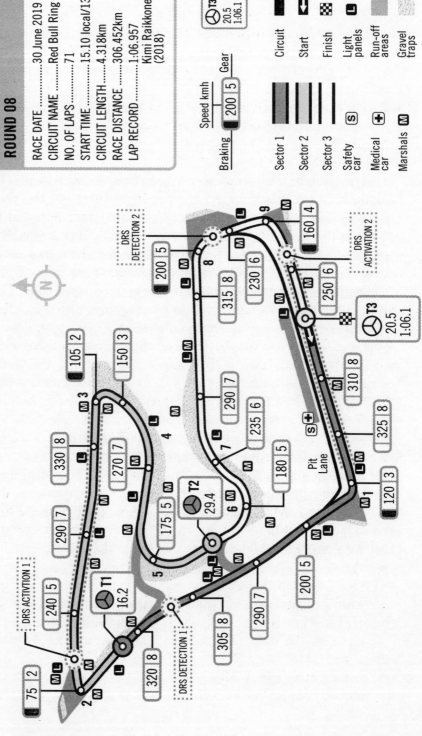

Austrian GP
ROUND 08

RACE DATE	30 June 2019
CIRCUIT NAME	Red Bull Ring
NO. OF LAPS	71
START TIME	15.10 local/13.10 GMT
CIRCUIT LENGTH	4.318km
RACE DISTANCE	306.452km
LAP RECORD	1:06.957 Kimi Raikkonen (2018)

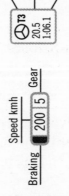

Timing sector — Sector time — Lap time
T3 20.5 1:06.1

Speed kmh — Gear
200 5

Braking

Sector 1
Sector 2
Sector 3

Safety car S
Medical car +
Marshals M

Circuit
Start
Finish
Light panels L
Run-off areas
Gravel traps

N

DRS DETECTION 2
DRS ACTIVATION 2
DRS ACTIVATION 1
DRS DETECTION 1

Pit Lane

T1 16.2
T2 29.4
T3 20.5 1:06.1

DRS ZONE

There will be three DRS zones. The first has a detection point 160 m before Turn One with an activation point 102 m after Turn One. The second zone will have a detection point 40 m before Turn Three and an activation point 100 m after Turn Three. The detection point of the final zone is 151 m before Turn Ten, while its activation point is 106 m after Turn Ten.

FAST FACTS

- This will be the thirty-second Austrian Grand Prix. The inaugural race was held at Zeltweg airfield in 1964 but then immediately fell off the calendar. The grand prix returned in 1970 at the almost 6 km-long Österreichring which hosted the race until 1987. The race then fell off the schedule once more before making a comeback at a shortened version of the Österreichring, named the A1 Ring, from 1997 until 2003. The Red Bull Ring, welcomed Formula One back to Austria in 2014.
- Four-time F1 world champion Alain Prost is the most successful driver at the Austrian Grand Prix, with three wins to his name—in 1983 with Renault and then in, 1985 and 1986 with McLaren. Ronnie Peterson, Alan Jones, Mika Häkkinen, Michael Schumacher and Nico Rosberg are next on the list with two victories apiece.
- McLaren are the most successful team at this race, with six wins. The British team won at the Österreichring in 1984 with Niki Lauda and in 1985-'86 with Alain Prost. The team then took three wins during the period the track was known as the A1 Ring, with Mika Häkkinen victorious in 1998 and 2000, and David Coulthard winning in 2001. Ferrari are next on the list with five wins, while Lotus and Mercedes have four wins each.
- Niki Lauda, René Arnoux and Nelson Piquet share the record for most Austrian Grand Prix pole positions with three each. Hamilton is the only current driver with multiple pole positions at this race. The Briton started from the front in 2015 and 2016.
- The race on the A1 Ring/Red Bull Ring layout has been won from pole position on five occasions and all by different

drivers. Jacques Villeneuve started from P1 in 1997 with the Canadian being followed by Häkkinen in 2000, Michael Schumacher in 2003, Hamilton in 2016 and Valtteri Bottas last year.

• Two teams scored their one and only Formula 1 victory in Austria. In 1976 US Team Penske won at the Österreichring with Northern Ireland's John Watson at the wheel while the following year Australian future champion Alan Jones took the only win of Shadow's 104 starts in F1. Watson's win for Penske remains the most recent win for a US-based team in Formula 1.

• David Coulthard holds the record for victory from furthest back on the grid on this layout. The Scot's 2001 win for McLaren was delivered from a starting posItion of seventh. Overall, the honour goes to Jones whose 1977 win was scored from 14th place on the grid.

GREAT BRITAIN

2019 BRITISH GRAND PRIX
12–14 July 2019

Following hot on the heels of races in France and Austria, this week teams reach the British Grand Prix at Silverstone, Round 10 of the 2019 FIA Formula One World Championship.

The wide-open spaces of Silverstone couldn't be more different to the undulating Red Bull Ring. The Northamptonshire circuit is a driver favourite, with a barrage of fast, flowing corners, of which high-speed Copse and the ultra-quick changes of direction through Maggotts, Becketts and Chapel are the standouts.

That said, ever since Silverstone adopted its new 'Arena' layout in 2010, extra variety has been added to the circuit, with the intricate low-speed infield section offering a choice of racing lines and also complicating the set-up decisions teams have to make.

Silverstone is one of the easiest circuits on the F1 calendar for braking but one of the toughest on tyres, the unrelenting sequences of high-speed turns putting vast amounts of lateral energy into the rubber.

CIRCUIT DATA—SILVERSTONE
Length of lap: 5.891 km
Lap record: 1:30.621 (Lewis Hamilton, Mercedes, 2017)
Start line/finish line offset: 0.134 km
Total number of race laps: 52
Total race distance: 306.198 km
Pitlane speed limits: 80 km/h in practice, qualifying and the race

CIRCUIT NOTES
- The entire track was resurfaced for 2018.
- The longitudinal and lateral cambers of the track have been changed to assist drainage in Turns One, Six, Sixteen, Seventeen and Eighteen.

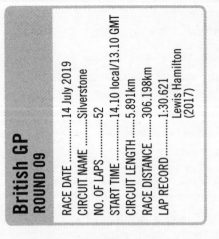

British GP
ROUND 09

RACE DATE ....14 July 2019
CIRCUIT NAME ....Silverstone
NO. OF LAPS 52
START TIME ....14.10 local/13.10 GMT
CIRCUIT LENGTH 5.891km
RACE DISTANCE 306.198km
LAP RECORD 1:30.621
                     Lewis Hamilton
                     (2017)

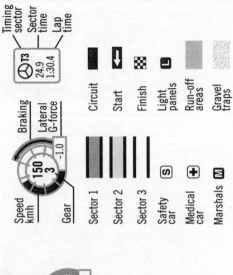

Timing sector
Sector time
Lap time

⊘ T3
24.9
1:30.4

Braking

Lateral G-force

Speed kmh — ⊘ 150 / 3 / -1.0

Gear

Sector 1

Sector 2

Sector 3

Ⓢ Safety car

✚ Medical car

Ⓜ Marshals

Circuit

Start

Finish

Ⓛ Light panels

Run-off areas

Gravel traps

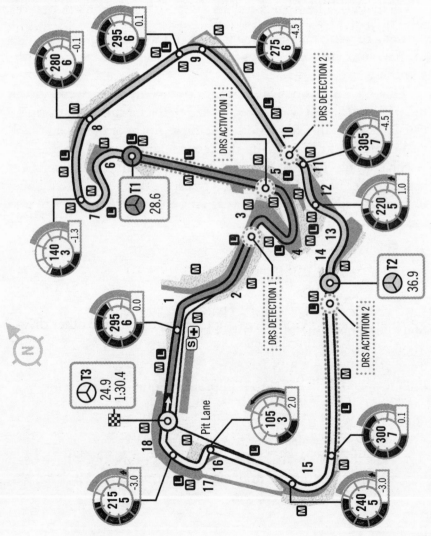

N

T3
⊘ 24.9
1:30.4

T1
⊘ 28.6

T2
⊘ 36.9

DRS ACTIVATION 1

DRS DETECTION 2

DRS DETECTION 1

DRS ACTIVATION 2

Pit Lane

280 / 6 / -0.1
295 / 6 / 0.1
275 / 6 / -4.5
140 / 3 / -1.3
305 / 7 / -4.5
220 / 5 / 1.0
295 / 6 / 0.0
105 / 3 / 2.0
300 / 7 / 0.1
215 / 5 / -3.0
240 / 5 / -3.0

- New kerb elements have been added behind the existing kerb on the exit of Turn Fifteen and at the apex of Turn Seventeen.

DRS ZONE
- Silverstone has three DRS zones this year. The detection point of the first zone is 25 m before Turn Three (Village), with the activation point 30 m after Turn Five (Aintree). The second detection point is at Turn Eleven (Maggotts) with the activation point at the exit of Turn Fourteen (Chapel). The final zone has a detection point 83 m before Turn Sixteen (Vale) and activation 62 m after Turn Eighteen (Club).

FAST FACTS
- This is the 70th F1 World Championship British Grand Prix. It is one of two ever-present races on the calendar, the other being the Italian Grand Prix. This is the 53rd race to be held at Silverstone. The British Grand Prix has also been held at Aintree (1955, 1957, 1959, 1961, 1962) and Brands Hatch (even-numbered years from 1964 to 1986).
- With seventeen victories, Ferrari are the most successful team at the British Grand Prix, three ahead of McLaren. At Silverstone, they're likewise ahead of McLaren with four-teent victories to twelve. Ferrari's first F1 victory came at this circuit, José Froilán González winning the 1951 British Grand Prix for the Scuderia.
- This was also González's first F1 victory. Three other drivers have taken a debut win at Silverstone. Giuseppe 'Nino' Farina won F1's first world championship round in 1950 for Alfa Romeo. Peter Revson won for McLaren in 1973, and Johnny Herbert took victory for Benetton in 1995. Three other drivers have taken a debut win at the British Grand Prix. They are Stirling Moss at Aintree in 1955 for Mercedes, Tony Brooks for Vanwall (in a car handed over to Moss after 26 laps) at Aintree in 1957, and Jo Siffert at Brands Hatch in 1968 for Lotus.

- The victory for Brooks/Moss in the 1957 British Grand Prix was Vanwall's first win and therefore the first F1 win for a British constructor. It was also the final time a victory was shared, and the third time overall that had happened, following shared wins for Juan Manuel Fangio and Luigi Fagioli at the 1951 French Grand Prix and Fangio with Luigi Musso at the 1956 Argentinian Grand Prix.

- Jim Clark, Alain Prost and Lewis Hamilton are tied on five victories apiece at the British Grand Prix. Prost (1983, 1985, 1989-90, 1993) and Hamilton (2008, 2014-17) have taken all of their wins at Silverstone, Clark won at all three venues, beginning at Aintree in 1962, taking Silverstone wins 1963, 1965 and 1967 and a Brands Hatch victory in 1964. Prost's 1993 victory made him the first driver to win fifty grands prix.

- A sixth victory this weekend would give Hamilton the outright record for British Grand Prix wins.

- Nigel Mansell has a record seven consecutive British Grands Prix fastest laps, beginning at Brands Hatch in 1986, followed by six more at Silverstone. Mansell also took another fastest lap on home soil, his first also came at Brands Hatch, in the 1983 European Grand Prix.

- Daniel Ricciardo made his F1 race debut at Silverstone. The Red Bull driver was loaned to the Spanish HRT team for the second half of the 2011 season.

- The Williams team had their first ever F1 victory at Silverstone, courtesy of Clay Regazzoni in 1979. In 1997, they won their hundredth at the same venue, courtesy of Jacques Villeneuve.

- While the track has been used in this configuration since 2010, the grid has only been in its current location since 2011. Hamilton the only driver is to win from pole position. Hamilton is also the winner from furthest back on this layout, winning from P6 in 2014. In the entire history of the race at Silverstone, that has only been bettered by Emerson Fittipaldi, the Brazilian winning from P7 for McLaren in 1975.

GERMANY

2019 GERMAN GRAND PRIX
26–28 July 2019

Round Eleven of the 2019 FIA Formula 1 World Championship sees teams and drivers return to the Hockenheimring.

Given the nature of the circuit it should mean that Kimi Räikkönen's 14-year-old lap record will come under threat this weekend.

Located in the Baden-Württemberg region, Hockenheim is usually considered something of a power circuit thanks to a sequence of fast straights in the first half of the lap.

The last generation of F1 cars routinely reached speeds of more than 300 km/h in these sections but a large proportion of any lap time reduction is likely to come from the medium- and low-speed corners that follow where the greater downforce generated by F1's current cars will come into its own. Add in a third DRS zone on those fast straights and the gains could be significant.

There is a trade-off required, however. The quick straights accent low-drag and top-end speed, but the Turn Six hairpin and the low-speed corners of the stadium section put the focus on good traction and downforce. It's not an easy balancing acts for teams.

CIRCUIT DATA—HOCKENHEIMRING
Length of lap: 4.574 km
Lap record: 1:13.780 (Kimi Räikkönen, McLaren, 2004)
Start line/finish line offset: 0.000 km
Total number of race laps: 67
Total race distance: 306.458 km

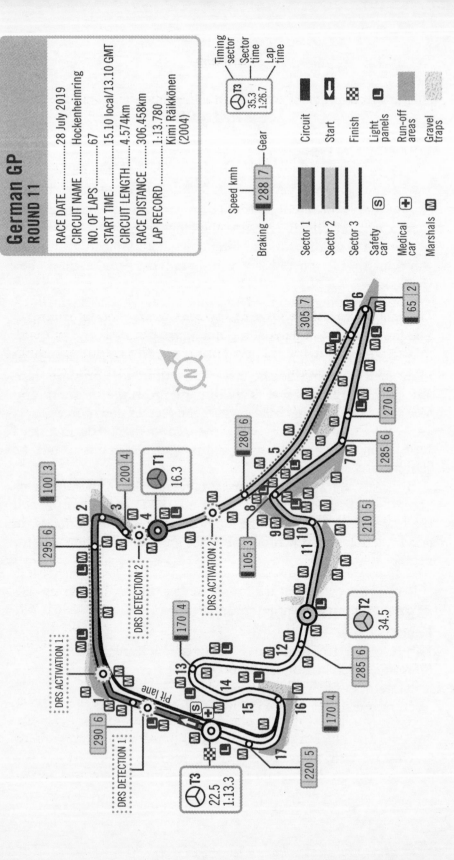

German GP
ROUND 11

RACE DATE	28 July 2019
CIRCUIT NAME	Hockenheimring
NO. OF LAPS	67
START TIME	15.10 local/13.10 GMT
CIRCUIT LENGTH	4.574km
RACE DISTANCE	306.458km
LAP RECORD	1:13.780 Kimi Räikkönen (2004)

Timing sector
Sector time
Lap time

T3
35.3
1:26.7

Speed kmh
288 | 7
Gear

Braking
288 | 7
Gear

Circuit
Start
Finish
Light panels
Run-off areas
Gravel traps

Sector 1
Sector 2
Sector 3

S Safety car
✚ Medical car
M Marshals

N

T1
16.3

T2
34.5

T3
22.5
1:13.3

DRS ACTIVATION 1
DRS DETECTION 1
DRS DETECTION 2
DRS ACTIVATION 2

Pit lane

Pitlane speed limits: 80 km/h in practice, qualifying and the race

CIRCUIT NOTES
- Tyre barriers have been upgraded through the addition of tyres, tube inserts or conveyor belting in Turns One, Eight, Twelve, Thirteen and Seventeen.
- A new double kerb has been installed on the exit of Turn Seventeen.

DRS ZONE
This year there will be three DRS zones at the Hockenheimring. The first zone has a detection point at the exit of Turn Four and an activation point 140 m after Turn Four. The second and third zones share a detection point, 20 m after Turn Sixteen. The second activation point is located 60 m after Turn Seventeen, while the third is located 60 m after Turn One.

FAST FACTS
- This will be the sixty-fourth edition of the Formula One World Championship German Grand Prix. The race was not on the calendar in 1950, 1955, 1960, 2007, 2015 or last year. This is the thirty-seventh German GP to take place at the Hockenheimring.
- In addition to the Hockenheimring, the German Grand Prix has been held at two other venues. The Nürburgring has hosted the race 26 times (from 1951-'54 1956-'58, 1961-'69, 1971-'76, 1985 and most recently in 2009, 2011 and 2013). The four-corner, 8.3 km AVUS circuit in Berlin hosted a single race, in 1959.
- Despite recent biennial appearances, Hockenheim remains the seventh-most-visited venue in F1 history. Only Monza (67), Monaco (65), Silverstone (52), Spa Francorchamps (50), the Nürburgring (40) and Montreal's Circuit Gilles Villeneuve (39) have hosted more races.
- Ferrari are by far the most successful constructors at the

German Grand Prix, with a massive twenty one wins. Eleven of the Scuderia's win have come at Hockenheim, including its most recent German Grand Prix win, courtesy of Fernando Alonso in 2012.

- Williams are next on the list of most successful constructors, with nine German Grand Prix wins. All were scored at Hockenheim, with the first being delivered by Alan Jones in 1979 and the most recent being scored by Juan Pablo Montoya in 2003.
- Michael Schumacher and Lewis Hamilton are the most successful drivers at the German Grand Prix, winning four times each. All of their victories came at the Hockenheimring.
- Only four German drivers have won their home Grand Prix. Apart from Michael Schumacher and Vettel, Nico Rosberg won in Hockenheim in 2014, while in 2001 Ralf Schumacher took the final win on the old 6.8 km Hockenheimring before the circuit was reconfigured to it current 4.574 km layout.

HUNGARY

2019 HUNGARIAN GRAND PRIX
2–4 August 2019

Budapest welcomes Formula One this week as the teams assemble at the Hungaroring for the Hungarian Grand Prix—the twelfth round of the 2019 F1 World Championship. For many in the F1 paddock it has been a hectic few days. Back-to-back with the German Grand Prix, Hungary represents a huge logistics effort for teams, pushed to their limits to transfer cars, garage equipment and motorhomes the 800km between the two circuits. The twisting Hungaroring is similar in characteristic to a street circuit—lacking the walls but retaining the tight radius corners, bumpy surface and low grip. It has something of a mixed reputation among drivers; common consensus claims it to be a wonderful track for a qualifying lap but a difficult place to race, given the paucity of overtaking opportunities. In close battles, good strategy has frequently been the decisive factor, more so than at other permanent circuits.

High track temperatures can be a factor as can be the frequent thunder storms. Teams run their maximum downforce packages in Hungary to cope with the many slow corners. The issue that will occupy the minds of engineers during the practice sessions is the need to maximise traction to get the best return from the many low-gear acceleration points.

CIRCUIT DATA—HUNGARORING
Length of lap: 4.381 km
Lap record: 1:19.071 (Michael Schumacher, Ferrari, 2004)
Start line/finish line offset: 0.040 km
Total number of race laps: 70
Total race distance: 306.630 km
Pitlane speed limits: 80 km/h in practice, qualifying and the race

Hungarian GP
ROUND 11

RACE DATE .... 4 August 2019
CIRCUIT NAME .... Hungaroring
NO. OF LAPS 70
START TIME .... 15.10 local/13.10 GMT
CIRCUIT LENGTH 4.381km
RACE DISTANCE 306.630km
LAP RECORD 1:19.071
Michael Schumacher
(2004)

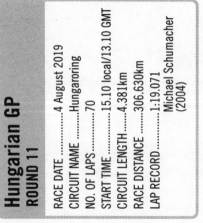

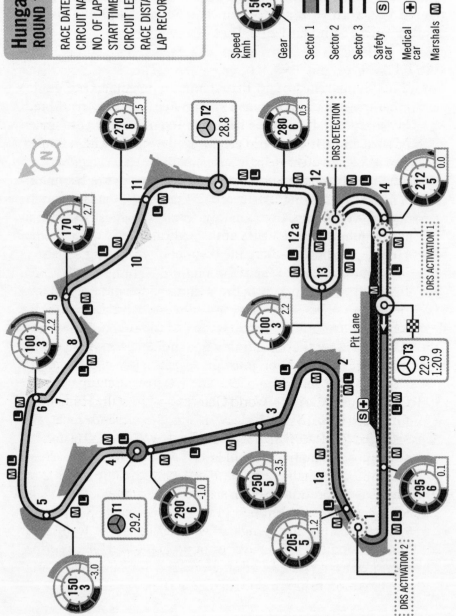

CIRCUIT NOTES

- A new debris fences has been installed on the right between Turns 3 and 4.

DRS ZONES

There will be two consecutive DRS zones sharing a detection point 5 m before Turn 14. Activation points are 130 m after the apex of Turn 14 and 6 m after Turn 1.

FAST FACTS

- The Hungarian Grand Prix made its Formula One World Championship debut in 1986 at the newly-constructed Hungaroring. It has been held at this venue every year since. Monza and Monte Carlo are the only circuits with a longer run of consecutive races.
- The race has been held thirty-three times. Lewis Hamilton is the most successful driver in the history of the Hungarian Grand Prix with six wins. McLaren are the most successful team with eleven victories at this circuit.
- Honda and Ferrari share the distinction of having a victory in each decade of the race's operation.
- In the last ten outings, the Hungarian Grand Prix has provided debut victories for Fernando Alonso (2003), Jenson Button (2006) and Heikki Kovalainen (2008).
- The 2011 Hungarian Grand Prix holds the distinction of being the race with the most pit stops: eighty-eight in total.
- Both Nigel Mansell in 1992 and Michael Schumacher in 2001 won the Drivers' World Championship at the Hungarian Grand Prix. In Mansell's case it was the eleventh race of a sixteen-race season, for Schumacher it was the thirteenth of seventeen. Schumacher holds the record for the earliest conclusion to the Championship, taking the title in 2002 at the French Grand Prix with six races remaining.
- Williams secured the 1996 Constructors' World Championship in Hungary with a one-two formation finish—Jacques Villeneuve leading Damon Hill over the line. Ferrari repeated both the one-two finish and securing the Championship in 2001, 2002 and 2004.

- The 1992 Grand Prix was memorable for more than Mansell claiming the Drivers' crown. It was the last F1 grand prix to feature pre-qualifying and also the final race for the Brabham. Damon Hill qualified twenty-fifth and finished eleventh (last).
- Hamilton made a small piece of history at the 2009 Hungarian Grand Prix by becoming the first driver to win a Grand Prix in a hybrid car. The McLaren MP4/24 powered by a KERS-equipped Mercedes FO 108W engine would win again in Singapore. Kimi Räikkönen, in Belgium, took a solitary victory for Ferrari's KERS-equipped Ferrari F60. The rest of the season was dominated by the conventional Mercedes and Renault engines powering the Brawn BGP001 and Red Bull Racing RB5 respectively.

BELGIUM

2019 BELGIAN GRAND PRIX
30 August–1 September 2019

The Belgian Grand Prix at Spa-Francorchamps is one of the calendar's true classics and one of its toughest tests. The 7.004 km circuit features every kind of challenge. From the run down through Eau Rouge and up the steep incline towards the blind Raidillon corner, to the flat-out blast of the Kemmel Straight. Through Les Combes and the technically difficult stretch down through Rivage, Pouhon and Fagnes and on to the fearsomely fast Blanchimont left-hander, Spa-Francorchamps is a circuit that, despite myriad alterations over the years, still pushes man and machine to the limit.

Spa is one of the season's fastest tracks, with average speeds of 230 km/h, and the stretch from the exit of La Source to Les Combes sees the throttle wide open for twenty-three seconds—the longest single period on the calendar.

Set-up is tricky too, with the key to success being the right balance between low downforce for the high-speed first and third sectors and good grip for the twistier middle sector.

And then there's the weather. The Ardennes defines the phrase 'four seasons in one day' and while one end of the circuit can be bathed in sunshine, the opposite side can be drenched with rain. The changeable conditions can present a real headache for teams, especially with regard to tyre choice.

CIRCUIT DATA—SPA-FRANCORCHAMPS
Length of lap: 7.004 km
Lap record: 1:46.286 (Valtteri Bottas, Mercedes, 2018)
Start line/finish line offset: 0.124 km
Total number of race laps: 44
Total race distance: 308.052 km
Pitlane speed limits: 80 km/h in practice, qualifying, and the race

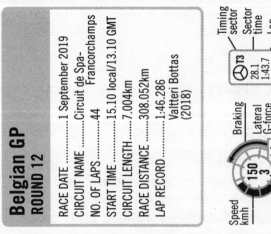

Belgian GP
ROUND 12

RACE DATE ....1 September 2019
CIRCUIT NAME ....Circuit de Spa-Francorchamps
NO. OF LAPS 44
START TIME ....15.10 local/13.10 GMT
CIRCUIT LENGTH......7.004km
RACE DISTANCE 308.052km
LAP RECORD...........1-46.286
Valtteri Bottas (2018)

Legend

Speed kmh / Braking / Lateral G-force / Gear

Timing sector / Sector time / Lap time

- Circuit
- Start
- Finish
- Light panels
- Run-off areas
- Gravel traps

Sector 1
Sector 2
Sector 3

S Safety car
✚ Medical car
M Marshals

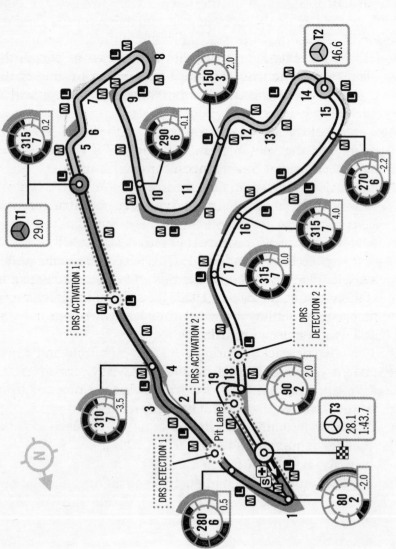

DRS ACTIVATION 1
DRS DETECTION 1
DRS ACTIVATION 2
DRS DETECTION 2
Pit Lane

T1 29.0
T2 46.6
T3 28.1 1:43.7

CIRCUIT NOTES
- Other than routine maintenance, no changes of significance have been made.

DRS ZONES
There will be two DRS zones at Spa-Francorchamps. The detection point for the first is located 240 m before Turn 2, with the activation point 210 m after Turn 4. The second zone has a detection point 160 m before Turn 18 and an activation point 30 m after Turn 19.

FAST FACTS
- This is the sixty-fourth Belgium Grand Prix as part of the World Championship. The race featured as a round of the original F1 World Championship in 1950 It was not held in 1957, 1959, 1969, 1971, 2003 and 2006.
- Three circuits have hosted the race: Nivelles in 1972 and 1974 Zolder in 1973, 1975-1982 and 1984. The remainder have been held at Spa-Francorchamps.
- Michael Schumacher is the most successful driver with six victories. Ferrari is the most successful constructor with seventeen wins.
- The Spa- Francorchamps circuit was originally a road course forming a triangle between Francorchamps, Malmédy and Stavelot. It held its first motorcycle race in 1921 and first car race in 1922. It has been modified many times since, settling roughly on its current layout in 1979 and was first used by F1 in 1983.
- The current track featuring a Bus Stop chicane and a new pit entry first appeared in 2007. On this version of the circuit the race has been won from pole five times and from no further back than sixth.
- Famously Jordan Grand Prix gave an F1 debut to a young Michael Schumacher at this race in 1991.

ITALY

2019 ITALIAN GRAND PRIX
6–8 September 2019

Hot on the heels of last weekend's Belgian Grand Prix, Formula One's teams and drivers return to action this weekend at one of the season's most storied circuits, high-speed Monza, home of the Italian Grand Prix.

The race has featured on every Formula One schedule since the Championship's first season in 1950 and all but one of those races have taken place at Monza—the last, true 'temple of speed' remaining in the sport.

The circuit's configuration of long straights and three fast curves broken by three chicanes rewards power, and with some seventy-five per cent of the lap run at full throttle teams with an advantage in this area traditionally thrive. Monza's layout also calls for teams to bring the lowest downforce packages used all season as they attempt to minimise drag.

Monza is not solely about speed, however. Setting up cars to deal with the challenge of high kerbs and to get good traction out of the few corners is also crucial to lap time. Despite the low number of corners, brake wear is also high at Monza, with each braking event occuring at high speeds. The paucity of corners means harvesting energy from the brakes can be challenging.

CIRCUIT DATA—AUTODROMO NAZIONALE MONZA
Length of lap: 5.793 km
Lap record: 1:21.046 (Rubens Barrichello, Ferrari, 2004)
Start line/finish line offset: 0.309 km
Total number of race laps: 53
Total race distance: 306.720 km
Pitlane speed limits: 80 km/h in practice, qualifying, and the race

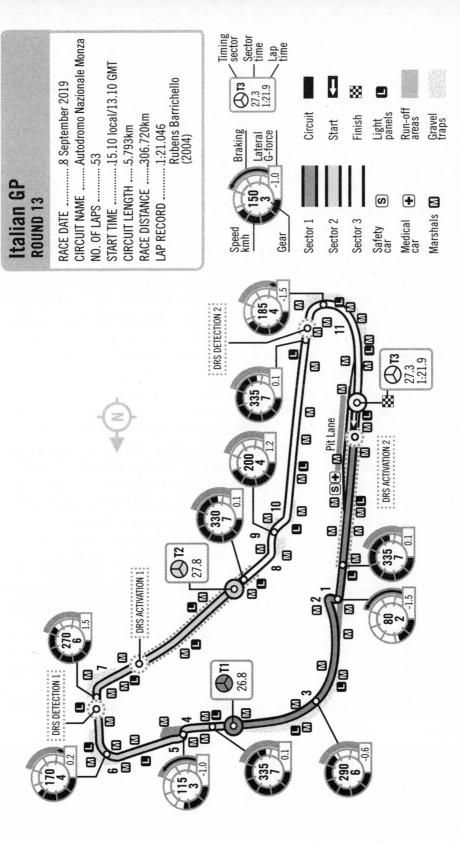

Italian GP
ROUND 13

RACE DATE ....8 September 2019
CIRCUIT NAME ....Autodromo Nazionale Monza
NO. OF LAPS 53
START TIME ....15.10 local/13.10 GMT
CIRCUIT LENGTH 5.793km
RACE DISTANCE 306.720km
LAP RECORD 1:21.046
Rubens Barrichello
(2004)

Speed kmh
Gear
Braking
Lateral G-force
150
3
-1.0

Sector 1
Sector 2
Sector 3
Safety car — S
Medical car — +
Marshals — M

Circuit
Start
Finish
Light panels
Run-off areas
Gravel traps

Timing sector
Sector time
Lap time
T3
27.3
1:21.9

N

DRS DETECTION 2

185
4
-1.5

335
7
0.1

200
4
1.2

330
7
0.1

T2
27.8

270
6
1.5

DRS DETECTION 1

DRS ACTIVATION 1

170
4
0.2

115
3
-1.0

335
7
0.1

290
6
-0.6

T1
26.8

80
2
-1.5

335
7
0.1

T3
27.3
1:21.9

Pit Lane

DRS ACTIVATION 2

CIRCUIT NOTES

- Double kerbs have been installed on the exit of Turn Six, Seven and Ten.

DRS ZONES

There will be two DRS zones in Italy. The detection point for the first zone will be 95 m before Turn Seven, with the activation point 210 m after Turn Seven. The second detection point will be 20 m before Turn 11, with the activation point 115 m after the finish line.

FAST FACTS

- This will be the seventieth Italian Grand Prix. The race has been ever-present the on calendar since the inaugural Formula One World Championship in 1950 and all but one Italian Grand Prix has been held at Monza. The race moved to Imola in 1980 while renovation work was carried at the circuit outside Milan.
- Michael Schumacher is the most successful driver at this event. The German has five wins to his name (1996, 1998,2000,2003,2006) and all were recorded at Monza. Nelson Piquet is next on the list with four wins. The Brazilian is the only driver to have taken an Italian GP win away from Monza, winning that sole Imola event for Brabham.
- Ferrari is the most successful team with eighteen victories. McLaren holds second place with ten wins, while Mercedes are third with seven victories.
- Seven drivers have taken their maiden Formula One win in Italy. Sebastian Vettel is the most recent, winning for Toro Rosso in 2008. The others are Juan Pablo Montoya (2001), Peter Gethin (1971), Clay Regazzoni (1970), Ludovico Scarfiotti (1966), Jackie Stewart (1965) and Phil Hill (1960).
- Just two manufacturers have landed a maiden win in Italy and curiously both outfits are Italian. Juan Manuel Fangio gave Maserati the first of nine F1 wins at Monza in 1953, while Vettel's win was the first and only win to date for Toro Rosso.

- This year makes the fifty-second anniversary of Honda's only Italian Grand Prix victory to date as a constructor. The team's 1967 win came courtesy of late F1 great John Surtee. At the wheel of the V12 powered RA 3000 car Surtees claimed the lead on the finish straight in a thrilling end to the race beating Jack Brabham by just two tenths of a second.

SINGAPORE

2019 SINGAPORE GRAND PRIX
20–22 September 2019

With the core European season complete, F1's teams and drivers this weekend head for South East Asia and into the night for Round Fifteen of the 2019 FIA Formula One World Championship, the Singapore Grand Prix.

Formula 1's original night race, which joined the calendar in 2008, presents F1's drivers and teams with a unique set of challenges, with the scheduled sixty-one laps under the lights of the Marina Bay Street Circuit being among the toughest faced all season.

For drivers, the major tests come in the shape of heat, humidity and the duration of the race. Here, cockpit temperatures often rise above 50°C making the race physically and mentally demanding. Add in a long, tight circuit featuring twenty-three corners and the high likelihood of safety car interventions, both of which often lead to the race edging towards or reaching the allotted two-hour for the race, and Singapore represents a true test of endurance.

For teams, the challenge centres on ensuring sufficient cooling. With few straights and with the boulevards of Marina Bay edged by tall buildings, keeping temperatures in check is a difficult task and teams will bring a variety of solutions to boost air flow to crucial components. The twenty-three corners also make the race tough on brakes and gearboxes.

With upwards of eighty gear changes per lap and brakes deployed more times than at any other circuit on the calendar, the Singapore Grand Prix stretches machinery to the limit.

CIRCUIT DATA—MARINA BAY STRET CIRCUIT
Length of lap: 5.063 km
Lap record: 1:41.905 (Kevin Magnussen, Haas, 2018)
Start line/finish line offset: 0.137 km
Total number of race laps: 61
Total race distance: 308.706 km

Singapore GP
ROUND 14

RACE DATE ....22 September 2019
CIRCUIT NAME ......Marina Bay Street Circuit
NO. OF LAPS..........61
START TIME ....20.10 local/12.10 GMT
CIRCUIT LENGTH ...5.063km
RACE DISTANCE......308.706km
LAP RECORD..........1-41.905 Kevin Magnussen (2018)

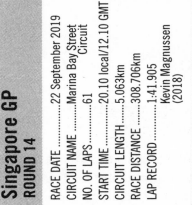

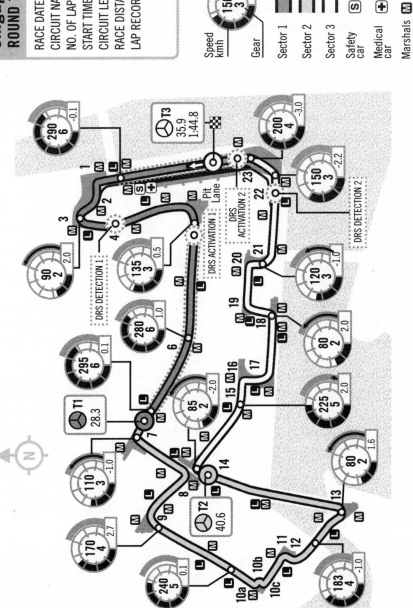

Pitlane speed limits: 60 km/h in practice, qualifying and the race

CIRCUIT NOTES
- The track has been resurfaced around Turn 1, between Turns 5 and 7, between Turns 15 and 17 and around Turn 23.
- The track has been slightly re-aligned around Turns 16 and 17. This means the track length is marginally reduced, from 5.065 km to 5.063 km

DRS ZONES
There will be two DRS zones in Singapore. The first detection point will be at the exit of Turn Four and the first activation point will be 53 m after Turn Five. The second detection point will be 180 m before the apex of Turn 22, and the activation point will be 48 m after apex of Turn 23.

FAST FACTS
- This is the twelfth running of the Singapore Grand Prix as a round of the FIA F1 World Championship. The race has been held every year since 2008, always at the Marina Bay Street Circuit.
- Sebastian Vettel and Lewis Hamilton are the most successful drivers at the Singapore Grand Prix with four wins each. The German scored a hat-trick of victories between 2011-2013 while racing for Red Bull Racing and also won for Ferrari in 2015. Lewis Hamilton's win here last year, allied to victories in 2009 with McLaren and 2014 and 2017 with Mercedes, while Fernando Alonso has two wins, with Renault in 2008 and with Ferrari in 2010.
- The only other winner at this race is Nico Rosberg, who won with Mercedes in 2015. Thus, every winner of the Singapore GP has a world title to his name.
- Mercedes are the most successful team here with four victories. Hamilton won in 2014, 2017 and 2018 and Rosberg in 2015.
- Only three drivers have taken part in all 11 F1 races held in Singapore to date: Hamilton, Vettel and Alonso. Of the

current drivers Kimi Raikkonen is next on the list with nine starts. The Finn raced the first two grands prix in Singapore but left F1 for two seasons, in 2010 and 2011.

- Despite this race being dominated by a small number of teams, none has managed a one-two finish in Singapore.
- Red Bull Racing lead the way, by quite some margin, in terms of podium finishes in Singapore. The Milton Keynes squad have scored twelve podiums in Singapore, more than double the total of closest rivals Ferrari and Mercedes who have six each. As well as Vettel's three wins, Red Bull Racing have six second places, (Vettel in 2010 and 2014, Daniel Ricciardo from 2015-'17, Max Verstappen in 2018) and three third places (Mark Webber in 2010 and 2011 and Ricciardo in 2014).
- The only drivers to win from a grid position other than pole are Alonso from fifteenth in 2008, Vettel from third on the grid in 2012 and Hamilton, who won in 2017 from a starting place of fifth.

RUSSIA

2019 RUSSIAN GRAND PRIX
27–29 September 2019

This week, teams and drivers head to the Sochi Autodrom for Round Sixteen of the 2019 FIA Formula One World Championship: the Russian Grand Prix.

After examining the opposing ends of the speed spectrum in Monza and Singapore, Sochi represents something of a return to the middle ground for F1. The key characteristic of the circuit is the proliferation of 90°, medium-speed corners. Despite several bumps appearing over the last couple of years, Sochi remains a smooth circuit and has relatively flat kerbs. This will encourage teams to run their cars very stiff, potentially raising rear ride-height to help with turn-in.

The straights in Sochi are relatively long, which raises questions regarding downforce levels. More downforce makes the car more predictable and easier to position accurately in the corners—but at the cost of lower speed on the straights.

Sochi has the reputation of being a circuit with extremely low tyre degradation.

CIRCUIT DATA—SOCHI AUTODROM
Length of lap: 5.848 km
Lap record: 1:35.861 (Valtteri Bottas, Mercedes, 2018)
Start line/finish line offset: 0.199 km
Total number of race laps: 53
Total race distance: 309.745 km
Pitlane speed limits: 60 km/h in practice, qualifying, and the race.

CIRCUIT NOTES
- The track has been resurfaced on the approach to Turns 1 and 8. A section of the pit entry has also been resurfaced.

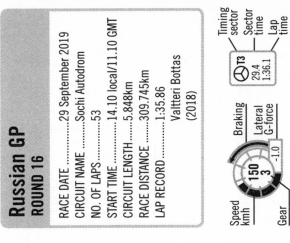

Russian GP
ROUND 16

RACE DATE ....29 September 2019
CIRCUIT NAME ....Sochi Autodrom
NO. OF LAPS 53
START TIME ....14.10 local/11.10 GMT
CIRCUIT LENGTH 5.848km
RACE DISTANCE 309.745km
LAP RECORD 1.35.86
Valtteri Bottas
(2018)

Timing sector
Sector time
Lap time

T3
29.4
1.36.1

Braking
Lateral G-force

Speed kmh
150
3
-1.0

Gear

Circuit

Start

Finish

Light panels

Run-off areas

Gravel traps

Sector 1

Sector 2

Sector 3

Safety car

Medical car

Marshals

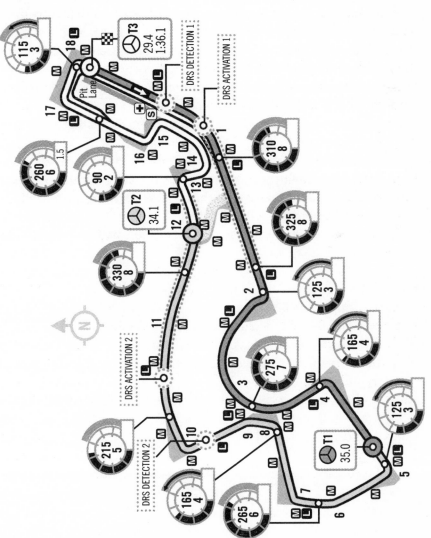

DRS ZONES
The first of two DRS zones has its detection point 72 m after Turn 18. Activation is 95 m before Turn 1. Zone Two's detection is 72 m before T10, with activation 203 m after the corner.

FAST FACTS
- This is the sixth FIA Formula One World Championship Russian Grand Prix. The race appeared on the calendar in 2014 and each race has been held at the Sochi Autodrom.
- Mercedes have a clean sweep of victories—albeit with three different drivers. Lewis Hamilton won the race in 2014, 2015 and 2018, Nico Rosberg took victory in 2016 and Valtteri Bottas won in 2017.
- Mercedes have taken four of the five pole positions in Russia to date. Hamilton was on pole for the inaugural event in 2014 and Rosberg had back-to-back poles in 2015 and 2016. Sebastian Vettel broke the chain in 2017 starting from P1 for Ferrari. Bottas was on pole in 2018. The race was won from pole position in 2014 and 2016, from second in 2015 and 2018 and from third on the grid in 2017.
- Ferrari have two of the five fastest laps at this circuit, thanks to Vettel in 2015 and Kimi Räikkönen in 2017. Bottas set the fastest lap at the inaugural race, driving for Williams, and Rosberg did so in 2016, as part of a dominant performance that saw him take pole, victory and fastest lap while leading every lap of the race. It was the first time Rosberg had achieved a so- called 'grand chelem', though he would do it again seven weeks later in Baku. His is the only such performance recorded in Sochi. Hamilton had the fastest lap in 2018.
- Hamilton's second place in 2016 came from P10 on the grid—the furthest back from which a driver finishing on the podium has started.
- Eight of the current field have contested every Russian Grand Prix: they are Bottas; Marcus Romain Grosjean; Hamilton; Nico Hülkenberg; Pérez; Räikkönen; Daniel Ricciardo and Vettel.

- Underlining the reputation of the Russian Grand Prix no two-stopper has finished higher than fifth.
- In 2014 and 2015, Mercedes secured the Constructors' Championship title in Russia. The race subsequently moved to an early-season slot.

JAPAN

2019 JAPANESE GRAND PRIX
11–13 October 2019

After a tense and intriguing battle by the Black Sea in Sochi, Formula 1 is back in action a fortnight later as teams and drivers head to legendary Suzuka for Round Seventeen of the 2019 FIA Formula One World Championship: the Japanese Grand Prix.

A favourite of fans and F1 personnel alike, Suzuka, which is this weekend celebrating hosting its thirty-first FIA Formula 1 race, is one of the sport's classics circuits, renowned for the exacting nature of its layout, which tests drivers and engineers in equal measure.

The figure-of-eight circuit features every kind of corner. From the precision required to perfectly thread a car through the first sector's intricate 'Esses', where balance is at a premium, to the risk and reward nature of the braking zones for the Degner curves, and making the most of the long high-G arc of the Spoon Curve and the flat out blast of 130R, stitching together a flawless lap of Suzuka is on the season's great challenges for drivers.

The circuit is no less taxing for teams and the fast and flowing nature of the layout—especially through sections such as the 'Esses', where rapid changes of direction put the accent on good balance—makes arriving at the perfect set-up a tricky task. Suzuka is also tough on tyres, with the many fast corners putting high lateral loads though the rubber. A fascinating battle awaits.

CIRCUIT DATA—SUZUKA INTERNATIONAL RACING COURSE
Length of lap: 5.807 km
Lap record: 1:31.540 (Kimi Räikkönen, McLaren, 2005)
Start line/finish line offset: 0.300 km
Total number of race laps: 53
Total race distance: 307.471 km
Pitlane speed limits: 80 km/h in practice, qualifying and the race

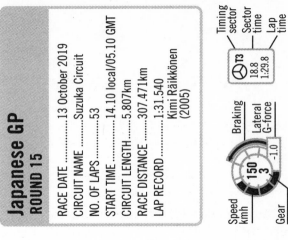

Japanese GP
ROUND 15

RACE DATE ....13 October 2019
CIRCUIT NAME ....Suzuka Circuit
NO. OF LAPS 53
START TIME ....14.10 local/05.10 GMT
CIRCUIT LENGTH ...5.807km
RACE DISTANCE 307.471km
LAP RECORD 1:31.540
                  Kimi Räikkönen
                  (2005)

Timing sector — T3

Sector time — 18.8
Lap time — 1:29.8

Speed kmh — 150
Gear — 3
Braking
Lateral G-force — -1.0

Sector 1
Sector 2
Sector 3

Circuit
Start
Finish
Light panels
Run-off areas
Gravel traps

S — Safety car
➕ — Medical car
Ⓜ — Marshals

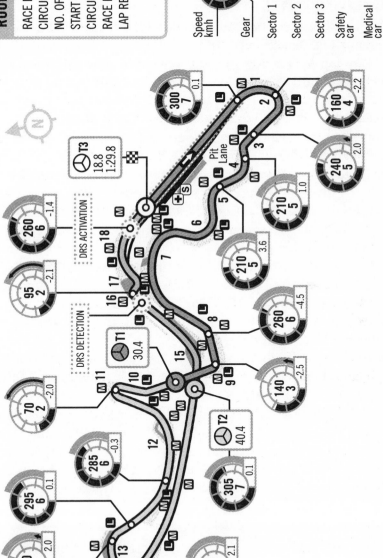

DRS ACTIVATION

DRS DETECTION

T3 — 18.8 / 1:29.8

T1 — 30.4

T2 — 40.4

Pit Lane

CIRCUIT NOTES

- New double kerbs have been installed on the exit of Turns 13 and 14.
- Tyres with tube inserts and additional conveyor belts have been installed in sections of the tyre barriers around the outside of Turns 2, 5, 7, 8 and 15.

DRS ZONES

There will be just one DRS zone at Suzuka located on the main straight. The detection point
is 50 m before Turn 16 and the activation point is 100 m before the control line.

FAST FACTS

- This is the thirty-fifth Japanese Grand Prix, and the thirty-first to take place at Suzuka. The race debuted at the Fuji Speedway in 1976 and hosted a second edition in 1977 before dropping off the schedule for a decade. The race returned in 1987 at Suzuka and save for a brief spell at Fuji in 2007 and 2008 it has been staged at the Mie prefecture circuit each year since.
- Michael Schumacher is the most successful driver at the Japanese Grand Prix with six victories winning for Benetton in 1995 and Ferrari in 1997, 2000, 2001, 2002 and 2004.
- McLaren are the most successful team at the Japanese Grand Prix with nine victories. Two of those victories are, however, at Fuji, James Hunt's 1977 win at the track being scored thirty years prior to Hamilton's. At Suzuka McLaren are tied with Ferrari on seven wins each.
- Michael Schumacher also holds the record for Japanese GP pole positions with eight. It's not only a Japan and Suzuka record but also a joint record for most poles for a driver at any grand prix. Schumacher shares the record with Ayrton Senna who was on pole eight times at the San Marino Grand Prix.
- Statistically, pole position is not crucial for victory at Suzuka. In its thirty grands prix to date, the man on pole position has won fifteen times. Second position on the grid has yielded victory eleven times. Only Räikkönen has won from

further back than sixth on the grid. He scored his 2005 victory from a starting place of P17.

• Alessandro Nannini is the only driver to take a maiden F1 win at the Japanese Grand Prix. However, five drivers have scored their maiden podium finish at this race: Roberto Moreno and Aguri Suzuki in 1990, Mika Häkkinen in 1993, Heikki Kovalainen in 2007 and Kamui Kobayashi in 2012. Only three Japanese drivers have scored podium finishes in F1: Suzuki and Kobayashi at their home race and Takuma Sato who finished third at the 2004 US GP.

• In all twenty Japanese drivers have made F1 appearances, with seventeen making grand prix starts. The most prolific is Ukyo Katayama who made ninety-four starts between his 1992 debut in South Africa and his final race, the 1997 European Grand Prix. Across those six seasons he scored five points, finishing fifth at the Brazilian and San Marino races in 1994 and sixth at the British Grand Prix in the same year.

MEXICO

2019 MEXICAN GRAND PRIX
25–27 October 2019

The FIA Formula One World Championship this week arrives in the Americas, with Round Nineteen taking place at Mexico City's Autódromo Hermanos Rodríguez, home of the Mexican Grand Prix.

Situated almost 2,300 m above sea level, the circuit is F1's highest altitude track, some 1,500 m higher than the next on the list, Brazil's Interlagos, and this presents a particular set of challenges. At this altitude the thinner air leads to lower levels of downforce and thus teams are able to bring higher downforce packages to this high-speed circuit where normally the opposite might be the case. There's less oxygen going to the engine, too, although the negative impact of this on ICE performance is mitigated by the effect of turbo. However, in order to create the necessary pressure the turbo has to spin faster, and thus this race is particularly demanding on that element of the power unit. A slippery and smooth track surface lead to low rates of tyre wear and degradation.

CIRCUIT DATA—AUTÓDROMO HERMANOS RODRÍGUEZ
Length of lap: 4.304 km
Lap record: 1:18.741 (Valtori Bottas, Mercedes, 2018)
Start line/finish line offset: 0.230 km
Total number of race laps: 71
Total race distance: 305.354 km
Pitlane speed limits: 80 km/h in practice, qualifying and the race

CIRCUIT NOTES
• Other than routine maintenance no changes of significance have been made.

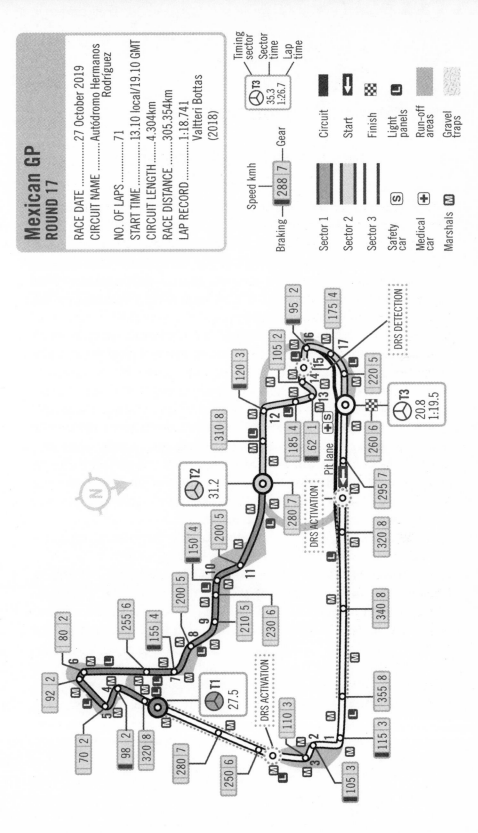

Mexican GP
ROUND 17

RACE DATE ....27 October 2019
CIRCUIT NAME ....Autódromo Hermanos
                                      Rodríguez
NO. OF LAPS........................71
START TIME.............13.10 local/19.10 GMT
CIRCUIT LENGTH.........4.304km
RACE DISTANCE.........305.354km
LAP RECORD..............1:18.741
                                      Valtteri Bottas
                                      (2018)

Timing sector
Sector time
Lap time

T3
35.3
1:26.7

Speed kmh
288 7
Braking — Gear

Sector 1
Sector 2
Sector 3

Circuit
Start
Finish
Light panels
Run-off areas
Gravel traps

S Safety car
✛ Medical car
M Marshals

DRS ZONES

There will be two DRS zones in Mexico, sharing a detection point, located at the exit of Turn 15. The first activation point will be 323 m after Turn 17 and the second will be 116 m after Turn 3.

FAST FACTS

- This will be the twentieth World Championship Mexican Grand Prix. The race has been part of the F1 calendar in three distinct phases: from 1963-1970; from 1986- 1992, while this latest iteration of the race joined the schedule in 2015. All of the races have taken place at the circuit that began life as the Magdalena Mixhuca circuit and was later re-christened the Autódromo Hermanos Rodríguez.

- The current layout has seen three different winners since the race's 2015 return. Nico Rosberg won the inaugural event on the new circuit in 2015, Lewis Hamilton was victorious in 2016 and Max Verstappen won in 2017 and last year.

- Lotus, McLaren and Williams are tied as most successful constructor at the Mexican Grand Prix, with three wins each. Lotus' victories were scored in 1963 and 1967 with Clark and in 1968 with Graham Hill. McLaren won in 1969 with Denny Hulme, in 1988 with Alain Prost and in 1989 with Aytron Senna. Williams won twice with Nigel Mansell, in 1987 and 1992 and also in 1991 with Patrese.

- As with victory, pole position at the latest version of the Autódromo Hermanos Rodríguez has been taken by a different driver at each of the four events held so far. Nico Rosberg won from pole in 2015, as did Hamilton in 2016. Sebastian Vettel began the 2017 race from pole but finished in fourth place. Daniel Ricciardo failed to finish after taking pole last year.

- Five drivers on the current grid have been classified in the top three here: Hamilton, Ricciardo, Räikkönen, Verstappen and Valtteri Bottas.

USA

2019 UNITED STATES GRAND PRIX
1–3 November

Formula One teams and drivers head to Austin, Texas this weekend and the Circuit of the Americas—home of the 2019 FIA F1 United States Grand Prix.

Despite being a relatively new addition to the F1 calendar, with the circuit making its debut in 2012, COTA has already made a name for itself as a track capable of showing off F1 cars at their best. It features a first sector with high-speed changes of direction but with a balanced layout. The whole of the second half of the lap at COTA is built around a serious of medium and low-speed corners. It is this characteristic that prompts tyre supplier Pirelli to move to softer tyres for the US Grand Prix.

While COTA has a predominantly smooth surface, in the last few years the track has settled and now features several prominent bumps, some of which are located in braking zones and have the ability to unsettle a car. This gives engineers and drivers something to ponder: the softer their car, the easier it will ride the bumps, but at the cost of lost performance through the corners. The circuit has attempted to grind down some of the undulations, and in doing so last year produced some interesting variations in the grip level.

CIRCUIT DATA—CIRCUIT OF THE AMERICAS
Length of lap: 5.513 km
Lap record: 1:37.392 (Lewis Hamilton, Mercedes, 2018)
Start line/finish line offset: 0.323 km
Total number of race laps: 56
Total race distance: 308.405 m
Pitlane speed limits: 80 km/h in practice, qualifying and the race

United States GP
ROUND 17

RACE DATE ....3 November 2019
CIRCUIT NAME ....Circuit of the Americas
NO. OF LAPS...........56
START TIME ....13.10 local/18.10 GMT
CIRCUIT LENGTH......5.513km
RACE DISTANCE 308.405km
LAP RECORD...........1:37.392
Lewis Hamilton
(2018)

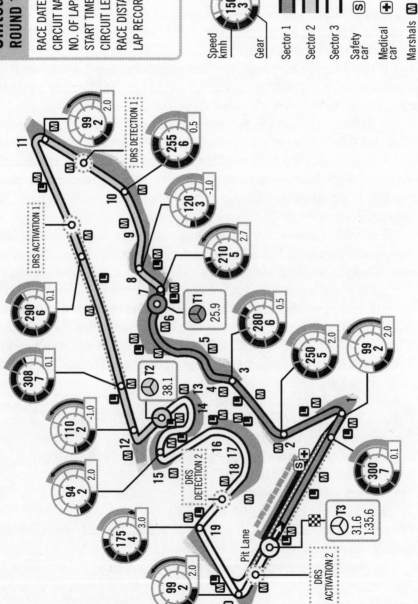

CIRCUIT NOTES
- Three bumps similar to those on the exit of Turns 11, 15 and 19 have been installed behind the exit kerb at Turn 1.
- Kerbs 2 m long, 1 m wide and 50 mm high have been installed behind the apex kerbs in Turns 16 and 17.

DRS ZONES
There will be two zones at COTA. The detection point of the first will be 150 m after Turn 10, with the activation point 250 m after Turn 11. The second zone's detection point will be 65 m after Turn 18, with the activation point 80 m after Turn 20, on the start/ finish straight.

FAST FACTS
- This is the forty-first FIA Formula One United States Grand Prix. The race debuted in 1959 at Sebring. It has subsequently been held at Riverside (1960), Watkins Glen (1961-80), Phoenix (1989-91) and Indianapolis (2000-2007). This is the eighth consecutive running at the purpose-built Circuit of the Americas.
- The USA has also hosted other grands prix. The US Grand Prix West ran at Long Beach between 1976-1983, The Caesars Palace Grand Prix (1981-82) was held in Las Vegas; the Detroit Grand Prix ran between 1982 and 1988, and Dallas hosted a one-off grand prix in 1984. Between 1950 and 1960 the Indianapolis 500 was also officially included as a round in the Formula One World Championship.
- See the comprehensive section earlier in the book on F1 in the US for more details.
- Ferrari are the most successful team at the US Grand Prix, scoring their nine wins at Watkins Glen in 1975, 1978 and 1979, and at Indianapolis in 2000, 2002-2006.
- Lewis Hamilton is the most successful driver at the US Grand Prix. He is also the only driver to win the race at more than one venue. He has a victory at Indianapolis, in 2007 with McLaren, and has won five of the six races held at COTA to date, once with McLaren in 2012 and with Mercedes from 2014 to 2017.

- Three titles have been decided at COTA. Red Bull Racing secured the Constructors' Championship at this track in 2012, when it hosted the penultimate round of the season, and Mercedes took the Constructors' Championship in 2017 at the seventeenth round of twenty. Lewis Hamilton became a three-times Drivers' World Champion here in 2015.
- The US Grand Prix has often been an end-of-season race, and thus it has been the venue for many other championship deciders. The Constructors' Championship was settled at Watkins Glen on five occasions, in favour of Brabham (1966), Lotus (1970, 1973), McLaren (1974) and Ferrari (1976). The Drivers' title has previously been won at Sebring by Jack Brabham (1959) and at Watkins Glen by Jochen Rindt (1970—posthumously), Emerson Fittipaldi (1974) and Niki Lauda (1977).

BRAZIL

2019 BRAZILIAN GRAND PRIX
15–17 November 2019

Formula One this weekend moves from North to South America for Round Twenty of the 2019 FIA Formula One World Championship, the Brazilian Grand Prix. And the penultimate event of this campaign takes place at one of the sport's most venerable circuits, the Autódromo José Carlos Pace in Interlagos, São Paulo.

The Interlagos circuit made its calendar debut in 1973 and has been a fixture on the schedule since 1990, making it the eighth most visited venue in the history of the sport. And despite the current 4.309 km layout being the second shortest by length after Monaco, Interlagos remains a testing venue for drivers and teams. São Paulo's circuit is at altitude, though at only 800 m compared with Mexico's 2,200 m the effects are less pronounced. Nonetheless, there is a reduction in downforce and turbos will work harder in the thinner air. The steep rise and fall—for example, the 40 m incline from Turn 12, Junção, to the braking point at Turn 1—means it's tougher on combustion engines than many other circuits.

Arriving at the perfect set-up can be tricky as teams needs to balance a desire for high levels of downforce in the tight and twisting infield section against the need to minimise drag on the straight between Turns 3, the Curva de Sol, and Turn 4, Descida do Lago and especially on the long sweep from Turn 12 to Turn 1.

The Brazilian GP can be unpredictable largely thanks to the often inclement weather and the weekend can spring many surprises.

CIRCUIT DATA—AUTÓDROMO JOSÉ CARLOS PACE
Length of lap: 4.309 km
Lap record: 1:11.540 (Valtori Bottas, Mercedes, 2018)
Start line/finish line offset: 0.030 km
Total number of race laps: 71

Brazilian GP
ROUND 19

RACE DATE .... 17 November 2019
CIRCUIT NAME ...... Autodromo Jose Carlos Pace
NO. OF LAPS 71
START TIME .... 15.10 local/17.10 GMT
CIRCUIT LENGTH 4.309km
RACE DISTANCE 305.879km
LAP RECORD .... 1:11.540 Valtteri Bottas (2018)

Timing sector
Sector time
Lap time

T3
17.4
1:12.3

Braking
Lateral G-force

Speed kmh
150
3
-1.0

Gear

Circuit	
Start	
Finish	
Light panels	L

Sector 1
Sector 2
Sector 3

Safety car — S
Medical car — ✚
Marshals — M

Run-off areas
Gravel traps

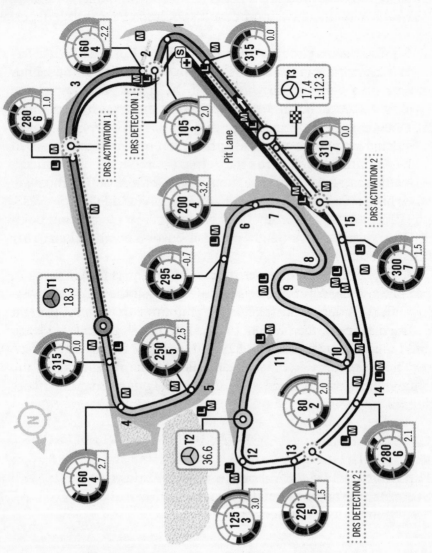

Total race distance: 305.879 km
Pitlane speed limits: 80 km/h in practice, qualifying and the race

CIRCUIT NOTES
- There is a new double kerb on the exit of Turn 4.

DRS ZONE
There are two DRS zones in Interlagos. The first has a detection zone point at the apex of Turn Two, with activation 30 m after Turn Three. The second zone has its detection point 30 m after Turn 13, with an activation point 160 m before Turn 15.

FAST FACTS
- This is the forty-seventh Brazilian Grand Prix. The race has been on the F1 calendar annually since 1973. After five events in São Paulo, the race moved to Rio's Jacarepaguá circuit in 1978, returned to Interlagos in 1979 and 1980 before moving to Rio between 1981-1989. The event returned to Interlagos in 1990 and has been here since.
- Alain Prost is the most successful driver at The Brazilian Grand Prix with six wins (1982, 1984, 1985, 1987, 1988, 1990). All but the last of Prost's wins were scored at Jacarepaguá. The most successful driver at Interlagos is Michael Schumacher with four wins at the São Paulo track.
- McLaren are the most successful team with twelve wins. Ferrari are next on the list with eleven victories.
- Five drivers have visited the podium for the first time in Brazil: Jochen Mass (P3, 1975); Elio de Angelis (P2, 1980); Mauricio Gugelmin (P3, 1989); Damon Hill (P2, 1993), and Nick Heidfeld (P3, 2001). Heidfeld's 2001 podium was the beginning of his march to an F1 record he undoubtedly wishes that he never held—that of driver with the most podium finishes without a win. Heidfeld has thirteen.
- Nico Hulkenberg landed the only pole position of his career to date at Interlagos in 2010. Only two other drivers have secured a maiden pole position at the Brazilian GP: Ronnie Peterson (1973), and James Hunt 1976.

ABU DHABI

2019 ABU DHABI GRAND PRIX
29 November–1 December 2019

Round Twenty-one of the 2019 FIA Formula One World Championship takes place this weekend at the Yas Marina Circuit, home of the Abu Dhabi Grand Prix. This is the final destination of a season that began on 17 March in Melbourne.

F1's only day/night race, the Abu Dhabi Grand Prix has established itself as a popular end-of-season destination and, also a favoured testing venue, regularly hosting a post-season test. This is partially because the facilities are excellent but also because the circuit offers a variety of challenges that test every aspect of car performance.

The three sectors of the lap are quite different: the first features high speed turns, the second has long straights, while the final sector around the marina is low-speed and highly technical. The cars also experience heavy braking demands but also need good traction out of the low-speed corners, tight chicanes and hairpin.

As is the case with the night race in Bahrain, the first and third practice sessions take place in full daylight. Their usefulness in preparing for twilight qualifying and a twilight race is limited, as track temperature changes fundamentally alter the car balance. Thus, much greater emphasis is placed on FP2, which shares a start time of 17.00—half an hour before sunset—with both qualifying and the race.

CIRCUIT DATA—YAS MARINA CIRCUIT
Length of lap: 5.554 km
Lap record: 1:40.279 (Sebastian Vettel, Red Bull Racing, 2009)
Start line/finish line offset: 0.115 km
Total number of race laps: 55
Total race distance: 305.355 km
Pitlane speed limits: 80 km/h in practice, qualifying and the race

Abu Dhabi GP
ROUND 20

RACE DATE ....1 December 2019
CIRCUIT NAME ....Yas Marina Circuit
NO. OF LAPS 55
START TIME ....17.00 local/13.00 GMT
CIRCUIT LENGTH......5.554km
RACE DISTANCE 305.355km
LAP RECORD 1.40.279
Sebastian Vettel (2009)

Timing sector
Sector time
Lap time

Braking
Speed kmh
Lateral G-force
Gear

Circuit
Start
Finish
Light panels
Run-off areas
Gravel traps

Sector 1
Sector 2
Sector 3
Safety car S
Medical car
Marshals M

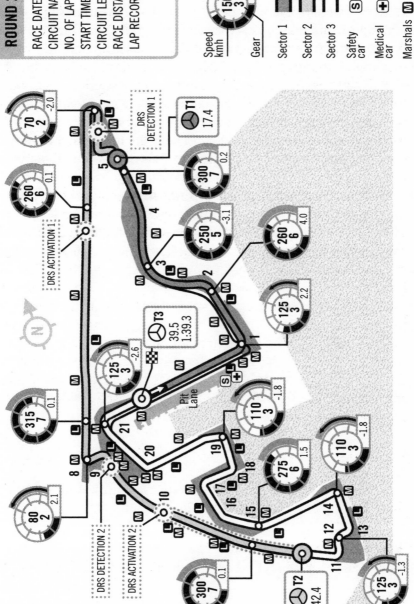

CIRCUIT NOTES
- Additional TecPro has been installed in parts of the barriers at turns 8 and 21.

DRS ZONES

There will be two DRS zones at Yas Marina. The first detection point will be 40 m before Turn 7, with the activation point 390 m after Turn 7. The second detection point will be 50 m after Turn 9 with the activation point at the apex of Turn 10.

FAST FACTS
- This is the tenth Abu Dhabi Grand Prix. It first appeared on the calendar in 2009 and has been a fixture ever since.
- Hamilton is the only driver to have the distinction of winning the race for two constructors taking his first Abu Dhabi victory for McLaren and his latest with Mercedes.
- The Abu Dhabi Grand Prix has always been held in November apart from this year's race weekend where it begins on 29 November with the race being held for the first time on December 1st. It has hosted the season finale six times.

TECHNICAL

AERODYNAMICS OF FORMULA ONE

In strange structures far from the racetrack, seemingly endless hours and excessive amounts of budget are spent in the pursuit of marginal gains. Aerodynamicists search for minute ways to maximize the amount of downforce created while minimizing the amount of drag produced to obtain the maximum results from the aerodynamics of the car. From inside Formula One, Willem Toet, former Head of Aerodynamic at the Sauber F1 Team explains how the work done in wind tunnels and in CFD (Computational Fluid Dynamics) can improve track lap times.

Why is so much money and energy spent looking at the shapes of Formula 1 (F1) cars? Fundamentally because it pays dividends. If you can reduce the drag of the car you will go faster on the straights. If you can use the shape of the car to generate some downward pressure (usually called downforce) onto the tyres, then the car will go faster around the corners. Research into aerodynamics has allowed cornering speeds in "high speed" corners to be much higher than that which is possible without the use of aerodynamic aids, although it has reduced ultimate top speeds. Track lap times have improved significantly.

The aerodynamics of racecars is intensely researched and 5–10 per cent downforce increases have been possible if rules do not change too much between seasons. Due to the nature of the vehicles, the aerodynamics of F1 cars are quite different to that of road cars—with drag coefficients of between 0.7 and 1.0 (it used to be even higher but rules restrict how much area can be used for aerodynamic devices)—this is between about two and four times as much as a good modern road car. This is partly due to the rules (running exposed wheels is part of the definition of an open-wheeled racing car) and partly because downforce is usually much more important than drag.

Aerodynamic research in F1 has been an area of high investment in the past thirty years. Assuming no regulatory limitations, this trend would continue while the bodywork rules are changed continually or while changes to the shape of the cars continue to provide significant improvements in lap time around the F1 circuits of the world. However, agreements between teams started to limit investment and now rules have been introduced officially to limit how much research is done into aerodynamics in wind tunnels and in CFD (Computational Fluid Dynamics). Naturally teams will optimize their resources to still obtain the maximum they can from the aerodynamics of the cars.

To investigate the aerodynamics of an F1 car the teams use various methods of research. Tests are conducted using scale models of the cars in a wind tunnel fitted with a "rolling road". Computers are used to mathematically simulate the flow of air around and through the cars and to model vehicle behaviour on the track. In the past, the real cars used to be tested as well in wind tunnels and on special straight-line test facilities, but this is now banned. Cars are tested on the real tracks of course, but that too is limited to fewer test days than was possible in the past. Each of the top ten F1 teams has somewhere between fifty and 150 people working solely on aerodynamic research. It is quite difficult to be sure about how many people work on aerodynamics as generally the teams do not talk about it. Despite the limits on track testing and on aerodynamic research that have been imposed by the rule makers (the FIA) and by agreements between the teams, the amount of research done is "significant". Even a "small" team of fifty people can do a lot of work!

Teams use computer simulation more and more to predict performance and to analyze many "what if?" scenarios. These simulations are then constantly improved by comparing them to the realities of racing and testing. From these tools we know that the drag of the cars does slow them down quite a lot but typically, on an average racetrack, it slows them by about 3–5 per cent in lap time. In other words, if drag were to be reduced to zero, the gain in lap time at a typical track would normally be a bit less than 5 per cent. However, if we remove the present levels of downforce then lap times get slower by about 25 per cent or so.

In the present F1 environment, other performance factors that are normally very important have been limited more severely, for example the tyres are all provided by a single supplier and are carefully randomly selected for the teams by the rule makers and tyre supplier together so there is no chance of one team getting an advantage.

In the five years to 2014 engine specifications were, effectively, frozen. For 2014 there was a completely new powertrain formula but the idea is that these powertrains will also be virtually frozen once a reasonable level of parity is established. Cars must race above a certain minimum weight (to protect against dangerous construction as low weight helps lap time). Suspension kinematics is relatively free so this is an area where the teams can make a difference, but suspension must be passive. However, because aerodynamics is so dominant, even this is compromised to ensure aerodynamics benefits are maximized.

The wind tunnel models used for testing are either 50 per cent or 60 per cent (60 per cent upper limit in F1) of full scale and are tested up to sixty hours per week. In the past the tunnels were used twenty-four hours per day, seven days per week and some teams had more than one wind tunnel working, but rules now limit that. The floor of the wind tunnel is replaced with a "rolling road" (a fancy name for conveyor belt) and a boundary layer removal system (that removes the slow-moving air that builds up on a stationary surface) to simulate the fact that the car rolls over the ground.

These rolling roads and boundary layer control systems are essential for racing car work and are a science in themselves. Most teams test their models at 50 m/s (=180 km/h), which is the highest speed the teams are permitted to use by the regulations (more was possible in a few facilities which is why the limit was imposed. The Sauber wind tunnel is one of the best in F1, capable of testing full-scale cars on a rolling road at speeds up to 300 km/h.). To approach a realistic representation of the aerodynamics on a real (full-scale) car, it is best to test a large model as fast as possible, allowing for all the difficulties involved.

All simulation methods, whether computer or wind-tunnel testing, have their strengths and their limitations. One way that teams can make a difference to performance is through the understanding of these factors and the methods employed to take advantage of the strengths and to cover the weaknesses of each type of simulation. The other way is through the quality and/or volume of testing the teams do. Real-car track testing is a vital part of this process but is too slow, imprecise and expensive a method to be the only sort of testing a team should undertake. The variations in temperature, wind, track condition, tyres, driver input variations, and so forth is why track testing is not as precise as testing in a controlled environment. It is, though, the most important reality we try to simulate. Track testing is also limited by regulation so the teams experiment with new parts mainly on Friday practice sessions at a Grand Prix weekend.

The highest proportion of aerodynamic research money and energy is spent by most teams on the wind-tunnel testing of scale models of the car. The models are not usually constructed in the same way or using the same materials as a real car. They are designed to simulate both the internal and external shape of the cars while enabling the teams to change the design of the model shape more simply than would be possible on a miniature replica of the real car. An average example might be a 50 per cent scale model of the car using a wind speed of 50 m/s (=180 km/h). The model is usually suspended from the roof of the tunnel and is packed full of motors, load cells, pressure-measuring equipment, computers and other electronics. Sometimes wheels are not attached directly to the model but are held in place via mounts from outside the model. This has been found to give better overall repeatability of force measurement.

However, wheels-on-model is more accurate and is more commonly used. The teams routinely conduct tests over a range of ride heights and pitches (differences in front and rear height to the ground) while assessing model (as well as wheel) forces and scanning pressures. The effects of exhaust gas, roll, yaw and steer are conducted regularly as well. Graphical or tabulated results are displayed on monitors during the tests and the final result is seen shortly after the last measurements are taken. Every team is different so this is only a guide. High-speed dynamic movement of the models has been tried by some ambitious teams but the mechanical forces involved are so high that this has not proven to be a reliable development method. However, there has been a strong trend toward continuous motion of the model in the tunnel (a sort of slow-motion Grand Prix simulation).

Mathematical modelling and computational fluid dynamics (CFD) are the areas of the most rapid growth in effort in racing car aerodynamics at the moment. Computers are used to back up real-car and rig testing of things like water and oil cooling, assessing what level of drag and downforce will give the best lap time at a particular track in any given conditions, etc. In-house circuit simulation and lap-time prediction programs are used to assess the effect of aerodynamic gains (as well as engine power, gear ratios, gear-change time, weight, centre of gravity height, cooling, mechanical set-up, etc.) on lap time. Driver simulators take this world of simulation yet another step closer to the reality of a car on track.

CFD is coming into its own as far as racing car aerodynamics are concerned. Modern super computers allow the use of mathematical models that mean complete and reasonably realistic full-vehicle aerodynamic simulations are now possible, if a little slow. The teams have now mainly settled on a CFD method called Navier Stokes which copes well with the realities of racing cars. Some teams are combining the use of commercially available packages with in-house computer programs/enhancements to maximise the gains that can be made using the computers. It will be some time before it is possible to dispense with wind tunnel testing because wind tunnels allow us to very quickly test hundreds of combinations of conditions and vehicle attitudes.

Both wind-tunnel testing and CFD are now limited by the FIA in its Sporting Regulations. In the wind tunnel, teams are limited by wind-on time (about fifteen hours per week) plus a maximum of eighty runs per week and sixty hours per week tunnel occupancy. CFD simulations are limited to a certain number of teraflops of solver time. Together, wind-on time and teraflops are limited to thirty units in total so, if we use fifteen hours of "wind on" time per week, we can use fifteen teraflops of computer power to solve CFD cases.

All the methods of improving car aerodynamics have their limitations. Testing everything you want to try on a real car is very expensive (engines, tyres, travel to the test tracks, personnel, etc) and has limited precision—plus this sort of activity is strictly limited. Atmospheric, track, tyre and driving changes, for example, mean that small (aerodynamic) steps cannot be reliably assessed. Wind tunnel model testing works reasonably well in a straight line but realistic tyre shape changes at the contact patch are difficult to match to reality and important to aerodynamics. Of course more aerodynamic downforce is only really needed when the driver is not able to drive at full throttle, such as when accelerating at low speed, cornering or braking. To simulate cornering in a wind tunnel is simply not practical as a racing car on the limit of adhesion is sliding all the time and the angle that the air approaches the front and the rear of the car is not the same. It is possible to steer the wheels of the model and to yaw the model.

Of course any limitation irritates engineers, so improvements are constantly sought and we get ever closer to being able to simulate real cornering. The more realistic the simulation of the tyre deformation, the more likely that the model tyres will wear out and this can restrict what a team can achieve because model tyres (also supplied by Pirelli) are restricted to twelve sets per year. While real-cornering simulation is not quite there yet for wind tunnel testing, these sorts of cases are at least theoretically possible using CFD. However, assessing sensitivity of forces to ride height, pitch, roll, yaw, steer and sliding through a corner are significantly slower than in a wind tunnel.

Generally, the approach taken today is to evolve from a baseline using wind tunnel testing and CFD, with most (but not all) CFD results checked in the wind tunnel, and then to make an update for the real car. This update is then tested on the real car to ensure that there are actually benefits. By conducting thousands of tests in the wind tunnel and using CFD for every real-car update, the aerodynamic step is usually large enough that the improvement is obvious to the drivers and quickly seen as an improvement in lap time. Should an update fail to impress, it is back to the drawing board for the Aerodynamicists to try to understand why. It is for reasons of updates to the car not performing particularly well and research into why this happened that some teams test in the wind tunnel in a yawed and steered condition (for example). Furthermore, it will continue to be the main driving force behind future improvements in the simulation techniques that the teams use.

Much of what the teams do is limited by the (bodywork) rules that govern the sport. It is because of the rules that there are flat-stepped floors on race cars with no car-to-ground bridging devices, the teams run exposed rather that covered wheels, have an open cockpit of certain minimum dimensions and virtually none of the wings or aerodynamic devices is movable or even flexible. Driver-controlled rear wing movement (upper element only, DRS) is allowed with extremely strict limitations and limited driver-initiated deployment under control of the rule makers. No material (even solid steel) is infinitely rigid and most teams have experimented with the limits of flexibility of the so-called rigid aerodynamic devices. As a result, the rule makers regularly adapt and refine specific flexibility limitations where they add a load to certain parts of the car and measure the deflection, which must be less than a rule-dictated limit. Suspension (mainly) parts cannot be wing-shaped and have to be of neutral section, i.e. the same top and bottom shapes, and have to be fitted "horizontally" with a tolerance of ± 5 degrees (more than enough to be able to play with). Rules also govern overhangs, heights, widths, etc. Despite the limitations of the rules, teams are able to work in many areas and continually increase the downforce without increasing the drag. Much of the work done now involves the understanding of airflow in three dimensions and it is mainly as understanding improves that aerodynamic efficiency of the cars is increased. It really is not possible to work on one part of the car in isolation (at least not for long) as everything interacts.

Many of the technical regulations change from time to time for reasons of safety. For example, there are tests for front impact, rear impact, side impact, top crush, floor (fuel cell) puncture— none of which may damage the chassis of the car. The cockpit must be a certain minimum dimension and shape, with energy-absorbing foam around the driver's head, shoulders and legs, and a driver's seat that can be removed from the car with the driver still seated in it. These safety regulations obviously influence what the teams can do aerodynamically speaking with the shape of the car.

Most of the ideas received by various teams from untrained enthusiasts are either illegal or more relevant to supersonic flow (which works more in line with untrained ideas of flow geometry) than to the subsonic flow on racing cars. It is, for example, not intuitive to people without aerodynamic training that there is more likely to be separation around a wing (a stall) at low speed (70 km/h, say) than at high speed (250 km/h). The other most common idea presented to reduce drag is the use of a dimpled or rough surface, via a "golf-ball" or shark skin effect. This and many other surface-finish treatments have been tried by most teams and found to be of no or, at best, little benefit. This is partly because skin friction only changes the drag of a Formula 1 car a very small amount (it is a much bigger deal for aircraft, for example). Research into surface treatments and micro-vortex generators continues.

Racing car wings are installed "upside down" compared to aircraft wings. This means that, on a racing car, the more curved or convex surface faces downward and rearward, while the flatter or sometimes concave surface faces upwards or forwards. On racing cars, it is the underside of the wing which is relatively more important than the top surface. Wings work because of air speed differences (caused by the shape of the wing) which in turn cause pressure differences—the faster the local flow caused by the shape of the wing, the lower the pressure and vice-versa. Wings working in "ground effect", that is wings reasonably close to the ground, are in general more effective (produce more downforce) than those a long way from the ground. Increasing the angle of the wing slows down the air on top of the wing and thus increases its static (surface) pressure, while speeding up the air under the wing leading edge decreases the static pressure there. The mid part of the front wing is a fixed neutral section dictated by regulation. There is no limit to the angle of attack of the rest of the front wings as such other than aerodynamic stall but the rules limit wing position (the wing has to fit into a number of boxes or zones). The optimum front wing design is mainly dictated by the influence the front wing then has on the flow to the underbody of the car and the rear wings. Despite the regulations, the front wing still contributes a high proportion of the downforce of the car. For performance reasons all the front wing shapes are three-dimensional in that the shape is different inboard to outboard.

The aerodynamic set-up of a modern F1 racing car is unlikely to be the same at any two races in a year. Aerodynamic settings (such as the front and rear wings) and hence the drag of the car are optimized to suit individual circuits. In addition, different brake ducts (for circuits where brakes are used more or less than an "average" circuit) and engine cooling exit ducts are fitted. Then, as a result of aerodynamic research, regular aerodynamic updates are made that change some feature of the car. These might be wings or body parts with a totally new shape. There are of course other settings and updates (for example suspension settings and suspension parts, electronics, engine, etc.), that are not directly aerodynamic, that ensure that the car is certainly never raced twice in the same configuration.

The downforce produced by the cars aerodynamically makes a big difference to grip. In a high-downforce configuration the cars produce their own weight (including driver) in aerodynamic download by around 36 m/s (=129 km/h or 80 mph). This means that if, at that speed, you were upside down on the roof of a theoretical "tunnel" you would stay there. In truth, in order to maintain control over the vehicle you would need enough grip to steer the car and to apply enough power to overcome the very high drag of the car. So you would really have to go at about 45 m/s (=162 km/h or 100 mph) to drive one of our cars upside down in a straight line.

BRAKES

IT'S ALL ABOUT HOW FAST YOU CAN SLOW DOWN

Formula One brake discs glow red hot at temperatures up to 1200°C and drivers experience forces in excess of 5.5g when decelarating into corners. In a full Formula One season, teams will go through up to ten sets of calipers (i.e. 4 x 10 components), from 140 to 240 brake discs and from 280 to 480 brake pads.

Exceptional progress has characterized the last ten years of Formula One racing, confirming its role as the most technologically advanced test bench on the planet. This is true not only for the engineers and the leading manufacturers but also for producers of components like braking specialists Brembo.

From 2008 to 2018, the braking systems were at the core of developments and increases in performance were of remarkable dimensions. Improvements have also influenced the way drivers brake which is decidedly different with respect to ten years ago.

Today's single-seaters are clearly very different from those of 2008 and the changed braking behavior cannot and should not be attributed solely to the brakes. The race cars have different weight distributions and aerodynamic loads but even more importantly their tyres are wider (and the tyre manufacturer is different). All of these factors play a significant role in differentiating braking performance.

Similarly, the evolution of the Brembo braking systems has seen enormous change over the last ten years. To demonstrate this, we have compared all of the braking data for the single-seaters in the 2008 Canadian GP and the 2018 Canadian Grand Prix.

STOPPING DISTANCE: -22%

The most surprising data stems from a comparison between the two Grand Prix races regarding the stopping distance which went down by a full 22.2%. In 2008, braking at Circuit Gilles Villeneuve required on average 371 feet; this year, 289 feet were enough. Naturally, we are talking about an average since data varies significantly even though the trend is the same. On the second to the last corner, the one that leads to the Wall of Champions, this year the single-seaters traveled 322 feet while braking and ten years ago, at the same spot, they needed 384 feet to brake.

BRAKING TIME: -15%
Although noteworthy, the reduction in braking time did not experience the same dramatic decrease as the stopping distance. From 2008 to 2018 in Montreal, the time spent braking per lap went down by a few seconds, a figure equivalent to a 15.5% reduction.

This may seem minimal, but to demonstrate its importance, we have provided this statistic: ten years ago, on three of the corners of the Canadian circuit, the drivers used their brakes for more than two seconds and on one of these turns, they did so for a good three seconds. This year, the most time spent braking was 2.44 sformer econds at turn ten and 2.00 seconds at turn thirteen.

LOAD ON THE BRAKE PEDAL: +4%
While the braking distance went down by 22%, the time spent braking decreased by 'only' 15% for one reason: the force drivers apply to the brake pedal has increased as has the power of the Brembo braking systems.

In 2008, on average, the drivers applied a load measuring 284 lb on the pedal at each corner of the Canadian GP. This year, the average load measured 295 lb. This 4% increase has made the driving style of each of the drivers even more important.
Besides there being more force applied by the driver the power of the Brembo braking systems has increased just as significantly. From 2008 to today the properties of the aluminum-lithium alloy used on the brake calipers have evolved.

Today's calipers are characterized by more complex geometries which are heightened by continuous research into optimizing the stiffness to weight ratio and by more and more efficient shapes to obtain the cooling these single-seaters require.

DECELERATION: +12%
Faster, wider tyres (resulting in a growing ability to dissipate brake torque) and a higher performing Brembo braking system

submit drivers to a deceleration that is far greater to that of the past. In 2008, the average peak deceleration per lap in Montreal was 4.2 G, and in 2018 this same figure went over 4.7 G. This is an increase of 11.9%.

On Turn Eight of the Canadian GP, the drivers experience 4.9 G of deceleration compared to 4.4 G in 2008. The difference found on Turn One is even more significant, both overall and in percentage: it has gone from 3.7 G ten years ago to 4.8 G this year.

Similar variations were registered on the other tracks that hosted a Formula One World Championship race in 2018. All of this would be even more evident on a track like Monza, where the peak deceleration in 2008 never went over five G. However, this year, according to calculations made on a simulator, none of the six braking sections will be lower than 5.1 G and when the cars enter the Parabolica, they will go well over 6 G.

BRAKE DISCS: FROM 200 TO 1,400 HOLES (+600%)
One of the components on the braking system that went through a visible transformation is the brake disc.

Over the course of the last ten years advancements in research enabled Brembo to progressively increase the number of holes and decrease the dimensions. Ten years ago, in 2008, there were about 200 ventilation holes on a Formula One brake disc.

Barely four years later, the number tripled reaching 600 holes. Innovation continued and on the Formula One single-seaters racing in 2014, the discs had more than 1,000 ventilation holes.

Increasing the surface of the disc exposed to ventilation ensures greater heat dispersion and a reduction in operating temperature. The temperature of the carbon discs used in Formula One can get up to 1,832°F for brief periods.

Since 2017, the discs have grown in size from 28 to 32 mm, which allows more space for the ventilation holes and results in further advancements in the evolution of braking system cooling.

Today, each Brembo brake disc can have up to almost 1,400 ventilation holes in the most extreme version, which is about 100 more than the number of holes on the discs used in 2017.

The holes, positioned in four different rows, measure 2.5 mm in diameter and are made one-by-one by a precision machine. It takes twelve to fourteen hours to make all of the holes on a single disc. At this level, precision is everything: the mechanical component tolerance is only four-hundredths.

BRAKE PADS: ENERGY DISSIPATED +10%

The brake pads have also undergone significant change over the last ten years both in size and in geometry. The overall area of each one increased by less than two per cent (from 4,000 mm to 4,070 mm), but they are now longer than in the past: In 2008 they measured 106 x 25 mm, while in 2018 they are 185 x 22 mm.

These days, the pads have to dissipate a lot more energy. In Canada ten years ago, the temperature of the discs at Turn Ten got up to a maximum of 1666°F and this year they got to over 1832°F at the same spot.

To remedy this problem more in-depth research went into the shape of the pad itself. The pads have ventilation holes that are customized according to the requirements of each team.

BRAKE CALIPER: +15% LIGHTER

Over the course of the last ten years the brake caliper has experienced a somewhat inconsistent evolution. On one hand, the choices available for the track became simpler, on the other hand, the amount of personalized developments for each team has become more and more prevalent.

In 2008 there were different calipers depending on the circuit the single-seaters were racing on, which caused some issues in terms of selection and made replacing them in an emergency with ones designed for different tracks impossible. However, for a few years now the teams use just one type of caliper for all of the circuits raced during the season.

At the same time, development became increasingly complex.

Today, contrary to ten years ago, Formula One requires braking systems that are highly customized according to the different design choices made for each single-seater. Each team Brembo supplies asks for an increasingly tailor-made braking system that is closely integrated with the design of the single-seater and is subject to continuous developments over the course of the season.

For example, the brake caliper is perfectly integrated with the cooling system for the corner of the car (air ducts, drums, deflectors, etc.) and with the aerodynamic solutions developed by the individual teams making each component unique.

In addition driver preferences influence the different combinations of stiffness and weight. There are teams that prefer lighter calipers because they need to lower the weight of the car, even though they lose in terms of stiffness. Others prefer stiffness to the detriment of mass.

Overall in the face of a weight reduction of just fifteen per cent compared to 2008, the brake caliper processing is now much more complex.

BRAKE-BY-WIRE

Another significant innovation introduced during the last ten years is Brake-By-Wire [BBW]. The need to guarantee proper braking force to the rear axle apart from the output torque generated by the electric motors led to the introduction of another innovation in 2014: Brake-By-Wire (BBW).

Under normal operating conditions the rear system is no longer activated directly by the driver but by a high-pressure hydraulic system on the car much like the ones for suspension and power steering. An electronic vehicle control unit keeps continuous track of the braking force linked to the two MGUs as well as the braking distribution imposed by the driver.

The amount of energy dissipated on the rear axle is moderated by the reduction in friction since it is recovered in part by the MGU-K: the result is a less cumbersome and lighter caliper. In addition to the traditional 6-piston calipers, the maximum allowed by regulation, Brembo supplies several teams with 4-piston calipers to be used at the rear which responds to their requests for lighter systems.

The key characteristics of a Formula One Brake System can be seen in this diagram as well data comparisons with a standard road car system.

F1 Brake System

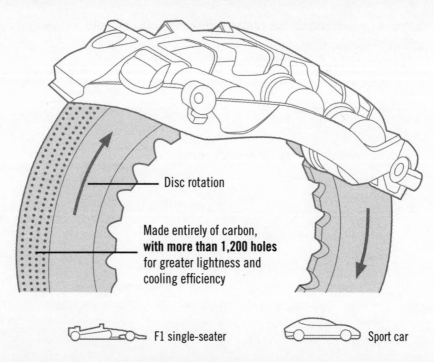

Disc rotation

Made entirely of carbon, **with more than 1,200 holes** for greater lightness and cooling efficiency

F1 single-seater   Sport car

Brake disc   **F1:** carbon disc   **Sport car:** cast iron disc

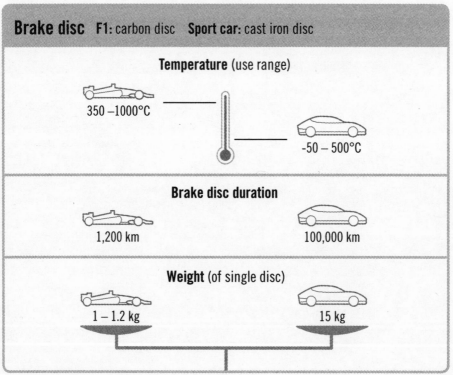

Temperature (use range)

350 –1000°C   -50 – 500°C

Brake disc duration

1,200 km   100,000 km

Weight (of single disc)

1 – 1.2 kg   15 kg

Brake pads

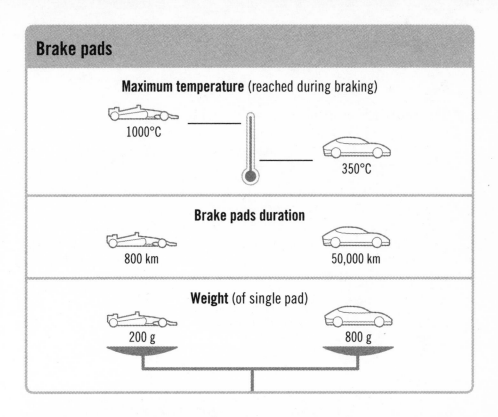

Maximum temperature (reached during braking)

1000°C

350°C

Brake pads duration

800 km

50,000 km

Weight (of single pad)

200 g

800 g

Brake caliper **F1:** Al-Li Alloy monobloc caliper **Sport car:** Al monobloc caliper

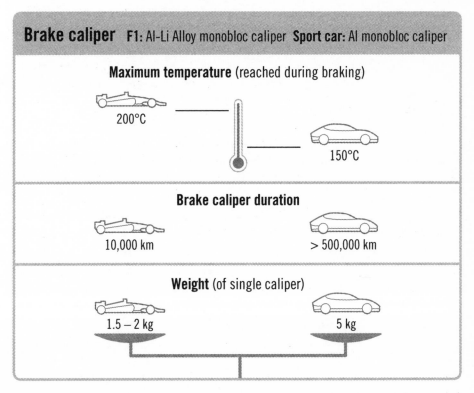

Maximum temperature (reached during braking)

200°C

150°C

Brake caliper duration

10,000 km

> 500,000 km

Weight (of single caliper)

1.5 – 2 kg

5 kg

DATA

THE FASTEST MEN IN F1—THE IT MEN

Data is key to the modern Formula One team and, with the difference between winning and losing being so small, the handling of data represents an opportunity to gain vital fractions of a second. Each lap more than 4 MB of data relating to speed, g-forces, pressures, temperatures and engine performance are transmitted from the race car to the pit system via real-time radio transmissions adding up to a massive 25 GB of telemetry data collected per three-day race weekend. Here we look at how two of the teams and their IT partners meet the data challenge to gain that crucial advantage.

THE DATA WRANGLERS

Graham Hackland, formerly of Lotus F1 Team and now at Williams, explains the role of data during the race weekend: "All of the teams arrive at the circuit with a base configuration for the car that they've done in simulation back at the factory, or from their experience of their previous years at the track, and very quickly on the Friday they have to get as close as they can to the set-up for the car that they think they're going to qualify with. Getting the data up to speed so it can be fed back into the car and analyzed to get the most out of the set-up is absolutely paramount.

"There is a large team back in the factory working on the real-time data that's coming off the car so that by the Saturday, it becomes even more critical that the performance of your data and the applications that we develop are spot on. Being able to access the right data at the right time means that engineers can be faster in getting new and effective ideas into the car and onto the track, and therein lies the competitive edge. By the time of the Grand Prix on Sunday, they have a strategy system that, at the press of a button and within three minutes, can run 10,000 race simulations based on the current situation; for instance it's started raining, there is a crash, track temperature, your competitors, the tyres you've got, the tyres your competitors have got. All of that data collected from the sensors on the car is factored in. This can be done continually at the press of a button, based on current real-time data."

The data wranglers in F1 may very well be the fastest men in the sport as they collect, process and disseminate vast amounts of crucial data at unheard of speeds. According to Hackland, "In less than a second (absolute real-time terms), we're getting the data, processing it and delivering it to the team sitting on the pit wall. Lap by lap, corner by corner, sector by sector, they are getting the data they need in realtime so as it's happening on the car, it's on the pit wall or at the mobile data centre in the back of the garage."

At any point in time, up to thirty engineers may be accessing a single file from either of the two live or the two back-up storage clusters. While the Race Team at the track are analyzing the data to improve performance in minuscule increments, there is an even bigger team back at the factory that are hard at work on larger sets of data to analyze performance in terms of the bigger, long-term picture. Speed, capacity and availability are the key indicators, but these are nothing without reliability. Teams will expect 100 per cent reliability from the car and they expect the same from the IT as well. For the past seven seasons, Lotus has run NetApp at the track with zero downtime; that is, a 100 per cent record for seven consecutive seasons for five days at a time, Wednesday to Sunday. At the end of the five days, the whole system is shut down and either flown or trucked back to the factory. The system has to maintain reliability and performance despite the rugged trackside and transport environments.

There are many in Formula One who talk about how important data is to the sport and to the business and even some who believe that no racing could take place without it. Hackland is quick to provide some perspective. "Sometimes, we IT people think they can't do anything without what we provide, and the reason is that the engineers absolutely need IT for the running of their jobs. The reality is that we should just be in the background providing the race team with the services they need to engineer the car. At the end of each race weekend, my hope is that they don't mention IT at all, then I know we have done our job."

These days, Formula One teams are looking for much more

agility in terms of the way they handle data—they need to provide the capability to consume the resources at business level rather than having to refer to IT. Lawrence James, Alliances and Solutions Manager at NetApp, explains: "What we do for F1 is simple: the ability to provision, expand and scale seamlessly. For instance, they've got elastic demand coming through where they need to provision more capacity, and they can do that really quickly. And it's the guys that actually need that capacity who can instigate the commands rather than having to go through IT all of the time. It's automated and self-provisioning, which is key for agility."

He continues: "What is expected these days is that the business and IT are working as a unit and the IT is enabling the business. IT is used in Formula One to effectively *enable* their engineers, both trackside and back at the factory, so that when they need capacity trackside or when they need to get data back to HQ quickly, they can do that. They can provision it themselves in a future-proof, self-sufficient way."

NetApp, in its partnership with Lotus, has moved away from storage islands towards a converged infrastructure so that rather than being a modular approach, it is an integrated approach to both networking and storage so that the two levels work in tandem with each other effectively, virtualizing each layer. James poses the question: "So how do you retire the old, introduce the new, but make it totally transparent to the applications that are running? Our agile data infrastructure does just that: it collapses all of those layers, it virtualizes those layers. When I want to retire an old piece of storage, I can transparently migrate all the data. The application doesn't see anything and isn't disrupted. I can bring in the new. I can rebalance. I can replicate so as to protect the data as well but totally transparently to the server layer and to the application layer."

Agile data is crucial in Formula One. The need to restore data from a few days ago (or even earlier in the season) so that it can be analyzed again and again is vital in the search for any performance advantage. James elaborates: "NetApp intelligently manages the Lotus data by protecting it very efficiently. They use a lot of our ability to copy data in the form of snapshots but with a difference in that the snapshots are created locally but don't consume any more physical storage. We provide the ability to grab data and to grow it efficiently by the use of 'snap mirror'; i.e. replicating from A to B and 'snapshotting' at A or B to create point-in-time copies which are spatially efficient. So, in other words, they are not consuming two, three or four times the capacity with every copy that they make."

Formula One provides NetApp with an opportunity to demonstrate what it does and the capability of the company's gear in a number of different environments from business applications to fluid dynamics through to the race situation. As James adds: "Let's face it; it's a great talking point. It's very positive in terms of talking about it in front of our clients. This technology would work wherever you put it. It's proved itself. There are no excuses for it; it's been there, it's done the job. It's been taken from one side of the world to the other. It never fails."

EVERY MILLISECOND COUNTS

Thanks to increasing high-speed connectivity the back-end is the new front line. When Tata Communications first entered Formula One the Indian Telco giant became Formula One's official connectivity provider. Here was a company that owned the world's largest (and only) round-the-world sub-sea cable network—over 20,000 route kilometres of sub-sea and terrestrial network fibre—allowing a data transfer capacity of one terabit per second. Back then, it was clear that Tata Communications was one of the few companies in the world with the technology to cater for and improve upon Formula One's colossal, split-second connectivity requirements.

Mehul Kapadia, Managing Director of Formula One Business at Tata Communications, and his team were looking forward to showcasing their talents on a global platform by providing the infrastructure for Formula One's connectivity and communications in all twenty race locations and offices worldwide. Melbourne 2012 was Tata Communication's first race, and it was here, and almost immediately, that Kapadia bumped into former CEO of the Mercedes Team, Nick Fry.

From that meeting came an agreement that would deepen the company's involvement in the race: to provide MERCEDES

AMG PETRONAS with trackside connectivity, enabling the team to transfer vital real-time data from the Silver Arrow cars at any Grand Prix location to its headquarters in the UK. The relationship with Mercedes puts Tata in the front-line, although, Kapadia explains, thanks to modern high-speed connectivity, the "front-line" can now be several hundred miles from the track.

"[On race days] we run a pit crew of about twenty people who from across the globe are actually running the operation," he says. "It's quite a task, but it's about practising what you preach. So if we are telling the industry that through Telecom you can save on operational cost by doing stuff backstage rather than having to send people to a lot of places, we also optimise it that way. We send these two people to the races; we don't send a battery of thirty people out there.

"There are specialists working out of London, out of India and also, at times, out of the US, depending on the need. We'd never operated within a level of a sport like Formula One before. It is a place for us to demonstrate our capability in delivering solutions and services across the world in crazy timelines, to modify our processes to suit our customers' needs, create response teams, which are so much in the backend but still able to deliver at the front-end."

For Mercedes, the data has to come back to Team HQ in Brackley where it's analyzed and then sent back to the racetrack. The goal is to decrease latency—the split-second time delay in transferring data—and, in the pursuit of efficiency and a competitive edge, every millisecond counts. Through its global network, Tata Communications was able to upscale Mercedes' connectivity to make it three times faster.

"The laws of physics mean latency can't completely go away," says Kapadia. "There will always be latency. Right now, when I'm talking to you, you can immediately hear me but if you were at a distance, the voice would take more time to travel. It's sheer physics. How do I ensure that even when you are in Australia I can minimize that latency? If there are x-hundred milliseconds happening, I reduce a few tens of milliseconds out of it. That also helps because if you can get it faster, if you can analyze it faster, you are going to make your decision a split second faster.

"It seems simplistic, but when you scale it up that much—by three times—imagine the amount of potential you've opened for those engineers. Let's not kid ourselves; we are a telecom player, we are not going to change a particular component on the car. But it can enable the people who *are* doing that to do their work with more flexibility, and three times faster."

Tata Communications hosts technical workshops with Mercedes during which the company explains the depth of its own services and listens to the needs of its client; although the relationship with Mercedes is that of service provider and customer, as opposed to an in-kind technical partnership or sponsorship. There is, however, a marketing partnership in existence. The opportunity to align itself with the Mercedes brand and its assets is just too attractive, says Kapadia, but he hastens to add that this agreement is independent of the company's role as a service provider. "This is truly a success, where you can have win-win between partners. It's not actually about sponsorship, I think. Formula One is way beyond that."

The deal with Mercedes is a multi-year contract and while immediate plans are under wraps, Kapadi sees an opportunity for all of the teams to improve their connectivity. "The way I look at it is that this is an opportunity to look at all the teams. Mercedes is definitely the team that we started work with, but all the other teams also need to look at getting into a strong relationship with a strong Telco that has the capability and the commitment to the sport.

"I'm sure what people are getting today is good. It's not about bad becoming good, it's about how you can better what is already there. Three times capacity is not to say that one times capacity was bad. It is just that three gives you the opportunity to do more. Our theme for the year is to provide to our customers the speed to lead. This is our way of saying that we truly believe that, with our kind of fibre capability globally, our kind of telecom experience, and our kind of data centre technology, we can help teams to look at telecommunications in a different way."

FUEL

While the latest generation of Formula One cars have been great to watch, their extra weight and downforce has lead to more time on the throttle and ultimately more fuel being burned.

So as to avoid the 'lift and coast' scenario of recent years where drivers have been forced to save fuel so as to make it to the end of the race it has been agreed by the teams, Formula One and the FIA to increase the race fuel allowance from 105kg to 110kg for the 2019 season. This it is hoped will allow the drivers to push flat out for the entire race distance utilising the engine at full power at all times.

This could add a new strategic element as teams may choose to carry less fuel to save weight combined with fuel saving at certain stages to gain an advantage. However the new regulation will still mean that the most energy efficient power units will prosper at the expense of those with heavier fuel consumption.

F1 fuels contain over two hundred ingredients providing one hundred ignitions per cylinder per second and during a season more than twenty F1 fuel formulas are produced. Below we examine how the fuel suppliers in Formula One: Shell, ExxonMobil, BP Castrol and Petronas embrace the new philosophy—optimisation of energy efficiency—that will bring Formula One ever closer to the car industry and the everyday motorist.

FUELS: AN ESSENTIAL CONTRIBUTION TO ENERGY SAVINGS

The power of an engine is down to the quality of its combustion. Optimising the performance of a turbo engine also comes from maximising the flexibility of the engine over a wide rev band and a large number of setups. In F1, igniting the air-fuel mixture and burning it as quickly as possible is an ongoing preoccupation.

If fuel pump petrol can be likened to ready-to-wear, that used in Formula 1 is a bespoke product. The supplier produces the fuel formula and as soon as it has been tested and validated by the team then homologated by the FIA it is transported to the circuits.

The Formula One fuel regulations are strict. They control the formulation by limiting the hydrocarbon content that goes into the final product. An F1 car must race on fuel that is very similar to the unleaded super at the pump and complies with draconian restrictions: except for one point—the octane rating is not limited. Thus, despite an apparent rigour, there is room for manoeuvre which allows the researchers to make a competitive difference. As long as the ingredients which make up the F1 fuel are regulated and their proportions controlled then the recipe is almost open to interpretation.

OPTIMISING THE INJECTION

The power units to be used in the 2019 season have direct injection so the fuel is injected directly into the combustion chamber as in a modern diesel engine: maximum revs are limited to 15 000 rpm. In reality, the combination between the search for reliability, the fuel flow limit and the way the lean mixture works imposes a working rev band of around 11 000 rpm. Nonetheless, because of direct injection the power unit should be fed by a fuel that vaporises very quickly.

The injection is triggered during the compression phase just before the ignition and the power stroke. It is managed electronically to be as quick as it is accurate. The high pressure injection favours vaporisation while the spray of petrol goes into fresh gases and the vaporisation can also be enhanced by the quality of the fuel.

The sprays should be very short to vaporise quickly without wetting the surface of the pistons or the cylinder sleeves too much. In the past, indirect injection above the valve took more time and the temperature and pressure were less critical.

STABILISING COMBUSTION

Running an electric motor on the shaft of the turbocharger by the exhaust gases to generate electricity is an innovative technology to harvest energy. It is efficient, however, only when it can pass the largest quantity of gas at the highest possible speed over the turbo's hot turbine placed in the stream of the exhaust gases. The solution? Make the petrol engine work like a diesel with a considerable excess of air thus creating a very lean fuel/air mixture. In addition to rapid ignition, Total formulates a fuel that provides stable combustion in lean mixture conditions. It must also ensure the cooling and the behavior of the fuel pumps including the feeding pump in the fuel tank, which raises the pressure by a few bars, and feeds the high-pressure pump generating the injection pressure.

MASTERING KNOCKING

The role of the fuel can be summed up in just a few words. To liberate the power, it has to combust very quickly and thus needs to be vaporised very rapidly in a homogenous manner. After ignition, the spread of the flame must be almost instantaneous without generating knocking. Turbo engines are particularly prone to this phenomenon as they have a higher thermal load than normally-aspirated motors. This was one of the challenges of the 2018 season that needs to be met in 2019 and beyond.

Knocking is uncontrolled combustion causing explosions, which spread at high speed in the combustion chamber. This explosive phenomenon produces high-speed pressure waves that bounce off the walls causing oscillation with large amplitude in pressure. The consequences are: sharp sounds, destruction of the internal dynamics of gasses in the combustion chamber, and heat transfer between the burnt gases and the metal. Thus, in a few seconds a piston can be holed or destroyed by fusion. The aerodynamics of the combustion chamber, the flow from the injectors, the design of the plugs, the electronics and the quality of the fuel all have to be taken into account. The key is to create a fuel with a much higher octane rating.

ENERGY CONTENT AND DENSITY

The 110kg of fuel allowed for the race has to be formulated in such a way that it contains the maximum amount of energy that the engine can use. This bespoke formulation has a few secrets. Out of the 110 kg fuel load a 0.025 difference in the density leads to a reduction of 5 litres in the contents and the size of the fuel tank. Thus suppliers formulate their fuels to meet the requirements of the power unit without penalising the design of the chassis. A single aim: find the best possible compromise in terms of density to meet the needs of the chassis (size of the fuel tank) and of the engine while ensuring bulletproof resistance to the temperature. This is a crucial point as the storage batteries are installed under the fuel tank, which they heat.

INGREDIENTS OF NON-FOSSIL ORIGIN
Since 2008, the law imposes ingredients of non-fossil origin in fuels—the bio-fuels. One of the fundamental elements in the recipe is the obligation to incorporate 5.75 per cent (in mass) of renewable ingredients in the fuels. These non-fossil molecules may contain oxygen as well as ethanol and hydrocarbons obtained from decomposition by bacteria of vegetable waste, which are not part of the food consumption chain. They are the second generation or renewable bio-fuels.

NB: The oxygen sometimes found in these bio-ingredients limits the calorific power, hence the energy available in the fuel, but it provides ingredients like alcohol, which give a high octane rating. Analysing the combustion is vital to find the best compromise on the turbo engine between reliability provided by the high octane rating and the maximum power available.

ADDITIVES
Additives are crucial for the reliability of the engine, both to avoid failure and also the progressive loss of power during its life cycle. The work on the resistance to knocking and in the field of lubrication answers these problems. While each of the teams has acquired in-depth knowledge about the optimisation of parts each fuel supplier knows how to mix additives with the fuel to reduce friction on the rings, prevent deposits forming on the pistons crowns and the hot areas of the engine, lubricate the high pressure petrol pumps and prevent the injectors from cocking. These active molecules have different properties: cleaning, anti-corrosion, anti-oxidation, reduction of emulsion with the air, modification of the frictions, amelioration of the combustion and the octane rating.

PRACTICALLY SPEAKING: ONGOING DIALOGUE
Formulating the best possible F1 fuel means knowing all the secrets of the engine. There needs to be complete openness between the fuel supplier and the team in the F1 factory and the engineers need to be in permanent contact. Certain parts of the engine are tested in conjunction with the fuel supplier. The shared experience means that collaboration on the design of the combustion chamber to optimise its functioning whether through simulation or tests on real parts is a major advantage.

THE FINAL RESULT
It is a fuel comprising dozens of ingredients specially formulated for the 2019 F1 power unit guaranteeing top-class performance. The V6 turbocharged engine is fed by a lead-free super petrol with a high octane rating (anti-detonation properties and power gain), excellent combustion stability (anti-knock), and a high energy content.

DEVELOPMENT
Numerous evolutions of F1 fuels are tested every season. Once the optimum formulation has been chosen and validated by the team the supplier homologates the product with the FIA (Fédération Internationale de l'Automobile). It's the birth certificate of the fuel. Some ten litres are sent to the Federation's laboratory in Great Britain to receive the legislator's agreement. The analysis of this sample by gas chromatography gives the genetic code of the fuel, which will serve as a reference until the homologation of the next batch. Another barrel of 25 litres is sent to one of the FIA's service providers for the calibration of the cars' fuel flow metre. Each time the formulation changes a new validation is required. The homologation process usually takes three to four weeks.

PRODUCTION
 F1 fuels are produced in different volumes from 200 litres for specific tests to large volumes for grand prix. Twenty to 100 cubic metres are produced per cycle which guarantees an autonomy of

8 to 10 race weekends for teams as well as for the test beds. Production takes several days, and putting the fuel into barrels is done quickly to ensure the homogeneity of their contents. In the middle of production a barrel is divided up into several samples for the FIA and for our own references. Finally, each barrel is numbered, a crucial stage that requires precision. Certain ingredients represent less than 1 per cent of the mixture. The supplier may have to bring several specific fuels to the circuits depending on the choice of the teams.

ANALYSING CONFORMITY AT THE GRAND PRIX
Despite the multiple hurdles (customs, sales and safety regulations, etc.), which differ from country to country a fuel supplier cannot make mistakes when it comes to transporting the fuels to the grand prix. The FIA takes fuel samples on a random basis during race weekends and also takes a sample from the cars of the drivers who finish in the top three meaning that fuels have undergone the highest number of checks over the past few seasons. Numerous parameters may alter a fuel compared to its homologated content: a solvent still present after cleaning the fuel pump or the fuel tank and evaporation of the lightest molecules if a car has run with a low fuel load. The alteration of the formulation compared to its reference may lead to the disqualification of a driver or his team. To ensure that the fuel used always complies with the registered genetic code Total brings a chromatograph to the circuits. This machine used for checking can identify the molecules present in the fuel on a daily basis and ensures that the fuel complies in real time.

LUBRICANTS
Unlike the restrictions placed on fuels the FIA technical regulations allow considerable freedom in the field of F1 lubricants where the challenge is to ensure reliability while searching for performance. The use of a wide range of ingredients and additives are used to formulate the most suitable products that contribute to power and energy saving, protect the mechanical parts, cool the engine, evacuate air and obtain a high level of

thermal stability. The influence of lubricants is not just limited to the engine (lubricants and cooling liquid) but also plays a role in terms of wheel bearings (grease), power steering (hydraulic fluid), brake liquid, KERS (cooling liquid), gearbox (lubricant), transmission (grease) and the DRS operation system (hydraulic fluid).

POWER UNIT

LONG LIVE THE POWER UNIT

Since the revolutionary technological changes of 2014 significant improvements have been made to Formula One Power Units so much so that thermal efficiency, a measure of how well an engine turns fuel burned into usable energy, has now exceeded fifty percent. The turbulent jet injection utilised in Formula One means a much leaner fuel burn so that less energy is wasted as heat and more of it is converted to work far in excess of the average road car which is only around 25-30 per cent thermally efficient. The Power Unit rules position Formula One firmly at the cutting edge of automotive technology, redefining what's possible in the field of engineering and actively encouraging innovation to stretch technological boundaries.

2019

In 2019 the challenge will be to get the balance right between performance and reliability as each driver will be restricted in the number of elements of the power unit that can be used before a grid penalty is imposed.

Each driver is only permitted to use three internal combustion engines (ICE), three motor energy units- heat (MGU-H) and three turbochargers (TC) but only two energy stores (ES), two control electronics (CE) and two motor energy units-kinetic (MGU-K) before a ten-place grid penalty is given. If other additional elements are then used then a further five-place grid penalty shall be given. If a driver receives grid penalties of fifteen places or more then they will be required to start from the back of the grid.

The reduction in the number of power unit components that can be used per driver per season without incurring grid penalties means that durability has to be extended to withstand the higher distances the hardware now has to run. This equates to a very significant forty per cent increase and the challenge has been to focus on increasing the life of the hardware without losing performance.

In addition to the changes coming from the Sporting Regulations the teams have sought to improve the power unit in other areas as well. They have changed the packaging of the power unit for the benefit of overall car performance to achieve the best overall integration with the chassis, the transmission and the aerodynamic surfaces. They have also worked hard to improve combustion efficiency and hardware friction reduction in partnership with their fuel and lubricant suppliers.

In 2019 there will be four engine manufactures:
- Mercedes who will also supply Racing Point Force India and Williams,
- Ferrari who will also supply Sauber and Haas
- Renault who will also supply McLaren
- Honda who will supply Red Bull and Toro Rosso.

TECHNOLOGY AND TERMINOLOGY
Power Unit— In regulatory terms, The Power Unit comprises six different systems:

- The Internal Combustion Engine (ICE)
- Motor Generator Unit-Kinetic (MGU-K)
- Motor Generator Unit-Heat (MGU-H)
- Energy Store (ES)
- Turbocharger (TC)
- Control Electronics (CE)

The Formula One powertrain is far more than simply an internal combustion engine and has been designed from the outset with hybrid systems integral to its operation.

ICE
The Internal Combustion Engine (ICE) is the traditional fuel-powered heart of the Power Unit previously known simply as the engine. From 2014 this has taken the form of a 1.6 litre turbocharged V6 configuration with direct fuel injection up to 500 bar of pressure. Where the old V8 engines could rev up to 18,000 rpm the current ICE is limited to 15,000 rpm. This reduction in crankshaft rotational speed coupled with the reduction in engine

capacity and number of cylinders reduces the friction and thus increases the total efficiency of the Power Unit.

TURBOCHARGER

The turbocharger is an energy recovery device that uses waste exhaust energy to drive a single stage exhaust turbine that in turn drives a single stage compressor via a shaft thereby increasing the pressure of the inlet charge (the air admitted to the engine for combustion). The increased pressure of the inlet charge offsets the reductions in engine capacity and RPM when compared to the pre-2014 V8, thus enabling high power delivery from a down-speeded, down-sized engine. The turbocharger is the key system for increasing the efficiency of the ICE.

ERS

Energy is recovered and deployed to the rear axle via a Motor Generator Unit. The MGU-K (for 'Kinetic') is permitted twice the maximum power of the pre-2014 motor (120kW or 161hp instead of 60 kW or 80.5 hp). It may recover five times more energy per lap (2MJ) and deploy ten times as much (4MJ) compared to its pre-2014 equivalent equating to over 30 seconds per lap at full power. The rest of the energy is recovered by the MGU-H (for 'Heat") an electrical machine connected to the turbocharger. Where the pre-2014 V8s offered one possible 'energy journey' to improve efficiency via KERS there are up to seven different efficiency enhancing energy journeys in the ERS system.

MGU-K

The Motor Generator Unit- Kinetic (MGU-K) has double the power capability of the pre-2014 used KERS motors but operates in an identical way. Some of the kinetic energy that would normally be dissipated by the rear brakes under braking is converted into electrical energy and stored in the Energy Store. Then, when the car accelerates, energy stored in the Energy Store is delivered to the MGU-K which provides an additional boost up to a maximum power of 120 kW (approximately 160 hp) to the rear axle for over 30 seconds per lap.

MGU-H

The Motor Generator Unit-Heat (MGU-H) is a new electrical machine that is directly coupled to the turbocharger shaft. Waste exhaust energy that is in excess of that required to drive the compressor can be recovered by the turbine, harvested by the MGU-H, converted into electrical energy and stored in the Energy Store. Where the MGU-K is limited to recovering 2 MJ of energy per lap, there is no limit placed on the MGU-H. This recovered energy can be used to power the MGU-K when accelerating or can be used to power the MGU-H in order to accelerate the turbocharger, thus helping to eliminate 'turbo lag.' This technology increases the efficiency of the Power Unit and most significantly provides a method to ensure good driveability from a boosted, down-sized engine.

ES

The Energy Store (ES) does exactly what it says on the tin; storing the energy harvested from the two Motor Generator Units (MGUs) for deployment back into those same systems. It is capped in terms of maximum and minimum weight: the maximum (25 kg) setting engineers an aggressive target while the minimum (20 kg) means weight reduction will not be chased at all costs.

KJ V MJ V KW

A joule (J) is a unit of energy; (kinetic, heat, mechanical, electrical etc.) A kilojoule (kJ) is equal to one thousand joules whilst a megajoule (MJ) represents one million joules. To put this into context, kJ is a unit often used to describe the energy present in nutritional goods while 1 MJ represents the approximate kinetic energy of a one-tonne vehicle travelling at 160 km/h. Meanwhile, a watt (W) is a unit of power that quantifies a rate of energy flow; with a kilowatt (kW) equal to one thousand watts. This unit is commonly used to express the power output of an engine, where 1 kW is equal to 1.34 horsepower.

MERCEDES-AMG F1 M09 EQ POWER+ TECHNICAL
SPECIFICATION

Power Unit Specification
Type: Mercedes-AMG F1 M09 EQ Power+
Minimum Weight: 145 kg
Power Unit Perimeter: Internal Combustion Engine (ICE)
Motor Generator Unit: Kinetic (MGU-K)
Motor Generator Unit: Heat (MGU-H)
Turbocharger (TC)
Energy Store (ES)
Control Electronics (CE)
Power Unit Allocation: Three ICE, TC & MGU-H per driver per
season

TWO MGU-K, ES, CE PER DRIVER PER SEASON

Internal Combustion Engine (ICE)
Capacity: 1.6 litres
Cylinders: 6
Bank Angle: 90
No of Valves: 24
Max rpm ICE: 15,000 rpm
Max Fuel Flow Rate: 100 kg/hour (above 10,500 rpm)
Fuel Injection: High-pressure direct injection (max 500 bar, one
injector/cylinder)
Pressure Charging: Single-stage compressor and exhaust turbine
on a common shaft
Max rpm Exhaust Turbine: 125,000 rpm

ENERGY RECOVERY SYSTEM (ERS)

Architecture: Integrated Hybrid energy recovery via electrical
Motor Generator Units
Energy Store: Lithium-Ion battery solution of minimum 20 kg
regulation weight
Max energy storage/lap: 4 MJ
Max rpm MGU-K: 50,000 rpm

Max power MGU-K: 120 kW (161 hp)

Max energy recovery/lap MGU-K: 2 MJ

Max energy deployment/lap MGU-K: 4 MJ (33.3 s at full power)

Max rpm MGU-H: 125,000 rpm

Max power MGU-H: Unlimited

Max energy recovery/lap MGU-H: Unlimited

Max energy deployment/lap MGU-H: Unlimited

Mercedes-AMG F1 W09 EQ Power+ Technical Specification

Chassis

Monocoque: Moulded carbon fibre and honeycomb composite structure

Bodywork: Carbon fibre composite including engine cover, sidepods, floor, nose, front wing and rear wing

Cockpit: Removable driver's seat made of anatomically formed carbon composite, OMP six-point driver safety harness, HANS system

Safety Structures: Cockpit survival cell incorporating impact-resistant construction and penetration panels, front impact structure, prescribed side impact structures, integrated rear impact structure, front and rear roll structures, titanium driver protection structure (halo)

Front Suspension: Carbon fibre wishbone and pushrod-activated torsion springs and rockers

Rear Suspension: Carbon fibre wishbone and pullrod-activated torsion springs and rockers

Wheels: OZ forged magnesium

Tyres: Pirelli

Brake System: Carbone Industries Carbon / Carbon discs and pads with rear brake-by-wire

Brake Calipers: Brembo

Steering: Power-assisted rack and pinion

Steering Wheel: Carbon fibre construction

Electronics: FIA standard ECU and FIA homologated electronic and electrical system

Instrumentation: McLaren Electronic Systems (MES)

Fuel System: ATL Kevlar-reinforced rubber bladder

Lubricants & Fluids: PETRONAS Tutela

Transmission
Gearbox: Eight speed forward, one reverse unit with carbon fibre maincase
Gear Selection: Sequential, semi-automatic, hydraulic activation
Clutch: Carbon plate

Dimensions
Overall Length: Over 5000 mm
Overall Width: 2000 mm
Overall Height: 950 mm
Overall Weight: 733k

SAFETY

When Kimi Räikkönen hit the wall head-on at Silverstone in 2014 at 240 km/h, he experienced a 47 g impact. The fact that he was able to walk away from the accident with minor injuries is a testament to the level of safety that exists in modern Formula One. From track safety, cockpit safety, crash tests, medical provision, helmets, HANS (Head & Neck Support), clothing and deployment of the Safety Car, Formula One sets the highest standards in safety and continually strives to improve every aspect taking nothing for granted. For the most comprehensive exploration of safety in F1 please go to www. formula1.com/inside_f1/safety where F1 Global Partner Allianz in association with the official Formula One Website examine each aspect in extensive detail. Below we take a look at two aspects of safety in F1, the Safety Car and Track Design, from the perspective of two key Formula One experts: Bernd Mayländer and Philippe Gurdjian.

BERND MAYLÄNDER—THE SAFETY CAR DRIVER

Always in the background and still a vital part of Formula One: Bernd Mayländer, the Official Formula One Safety Car driver. The FIA is responsible for the deployment of the Official Formula One Safety Car and sends it onto the track in hazardous situations. Bernd Mayländer gives exclusive insights into his unique role.

The Car

Tell us about the Official Formula One Safety Car, Bernd:
"The Safety Car is a 525-HP Mercedes Benz SL 63 AMG. It is not a standard road car. In order to ensure the best possible reliability even in tropical temperatures, the vehicle incorporates large additional coolers for engine oil, transmission oil, cooling water and power steering. Despite a larger braking system including brake cooling, additional cooling measures, lighting system and communications equipment the Safety Car is significantly lighter than the road version. It has been possible to dispense with all the mechanical and hydraulic components

of the convertible roof. Also, the sound-absorbing materials, which serve primarily to improve the driving comfort, have been removed. The result is a weight reduction of 220 kg and a Safety Car that only weighs 1750 kg."

When are you deployed onto the track?
"According to the official regulations of the Fédération Internationale de l'Automobile (FIA), the car is deployed 'if competitors or officials are in immediate physical danger but the circumstances are not such as to necessitate stopping the race', for example after an accident or in severe rain showers."

What's the role of the Official Formula One Safety Car?
"It takes up its position at the front of the field and leads the Formula One cars around the track at reduced speed until the dangerous situation has passed. All the cars, beginning with the race leader, must line up behind the Safety Car."

Who decides when you should take to the track?
"The decision is made by the FIA race director, Charlie Whiting. He also decides when the Safety Car phase is finished."

How are the drivers informed about the Safety Car phase?
"The drivers are notified by the marshals and light-panels that show yellow flags together with the letters "SC". Additionally the driver is informed via radio by the team and a warning light inside the cockpit flashes until the Safety Car phase is over."

How long does the Safety Car remain on the circuit?
"It will remain until the hazardous situation is under control and the FIA feel that it is safe to resume. The laps completed during the Safety Car phase count as normal race laps. If the specified number of laps is completed, a race can also come to an end behind the Safety Car."

What influence does a Safety Car phase have on the race strategy?
"As a rule, the teams use a Safety Car phase for an unscheduled pit stop, because it involves a much smaller loss of time than if

the field is racing at full speed. If a team manages to bring its driver into the pits at exactly the right time, it can result in a crucial advantage. Because the field is pressed up close together during a Safety Car phase, it also increases the excitement for the spectators."

Since when has the Safety Car been used in Formula One?
"Its first introduction was in 1973 at the Canadian Grand Prix. However, the FIA laid down clear guidelines for the role of the Safety Car in 1992."

The Driver

In 2000 the FIA entrusted the task of driving the Official Formula One Safety Car to Bernd Mayländer, a successful touring-car driver. He knows how to keep the pace during the safety period just high enough so that the race-car tyres do not cool down too much. Bernd started his career in karting at the end of the 1980s. In the following years he progressed to Formula Ford, the Porsche Carrera Cup, the FIA GT Championship and the Deutsche Tourenwagen Meisterschaften (DTM) before becoming the Official Formula One Safety Car driver in 2000.

A part of Formula One—Bernd Mayländer outlines his work environment

"The Safety Car is deployed on Formula One race weekends, so my working week generally starts on Thursday and ends on Sunday. Besides Formula One, the car is also used in other racing series over the course of the weekend, such as the GP2 Series, Porsche Supercup, etc. The same rules and regulations apply as in Formula One. Even if this means additional work for me, it ensures the same safety standard in all series and this is our main objective.

"Our safety team consists of two Safety Cars and a pair of medical cars—we transport approximately 3.5 tons of material from race to race, which we store in a small area on the pit lane or next to it. Along with my co-driver Peter Tibbetts, I am responsible for the Official Formula One Safety Car. The medical car is staffed by an additional driver and the F1 rescue coordinator of the FIA. Two mechanics take care of our cars, and remain present at all times. My co-driver and I have been working together since 2000—we always work as a team! Our small team is part of the FIA and is coordinated by the Race Director Charlie Whiting, and FIA observer Herbie Blash in Race Control. During a race, I am permanently in radio contact with Herbie, who keeps me up-to-date on all the racing action."

A typical Formula One race weekend
Thursday
"Generally I arrive on Wednesday evening, at European races early on Thursday morning. We meet at the racetrack at around 10 a.m. First, I go to the FIA office, where we have a short meeting and go through the important documents for the race weekend, such as race schedules, circuit maps, rules and regulations etc. Then I get changed into my race overalls and I am in the Safety Car at 1.35 p.m. Between 2 p.m. and 3 p.m. the first circuit test takes place. The Safety Car is therefore the first car that enters the circuit each race weekend.

"The track test is very important because both the car and the track are being tested, also the radio system, the GPS systems, as well as the cameras. Then, I forward our test results to Charlie Whiting, change into my official FIA clothing and attend the Drivers Briefing for the GP 2 series. The meeting takes roughly ten to thirty minutes, depending on the topics and how much needs to be discussed. After that I return to the hotel. I usually spend the evening exercising or I go for dinner with the teams and sponsors. It depends on which city we are in—cities like Melbourne and Istanbul obviously offer more possibilities to go out in the evening than others."

Friday
"Friday morning we leave the hotel at around 7 to 7.30 a.m. After arriving at the circuit we have a brief meeting with Charlie Whiting, the press, the technical and software department and with my team. Afterwards we perform another GPS test of the circuit—this test is performed from Thursday through to Sunday. This is very important because a track system is built into the

Safety Car and all other Formula One race cars, which not only provides an exact location of the vehicles but also transmits the flag signals on the side of the track to the display in the car. Tests have shown that the driver can see them much better on the display—this goes a long way towards increasing safety at the circuit. I follow the practice session on the monitor in the FIA trucks, but I am not in my car because there is no Safety Car during the practice session. I can always be reached though, in case the Safety Car is needed.

"The Formula One drivers briefing takes place at 5 p.m. and during the driver briefing the previous race and the current race are analyzed and we discuss what can be improved and how. The meeting is led by Charlie Whiting, and all Formula One drivers and test-drivers, FIA race stewards and I are present. After the meeting I return to the hotel. I try to exercise or go for dinner with friends—it is completely up to me how I plan my evening."

Saturday

"Saturday morning the FIA arrive at the track very early and have another meeting and this is followed by a GPS test, then I watch the third practice session. Directly after Formula One qualifying, the countdown starts for the first GP2 race. The GP2 race on Saturday afternoon is principally the same as the Formula One event, just at a different time and with different cars. Saturday evening we usually socialize a little, but we tend not to stay up that late—because Sunday is the all-important race day."

Sunday

"On Sunday we arrive even earlier at the track. It is one of the greatest moments of the weekend—to see how the circuit and the people slowly awake and embrace the exciting day ahead. The toughest part of the day for me begins right after the GPS test. After the second GP2 race, the Porsche Supercup takes place and at 1 p.m. the showdown for the Formula One race begins. At 1.10 p.m. my boss Charlie Whiting brings the Official Formula One Safety Car to the starting grid and hands it over to me. I check again whether the camera and the radio function properly and I make sure I get the most recent weather update—which is a very important part of my race preparation.

"At 1.50 p.m. I join my co-driver in the car. We adjust our helmets, buckle up and check the radio frequency. At 1.55 p.m. we leave the starting grid and park the car in the agreed parking position for the first lap. As soon as all cars have completed the first curve, I am told to move the Safety Car to the parking position for the rest of the race by my colleagues in Race Control. I observe the race on the TV monitor in the car and I also watch the weather. I usually communicate two to three times with Race Control to check whether all frequencies function properly and to receive further weather updates.

"When I get a command, I always have to confirm it by stating what I am currently doing. It is like the relationship between an airplane pilot and air traffic control: when the pilot receives the order he then confirms it and also re-confirms the update of his/her new position. In addition, our mechanics also follow the radio on the pit lane. If the race is finished without a Safety Car phase—which is thankfully usually the case—I wait for the last race car and I follow it. With this, I notify the marshals that there are no other cars coming behind me and that they are able to enter the circuit. If no support race takes place, my day usually ends there. There are races after which I leave straight away and others where we depart on Monday morning. When my work is done it is nice to spend Sunday evenings at home."

Bernd Mayländer on track
"During the race I am constantly in the Safety Car and I follow the race on the monitor in my car and also listen to the radio, which connects me to Race Control. If the weather conditions worsen, or an accident occurs, I communicate with Race Control several times. I give them my opinion of the situation and I wait for their feedback. Race Control then decide whether I will be deployed or not. Along with the information I provide, Race Control takes the information of the weather station and the teams into consideration.

"If Race Control sees potential for the deployment of the car, I get the command—'Safety Car stand-by!' I prepare for deployment and wait for further commands. If I receive a 'Safety Car stand-down!' the dangerous situation no longer exists, and there is no need for me to go on the track. If I hear 'Safety Car GO!' I immediately drive onto the circuit and try to quickly go in front of the leading car, so that the race cars can line up behind me.

"During a Safety Car phase, safety is the most important element; however I still need to maintain a certain level of speed. This is so the race cars do not overheat from the lack of cooling air or that their tyre pressure does not decrease. The teams have also an impact on the velocity. They inform Race Control if they want me to speed up or slow down.

"I tend to drive at my limit during the Safety Car phase—the Safety Car often seems slower than it is. Just to give an example: A Formula One race car is on average thirty-five to fifty-five seconds faster with every lap it completes, depending on the length of the track. This means that a Formula One car can overtake the Safety Car every three laps. It is incredible how fast these cars are. I then stay on the circuit until the hazardous situation has been overcome. This is the decision of Race Control. At the end of the second section I switch off the warning lights. Before taking the next possible exit, I turn into the pit lane and the grid is released. Overtaking is only permitted after having crossed the start/finish line."

Safety is essential—Bernd Mayländer about safety in Formula One

"In the field of safety, a lot has changed over the past few years. Regardless of which Formula One topic you speak about, whether it is the race car, the circuit, or the procedure of a Safety Car deployment—everything is being actively thought about and there is always room for improvements. There are different departments within the FIA that are responsible for safety in Formula One and there are many regulations that are created in co-operation with the Formula One teams. These intensive exchanges with the drivers ensure constant improvement. Currently, we already are at a very high level and strive to continuously enhance safety standards in the future."

SAFETY BY DESIGN—PHILIPPE GURDJIAN

Philippe Gurdjian (1945–2014) was one of Formula One's most gifted practitioners. The organizer and facilitator of almost thirty Grands Prix across five different countries during his four decades in the sport, including the inaugural races in Malaysia, Bahrain and Abu Dhabi, Gurdjian was most closely associated with his role at the heart of the quest for improved circuit safety. Writing shortly before his untimely passing, Gurdjian reflected on the improvements in trackside safety over the past thirty years, and considered where future innovation can lead to even safer racing environments.

THE SAFETY IDEAL

Since I organized my very first Grand Prix at France's Paul Ricard Circuit in 1985, I have always concentrated my attention towards safety. When I first came to Formula One, at the height of the turbo age in the era of Jean-Marie Balestre, concerns about safety were rising as the speed of the cars grew ever faster. Paul Ricard, where I organized six Formula 1 Grands Prix, was notorious as one of the world's fastest and most dangerous circuits. To improve safety, we created "red zones" (no spectators and no marshals), removed the "fences system" inside the gravel traps and tripled the height of the safety rail over the Mistral Straight—as well as adding three further layers of guard rails. Following Elio de Angelis' fatal accident while testing at Paul Ricard in 1986, we took the decision to modify the circuit layout, removing the high-speed "S" of the Verrerie complex to better control the speed of the cars.

After the French Grand Prix moved to Magny-Cours in 1991, I remained the race promoter, and once again innovated improvements at the circuit to improve safety. The most significant of these came in 1994 when, as Formula One collectively focused on ways to make the cars and circuits safer after the tragedy of Imola, we introduced two new systems at Magny-Cours: the "AVD" (Visual Starting Aid) system, which saw twelve quadri-flashes placed along the grid to indicate the exact location of a problem at the start of a race, and the "AVP" (Visual Driving Aid) system, where flashing lighted signs backed up the flags used by the stewards in the event of an incident. Furthermore, we increased the size of the gravel trap at Turn One and pushed the guardrails back by 100 m—all executed in less than eight weeks at a then substantial cost of 6 million Francs. A year later, we were able to overhaul the pit lane and starting grid areas, installing armoured glass windows above the pit lane wall to protect the teams and marshals, introducing electronic control of the safety lights from the race manager's post, and adding flying start control and speed monitoring systems in the pit lane. Our work at Magny-Cours set a standard that was successfully applied to a new generation of racetracks.

DEVELOPING NEW SOLUTIONS

Working at Paul Ricard and Magny Cours was about upgrading and modernizing safety at existing facilities, and allowed me to develop solutions that could subsequently be fed into the design of new circuits and facilities. Bernie Ecclestone consequently gave me total freedom to execute my vision with the development of Paul Ricard into a High Tech Test Track (HTTT). We needed to create new solutions for the track layout, the pit lane and pit garages, the race control and the medical centre. In addition, the safety solutions had to satisfy the needs of all types of vehicles, from touring cars to Formula 1. With the freedom and trust granted by Mr Ecclestone, we were able to implement the development of three significant safety mechanisms at HTTT Paul Ricard: TECPRO barriers, a video tracking system, and asphalt run-off.

TECPRO barriers were developed in order to replace the archaic system of tyre barriers. Today, racetracks such as Monaco, Circuit of the Americas and Buddh International Circuit are using the TECPRO technology. Yas Marina Circuit in Abu Dhabi, which I created from scratch, and Singapore are the only racetracks equipped entirely with TECPRO barriers, but the safety, efficiency and lifespan of these new barriers means they are being seen as not only viable, but an essential component of new circuit design.

A unique Lighting System replacing flag marshals was also developed at HTTT Paul Ricard and applied in Abu Dhabi. The video tracking being linked to the race control room allowed the stewards to instantly follow the progress of each car around the circuit. In addition, I worked closely with COLAS [Group] to create and implement 25 hectares of run-off made of three different types of asphalt abrasiveness; replacing all the gravel traps on the new HTTT Paul Ricard. The old gravel traps used to cost a lot of money and required regular maintenance at that time in order to remain efficient and safe. They were also fundamentally flawed, as accidents such as Michael Schumacher's crash at Silverstone in 1999 showed, because cars were unable to brake on the gravel and couldn't reduce their speed before impact.

FROM THE PAST TO THE MODERN AGE

The solutions developed at Paul Ricard were extremely efficient and are now not only set as safety standards for new circuits, but have also been used to update historic tracks such as Silverstone, the Nürburgring and the Circuit de Catalunya. With HTTT Paul Ricard, I was able to demonstrate that before becoming the most modern and safest racetrack in the world, it was an obsolete and unusable facility. In Barcelona, we decided to implement some ECPRO barriers around the racetrack and, most importantly, we created a chicane between Turn Thirteen and Fourteen to reduce the speed of the cars entering the finish line. Thus, it is becoming crucial that old racetracks such as Spa, Monza, Le Mans and Montreal start investing more money and significantly update the safety for the drivers. I strongly believe that TECPRO barriers should become mandatory by the FIA in 2015 replacing all the existing tyre barriers which are extremely dangerous and displace energy inefficiently—as we have seen during enormous accidents at the 24 Hours of Le Mans in the past two years.

SAFETY FROM SCRATCH

Of course, updating historic circuits to make them safer is crucial, but it is a different consideration entirely to design a completely new circuit and implement the safety features as a key design component rather than an afterthought. With innovations in racetrack safety, so new possibilities have emerged. The most compelling of these has been the development of night races.

When Bernie Ecclestone decided to introduce the first night race in Singapore, he asked me to initiate the testing at HTTT Paul Ricard. An Italian company was chosen to find and develop the best solution. Such a task required us to take the drivers' visibility and the quality of the images on TV into consideration. Even though the drivers' visibility was an easy task, finding the most efficient solution for TV images was substantially more difficult. After several weeks of testing, we finally came up with the solution that allowed me to call Bernie and tell him he would host the first night race in Singapore in the safest conditions. The success of Singapore pushed other tracks such as Abu Dhabi and now Bahrain to replicate it. Talking about Bahrain, even though I had only ninety days to complete the racetrack constructions for the inaugural race ten years ago, I took an important decision to push back the guardrails by an additional fifteen metres. Today, I am extremely satisfied to see that this circuit has kept improving its safety and replaced most of the gravel traps with run-off areas.

Combining all of the lessons we have learned through the years, the most developed circuit in terms of design and safety is undoubtedly the Yas Marina Circuit in Abu Dhabi. I have to pay tribute to Khaldoon Al Mubarak and the Royal Family of Abu Dhabi for entrusting me. I was provided with all the resources I needed to build the most advanced, developed, modern, safest and unique racetrack in the world.

In terms of architecture, it is by far the most accomplished racetrack in the world, symbolizing the image of Abu Dhabi and featuring creative touches such as the tunnel at the pit lane exit, the new generation of garages, the team houses in the paddock and Paddock Club hospitalities, the media centre and the medical centre. From a spectator's point of view, it is the only track that has 55,000 covered seats, and where the positioning of the grandstands has been designed to bring the public closer to the action. Above all, the Yas Marina Circuit is the safest racetrack in the world featuring the entire range of solutions developed at HTTT Paul Ricard, including asphalt run-off areas, TECPRO barriers, lighting systems and painting solutions for the run off areas. New safety solutions are yet to be developed and "risk zero" will never exist. The investment behind each solution is definitely significant, however protecting the lives of the drivers, the crews, the marshals, the media and the spectators around the track remains the primary obligation, no matter what the costs.

Finally, I would like to thank the drivers, Charlie Whiting, Herbie Blash, Jean-Louis Piet and Professor Sid Watkins for their strong collaboration through the development of safety solutions during my work and over the last thirty years.

TYRES

Sole F1 tyre supplier Pirelli will simplify the naming system in 2019 and only use hard (white), medium (yellow) and soft (red) compound names so that on any given weekend the hardest compound will be just known as the hard, the softest will be known as the soft and the compound in between known as the medium. Pirelli will still let the fans and media know what the 'actual' compounds are as they change from race to race.

Below are Pirelli's technical notes on each tyre compound as well as their circuit-by-circuit tyre guide. At the end of the chapter is an interesting insight into the lifespan of a typical competition tyre as well as how barcodes are used to track performance so as to aid research into the next generation of tyres.

MEET THE 2019 COMPOUNDS

DRY COMPOUNDS

HYPERSOFT

First introduced last season in 2018 the Pink hypersoft tyre—named by fans following a social media survey—is the softest and therefore the fastest compound that Pirelli has ever made. The drivers got to sample it for the first time at a test following the 2017 Abu Dhabi Grand Prix, with Lewis Hamilton calling it the best tyre Pirelli has ever produced. The new Pink hypersoft is suitable for all circuits that demand high levels of mechanical grip, but the trade-off for this extra speed and adhesion is the fact that the hypersoft has a considerably shorter lifespan than the other tyres in the range. Getting the most out of it will be a key to race strategy.

ULTRASOFT

This is designed for use on tight and twisty circuits, sitting below the supersoft. It has a rapid warm-up and huge peak performance, but the other side of this is its relatively limited overall life. Introduced in the 2016 season, its purple markings were also chosen as the result of an innovative social media campaign, with fans voting for their preferred colour.

SUPERSOFT

The supersoft, roughly equivalent to the 2017 ultrasoft, is ideal for slow and twisty circuits or when a high level of mechanical grip is needed. The supersoft benefits from a reasonably fast warm-up time, which makes it good for qualifying as well, but the flip side to that important characteristic is of course increased degradation.

SOFT

This tyre has been nominated at every race in the past—something that could change in 2019—striking a very good balance between performance and durability, with the accent on performance. It's a very adaptable tyre that can be used as the softest compound at a high-severity track as well as the hardest compound at a low- severity track or street circuit.

MEDIUM

The medium is a versatile compound but sitting in the harder part of the spectrum, it often comes into its own on circuits that tend towards high speeds, temperatures, and energy loadings. The 2019 medium has previously demonstrated an ample working range and adaptability to a wide variety of different circuits.

HARD

The hard tyre sports an ice blue colour and is designed for the circuits that put the highest energy loadings through the tyres, with fast corners, abrasive surfaces, or high ambient temperatures. The compound takes longer to warm up but offers maximum durability which frequently means that it plays a key role in race strategy—and provides low degradation.

SUPERHARD

This was introduced as an insurance policy, just in case the performance of the 2019 cars didn't match expectations, so the plan—and the likelihood—is for it not to be used at all. The

superhard provides a tyre at the very opposite end of the spectrum to the hypersoft. It features orange markings: the traditional
colour for the hardest tyres in Pirelli's range.

WET COMPOUNDS

INTERMEDIATE
The intermediates are the most versatile of the rain tyres. They
can be used on a wet track with no standing water, as well as a
drying surface. This tyre evacuates 30 litres of water per second
per tyre at 300 kph. There are two compounds of intermediate
tyre, to best suit specific circuit conditions: these will be called
'base' and 'soft'.

WET
The full wet tyres are the most effective solution for heavy rain.
These tyres can evacuate 85 litres of water per second per tyre at 300
kph. As is the case for the intermediates there are 'base' and 'soft'
compounds of wet tyre, to best suit specific circuit conditions.

2019 FORMULA ONE TRACKS AND THEIR TYRE CHARACTERISTICS

Australian Grand Prix
The Australian Grand Prix is a race loved by teams and fans
alike. The atmosphere is great, the weather is usually warm and
the track is close to the vibrant city of Melbourne. With the
Australian circuit being a semi-permanent facility, there is a high
level of track evolution as the weekend goes on.

Bahrain Grand Prix
Bahrain is very tough on rear tyres in particular with a high level
of traction and grip required for a good lap time. As it is located
in the desert it is quite common to have sand on the track, which
can lower the grip levels, in particular at the start of a session.
This is a track where tyre management is important, with rear

traction in particular being the key to a strong qualifying and race pace. The grand prix starts in the late afternoon, so temperatures fall as the race goes on, affecting tyre behaviour.

Chinese Grand Prix
The Shanghai International Circuit has hosted some thrilling and unpredictable races in the past and a wide variety of pit stop strategies can work at this track. Although ambient temperatures can be quite low and the surface is relatively smooth, tyre degradation is sometimes high due to the unique track layout. Overall, it is a demanding circuit for the tyres: especially the front- left. The heavy braking that is a characteristic of this track tends to put more strain on the front tyres than the rears. Some graining is also possible as the tyres cool down on the long straights.

Azerbaijan Grand Prix
Baku is the fastest street circuit on the calendar, running through the centre of the Azerbaijani capital, with some tight ninety-degree corners as well as a few straights. The track was designed by renowned circuit architect Hermann Tilke and incorporates a number of unique features such as an extremely narrow uphill section, and a straight that runs the length of the seaside promenade.

Spanish Grand Prix
Barcelona is extremely well known to all the drivers and teams because of the many tests that have been held there, including both pre-season tests this year. The circuit itself has several medium to high speed corners that test every aspect of a tyre's performance and can lead to a notable degree of wear and degradation. The asphalt is traditionally abrasive and temperatures can be high. It is one of the most challenging circuits of the season for tyres, which is particularly hard work for the left-hand tyres, especially in Turn Three.

Monaco Grand Prix
Monaco is probably the most famous race of the season, taking place on a street circuit in the Principality. It is also the slowest

and least abrasive circuit of the year. Tyre wear is low: mechanical grip and high levels of low- speed downforce are very important here. Overtaking is nearly impossible, putting the emphasis on qualifying. With limited run-off areas and a high risk of incidents the safety car has often influenced the race outcome at this track in the past.

Canadian Grand Prix
The iconic Circuit Gilles Villeneuve is a semi-permanent track, infrequently used during the year, which means that at the beginning of the weekend the track is very 'green' and slippery. However, there is plenty of track evolution as more rubber gets laid down throughout the weekend. This track puts a lot of longitudinal stress through the tyres and is very demanding in terms of braking and traction. The surface provides little grip, which can lead to the cars sliding more. The rear tyres are particularly stressed at this track, due to the traction required out of the low and medium speed corners.

French Grand Prix
Located in Le Castellet, near Marseille in southeast France, Circuit Paul Ricard officially opened in April 1970 and hosted the French Grand Prix fourteen times between 1971 and 1999 (before the event moved to Magny-Cours). Now it's back for the second year in a row and while the track has been transformed beyond recognition in the intervening years but still maintains many of its most famous characteristics, including a long straight and a wide variety of technical corners.

Austrian Grand Prix
The Austrian Grand Prix re-joined the calendar in 2014, having been absent since 2003. During this period of absence, the track underwent extensive construction work once more to become the Red Bull Ring, in its latest incarnation. It now features two main straights and mostly sharp corners. As a result, average speeds are generally low, meaning that the cars have to rely on mechanical grip from the tyres more than aerodynamic downforce. As this is a clockwise circuit the emphasis is on the tyres on the right-hand

side of the car: especially during the double left-handers of Turn Five and Turn Six.

British Grand Prix

Silverstone is another challenging track for the tyres. Here, aerodynamics play a more important role than mechanical grip, due to a high average speed. The circuit features a technical layout, taking in a variety of very high-speed corners with some slower and more complex sections. This, together with an abrasive surface, tends to lead to a high wear rate: although the track will be resurfaced this year. Temperatures in Silverstone can often be rather low and there is always a risk of rain. But when dry, temperatures can equally be quite high, which means that a versatile compound choice is required for this track.

Hungarian Grand Prix

Hungary is the slowest permanent circuit of the year, which does not make it any easier on the tyres. It is a very twisty track and often slippery, in particular at the start of the weekend. This means that much more heat is put through the tyres than on a fast and flowing layout because the tyres are moving around more: particularly when it is hot, which is often the case in Hungary. Therefore, balancing the demands of speed and durability is key to getting the most out of the compounds, to keep degradation under control. Overtaking is traditionally difficult at this track, so drivers have an opportunity to use strategy to gain track position.

Belgian Grand Prix

Spa-Francorchamps is the longest and one of the most iconic circuits on the Formula 1 calendar, with extreme demands on the tyres. It is the track that puts the highest peak vertical load on the tyres during the season, for example, in the Eau Rouge to Raidillon section. The undulating surface at Spa also means that the tyres work hard as part of the car's suspension, placing heavy demands on the structure. On top of this, the weather can be very changeable—and because the track is so long, it is not unusual for it to be raining on one part of the circuit but dry in another.

Italian Grand Prix
The Italian Grand Prix is Pirelli's home grand prix, as Monza is just half an hour from company headquarters in Milan. There is always a special atmosphere thanks to so many passionate fans. The track is characterised by very high speeds, putting a lot of energy through the tyres, so the cars run the lowest downforce levels of the year. There are also a number of high kerbs, which mean that the tyres have to constantly absorb heavy structural impacts. Overall, this track puts some of the highest speeds through the tyres that they will face all year.

Singapore Grand Prix
Singapore is the season's only race held completely at night, run under powerful spotlights, with twenty-three corners. The circuit itself is low-grip and slippery; evolving considerably as more rubber gets laid down. Average speeds are contained, so degradation is not usually an issue provided that wheelspin—which can lead to overheating and blistering—is controlled out of the slower corners. The softest compounds are usually well suited for this race, and the fact that the high temperatures tend to fall as the race goes on can put an interesting spin on strategy.

Russian Grand Prix
Sochi is a medium-speed circuit with a variety of different corners, including one left-hander that has been inspired by the long triple apex Turn 8 at Istanbul Park. In total there are twelve right and six left-hand corners, with a 650-metre straight between the first and second turns. There has been little track evolution over the years and the surface is low-severity, as a result of which the softest compounds in the range are nominated.

Japanese Grand Prix
Suzuka is a little less aggressive on the tyres than in the past, but the circuit is still a difficult one for the rubber because of the track layout. It contains a wide variety of fast and flowing corners that place high lateral loads on the tyre but there are also some heavy braking areas and tighter corners. The first half of the lap is essentially a non-stop series of corners, which put plenty of heat

through the tyres with no significant straights where they can cool down.

Mexican Grand Prix

The Autodromo Hermanos Rodriguez in Mexico City has proved to be a huge success since returning to Formula 1 in 2015 for the first time since 1992. The highlights of the circuit include a very long pit straight and a huge stadium section in the last part of the lap, converted from a former baseball ground, which also hosts a unique podium ceremony. At an altitude of 2200 metres, the rarefied air could produce some of the highest top speeds of the year.

United States Grand Prix

The United States Grand Prix has already established itself as a favourite of teams and spectators alike. The track contains a variety of elevations, plus some slow and technical sections alternating with very fast parts. It's a good test of a tyre's all-round ability with traction demands out of slow corners just as important as lateral grip through the high-speed changes of direction that are another key characteristic of the 5.513-kilometre Circuit of the Americas.

Brazilian Grand Prix

Brazil is Pirelli's biggest market outside Italy, so this grand prix is always very busy for us. The track is one of the shortest but also one of the most challenging of the year. There are some big elevation changes and it can be bumpy, which makes it hard for the tyres to find traction and increases the physical demands on the drivers. The track was resurfaced quite recently, which had an effect on wear and degradation

Abu Dhabi Grand Prix

As has been the case in recent years, Abu Dhabi will host the season end and possibly even the title- decider. The track surface is generally smooth, so degradation is low. The circuit provides a variety of speeds and corners, so the tyres have to withstand a wide range of different demands, but none of them are particularly severe. As the race starts late in the afternoon and continues into dusk, ambient and track temperatures tend to fall as the race goes on, which alters the usual strategy calculations.

THE LIFE OF A COMPETITION TYRE

In Milan, the home of Pirelli, 150 research engineers work exclusively on Formula 1—and many more in other areas of motorsport. The starting points are the physics and chemistry labs, where new compounds and structures are tested. There are about 100 elements in each tyre and eighteen structural components. At the motorsport factory in Romania (with a back-up factory in Turkey), physical prototypes are built on the basis of the virtual model, with the compounds produced at Pirelli's Settimo Torinese plant in Italy. This is when the theory gets turned into practice: the compounds and structure are tailor-made and all the components are finally put together. The first physical tests take place at Pirelli's experimental test centre in Milan, where sophisticated machines simulate every race condition and measure all the stresses to which the tyres are subjected. Once various laboratory tests have been concluded, the tyres then get to experience a real circuit. The tyres that have successfully made it through the track tests are then eligible to form part of the final selection offered to teams for racing.

At the factories, there are two parallel Formula 1 production lines. One line makes the shoulder and the carcass of the tyre. At the same time, on a parallel line, the belt and tread pattern are produced. Natural rubber, synthetic rubber and other artificial fibres are among the key ingredients. The elements produced by the first two production lines are assembled on a third line— which represents the key part of the production process, as a recognisable Formula 1 tyre is born.

The barcode, which acts as the tyre's 'passport', is affixed to the tyre. This contains all the relevant data about the tyre and allows its usage to be tracked from production to race.

The next step, the vulcanisation period during which the tyre is 'cooked', determines the definitive characteristics of the compound and structure. It also seals in the barcode.

Finally, there is quality control, which takes in a visual check, weight check and an x-ray scan of the tyre. There is also shearography and a geometric check. A random sample of tyres is additionally taken from each batch to check structural integrity via a destructive test. The tyre is then ready for dispatch to a race or test. These exacting principles, used in Formula 1, are the same for other types of competition tyre, seen in a wide variety of races and rallies all over the world.

THE BARCODE: EACH TYRE'S PASSPORT
Pirelli will bring around 1800 tyres to each grand prix in 2019. They are allocated to the teams randomly with the help of a barcode; a process carried out by the FIA: the sport's governing body.

The tyres are manufactured at Pirelli's state of the art motorsport facilities in Romania. During the production process, each tyre is allocated a barcode provided by the FIA. This barcode is the tyre's 'passport', which is embedded firmly into the structure during the vulcanisation process and cannot be swapped. The code contains all the details of each tyre, making it traceable throughout the race weekend with Pirelli's RTS (Racing Tyre System) software, which can read and update all the data. For European events, the tyres are then transported to Pirelli's logistics and distribution hub at Didcot in the United Kingdom.

Once they arrive there, an FIA official receives a list of barcodes, which relate to the tyres that will be taken to the next grand prix. The FIA then allocates barcodes—and therefore tyres—to each individual team at random. Pirelli itself is not involved in this process at all, meaning that the Italian firm cannot influence which tyres are allocated to which teams—although a rigorous quality control process ensures that all the tyres leaving the factory are entirely identical.

Once at the circuit, the tyres are then allocated to the teams in strict compliance with the list that has been previously prepared by the FIA. The barcodes allow both the FIA and Pirelli to ensure that the right teams, according to the regulations, are using the correct tyres. Each team is allocated a Pirelli engineer, who works exclusively with that team for all of the year, but the database that every engineer works off allows the engineer to see only

information relating specifically to his or her team over the weekend, so that individual strategies are not compromised.
Development data is overseen by Pirelli's senior engineers, who
monitor all the information in order to assist the research team in
charge of shaping the next generation of tyres.

GLOSSARY

A: from Accident Data Recorder to Auxiliary Driving Features

Accident Data Recorder (ADR):
A module that collects accident data. Its installation has been required in every Formula One car since 1997. The ADR logs speeds and deceleration rates that occur in an accident. This data is analyzed to obtain findings about possible causes of the accident in order to further increase safety in Formula One.

Acoustic Signals:
Ten minutes before the start, an acoustic signal indicates that everyone except drivers, officials and technical staff have to leave the starting grid. Three minutes before the start there is another acoustic signal. At this time, the tyres must be properly fitted. Those who have not fitted their tyres within three minutes before the race starts receive a ten-second penalty. One minute before the start, the engines are started. By the time the fifteen-second signal is given, all team personnel must have left the grid and taken all equipment with them. If a driver then requires further assistance, he must raise his arm and he will be pushed into the pits.

Adjustable Rear Wing:
According to the moveable bodywork regulations introduced in 2011, drivers of suitably equipped cars can adjust the rear wing

from the cockpit, altering its angle of incidence through a set range. Also known as DRS (Drag Reduction System), it can be used at any time in practice and qualifying (unless race direction is suspending its use due to poor weather conditions or yellow flags in the activation zone), but only in the designated DRS zones. During the race it can only be activated when a driver is less than one second behind another car at pre-determined points on the track. The system is then deactivated once the driver brakes. In combination with ERS, it is designed to boost overtaking.

Aerodynamics:
The study of the interaction of air with solid bodies moving through it. The basic rule when designing cars for Formula One is simply to create as much downforce and as little air resistance as possible.

Air Box:
The air inlet behind the driver's head. The airbox channels the air necessary for the combustion process to the engine.

Allianz Center for Technology (AZT):
The AZT, based in Munich today, was founded as a full subsidiary of Allianz in Berlin in 1932. It has built an eighty-year reputation as a successful accident and damage research institute dedicated to practical knowledge and thorough analysis. Core areas of its expertise are risk management, consultancy services and damage reduction. The AZT conducts weekly crash tests to improve the safety of its 50 million motor insurance customers and other motorists. Eighty to ninety crash tests per year contribute to the development of technologies that help to reduce the incidence of traffic accidents and to minimize the resulting damage.

Apex:
The point at which the ideal racing line touches the inner radius of a corner.

Aquaplaning:
When there is more water between the tyres and the road than can be displaced by the tyre tread, the car "floats" and consequently cannot be controlled by the driver. Formula One races can be stopped if there is a danger of aquaplaning. Under very wet conditions, the Official Formula One Safety Car is generally used to keep the field at a lower speed.

Autoclave:
A pressure vessel, in which vacuum packed composite components are cured at 100–200° C for ten to twenty minutes up to twenty-four hours—depending on the piece and its purpose. This procedure lends the composite components their high strength while maintaining low weight.

Auxiliary Driving Features:
Traction control, automatic transmission or launch control are examples of auxiliary driving features. An expert team commissioned by the FIA may check at any time during the race weekend whether a car's electronics contain banned auxiliary driving features. In the 2004 season, launch control and automatic transmission were banned and since 2008 traction control is also no longer permitted.

B: from Balaclava to Briefing

Balaclava:
Fireproof face mask made of Nomex® brand fibre, a flame retardant synthetic fibre. It is worn under the helmet.

Black Flag:
The black flag—together with the respective car number—is shown to drivers who should stop at their pit or near the pit lane entrance. If for any reason a driver does not respond, the flag should not be shown for more than four successive laps. When the stewards decide to show the black flag to a driver, they also immediately inform his team. A black flag with an orange circle informs drivers of technical problems with their car that could

endanger themselves or others. They must go in for a pit stop immediately. They can then rejoin the race following repairs. The black/white flag together with the car number warns a driver about unsportsmanlike behaviour.

Blistering:
Formation of blisters on the tyres, caused by excessive use. The negative consequence is reduction in grip.

Blue Flag:
The blue flag is used when a faster vehicle approaches a lapped car from behind. The slower car has to make way immediately. The blue flag is also used at the pit lane exit to signal that a car is approaching on the track.

Boots:
Formula One shoes are ankle boots made of soft, cushioned leather. They have thin rubber soles with good grip to prevent drivers' feet from slipping off the pedals.

Brake Balance:
To gain a better balance when braking, the driver can adjust the brake force distribution between the front and the rear axle even during the race via a button on the steering wheel or via a lever at the cockpit wall.

Brake Discs:
Formula One brake discs are made of carbon. The discs may not be thicker than 28 mm and their diameter may not exceed 278 mm. Carbon brake discs and pads require an operating temperature between 350 and 550°C and reach up to 1,000°C during a braking process. Disc brakes were introduced in 1955.

Brakes:
The regulations call for two separate, independent hydraulic braking circuits operated from a single pedal. One circuit has to operate the brakes on the front axle, and the other the brakes on the rear axle, where a brake-by-wire system is in use from the

2014 season. This system electronically converts the driver's input on the brake pedal into braking force at the rear axle. Only one brake calliper and a maximum of six pistons are permitted per wheel. Brake callipers must be made of an aluminium alloy. Anti-lock braking systems (ABS) are not allowed. Full braking will bring a Formula One car from 200 to 0 km/h within 65 metres, all within 1.9 seconds. Anti-lock systems are prohibited, as are cooling systems using fluids. Force distribution may not change during the braking process.

Briefing:
At the meeting with the drivers and representatives from their teams convened by the race director before every Grand Prix, the discussions focus on current issues such as special features of the respective track or changes to the rules or weekend format. At the team briefings, the team managers, engineers and drivers set out the strategies for each day of the Grand Prix weekend. The subsequent review of the race day by this group, which forms the basis for future strategies and technical enhancements, is called the debriefing.

C: from Carbon to Cylinder

Carbon Fibre
A construction material for Formula One cars. The monocoque, for example, is made of epoxy resin reinforced with carbon fibre. These materials, when laminated together, give great rigidity and strength, but are very lightweight.

Carbon-fibre-reinforced Plastic (CFRP):
CFRP covers composite materials such as carbon and Kevlar® which, when combined with epoxy resins, provide high rigidity and strength and an extremely low weight. Many parts are produced from these materials, e.g. the monocoque.

Chassis:
The central part of a Formula One car, with the main component being the monocoque. All the other components are connected to

the strong, lightweight monocoque. The chassis walls must be at least 3.5 mm thick with 2.5 mm reserved for a casing with DuPont™ Kevlar® brand fibre. The geometry of the chassis suspension must not be modified while driving.

Checkered Flag:
The checkered flag (black/white) indicates the end of a practice session, qualifying session or race.

Chicanes:
Tight corners that race organizers use to break up long, straight stretches of a circuit for safety reasons. Chicanes force drivers to reduce their speed and serve as overtaking opportunities, too.

Cockpit:
This is the driver's workplace. The cockpit must be designed so that the driver can get out easily within five seconds. The width of the cockpit must be 50 cm at the steering wheel and 30 cm at the pedals. The opening must have a minimum length of 85 cm. For safety reasons, no fuel, oil or water lines may pass through the cockpit. The cockpit temperature may reach an average temperature of 50°C.

Computational Fluid Dynamics (CFD):
CFD makes the airflows surrounding the vehicle visible on the computer, and at the same time shows the effects of individual vehicle parts on each other and on the aerodynamics. The engineers can simulate these effects without even having to build the parts first. That saves time and money.

Computer Aided Design (CAD):
Intelligent computer programs provide efficiency and speed and make the designers' work much easier. Drawing boards have long been a thing of the past in modern racing factories.

Concorde Agreement:
This agreement specifies the rights and obligations of the teams and the FIA. It also calls for unanimity for important decisions. The sixth Concorde Agreement so far—after 1981, 1987, 1992,

1997 and 1998—was signed on 1 August 2009 and remained in effect until 31 December 2012. As of now, there is no current Concorde Agreement.

Crash Barrier:
Safety measure at track locations where there is no space for run-off zones.

Crash Tests:
The FIA specifies and defines two main types of crash tests: static and dynamic. The crash tests were introduced in 1985. Since the cars start with more fuel due to the refuelling ban, the FIA has issued stricter rules for crash tests. As of 2012, only cars that have passed the mandatory crash tests can be used in test drives. There are tests for front, side and rear constructions. They are carried out under the supervision of the FIA, usually at the Cranfield Impact Centre in Bedfordshire, England. The front impact crash test is done at a speed of 15 metres per second, the lateral at 10 m per second and the rear at an impact speed of 11 m per second. The deceleration measured on the chest of the dummy may not be in excess of 60 g within three milliseconds. A fourth dynamic impact test relates to the steering column which must collapse under a simulated head impact. The safety cell must remain undamaged after all the dynamic tests have been performed. The quick release for the steering wheel must also remain fully functional. In addition to the dynamic crash tests, the front, side and rear structures must withstand collateral pressure during static crash tests. The roll-over bar is tested in three directions: laterally with 5 tons, longitudinally with 6 tons and vertically with 9 tons. Deformation may not exceed 50 mm.

Curfew:
Since 2011 a curfew has been imposed on team members who work directly on the cars. During two six-hour time periods prior to the start of practice on Friday and Saturday they may not be present in the trackside facilities. The two time periods start eleven hours before the start of the first practice session on Friday and nine hours before the third practice session on Saturday,

respectively. Each team is entitled to six exceptions during the course of the season.

Cylinder:
Component in the engine where the power is generated. The upward and downward movement of the piston and the combustion of the fuel air mixture take place in the cylinder.

D: from Differential to Drivers

Differential:
A differential is connected between the drive wheels to compensate the speed differences between the outer and inner wheels when cornering.

Diffuser:
Air outlet at the rear of the car's underbody that has a strong influence on the aerodynamic properties. Rising to the rear, the tail ensures a controlled airstream on the underbody which generates low pressure under the car and supplies the downforce critical to fast cornering. The double diffusers introduced in 2009 have been prohibited since 2011. As of 2012 it is no longer permitted to blow fumes under the underbody to increase downforce.

Dimensions:
Whereas the length of a Formula One car is up to the designers, the width is limited to 1.80 m. The maximum width of the front wing must not exceed 1.65 m. The rear wing may not exceed 0.75 m in width and it may have no more than two wing elements. Car height is limited to 95 cm, measured from the lowest point.

Downforce:
Pressure that propels the Formula One car downward. It is generated by low pressure conditions under the body of the car, as well as by the angle of attack of the front and rear wings, and enhances the grip. Especially on slower circuits, this effect permits higher cornering speeds.

Drag Reduction System (DRS):
The Drag Reduction System (DRS) is a method to aid overtaking by altering the angle of the rear wing flap to reduce drag. Drivers are able to activate the system in designated DRS zones around a track. In practice and qualifying they can do so at will, during a race only if they are within one second of the car in front at the DRS detection point. DRS is deactivated again the first time the driver uses the brakes after activation. DRS may not be used during the opening two laps of a race. In wet conditions and with yellow flags race direction may choose to suspend the use of DRS.

Drive:
Two-wheel drive is the limit. Automatic and continuously variable transmissions are prohibited. As of 2014, ERS, the predecessor of which (KERS) has been permitted since 2009, has to be integrated into the power unit.

Driver's Seat:
The entire seat is one single unit and specially tailored to the respective driver. Drivers can be extracted from the cars together with their so-called rescue seats. In the normal seating position, the soles of the driver's feet must not protrude from the centre of the front axle. Since 1971 the cockpit must be designed in such a way that the driver can be rescued within five seconds. Since 1999, regulations have stipulated that the seat may no longer be installed as a fixed part of the car. The risk of damaging the driver's spine when removing him from the car is thus eradicated.

Drivers:
Each team can use four drivers per season. The drivers may be substituted on a race weekend up to the start of qualifying. Any later substitutions due to *force majeure* are at the discretion of the stewards. In the first and second free practice sessions the race teams may use two additional drivers, who must also be in possession of a super license, but not more than two cars.

E: from Electronic Control Unit (ECU) to Energy Store

Electronic Control Unit (ECU):
The unit that controls all the electronic processes in a Formula One car. The ECU has been standard since 2008 and is designed by a manufacturer specified by the FIA. The current ECU supplier is McLaren Electronic Systems.

End-plate:
Vertical border area on the front and rear wings that helps to streamline a car's aerodynamics.

Energy Recovery System (ERS):
For 2014, the notion of hybrid energy recovery has shed a letter (KERS has become ERS) but become significantly more sophisticated. Energy can still be recovered and deployed to the rear axle via a Motor Generator Unit (MGU), however this is now termed MGU-K (for "Kinetic") and is permitted twice the maximum power of the 2013 motor (120 kW or 161 hp, instead of 60 kW or 80.5 hp). It may recover five times more energy per lap (2 MJ) and deploy ten times as much (4 MJ) compared to its 2013 equivalent, equating to over thirty seconds per lap at full power. The rest of the energy is recovered by the MGU-H (for "Heat"); an electrical machine connected to the turbocharger. Where the V8 offered one possible "energy journey" to improve efficiency via KERS, there are up to seven different efficiency enhancing energy journeys in the ERS system.

Energy Store:
The Energy Store does exactly what it says on the tin; storing the energy harvested from the two Motor Generator Units (MGUs) for deployment back into those same systems. It is capped in terms of maximum and minimum weight: the maximum (25 kg) setting engineers an aggressive target, while the minimum (20 kg) means weight reduction will not be chased at all costs.

F: from Factory Shutdown to Fuel

Factory Shutdown:
All competitors must observe a factory shutdown period of fourteen consecutive days in August, during which time their wind tunnels and Computational Fluid Dynamics (CFD) facilities must not be used for Formula One activities.

Fading:
Technical term for the gradual loss of the brake effect after relatively long, heavy use. Occurs less with the modern carbon brakes than with conventional steel disc brakes.

F-duct:
This aerodynamic modification was introduced in 2010. A channel (duct) conducts air to the rear wing where it causes the flow to separate. This reduces downforce and aerodynamic drag, enabling the vehicle to achieve a higher end speed. The F-duct has been prohibited since 2011.

Fédération Internationale de l'Automobile (FIA):
The FIA is the international automobile umbrella organization and draws up the technical and sporting regulations for Formula One. It is based in Paris. Since 23 October 2009, Jean Todt has been the new FIA president. The FIA was founded in 1904.

Fire Extinguisher:
Every Formula One car must have a fire extinguisher that spreads foam around the chassis and engine area. It must be operable both by the driver and from outside the car.

Flags:
The cars are fitted with diodes that transmit the flag signals from the marshals to the drivers in the cockpits.

Formation Lap:
Thirty minutes before the start of a Formula One race, the pit lane is opened and the drivers may drive one or several

formation laps—in this instance the pit lane needs to be used. Vehicles that fail to finish the formation lap and are unable to reach the starting grid on their own power are not allowed to participate in the race. Fifteen minutes before the start, the pit lane is closed. If a car is still in the pits, it has to start from the pit lane.

Formula One:
The term "Formula One" was not introduced until after the Second World War. It was intended to identify top class motor racing. The first Formula One World Championship took place in 1950 under the direction of the FIA. The first race in the World Championship was the British Grand Prix on 13 May 1950.

Formula One Commission:
This commission consists of representatives from the teams, race organizers, engine manufacturers, sponsors, tyre manufacturers and the FIA. The commission decides whether changes to the regulations suggested by the FIA's technical committee should be implemented.

Formula One Teams Association (FOTA):
The FOTA was the association of all Formula One teams and was chaired by McLaren team principal Martin Whitmarsh. The FOTA represented the racing teams in negotiations with the FIA and, for example, made suggestions to regulation changes. It was founded on 29 July 2008 and dissolved prior to the 2014 season.

Free Practice:
During practice sessions on Friday and Saturday before a Grand Prix, the lap times are recorded, but they have no influence on the starting order or the result. The teams use them as an opportunity to set up their cars for the respective track and work on the tyre wear.

Front Wing:
Creates downward pressure on the front area of the Formula One car and is thus an important part of the aerodynamics.

Details of the front wing sometimes change for every new race—according to how much downward pressure is required for the respective circuits. Apart from that, the drivers make adjustments to the front wing, mainly modifying the angle of the second flap.

Fuel:
Only super unleaded petrol may be used in Formula One. It corresponds to a large extent to the fuel available at a conventional filling station with a minimum of 87 octane. However, the fuels contain additives that ensure faster and better combustion; in some cases, they are also lighter than commercially available petrol; 5.75 per cent of the petrol must originate from biological sources. Each team can choose its supplier independently, but it must submit two five-litre samples of the petrol used to the FIA before the season for test purposes.

G: from Gloves to Gurney Flap

Gloves:
Like the racing overalls, these are made of Nomex® fibre, a fire-resistant material. The close fitting gloves with suede leather palms provide the necessary sensitivity for steering.

Graining:
Due to excessive use, tyres show signs of corrosion and the rubber compound begins to disintegrate. This is referred to as graining. The negative consequence is reduction in grip.

Grand Prix Drivers Association (GPDA):
Association representing the interests of Formula One drivers.

Gravel Trap:
Run-off zone at a racing circuit that quickly slows down cars that have gone off the track. It is filled with small gravel stones of between 5–16 millimetres diameter and is about twenty-five centimetres deep.

Green Flag:
The green flag indicates the track is clear. The green flag is also waved after a spell of yellow flags.

Grip:
Describes how much the car adheres to the ground. High grip means high cornering speeds. Main factors of grip are the aerodynamics, the downforce created by the vehicle and the tyres' properties. Without grip, a vehicle will begin to slide or skid.

Ground Clearance:
The distance between the underbody and the surface of the track.

Ground Effect:
The contact force generated by an aerodynamically shaped underbody. In the late seventies and early eighties, sills were attached to the sides of the cars to create a vacuum underneath the vehicle that held it down on the track. The enormous resulting grip allowed for extremely high cornering speeds. The pure ground effect cars developed in the seventies were banned by the FIA for safety reasons in late 1982.

Gurney Flap:
L-shaped counterflap on the trailing edge of a car's wing, which was invented by the American race driver Dan Gurney.

H: from Hairpin to Helmet

Hairpin:
Very narrow turn. The most famous hairpin is the former Loews hairpin in Monaco, which is now known as the Grand Hotel hairpin.

Head and Neck Support (HANS):
Since the 2003 season the drivers have been given additional head and neck protection. The Head and Neck Support system consists of a carbon shoulder corset that is connected to the

safety belts and the driver's helmet. In case of an accident, HANS is intended to prevent a stretching of the vertebrae. Additionally, it prevents the driver's head from hitting the steering wheel. The HANS was invented by Jim Downing and Robert Hubbard.

Head Support:
The removable padding on the inside of the cockpit. The cockpit is fitted with removable padding around the driver's head, designed to absorb any impact. The two side pads must be at least 95 mm thick and the rear pad between 75 and 90 mm.

Helmet:
The helmet is made of carbon, polyethylene and Kevlar® and weighs approximately 1,250 g. Like the cars, it is designed in a wind tunnel to reduce drag as much as possible. Helmets are subjected to extreme deformation and fragmentation tests. As of 2011, the most vulnerable part of the helmet, the visor, is reinforced with Zylon strip to increase its impact performance and to provide even more effective head protection. Only helmets tested and authorized by the FIA may be used.

I: from Internal Combustion Engine to International Sporting Code

Internal Combustion Engine (ICE):
The Internal Combustion Engine (ICE) is the traditional, fuel-powered heart of the Power Unit; previously known simply as the engine. For 2014 this took the form of a 1.6-litre, turbocharged V6 configuration, with direct fuel injection up to 500 bar of pressure. Where the V8 engines could rev to 18,000 rpm, the ICE has been limited to 15,000 rpm since 2014. This reduction in crankshaft rotational speed coupled with the reduction in engine capacity and number of cylinders, reduces the friction and thus increases the total efficiency of the Power Unit. This down-speeding, down-sizing approach is the key technological change at the heart of the ICE structure.

International Court of Appeal:
The FIA's Court of Appeal is composed of professional judges, and its twenty-three members are appointed for a three-year term. In order for the court to make a legally binding decision, the presence of at least three judges is required, none of which may be of the same nationality as the parties involved. A Formula One team that is unwilling to accept a decision by the racing commissioners can appeal to the FIA's International Court of Appeal. In this case, a declaration of intent must be submitted within an hour of the decision. The FIA, too, can send a decision by the commissioners to the Court of Appeal. Since December 2009, the teams have been allowed to nominate one of the three judges.

International Sporting Code:
The FIA code that contains all the regulations governing international racing.

J: like Jump Start

Jump Start:
A jump or false start is committed by drivers whose cars start moving before all the lights on the starting grid have gone out. This is determined by sensors on the starting straight. A jump start normally results in penalties imposed by the race stewards.

K: from Kerbs to Kevlar®

Kerbs:
Raised kerbstones lining corners or chicanes on racing tracks. The kerbs provide additional safety as the drivers must reduce their speed when driving over them.

KERS (Kinetic Energy Recovery System):
KERS was used for the first time in the 2009 season. For the following year the teams agreed to suspend its use for cost reasons. In 2011 the system returned to Formula One, but was suspended again for the 2014 season with ERS taking its place. KERS recovered kinetic energy (which is normally wasted) under

braking and made it available to the driver for about 6.6 seconds as a 60kW boost when he pushed a button. This power boost could either be used once or in quantities during a lap. To prevent heavier drivers from being disadvantaged, the minimum weight of the car including the driver had been raised.

Kevlar®:
Highly durable artificial fibre used in the covering of the headrest. Combined to form a composite with epoxy resin, it has high strength, but is very lightweight.

L: from Logistics to Lollipop

Logistics:
The tour of Formula One around the globe demands sophisticated logistics. For every race, around 120 crates of different sizes have to be packed with the help of a twenty-page checklist. The two race cars are always part of the cargo—plus spare parts and tools, wheels and the pit lane equipment. The luggage also includes several engines. PCs and notebooks, secure data lines and radios are all part of the basic equipment of every team. For European races the equipment is transported to the venues by trucks, for races on other continents by chartered cargo planes.

Lollipop:
The signal pole with a sign saying "Gear" on one side and "Brake" on the other. During a pit stop, the chief mechanic posted in front of the car uses the sign to show the driver when he should apply the brake and when he should shift gear and drive off.

M: from Manufacturers to Motor Sport Safety Development Fund

Manufacturers:
Any manufacturers wanting to enter Formula One must prove to the FIA that they have designed and built the chassis of their racing cars. They are also obliged to compete in all the races in a

particular season and to prove that they possess the necessary technical and financial means.

Marshals:
Officials posted along the side of the track. They wave the flag signals and secure any possible accident sites; they also rescue any cars that have broken down.

Medical Car:
The Official Formula One Medical Car is staffed by a driver and the Formula One rescue coordinator of the FIA. Like the Safety Car, it is on standby at the exit of the pit lane during every practice session and race. Since 2009 it has been driven by the former Formula Three Champion Alan van der Merwe. Dr Ian Roberts, the official Formula One physician, is also on board.

Medical Centre
Every Formula One race and test circuit must have a state-of-the-art emergency service facility staffed by experienced physicians. A rescue helicopter must always be on standby, ready for lift-off.

MGU-H:
The Motor Generator Unit-Heat (MGU-H) is a new electrical machine that is directly coupled to the turbocharger shaft. Waste exhaust energy that is in excess of that required to drive the compressor can be recovered by the turbine, harvested by the MGU-H, converted into electrical energy and stored in the Energy Store. Where the MGU-K is limited to recovering 2 MJ of energy per lap, there is no limit placed on the MGU-H. This recovered energy can be used to power the MGU-K when accelerating, or can be used to power the MGU-H in order to accelerate the turbocharger, thus helping to eliminate "turbo lag". This new technology increases the efficiency of the Power Unit and most significantly provides a method to ensure good driveability from a boosted, down-sized engine.

MGU-K:
The Motor Generator Unit-Kinetic (MGU-K) has double the power capability of the previously used KERS motors and operates in an identical way. Some of the kinetic energy that would normally be dissipated by the rear brakes under braking is converted into electrical energy and stored in the Energy Store. Then, when the car accelerates, energy stored in the Energy Store is delivered to the MGU-K which provides an additional boost up to a maximum power of 120 kW (approximately 160 hp) to the rear axle for over thirty seconds per lap.

Monocoque:
French for single shell. A safety cell made of carbon-fibre composite that forms a protective shell around the driver. In some parts the monocoque even has sixty layers of carbon fibre. The "drivers' life insurance" is surrounded by deformable structures that absorb energy in an accident. The molding and binding process takes place within an autoclave at high levels of pressure and heat.

N: from NACA Duct to Nose

NACA Duct:
The NACA duct is a common form of low-drag intake design, originally developed by the National Advisory Committee for Aeronautics (NACA). It is a triangular air inlet on the surface of the car body.

Nomex®:
Artificial fibre that undergoes thermal testing in the laboratory. It is subjected to an open flame with a temperature of between 300–400°C that acts on the material from a distance of 3 cm— only if it fails to ignite within ten seconds can it be used for racing overalls. The drivers' and pit crews' underwear, socks and gloves are also made of Nomex®.

Nose:
Front part of a Formula One car, subjected to various crash tests for safety reasons. The nose also functions as a protruding crash structure protecting the monocoque.

O: from On-board Camera to Oversteering

On-board Camera:
A miniTV camera on board the racing car, which can be attached near the airbox, the rear mirror or the front or rear wing. It provides live footage throughout the race weekend.

Overall:
Protective suit with elastic cuffs on wrists and ankles made of two to four layers of Nomex® for drivers and pit crews. A completed multi layered overall undergoes fifteen washes as well as a further fifteen dry-cleaning processes before it is finally tested. It is subjected to a temperature of 600–800°C. The critical level of 41°C may not be exceeded inside the overall for at least eleven seconds.

Oversteering:
When oversteering, a car's rear wheels lose grip and break away. In order to get through the corner, the driver must decrease his steering angle or, in the case of extreme oversteering, even steer in the opposite direction—called opposite lock.

P: from Paddle to Push Rod

Paddle:
Manual gear shifter behind the steering wheel.

Parc Fermé:
Restricted area of the pit lane in which the FIA's technical stewards inspect the cars after each race to make sure they conform to technical regulations. Team members are not admitted to this area. As soon as a vehicle leaves the pit lane in qualifying, the Parc Fermé rule comes into effect as well but it is not linked with a

certain area. Up to the race the teams are only allowed to make minor changes to the car. For more extensive work such as repairs of accident damage FIA approval must be obtained. If modifications are made to the set-up (in case of expected weather changes, for instance), the respective driver must start from the pit lane. Three-and-a-half hours after the end of qualifying the vehicles are wrapped in special tarpaulins in the team garages and the wraps are sealed by the FIA. Overhead cameras are used for night-time monitoring to verify that the race teams comply with the ban on working on the cars. Five hours before the start of a Grand Prix race the wraps may be removed, but the Parc Fermé rules remain in effect.

Penalties:
The stewards can (amongst other things) impose time penalties, disqualification or a ban for subsequent races in case of violations of the rules. The race director can recommend time penalties for a false start, causing a collision, forcing another car off the track, not responding to a blue flag, and deliberately hindering another driver. The final decision for a stop-go and drive-through penalty, as well as places added to a driver's grid position, is made by three race stewards, the official Formula One race referee jury. Since 2010 they have been assisted by a race steward from the national automobile association and experienced former Formula One drivers or experienced drivers from other categories. The stewards may use the video footage and radio communications of the race teams to make their decisions. If drivers commit sport-related or technical violations during qualifying, the racing commissioners can cancel all their qualifying times. Additionally there are penalties for technical defects.

Pit Lane:
This is where changes to the car take place. During practice sessions the speed limit in the pit lane is 80 km/h, as it is during qualifying and races. On street circuits, where pit lanes are especially narrow, the speed limit is reduced to 60 km/h for practice, qualifying and race alike. The pit order acts in accordance with the teams' position in the Constructors' Championship of the previous season.

Pit Stop:
During a regular pit stop in a race, a team of twenty-seven mechanics changes the tyres on the car and possibly performs further mechanical or aerodynamics settings. Between 1994 and 2009, cars were also refuelled during pit stops. Refuelling has been banned since the 2010 season. It takes a well-trained crew less than three seconds to change all four tyres on a modern Formula One car.

Points:
Since the 2010 season, the first ten drivers in each race have been awarded points for the championship ranking. The winner of the Grand Prix is awarded twenty-five points, while the drivers that follow receive eighteen, fifteen, twelve, ten, eight, six, four, two and one respectively. The same points system is used for the Constructors' Championship. Both cars of each team can collect points in one race. For the last race of the 2014 season, double points were awarded for both the Drivers' and the Constructors' Championship, for the first time—although this scoring system was subsequently dropped for the 2015 campaign.

Pole Position:
First place in the starting order for the race, which is given to the fastest driver in qualifying. In 2014, Formula One introduces the Pole Position Trophy for the driver who earns the most Pole Positions during the season.

Power Unit:
In regulatory terms, the Power Unit comprises six different systems: the Internal Combustion Engine, Motor Generator Unit-Kinetic (MGU-K), Motor Generator Unit-Heat (MGU-H), Energy Store (ES), Turbocharger and the Control Electronics. The change in terminology reflects the fact that this new power-train is far more than simply an Internal Combustion Engine. Where the previous V8 format utilized a KERS hybrid system which was effectively "bolted on" to a pre-existing engine configuration, the new power unit has been designed from the outset

with Hybrid systems integral to its operation. The 1.6-litre V6 engine delivers approximately 600 bhp and gains additional 160 bhp through its ER system for about thirty-three seconds per lap.

Pull Rod:
A suspension layout where the suspension rockers are pulled. Long forgotten, it returned to Formula One in 2009, at first on the rear suspension. 2012 saw the return of vehicles with a pull rod layout on the front suspension for the first time in eleven years.

Push Rod:
This layout, where the suspension unit is operated with a strut, is used in the front and rear of most Formula One cars.

Q: like Qualifying

Qualifying:
The starting order for the race is determined during qualifying. The driver with the fastest lap time qualifies for the best starting place: pole position. Qualifying is conducted in shoot-out format in three individual sessions. In the first session the slowest seven drivers are eliminated, and seven more in the second one. The ten fastest drivers fight for the pole position in the third session. A driver who on his fastest lap in Q1 fails to post a time that is within 107 per cent of the fastest driver in qualifying is not allowed to contest the race. The top ten drivers of qualifying have to start the race on the tyres they have used for their fastest lap in the final qualifying session.

R: from Race Director to Run-off Zone

Race Director:
The FIA race director supervises the safety measures on the race weekend and makes improvements when necessary. Additionally, he decides whether the Safety Car should be deployed or whether the race should be stopped. If a driver does not behave in a

sportsmanlike manner or if he endangers a competitor, the race director can recommend a penalty. The current FIA race director is Charlie Whiting from the UK.

Race Distance:
The smallest number of laps needed to exceed a distance of 305 km (exception: Monaco, 260 km). The maximum duration of the race is two hours. The entire duration per Grand Prix, including possible interruptions, has been limited to four hours since 2012.

Race Stop:
If weather conditions are so poor as to endanger safe driving (e.g. heavy rain, snow, fog) or if a vehicle is blocking the track, a red flag signals that the race has been stopped. If a race is stopped during the first two laps, it is started again. If this is not possible, no points are awarded. If a race is stopped after the first two laps, it is restarted. In this case, half of the total points are awarded. The total number of points is awarded if 75 per cent or more of the race are completed.

Racing Line:
Also known as the ideal line, the racing line is the imaginary line on which the circuit can be driven in the fastest possible time. Due to the rubber build-up, this is also usually where the grip is best.

Rear Light:
Decreases the risk of pile-ups. When using wet weather tyres, the rear light must always be switched on. The red rear light must be positioned between 30 and 35 cm above the floor of the car. The rear light also lights up when a car is slowing down ahead of a corner while recovering energy on the rear axle.

Rear Wing:
Also known as rear wing assembly. Creates downward pressure, mainly upon the rear axle. The rear wing is adapted to the conditions of the tracks (the steeper it is, the more downforce is created). The settings and angles of the surfaces can be

additionally modified. These modifications are part of the set-up. To facilitate overtaking manoeuvres, the regulations allow the drivers to adjust the rear wing from the cockpit since 2011.

Red Flag:
The red flag is shown simultaneously at the starting line and around the circuit when a practice or a qualifying period or race is stopped.

Refilling/Refuelling:
Nitrogen and compressed air are the only gases that may be replenished during the race. Since 2010 refuelling during races has been banned. This has a big effect on race strategy as drivers have to pay more attention to tyre and brake conservation. As from 2019 the maximum amount of fuel for the race is 105 kilograms, drivers have to save fuel, too, to make it to the finish line.

Regulations:
The FIA draws up the sporting and technical regulations for Formula One. The technical regulations primarily aim at two important things: speed should be controlled in the interest of safety, while simultaneously retaining the ongoing technical development so critical to the nature of Formula One. In addition, safety is to be guaranteed in the event of an accident. To achieve these aims, the following factors have been limited: engine capacity, fuel composition, tyre size, tyre contact surface, minimum weight and width of the cars. The sporting regulations primarily control the "procedure of a Grand Prix weekend, such as qualifying, deployment of the Safety Car and the podium ceremony".

Roll-out:
The first test drive of a new racing car, usually at a private test.

Roll-over Bar:
If a car rolls over in an accident, the roll-over bar, a curved structure above the driver's head made of metal or composite materials, is intended to provide the driver with better protection.

Rubber Build-up:
This is a knock-on effect of the slow erosion of tyre surfaces. When tyres are driven on asphalt, the surface rubs off and leaves behind a layer of rubber on the road, which accumulates over the course of the racing weekend and progressively enhances grip. This erosion is influenced both by the vehicle set-up and the abrasive properties of the asphalt.

Run-off Zone:
Run-off zones are empty spaces directly beside the actual race-track. They are supposed to passively or actively decelerate cars that are out of control and prevent a collision with track walls or barriers. Only recently, an increasing number of asphalted spaces have been introduced at various circuits as drivers have a better chance of regaining control of their vehicle. Previously, gravel pits were more common. Although gravel has a decelerating effect, the chances of controlling the car are fairly low and the danger of getting stuck is rather high.

S: from Safety Belt to Suspension

Safety Belt:
The safety belt used by the driver in the cockpit is also known as a six-point harness and can be opened with a single hand movement.

Safety Car:
The Official Formula One Safety Car is deployed when the race director wants to reduce speed for safety reasons—for instance, after an accident or because the track is waterlogged after heavy rainfall—"whenever there is an immediate hazard but the conditions do not require the race to be interrupted". It moves onto the track regardless of what the current race leader's position is and all cars line up behind it. During a Safety Car phase there is an absolute ban on overtaking and the drivers have to reduce their regular lap time. The Official Formula One Safety Car was introduced in 1992. Since 2018 it has been a Mercedes-Benz AMG GTR with 585 horsepower and a 4.0 litre V8 biturboengine.

Safety Car Driver:
Since 2000, the Official Formula One Safety Car has been driven by Bernd Mayländer, a German former touring-car driver. He has raced in Formula Ford, the Porsche Carrera Cup, the FIA GT Championship and the Deutsche Tourenwagen Meisterschaft (DTM). His co-driver is Peter Tibbetts.

Scrutineering:
Scrutineering, the technical approval of the cars, takes place on the day before the first free practice session of a Grand Prix. The scrutineers of the FIA check whether the vehicles comply with regulations.

Set-up:
General vehicle tuning for all the adjustable mechanical and aero-dynamic parts (wheel suspension, wings, etc.). Specifically, the term describes the various possibilities for adapting a Formula One car to the conditions of a particular circuit. Included are, among other things, modification to the tyres, suspension, wings and engine and transmission settings.

Shake-down:
The final test drive of a newly prepared car before the team departs to a Grand Prix.

Sidepods:
Side cladding of the cockpit which is integrated in the mono-coque. The sidepods contain crash structures that absorb the forces arising from an accident or impact. The radiators are also located in the sidepods.

Skid Block:
A plate made of plastic or wood fitted to the underbody of a racing car. It is intended to prevent a strong suction effect, limiting excessively high speeds, especially in the corners, for safety reasons. It also acts as protection for the underbody.

Slicks:
Slicks are tyres without tread patterns. In 2009 slicks were reintroduced to Formula One in order to facilitate overtaking. Slicks provide around 20 per cent more grip compared to the grooved tyres used from 1998 until 2008.

Slipstream:
Low pressure area behind a Formula One car created by air currents. Driving in the slipstream can provide a boost to a car's speed, making it the ideal position for a pursuing vehicle to start an overtaking manoeuvre.

Spare Car:
Replacement cars are no longer permitted in Formula One. However, if a driver irreparably damages his car the team can prepare another car. If the driver changed his car between qualifying and race, he must start from the pits.

Speed Limiter:
The cruise control feature used in Formula One pit lanes. It is activated by pressing a button on the steering wheel. Speed is then reduced down to the pit lane limit.

Speed Limits:
At most of the tracks a speed limit of 80 km/h will be imposed in the pit lane during all sessions. However, this limit may be amended by the stewards following a recommendation from the FIA Formula One safety delegate, for example in Monaco, Melbourne or Singapore, where the pit lane is particularly narrow and a speed limit of 60 km/h is imposed. In the race, speeding leads to a drive-through penalty.

Stabilizers:
Rotary or torsion bars that connect right and left wheel suspensions flexibly to each other. The so called "rollbars" help to reduce the rolling movement of the chassis along the longitudinal axis and so provide more precise handling during load shifts.

Starting Grid:
Formula One uses a standing start. The deciding factor for the starting position of a driver is his time from qualifying. The driver with the fastest lap time starts from pole position. The cars line up at offset eight-metre intervals. Each row of the starting grid has two race cars, one slightly in front, with a distance of eight metres to the next row.

Starting Lights:
As soon as the last car is positioned on the starting grid, the five starting lights go on successively at one-second intervals. The race starts when all the lights go off at once.

Starting Number:
The maximum number of teams that may race in Formula One is thirteen, with two cars each. All cars have to be fitted with the starting number of the driver. For the 2014 season drivers were able to choose their starting number as Formula One moved from pre-assigned starting numbers to personal starting numbers the drivers are supposed to keep for their whole career in Formula One Only the reigning World Champion can choose to run number one. However, he may go with a different number, too. In this case, number one will not be given to another driver. The highest possible starting number is ninety-nine.

Steering Wheel:
A Formula One car's steering wheel is the control centre for the driver. He steers, clutches, changes gear and is able to influence electronic functions by means of numerous buttons. A small screen displays current car statistics. The design and the arrangement are adjusted to suit the individual driver.

Strategy:
Formula One teams can use their own race strategy. The number of scheduled pit stops is optional. However, the drivers have to cover at least one stint (section up to the next pit stop) on tyres with both prescribed compounds. Typically, there are two to three

pit stops. Depending on the race situation (for instance a Safety Car period), the teams may also change their strategy.

Super Licence:

Formula One driving licence issued by the FIA. In the interest of safety, it is only granted on the basis of good results in the junior series or, in exceptional cases, if other proof of ability can be supplied. It may also be granted under provisional terms. To get a Super Licence, a driver must demonstrate that he is capable of handling a modern Formula One car over a full race distance of about 300 kilometres in an appropriate amount of time.

Suspension:

Several years ago, the wheel suspension was the Achilles' heel of a Formula One car, but the use of composite materials has since made it extremely robust. Basically, double arms are used at the front and rear, and each team gives them a different aerodynamic shape.

T: from Tank to Tyres

Tank:

The fuel tank is a fibre-reinforced rubber hull that must yield flexibly when deformed. It must fulfil the FIA's rigid criteria. To avoid damage, the tank is also located within the monocoque and is thus encased in the survival cell, the car's best-protected area.

Team Order:

The clause prohibiting team orders was removed from the Sporting Regulations in 2011.

Technical Committee:

These FIA experts lay down the Formula One regulations. Every team's technical director is a member of the Technical Committee. The Committee makes recommendations to the FIA Formula One Commission. The decisions made by the Commission are in turn forwarded to the FIA's World Motorsport Council and must then be approved by the FIA's general assembly.

Technical Delegate:
The FIA technical delegate leads the team of technical inspectors (scrutineers). They check whether the cars meet the regulations. If the technical delegate does not think a car conforms to the rules, he submits a report to the racing commissioners, who are authorized to impose penalties.

Telemetry:
A system allowing a large quantity of data, e.g. concerning chassis and engine, to be recorded in the car and transmitted to the pits. There, the data is analyzed so as to determine any faults (a loss of brake fluid or a slow puncture, for example) at an early stage and to be able to improve the car's set-up.

Test Runs:
During test runs Formula One teams try out new developments and various set-ups on the car. However, the teams are substantially limited since 2009. Teams may not exceed 15,000 test km during a calendar year. From one week prior to the first race until 31 December, teams may only test during four two-day tests and during the Young Driver Test at the end of the season. In addition, each team may use four days for aerodynamics tests. Two promotional events, with a maximum distance of 100 kilometres each, are allowed without counting towards the total kilometre tally.

Time Penalty:
This is a penalty during the race for drivers who have violated regulations. Once his team has been informed by the racing commissioners, the driver must drive through the pit lane within the next three laps. He may not stop there to change tyres. Entering and leaving the pit lane costs the penalized driver valuable time. If the penalty is imposed during the last five laps, the driver no longer has to sit it—instead, he will have twenty-five seconds added to his final time. In more severe cases, race direction may impose a stop-and-go penalty, which requires the driver to park in front of his pit garage for ten seconds before rejoining the race. Again, no work on the car is allowed.

Torque:
Generated in the engine by the combustion pressure acting on the crankshaft via the pistons and the connecting rods. The maximum torque is a benchmark for the power and usability of the engine and the acceleration capacity of a racing car.

Traction:
This term describes the ability of a race car to apply its engine's power to the track.

Traction Control:
An electronic system, also called anti-slip control. It uses sensors to detect whether the wheels are spinning and then automatically reduces the engine power. This guarantees ideal acceleration, especially at the start, when leaving a corner and on wet tracks. Traction control has been prohibited since 2008.

Transmission:
A Formula One car may have a maximum of eight forward gears. A reverse gear is prescribed. The gear wheels in the transmission must be made of steel.

Turbocharger:
The turbocharger is an energy recovery device that uses waste exhaust energy to drive a single stage exhaust turbine that in turn drives a single stage compressor via a shaft, thereby increasing the pressure of the inlet charge (the air admitted to the engine for combustion). The increased pressure of the inlet charge offsets the reductions in engine capacity and RPM when compared to the V8, thus enabling high power delivery from a down-speeded, down-sized engine. The turbocharger is the key system for increasing the efficiency of the Internal Combustion Engine.

Turbo Engines:
The first turbo engine was used in Formula One in 1977. In qualifying, these engines boasted up to 1,400 bhp. They were banned from Formula One in 1989 and re-introduced for the

2014 Formula One season. The current engine format boasts 1.6-litre V6 engines which deliver approximately 600 bhp at 15,000 rpm. The new Formula One power units are closely linked to the ERS which provides additional 160 bhp for about thirty-three seconds a lap.

Tyres:

Sole F1 tyre supplier Pirelli will simplify the naming system in 2019 and only use hard (white), medium (yellow) and soft (red) compound names so that on any given weekend the hardest compound will be just known as the hard, the softest will be known as the soft and compound in between be known as the medium. Pirelli will still let fans know what the 'actual' compounds are as they change from race to race.

Tyre Stack:

Tyre stacks have been mandatory at racetracks since 1981. The tyre barrier consists of two to six rows of conventional car tyres that are bolted together and connected by rubber bands. This achieves an optimal absorption of the impact energy.

Tyre Warmer:

The tyres require an operational temperature of around 100°C to achieve optimal effectiveness. In order to rapidly reach this temperature, special electric blankets pre-heat the tyres up to 60–80°C. Cold tyres do not develop enough grip. If they are too hot, they wear out quickly.

U: from Understeering to Underwear

Understeering:

When front wheels lose grip but the back ones do not.

Undertray:

The aerodynamically shaped lower surface of a racing car creates an airflow, which in turn generates a vacuum under the car that provides better grip. However, continuous air ducts are banned in Formula One and are prevented by the skid block, which splits the airflow.

Underwear:
Under the racing overall, drivers wear a T-shirt, boxers, socks and a balaclava. All the underwear is made of fire resistant material made of Nomex® brand fibre.

V: like Valves

Valves:
The task of the engine-controlled valves is to open or close the inlet and outlet ducts at the right moment and so to allow the gases into or out of the combustion chamber. Each valve consists of a stem and a disc.

W: from Weight to World Champion's Title

Weight:
A Formula One car including the driver in full racing gear, with oil and brake fluid, must weigh at least 740 kg whilst on the track. The vehicles' construction weight is actually less. The teams can achieve a better weight distribution using additional weights, thus improving the handling. The technical commission of the FIA may, at any time, send cars to the electronic scales located at the entrance to the pit lane.

Wet Weather Tyres:
In wet weather, cars use special tyres that are better able to displace water from the track and optimize grip.

Wheels:
Formula One uses relatively small wheel sizes of thirteen inches. Most road cars are fitted with wheels ranging between sixteen and twenty inches. Instead, the wheel rims are much lighter due to the use of magnesium. The width of the rear wheels must be between 365 and 380 mm, and between 305 and 355 mm at the

front. The maximum wheel diameter is 660 mm for dry-weather tyres and 670 mm for wet-weather tyres.

Wheel Tethers:
Each wheel is connected to the chassis by means of high-performance tethers (PBO, Zylon). They are intended to prevent the wheels from flying off in the case of an accident. Each tether has to withstand a load of seven tons.

White Flag:
The white flag indicates that a slow vehicle is on the circuit.

Wind Tunnel:
The holy shrine of every Formula One team and indispensable for the development of a race car. Aerodynamic studies are carried out in the wind tunnel. Using various flow speeds, the engineers can simulate various car speeds and can test the effects of new vehicle parts or the aerodynamic behaviour of the entire car in various racing situations. Since 1 January 2009 teams may only test with models that do not exceed a scale of 60 per cent for cost reduction reasons. Additionally, tests in the wind tunnel must not exceed wind speeds of 50 m per second. For 2014, the wind tunnel rules have been tightened again in terms of, for example, how much time teams can spend evaluating in the wind tunnel.

Winglet:
Additional wing located on the car body just in front of the rear wheel. Prohibited since 2009.

Wings:
Fixed surfaces that are intended to increase downforce. The wings serve to press the car downwards more firmly. The secret of wing adjustment lies in finding the best compromise between high speed on straights (low downforce) and optimal performance in corners (high downforce). The front wings are 1,650 mm, the rear wings 750-mm wide. To facilitate overtaking, adjustable rear wings (DRS) have been permitted since 2011.

Wishbones:
The components connecting the wheel suspension and the chassis.
Wishbones are mounted at right angles to the vehicle's longitudinal
axis. These pivoting rods, which have also acquired aerodynamic
significance, must be made of extremely strong materials.

World Champion:
With seven titles to his credit, Michael Schumacher is the most
successful racer in Formula One history.

World Champion's Title:
In Formula One, two World Championship titles are awarded—
one for the drivers and one for the manufacturers. The Drivers'
Title has existed since 1950, and the Constructors' Title was
introduced in 1958. For the drivers, the points won in all the races
are added up. If several drivers have the same points total, the title
is determined by the final positions they achieved: the number of
first places, followed by the number of second places, etc. In the
Constructors' division, the points that both of the team's drivers
earn each race are added up.

X: like X-wing

X-wing:
Additional wings developed by the Tyrrell team and first used in 1997.
The X-wings created high levels of downforce. For safety reasons, the
FIA banned them before the Spanish Grand Prix in 1998.

Y: like Yellow Flag

Yellow Flag:
The yellow flag waved once indicates danger. When this is
shown, drivers should reduce speed, refrain from passing and
be prepared to deviate from their ideal racing line. If the yellow
flag is waved twice, drivers have to be prepared for a full stop.
The yellow flag with red stripes informs drivers that oil or water
is on the track.

Z: from Zip to Zylon

Zip:

While the zip on a driver's overall is hidden behind the layers of Nomex® fibre, it has to be able to withstand the same temperature that the suit will take in the event of a fire. It must not melt or transfer heat close to the driver's skin.

Zylon:

The safety cells' flanks are protected by a six-millimetre layer of carbon and zylon. The drivers' crash helmets feature a Zylon strip across the top of the visor since 2011 in order to enhance protection from flying objects. Zylon is also used for bullet-proof vests and is intended to prevent objects such as splinters from entering the cockpit. Padding has absorbed impact energy on the inside since 2002. Occupants of production vehicles are protected by airbags and side-impact protection in side crashes.

INDEX